WEAKNESS AND DECEIT

WEAKNESS

AND DECEIT

U.S. POLICY AND EL SALVADOR

by Raymond Bonner

𝕿imes BOOKS

Published by TIMES BOOKS, The New York Times Book Co., Inc.
130 Fifth Avenue, New York, N.Y. 10011

Published simultaneously in Canada by Fitzhenry & Whiteside, Ltd., Toronto

Library of Congress Cataloging in Publication Data

Bonner, Raymond.
  Weakness and deceit.

  Bibliography: p. 383
  Includes index.
  1. El Salvador—Politics and government—1979–
2. El Salvador—Foreign relations—United States.
United States—Foreign relations—El Salvador.
I. Title.
F1488.3.B65   1984   327.7307284   83–45921
ISBN 0–8129–1108–3

Designed by Betty Binns Graphics/Betty Binns

MANUFACTURED IN THE UNITED STATES OF AMERICA
84 85 86 87 88 5 4 3 2 1

FOR MY PARENTS

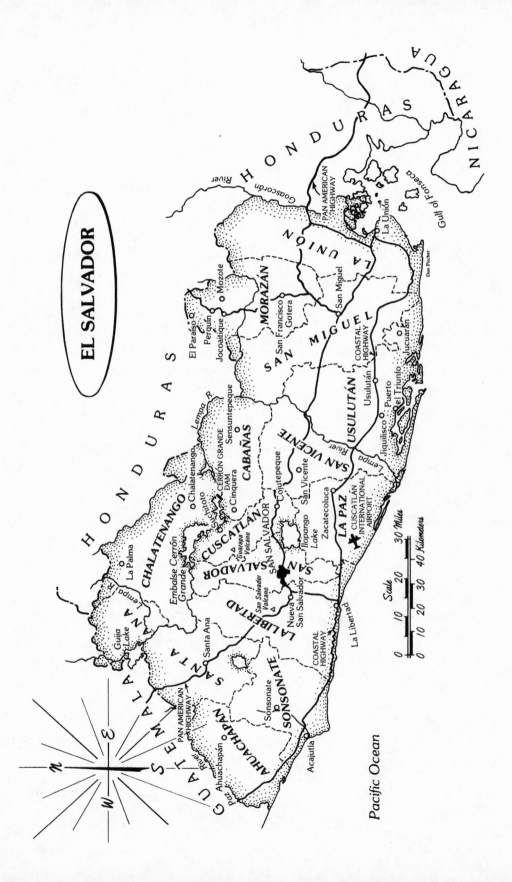

CONTENTS

CAST OF CHARACTERS

ABRAMS, ELLIOTT Assistant secretary of state for human rights and humanitarian affairs, 1981–present.

ÁLVAREZ CÓRDOVA, ENRIQUE Wealthy Salvadoran landowner; first president of the FDR; tortured and killed, November 1980.

CARPIO, SALVADOR CAYETANO Hard-line leader of the FPL; committed suicide in Managua, April 1983.

CARRANZA, COLONEL NICOLÁS Archconservative military commander, forced out of a command position by Carter administration pressure in December 1980; named head of the notorious Treasury Police in 1983; paid CIA informant.

CLARKE, MAURA American Maryknoll nun, murdered by Salvadoran soldiers on December 2, 1980.

DERIAN, PATRICIA "PATT" Carter's assistant secretary of state for human rights and humanitarian affairs.

D'AUBUISSON, ROBERTO Right-wing extremist, forced out of the military after the coup in October 1979; linked to the murder of Archbishop Romero and the American AIFLD workers; founder of the Nationalist Republican Alliance (ARENA).

DEVINE, FRANK J. Carter's first ambassador to El Salvador, 1977–1980.

DONOVAN, JEAN American lay missionary, murdered by Salvadoran soldiers on December 2, 1980.

DUARTE, JOSÉ NAPOLEÓN Christian Democrat; presidential candidate in 1972 elections widely believed to have been stolen by the army; member of the junta from March 1980 to April 1982.

ENDERS, THOMAS OSTROM Assistant secretary of state for Inter-American affairs, 1981–1983.

FARABUNDO MARTÍ, AGUSTÍN Communist organizer of peasants and workers, which led to uprising and *matanza* in 1932.

FORD, ITA   American Maryknoll nun, murdered by Salvadoran soldiers on December 2, 1980.

GARCÍA, JOSÉ GUILLERMO   Minister of defense, 1979–1983.

GUTIÉRREZ, COLONEL JAIME ABDUL   Member of junta, October 15, 1979–1983.

HAMMER, MICHAEL   American AIFLD worker, murdered in Sheraton Hotel dining room on January 4, 1981.

HERNÁNDEZ MARTÍNEZ, GENERAL MAXIMILIANO   Brutal architect of the *matanza* in 1932; ruled the country until 1944.

HINTON, DEANE R.   Reagan's first ambassador to El Salvador, replacing White, 1981–1983.

KAZEL, DOROTHY   American Ursuline nun, murdered by Salvadoran soldiers on December 2, 1980.

MAGAÑA, ÁLVARO   Named provisional president after elections in March 1982. Scheduled to be replaced after elections in March 1984.

MAJANO, COLONEL ADOLFO ARNOLDO   Member of junta—widely considered most liberal—from October 15, 1979 to December 1980.

MORALES EHRLICH, JOSÉ ANTONIO   Christian Democrat; vice-presidential candidate in 1977; member of junta from January 1980 to April 1983.

NUTTING, LIEUTENANT GENERAL WALLACE H.   Commander in chief, U.S. Southern Command, in Panama, from 1979 to 1983.

PASTOR, ROBERT   Carter's Latin America specialist on the National Security Council.

PEARLMAN, MARK   American AIFLD worker, murdered in Sheraton Hotel dining room on January 4, 1981.

RIVERA Y DAMAS, ARTURO   Became archbishop of San Salvador after assassination of Archbishop Romero; was still archbishop in March 1984.

ROMERO, GENERAL CARLOS HUMBERTO   Became president after fraudulent elections in 1977; ousted by a coup, October 15, 1979.

ROMERO, OSCAR ARNULFO   Archbishop of San Salvador and the country's most outspoken and respected human rights critic; murdered while saying mass, March 24, 1980. (No relation to General Romero.)

UNGO, GUILLERMO MANUEL   Social Democrat. Duarte's running mate in 1972 elections. Succeeded Álvarez as head of the FDR; still serving as such in March 1984.

VIDES CASANOVA, CARLOS EUGENIO   Colonel and commander of the National Guard following the October 1979 coup, holding that post when the four American churchwomen and AIFLD workers were killed. Promoted to general, and became minister of defense, replacing García, in 1983.

VILLALOBOS, JOAQUÍN   Founder of the ERP; executioner of Roque Dalton García; in 1984 he had emerged as the most prominent leader of the FMLN and was widely considered the best military commander on either side of the war.

WHITE, ROBERT E.   Carter's second ambassador to El Salvador, replacing Devine in March 1980, serving until Reagan administration fired him quickly after coming into office.

WAGHELSTEIN, COLONEL JOHN DAVID   Widely regarded as one of the most knowledgeable guerrilla war experts in the U.S. Army; was an adviser to the Bolivian Army when Che Guevara was trapped and killed; senior U.S. military adviser in El Salvador, 1982–1983.

ZAMORA, RUBÉN   Member of the FDR political-diplomatic commission who frequently spoke to groups in the United States until Reagan administration lifted his visa in 1983.

ABBREVIATIONS AND ACRONYMS

AIFLD   American Institute for Free Labor Development. *Ostensibly an independent labor organization, has long been an instrument for U.S. foreign policy, with links to the CIA.*

ANEP   National Association of Private Enterprise. *Powerful Salvadoran business organization.*

ARENA   Nationalist Republican Alliance. *Ultraright-wing political party founded by D'Aubuisson in 1981.*

FDR   Democratic Revolutionary Front. *Political wing of the revolution; coalition of dissident Christian Democrats, Marxists, priests, professionals, and the popular organizations; aligned with the FMLN.*

FMLN   Farabundo Martí National Liberation Front. *Coalition of five guerrilla groups.*

ERP   People's Revolutionary Army. *Founded in 1972. In 1984 one of the two strongest guerrilla organizations.*

FPL   Popular Forces of Liberation. *Founded by Carpio in early 1970's. In 1984 one of the two strongest guerrilla groups.*

FARN   Armed Forces of National Resistance. *Third largest of the five guerrilla groups; considered the most moderate.*

ISTA   Salvadoran Institute for Agrarian Transformation.

ORDEN   *Rural paramilitary organization set up by the government in the 1960's; officially abolished after the coup in October 1979, but its members continued to operate.*

PDC   Christian Democratic party.

PCN   National Conciliation party. *Official government/military party, which ruled the country from 1961 to 1979.*

CHRONOLOGY

1932
The *matanza*. Peasant uprising inspired by Agustín Farabundo Martí crushed by General Maximiliano Hernández Martínez. His soldiers kill up to 30,000 peasants, and he rules the country until 1944.

1972
Military steals election from José Napoleón Duarte and Guillermo Manuel Ungo.

1977
JANUARY   Jimmy Carter becomes President of the United States, vowing to make human rights "the soul of our foreign policy."

FEBRUARY   Another fraudulent presidential election in El Salvador; General Carlos Humberto Romero becomes president.

MARCH   U.S. congressional hearings into the Salvadoran election, probably the first ever devoted exclusively to El Salvador. Father Rutilio Grande assassinated in El Salvador.

JUNE   Carter sends Frank J. Devine as ambassador to El Salvador, replacing Ignacio E. Lozano, Jr.

JULY   U.S. congressional hearings into religious persecution in El Salvador.

1979
JULY 19   Sandinistas topple General Anastasio Somoza Debayle in Nicaragua.

OCTOBER 15   General Romero deposed by a coup in El Salvador. Junta formed with Colonel Jaime Abdul Gutiérrez and Adolfo Arnoldo Majano, Guillermo Manuel Ungo, Ramón Mayorga Quiros, and Mario Antonio Andino. Within the next few weeks Carter administration announces its intention to provide "nonlethal" military aid, the first since 1977, and a team of U.S. military advisers arrives.

1980

JANUARY 3–5 Government collapses when Ungo, Mayorga, and Andino resign, along with nearly every minister and deputy minister, because of the army's unwillingness to submit to civilian control and because of the increasing repression. Defense Minister Colonel Jose Guillermo García refuses to resign. Christian Democrats join the government. New civilians on the junta are two Christian Democrats, José Antonio Morales Ehrlich and Héctor Dada Hirezi, and José Ramón Avalos Navarrete.

JANUARY 22 Unity of the popular organizations. An estimated 100,000 march through the capital streets.

MARCH 3 Dada resigns from junta because "We have not been able to stop the repression."

MARCH 6–7 Government announces land reform and nationalization of banks and export trade.

MARCH 9 Duarte joins junta.

MARCH 10 Seven leaders of Christian Democrats leave the party, declaring that "a program of reforms with repression runs contrary to the fundamentals of the Christian Democrats."

MARCH 11 Robert E. White presents his credentials as ambassador.

MARCH 24 Archbishop Oscar Arnulfo Romero assassinated while saying mass.

MARCH 25 House committee holds hearing on Carter administration's request for $5.7 million in "nonlethal" military aid for El Salvador. The aid request is a marked departure in policy for the United States, which provided El Salvador with a total of $16.8 million during the entire period from 1946 through 1979.

MARCH 26 Three more high-level Salvadoran government officials resign.

MAY 7 Roberto d'Aubuisson arrested for plotting a coup. Supporters surround White's residence, chanting, "Get out of El Salvador, Communist. Go to Cuba." D'Aubuisson released several days later.

JUNE 26 Soldiers storm the National University, killing at least fifty. Government closes university, which remains closed today.

OCTOBER Another team of U.S. military advisers secretly enters El Salvador. Leftist opposition rejects offer of Salvadoran bishops to mediate a settlement.

NOVEMBER 4 Ronald Reagan elected President of the United States.

NOVEMBER 27 Enrique Álvarez, four other FDR leaders, and a sixth person seized from a Catholic high school, tortured, and killed.

NOVEMBER 28 Salvadoran business leaders meet with President-elect Reagan's foreign policy advisers, including Jeane Kirkpatrick, and are assured of receiving more military aid under the new administration.

DECEMBER 4 Bodies of four American churchwomen—Maura Clarke, Jean Donovan, Ita Ford, and Dorothy Kazel—found.

DECEMBER 5 Carter administration suspends aid to El Salvador and dispatches a high-level team led by former Assistant Secretary of State William Rogers.

DECEMBER 7 Junta's most liberal member, Colonel Majano, ousted.

DECEMBER 13 Duarte named president of the four-man junta.

DECEMBER 17 Carter administration restores economic aid.

DECEMBER 26 Guerrilla commander Fermán Cienfuegos declares that situation in El Salvador will be "red hot" by the time Reagan arrives in the White House.

1981

JANUARY 4 AIFLD workers Michael Hammer and Mark Pearlman gunned down in the Sheraton Hotel.

JANUARY 10 Guerrillas launch "final offensive."

JANUARY 13 Purported landing of boats from Nicaragua.

JANUARY 14 Military aid, suspended after killing of the churchwomen, resumed.

JANUARY 16 Carter administration announces immediate delivery of an additional $5 million in military aid.

JANUARY 20 Reagan inaugurated.

FEBRUARY 1 White removed as ambassador.

FEBRUARY 23 Reagan administration releases white paper, charging that the situation in El Salvador is a "textbook case of indirect armed aggression by Communist powers through Cuba."

MARCH 2 Reagan administration dispatches twenty additional military advisers and announces an additional $25 million in military aid. In public statements and testimony to the Senate Foreign Relations Committee during following weeks, senior administration officials say aid will not be linked to human rights performance.

APRIL 6 Archbishop Arturo Rivera y Damas quietly seeks to act as mediator in a negotiated settlement of Salvadoran conflict; rejected by Reagan administration in private meeting in Washington.

JUNE 1 Deane Hinton presents his credentials as ambassador.

AUGUST 28 Mexico and France, in a joint communiqué, recognize the FDR-FMLN as a "representative political force."

OCTOBER 7   In address to the UN General Assembly, senior member of Nicaragua's Sandinista government, Daniel Ortega, proposes internationally supervised negotiations in El Salvador, without preconditions.

1982

JANUARY 10   The first group of young Salvadoran men arrive in the United States for military training, program will eventually train approximately 1,000 troops at Fort Bragg and 500 officer cadets at Fort Benning.

JANUARY 18   Commanders of five guerrilla organizations sign a letter to President Reagan offering to negotiate without preconditions.

JANUARY 27   Reports about government massacre of peasants in Mozote and surrounding villages appear in *The New York Times* and *The Washington Post.* A guerrilla sabotage raid on Ilopango Air Base destroys several U.S.-supplied helicopters.

JANUARY 28   President Reagan certifies that the Salvadoran government is making progress in adhering to international human rights standards, is investigating the murders of the churchwomen and AIFLD workers, and is continuing the land reform (certification law was passed by Congress in 1981 as a condition for continued military aid).

JANUARY 31   At least twenty persons killed after being dragged out of their homes by soldiers who stormed the poor capital barrio of San Antonio Abad. Widely reported in the press.

MARCH 28   Constituent Assembly elections. Christian Democrats emerge with plurality of vote, but not a majority. D'Aubuisson's ARENA party and the PCN, the traditional military party, together have enough votes to name D'Aubuisson president. Reagan administration applies intense pressure to block D'Aubuisson from becoming president.

APRIL 29   At the behest of the military high command, newly elected Constituent Assembly names Álvaro Magaña the country's provisional president.

MAY   Constituent Assembly, in one of its first acts, suspends provisions of the land reform.

JULY 27   Reagan administration issues second certification.

OCTOBER   Leaders of FMLN and FDR send a letter to President Magaña offering to negotiate without preconditions. Letter delivered by Archbishop Rivera y Damas.

OCTOBER 29   Ambassador Hinton, departing from the Reagan administration's policy of "quiet diplomacy," tells the U.S.-Salvadoran

Chamber of Commerce that a "Mafia" which carries out the murder of innocent civilians and American citizens "must be stopped."

NOVEMBER 8 In a cover story *Newsweek* magazine reveals details about the Reagan administration's so-called secret war against Nicaragua, being fought from Honduras by "counterrevolutionaries" trained and supplied by the United States.

1983

JANUARY 21 Reagan administration issues its third certification.

APRIL 12 Guerrilla leader Salvador Cayetano Carpio commits suicide in Managua, Nicaragua, a few days after one of his top aides, Comandante Ana María, is bludgeoned to death, revealing publicly splits within the Salvadoran guerrilla forces.

APRIL 27 Reagan takes his Central America policy to a joint session of Congress, one of the few times in history that an American President has addressed the joint body on a foreign policy issue.

MAY 25 Lieutenant Commander Albert A. Schaufelberger III assassinated by a guerrilla faction while sitting in his car, waiting for his girl friend, at the Catholic university in San Salvador.

MAY 28–29 Reagan shakes up his Central America team, removing Thomas Enders as assistant secretary of state for Inter-American affairs and Hinton as ambassador to El Salvador.

JUNE One hundred U.S. military advisers begin training Salvadoran troops in Honduras.

JULY 20 Reagan names former Secretary of State Henry Kissinger to head a twelve-man National Bipartisan Commission on Central America.

JULY 20 Reagan administration certifies for the fourth time that Salvadoran government is making progress on human rights, implementation of land reform, and investigations into the murders of American citizens. To date, no one has been brought to trial for the deaths of the churchwomen or the AIFLD workers.

NOVEMBER 30 President Reagan vetoes a bill that would have continued the certification requirements.

DECEMBER 30 Guerrilla forces, in their largest and most successful action of the war, attack military base at El Paraíso, killing at least 100 government soldiers, who are buried in a mass grave.

1984

JANUARY 1 Guerrillas destroy Cuscatlán suspension bridge.

JANUARY 11   Kissinger commission releases its report.

FEBRUARY   Reagan administration announces that it will seek a supplemental $178.7 million in military aid for El Salvador for fiscal year 1984 and $132.5 million for 1985.

MARCH 25   Scheduled date for Salvadoran presidential elections.

INTRODUCTION

THIS book is about turmoil and revolution and the United States response. Though the focus is on the caldron in a country called El Salvador, the issues are broad, with parallels from the past and lessons —it is hoped—for the future.

"We are going to have more revolutions, but we still haven't learned how to deal with them," observed one of President Jimmy Carter's senior foreign policy advisers during an interview for this book.

Today it is El Salvador. The question is not if but how soon it will be Guatemala, where the poverty and repression that spawned the revolution in El Salvador are replicated—and the U.S. interests far greater. After that it may be the Philippines, Chile, South Korea, Turkey, or any one of dozens of other nations around the world—just about anywhere but Europe and North America.

In the late summer of 1980 I was talking with the person in charge of editorials at one of the country's major dailies. Peering over the top of his glasses, he asked, "What should the United States policy be in El Salvador?" I had spent several months in Bolivia and Guatemala, in addition to two short visits to El Salvador, and I replied, "Ask me about Bolivia, or Guatemala, or any country, I'll probably have an opinion. But El Salvador, boy, I just don't know. I guess we're doing the right thing."

During the next two years I returned to El Salvador many times, as a reporter for *The New York Times*. My experiences there are the foundation for this book. But it was after returning to the United States that I began to probe—a quest to understand what has led to the extensive U.S. involvement in such a tiny country. What I gleaned, what appears in these pages, is the culmination of interviews—principally with senior U.S. Foreign Service officers who were posted in El Salvador from 1979 until late 1983 but also with diplomats who served in neighboring countries and State Department officials who were involved with developing the policy. They talked candidly, but most insisted that their names not be used. It was an understandable request. They are still in the government; what they told me ran counter to public accounts. As crucial as the interviews were to an understanding of what the United States has been doing in El Salvador, maybe more so were the reams of confidential documents. Some of these were released under the Freedom of Information Act; the most critical ones were provided to me through a variety of other channels.

THIS book owes a great deal to many people, in addition to those Foreign Service officers who gave their honest assessments.

Among the individuals who shared their insights and understanding of El Salvador and Central America were Aryeh Neier, Michael Posner, Diane Orentlicher, Heather Foote, Ricardo Stein, and Janet Shenk. In addition to her vast knowledge about Central America, Cynthia Arnson provided access to her files, including copies of all articles about El Salvador—filed chronologically and by subject—from *The New York Times* and *The Washington Post,* dating back to the mid-1970's. The reporting in those newspapers was indispensable. Among the journalists whose dispatches are not adequately mentioned in this book, four deserve mention, for the assistance and camaraderie they provided when I worked with them in El Salvador and for their continuing excellent reporting from the region: Julia Preston of the *Boston Globe* and National Public Radio ; Sam Dillon of the *Miami Herald;* Juan Vasquez of the *Los Angeles Times;* and Robert Rivard of *Newsweek.*

Carolyn Croak in the State Department's Freedom of Information Act office responded to my voluminous FOIA requests with courtesy and cheerfulness that should be a model for others. Jay Peterzell shared with me the many documents the Center for National Security Studies obtained under the FOIA. Alan Morrison and Eric Glitzenstein represented me, without charge, in my lawsuit to require the State Department to disgorge more documents. Rachel Burd transcribed hours of taped interviews. The researchers at *The New York Times* located every detail and fact that I needed during the crucial final weeks. In this day of word processors and computers, I would not have made it to the finish line on time without the always available assistance of Howard Angione, Jed Stevenson, and Torin Roher.

But whatever material I gathered from all the sources would have been little more than a mass of reporting had it not been for my colleague at *The New York Times* Leslie Bennetts. In addition to encouraging me to write this book, she read the manuscript in its entirety and provided truly caring editing and polish. John Dinges and James LeMoyne, each of whom has a considerable depth of knowledge about and experience in El Salvador and Latin America, also read the manuscript. Their perceptive criticisms and input—additions and corrections—made it a better book. During long runs around Central Park, Ben Cheever listened for miles, then offered suggestions that gave the book much of its direction.

"In the beginning . . ." This book would not have been possible without the support of several very important people at *The New York Times.* A. M. Rosenthal, *The Times'* executive editor, hired me, a lawyer-turned-journalist. Then two years later, when I was bursting with the need to write this account, he allowed me to take several months away from the paper in order to do so. My foreign editors at *The Times,* Robert Semple and Craig Whitney, provided guidance and patience while I was in the field. And I shall forever feel a particular warmth and gratitude for two of my *Times* friends, Warren Hoge and Alan Riding. Each in his own very talented and caring way encouraged and taught me.

Legion are the horror stories about the clashes between authors and editors. But only the highest accolades were earned by the friendly and brilliant staff at Times Books. Jonathan Segal spent many hours with me, suggested structure and organization, provided broadening concepts, and answered minute questions. His associate, Ruth Fecych, gave the book the touches it needed. Other of Jonathan's colleagues— Sarah Trotta, Pamela Lyons, Pearl Hanig —took care of all those details that were essential to creating what is between these covers.

Though my name is on the cover—and I, of course, am solely responsible for its contents—this book was a team effort, aided by friends who went months without seeing me and listened to my obsession with El Salvador when they did.

RAYMOND BONNER
March 22, 1984
New York

PART ONE

1

THE STORY NOT TOLD

CAUTIOUSLY. Tensely. Down Calle Arce we crept, past the smoldering hulks of beat-up buses and overturned passenger cars. The tropical afternoon heat was stifling, adding to the nervous sweat that soaked our khaki safari jackets. We were a handful of journalists, mostly European—a British cameraman, a French photographer among them—for El Salvador was still not a major or even a very important story in the United States.

The day's events had begun as another protest march, this one by students, who carried their hand-lettered banners with revolutionary slogans, some with triangular-folded red bandannas covering the lower portions of their startlingly young faces. It had erupted not surprisingly—almost predictably in view of the military's attitude toward dissent—into violence: Government soldiers took aim with their German-made G-3 automatic rifles; a few demonstrators tossed Molotov cocktails they had hidden in brown paper bags and fired pistols pulled from their waistbands.

But the story wasn't the demonstration.

We slowly worked our way east, to Fifteenth Calle, a leafy street of nondescript one- and two-story stucco houses on the edge of the downtown commercial district, the walls or metal pull-down shutters of stores and government offices so covered with revolutionary graffiti the place had the look of the New York City subway. On the pavement, in the dancing shadows created by the leaves overhead, on the east side of 15A, was the body of a man in his early twenties. The blood was still wet. A revolutionary banner lay next to him.

Soldiers repeatedly ordered us not to proceed farther. We would wait a few minutes, then begin to inch forward again. But we weren't all that confident that the soldiers wouldn't enforce their commands with

3

bullets; bursts of automatic-rifle fire sent us lunging to the ground, hugging the cement walls, scurrying into an auto repair garage.

A squad of National Guard soldiers, in their black puttees and helmets, sheathed machetes dangling from their waists, stormed by. Then came the camouflaged armored personnel carriers. At Third Calle they turned north—to the headquarters of the Christian Democrats, the country's major nonmilitary political party. We could hear the crackle of automatic rifles, the splintering thud of grenades. But we were not allowed to observe what was happening. A burly sergeant forced us to remain out of sight. This one was serious. We tried to sneak looks around the corner. At one point I caught a glimpse of soldiers hauling someone in blue jeans from a pile of people lying in the driveway. It would be some time before I connected that view with what had happened.

The Christian Democratic party headquarters had been occupied by the LP-28, one of the country's several mass-based, leftist organizations, on January 29, 1980. Today was February 12. The takeover had been peaceful. The demands were the usual ones: an end to the repression; the release of political prisoners. Among the hostages were the wife of the minister of education and the daughter of José Antonio Morales Ehrlich, a Christian Democratic member of the junta.

Christian Democrat leaders and the civilians on the junta had requested the armed forces high command not to take any military actions to dislodge the protesters. Historically, for nearly fifty years the military had ruthlessly ruled the country, always reacting with force—to demonstrations; to occupations; to protests by peasants, workers, students. The era of dictatorial military rule was to have ended with a coup in October 1979. The Christian Democrats, with strong backing from the United States, had joined in a ruling coalition with the military. Now the civilians were testing the military's commitment to resolving problems politically, peacefully, not with military force.

A FEW weeks following the incident at the Christian Democratic party headquarters, a congressional subcommittee in Washington held a hearing on a request by the Carter administration to send $5.7 million in military aid to El Salvador, the assistance marking a major shift in U.S. policy. Among those opposing the military assistance was the Washington Office on Latin America (WOLA), a nonprofit church-supported organization. The aid, argued Heather Foote, a staff member at WOLA, would go not to a moderate civilian government but to a government controlled by the military. The civilians' inability to stop the army from attacking the Christian Democratic party headquarters was one demonstration of that, she told the subcommittee.

Defending the administration's request was John Bushnell, the deputy assistant secretary of state for Inter-American affairs. Ms. Foote had misled the subcommittee, he contended, by relating "only two-thirds of the story about the Christian Democratic headquarters." He told the congressmen that the government forces had "been successful in holding their people back" and that they had tried to keep the situation at the party headquarters "under control."

Bushnell was right that only part of the story had been told. But what had not been told reflected less, not more, favorably on the government forces and rebutted his contention that they had acted with restraint. Bushnell did not tell the congressmen about the small tanks that had surrounded the headquarters or about the soldiers who had fired their automatic weapons into the demonstrators. Nor had he told the congressmen the rest of what had happened.

WHEN the shooting stopped, our small knot of reporters was allowed to approach the scene. The Christian Democratic headquarters is a plain two-story building. On the green stucco exterior is the simple drawing of a fish, the symbol used by the early Christians and today the party's logo. Facedown in the driveway were twenty-three members of the LP-28. Many were shirtless. Some were barefoot or wearing only socks. Boys and girls. They were trembling. Some sobbed convulsively. As they were marched—at gunpoint, hands behind their heads—to a military truck, the fear—of death, torture—that registered in their eyes was palpable. They were so young. Most were teenagers. Soldiers tossed them onto the flatbed, piled on top of one another. National guardsmen stood over them, jamming rifles into their backs.

Then we entered the headquarters. In the foyer were three bodies— a man and woman who appeared to be in their early twenties and a younger male. They had been shot. They lay in coagulating blood. The lower jaw of the older man had been hacked away with a machete. Blood soaked the woman's blue jeans around the groin. The green stucco building was eventually cleaned up and remained the party headquarters. During the next two years I would enter it frequently, to interview José Napoleón Duarte, as the president of the junta, or Morales Ehrlich, another junta member. I drank beer and watched the dancing when the Christian Democrats celebrated behind the wrought-iron gates, which were always guarded by men with heavy weapons. And every time I visited I would vividly remember those bodies. But on February 12 I had coldly recorded it all in my notebook and on film. The significance of what I was reporting did not register. It was my first time in El Salvador. I didn't know what the fighting was all about, who or what the LP-28 was, why students were burning buses, seizing embassies. I could not conceive that an army could be so brutal to its own citizens. It just didn't cross my mind that the occupants had been killed in other than a shoot-out.

But the events and the scenes played in my mind, sometimes as stills, other times as instant replays in slow motion. I kept seeing the low brick wall in front of the headquarters, where the soldiers had displayed the weapons they captured from the occupants: six home-made contact bombs; one beat-up .38 caliber pistol; one 357 Magnum Smith & Wesson; and five bullets. And then I flashed back on what I had seen as I crouched at the corner of Fifteenth and Third, stealing every opportunity to get a closer look: the man in blue jeans being hauled from the people lying prone in the driveway. Then I thought about where the bodies had been found. Inside. Behind walls. The window openings of the building had been filled in with cinder blocks. There were boxes behind them. There was no way that shots fired from the outside could have entered that building.

There hadn't been a shoot-out. It had been murder. After the lightly armed occupants had surrendered, releasing their hostages un-harmed, the soldiers ordered them all to lie on the ground, then had determined who the leaders of the takeover had been. They hauled them back inside—this is what I had glimpsed—hacked them with machetes, shot them. What I would not realize until many months later, until I learned more about the history of El Salvador, was that the army that day at the Christian Democratic party headquarters had behaved as it always had, ignoring civilian pleas for restraint, using excessive force against all dissent from the left.

In a Confidential* cable to Washington the U.S. embassy in El Salva-dor reported that the Christian Democrats had issued a communiqué "condemning security forces for violent dislodgment contrary to party's demand that the occupation be treated as political and not military matter." Bushnell did not tell the congressmen what the em-bassy had reported, just as he did not tell them about the murders.

---

*The classification system for government documents is: Unclassified; Limited Official Use; Confidential; Secret; Top Secret. Throughout this book, upper-case designates the classification as it appears on the document; lower case, the generic nature of documents. Thus "Confidential cable" means that the cable was classified by the sender as "Confidential."

But Bushnell also told the congressmen:

There are three categories of violence now going on in El Salvador. One is the violence which is paid-for, violence by the right-wing assassination groups, which is targeted on assassinating people. By and large this is not approved of, it is resisted by the security forces but it is a hard thing to stop. These people strike quickly and are gone.

A second form of violence comes from the left, where there is a conscious effort to provoke violence, to challenge the Government. At times they attack police posts; they move in and take over farms subject to land reform in order to put in different farmers. That challenges the authorities. When the authorities appear, fire fights result. It may be that peasants are killed as well as soldiers.

The third type of violence which, it is said is happening, and I think probably there is some, is what is properly called repression. I do not think we can call the violence caused by the left or the far right as repression. There have been cases where people who are part of the government security forces—the police, the Army—have taken action against people without provocation.

Our information is that that type is the smallest part of these three types of violence.

It is hard to imagine a more unrealistic picture of the violence in El Salvador. The security forces weren't trying to stop the right-wing assassination groups; the death squads were made up of members of the security forces. Leftists weren't attacking the land reform farms; government military units were. Peasants were not the unfortunate victims during fire fights; they were singled out for murder by government forces.

"We do not overlook the sins of the left," the archbishop of San Salvador, Oscar Arnulfo Romero, said during a Sunday homily a few weeks before Bushnell testified. "But they are proportionately fewer than the violence of the repression. The actions of the political military groups do not explain the repression." During the previous week, he recounted, leftists had killed three policemen and three or four local commanders, "no more than ten in all, which is the same proportion of 1.5 a day as in the preceding two months." On the other hand, he reported, the government and "so-called paramilitary forces" had killed seventy during that week. The deaths, he noted, "had almost nothing to do with repelling these subversive attacks. They are part, rather, of a general program of annihilation of those of the left, who by themselves would not commit violence or further it were it not for the social injustice that they want to do away with."

During the first three months of 1980 nearly 900 civilians, primarily peasants and workers, had been killed by the government forces, more than during all of the preceding three years, when El Salvador was receiving no U.S. military assistance because of the deplorable human rights situation. Now the Carter administration wanted to send military aid, and it had to present the Salvadoran situation in light of the policy, but not in light of the reality.

On February 28, in the village of Villa Victoría, department of Cabañas,* the combined forces of the National Guard, the Treasury Police, and the dreaded rural paramilitary force ORDEN killed seven peasants between the ages of nineteen and thirty-five and an old man who was eighty. Two days later, in nearby Cinquera, the army, National Guard, and ORDEN killed six peasants, ages sixteen to twenty-five. On New Year's Eve day soldiers seized a peasant in El Jícaro, tortured him in front of the Roman Catholic church, then took him to nearby El Terreno, where he was hanged from a tree in the main square and then shot. Also on New Year's Eve day, soldiers seized Josefina Guardado in the hamlet of Conacaste. The following day her body, bearing signs of torture and rape, was found tied to a bed; her throat had been cut. Within a three-week period eight members of the Guardado family were killed, including Antonia de Guardado, forty, and her two infant daughters. Prospero Guardado, twenty-three years old, was killed while shelling corn. Soldiers stole 150 colones ($60) before they shot him. In La Joya, Chalatenango, on January 13, the National Guard and ORDEN killed three Recinos brothers—ages eleven, sixteen, eighteen—and their fourteen-year-old friend. Every day tortured, decapitated bodies were found along the shoulders of dusty roads or in ravines among the garbage and shattered glass. There were twenty separate attacks against churches or church workers during the first two months of 1980. On January 22 National Police machine-gunned the El Rosario Church, where 300 refugees were being cared for. A few days later members of ORDEN and the National Guard raided the church of Ilobasco, shooting four of its occupants. The next day, in Aguilares, two young women who assisted the local priest were kidnapped, tortured, and assassinated. In February the church of El Rosario was again machine-gunned on successive days; three were killed, eighteen wounded while visiting

*Cabañas is one of El Salvador's fourteen departments, as the country's largest jurisdictional districts are called. The departments are the equivalent of states in the United States, provinces in Europe. In this book they will be called departments or provinces.

an exposition in front of the church. The house where the Jesuits lived was machine-gunned, as was the parish church of Nejapa.

Going back to Vietnam, the whole government is always trying to sell something to the American people," said a Foreign Service officer who served in El Salvador for Presidents Carter and Reagan. "Why not just tell the American people the truth? We're not used car salesmen for chrissake. Tell them what's happening and let them decide."

Decisions of state and foreign policy should be the property of the people of the United States," Secretary of State Edmund S. Muskie said during a meeting with the families of four American churchwomen murdered in El Salvador. The families and religious leaders were seeking information about what had happened. Muskie added, according to notes of the meeting kept by a brother of one of the murdered women, "All decisions of a government should rest on the will and support of the masses."

But government officials, especially in Washington, have not been honest about the situation in El Salvador. Distortions, disingenuous statements, tortuous interpretations, half-truths have characterized congressional testimony and public declarations. Salvadoran government atrocities have been covered up. Efforts by congressional committees to obtain information have been met with evasive answers.

When the Reagan administration invaded Grenada in October 1983, the press was kept off the island for several days and tightly controlled when allowed to enter. The manipulation of information about El Salvador has been more subtle, but nearly as invidious, at least from the perspective of an informed public as the bulwark of a democracy. Information that could help the American people decide on the correctness of the American policy has been withheld. Cable traffic— about the violence, the death squads, the military's responsibility for the deaths of thousands of peasants, the armed forces' control of the government—has been routinely overclassified, as Confidential or Secret, in order to prevent it from being released to the public.

The Freedom of Information Act (FOIA), adopted in 1966 and strengthened in 1974, provides the mechanism for the public to obtain access to the workings of agencies and officials. It applies to all federal agencies, including the State Department, Defense Department, and Central Intelligence Agency. The Reagan administration adopted regulations that made it more difficult to use the law.

In response to FOIA requests I made, the Defense Department con-tended that it couldn't locate the documents, even though they were identified by specific numbers and dates. They related generally to Salvadoran armed forces and contained information about the cor-ruptness among the officer corps, the inability of the Salvadoran Army to prosecute the war, the links between the officers and the death squads. It wasn't that the documents couldn't be located. Either the Defense Department was violating the law or it destroyed the docu-ments after the requests had arrived.

The State Department denied my request for scores of documents. It released others, but with substantial excisions, many times several pages. But some of the withheld documents and excised portions of others were made available to me through other channels. These leaked cables show that what the U.S. government withheld would not jeopardize American security, but they would embarrass the policy-makers and tell a story different from the one being presented pub-licly.

In one Secret cable that was denied under the FOIA, Ambassador Deane Hinton advised Washington that he was being selective in what he told reporters. "While I talk to the press about favorable trends, and there are some, there are also seriously adverse trends."

While the ambassador may have been less than forthcoming with journalists, by and large the reporting from the embassy to Washing-ton was honest during the Carter and Reagan administrations. "The distortions were in Washington, to fit a policy," said a diplomat who served Carter and Reagan in El Salvador.

The United States policy in El Salvador has never had the public support officials in Washington sought, and support declined as American involvement escalated. In March 1981, 43 percent approved of the way in which President Reagan was handling the situation in El Salvador, according to a *Newsweek* poll. A year later the approval rating had fallen to 33 percent. Similarly, according to the same poll, in 1981, 44 percent thought the United States should help the Salvado-ran government, and 47 percent said it should "stay completely out." One year later only 36 percent thought the United States should help the Salvadoran government, and 54 percent advocated staying com-pletely out. A *New York Times*/CBS poll in June 1983 found 52 percent saying the United States should "stay out" of El Salvador. If the reality of the situation in El Salvador had been known, if the American peo-ple had understood the ruthlessness of the armed forces against their own people—as revealed by confidential documents—it seems likely that there would have been even less public and congressional support for U.S. involvement.

Until four American churchwomen were murdered in December 1980, few Americans had ever even heard of El Salvador. Was El Salvador the country and San Salvador the capital, or vice versa? The number of academic or scholarly books about El Salvador, until recently, could have been read in a long weekend. In the 1960's blond Californians passed through in their search for the perfect wave; few other tourists were attracted by the beaches, tranquil volcanoes, placid lakes. Americans and Europeans in search of natural beauty and the rich Indian culture sojourned in neighboring Guatemala.

U.S. policymakers historically treated El Salvador in the same fashion—with scant interest. Understandably. It's a tiny country, a total area of some 8,124 square miles, barely the size of Massachusetts. From east to west the country measures no more than 160 miles; the average width, between Honduras and the Pacific, is a mere 60 miles. On a world globe it's a speck; even on a map of just Central America it's hard to locate, its alluvial valleys seemingly being shoved into the Pacific by much larger Honduras (43,277 square miles) and Guatemala (42,042). To the south Nicaragua is nearly seven times larger. El Salvador has no oil, no gold, no silver, no other minerals. Its people have been too poor to offer any significant market for American businesses. The amount of multinational investment has been too minuscule to have an influence on policy.

In 1977 the American ambassador to El Salvador, a California businessman who had been appointed by the Republican administration of Gerald Ford, told a congressional subcommittee that "the United States really has no vital interest in the country." And the head of the Latin American bureau in the State Department declared in the same year, "The United States has no strategic interests in El Salvador." Yet four years later President Reagan was declaring that what happened in El Salvador was critical to the security interests of the United States. The Soviet Union and its proxies "aren't just aiming at El Salvador," he warned, "but at the whole of Central and possibly later South America, and I'm sure, eventually, North America." By 1983 the U.S. involvement in El Salvador, and Central America, had become so crucial to the Reagan administration that the President sought support for his policy in an address to a joint session of Congress. He was only the seventh President in the nation's history to take a foreign policy issue to a joint session.

For the thirty-three years from 1946 to 1979, U.S. military assistance to El Salvador totaled a mere $16.7 million. In the first full fiscal year of the Reagan administration alone, it was five times that, or $82 million—and it continued to spiral. Economic aid, which totaled $199 million for the 1946–1979 period, reached $354.5 million for just three years from 1980 to 1982. By 1982 El Salvador had become the fourth largest recipient of U.S. largess. The tiny country of some 4 to 5 million people followed only Israel, a democratic country and one of America's most important allies; Egypt, a democratic country of some 44 million people and also of unquestionable strategic importance; and Turkey, with a population of 47 million and the location of important U.S. military bases. On a per capita basis, Salvadorans were receiving four times what the Turks got. And in February 1984 the Reagan administration announced that it would seek $312 million in military aid alone for El Salvador for 1984 and 1985, the equivalent of some $30,000 for every guerrilla fighter.

The policy, at least as publicly stated by both the Carter and the Reagan administrations, was to develop a moderate, democratic government in El Salvador. It can be argued that even a leftist, democratic government in El Salvador would not be inimical to U.S. interests, in view of the fact that all the Socialist governments in southern Europe in 1983, led by France, were staunch anti-Soviet U.S. allies. But even if the soundness of the U.S. policy in El Salvador is accepted, the question of whether or not it has been successful remains.

When the United States invaded Grenada in October 1983, President Reagan justified it in part because of the leftist "thugs" who, he said, had taken control of the tiny Caribbean island. But in El Salvador the effect, even if not the purpose, of the Reagan administration policy was to support rightist thugs. It was, as one disgusted diplomat remarked after the rape-murders of the four American churchwomen, a "genocidal, nun-killing junta" that the United States was backing. Privately U.S. diplomats in El Salvador routinely referred to the military as the Mafia. And contrary to the public statements by U.S. policymakers, the confidential documents reveal that it was not the civilians but the colonels and generals, many of them officers with fascist ideologies, who controlled the country.

In the 1980 presidential campaign candidate Reagan and the Republicans charged that during the Carter years the United States had become weak and had lost its power to influence world events. But what has the Reagan administration accomplished in El Salvador? What does it have to show in exchange for the expenditure of nearly $1 billion? The Salvadoran military has taken the money, listened to the lectures about the need to respect human rights, heard the threats that aid would be halted if they didn't—and gone on killing fellow countrymen.

In January 1981 two Americans working with the Salvadoran land reform program, Michael Hammer and Mark Pearlman, were gunned down, gangland style, while they were eating dinner in a restaurant of the Sheraton Hotel in San Salvador. The United States pressed the Salvadoran government to bring the murderers to justice.

Two years after the slayings President Reagan personally called the president of El Salvador, Álvaro Magaña, and pleaded with him to ensure that the accused killers were prosecuted. Reagan was ignored. The army officer who gave the orders to kill Hammer and Pearlman was released by the courts, and then, in what can be considered one of the most revealing statements of who runs El Salvador and how powerless the United States is, he was made a troop commander.

This is not an isolated example of American impotence in El Salvador. In spite of all the money poured in and the verbal threats and hand wringing, the murderers of the four American churchwomen had not been brought to justice by March 1984, more than three years after the crime. With the United States powerless to force the Salvadoran government to prosecute the killers of American citizens, it is not surprising that no Salvadoran military officer has been punished for the most extreme abuses of human rights.

The Reagan administration also didn't have much to show for its military expenditures of some $250 million. By 1984 the guerrilla forces were stronger, not by fractions, but by multiples, and a leftist military victory seemed more likely than when the administration had come into office three years earlier.

SINCE October 15, 1979 . . ." With that incantation U.S. policymakers have justified nearly everything that the United States has done, or tried to do, in El Salvador in recent years.

On October 15, 1979, a small group of military officers led a coup that overthrew the government of General Carlos Humberto Romero. The coup, according to the widely repeated interpretation, ended nearly half a century of an alliance between the armed forces and the oligarchy. The former had kept the peasants in check while the latter garnered enormous profits. U.S. policymakers insist that the coup ushered in a new era, one that saw "the transformation of the military from an institution dedicated to the status quo to one that spearheads land reform and supports constitutional democracy," as the assistant secretary of state for Inter-American affairs, Thomas Enders, declared.

That there was a coup by reform-minded younger officers is true. But in order to justify the policy of supporting the Salvadoran regime with torrents of aid, U.S. officials have focused on that single event and have ignored and distorted what followed. Indeed, accounts of how the coup came about and what transpired in subsequent weeks have been so mangled that it is difficult to separate the myth from the reality. The Reagan State Department even went so far as to rewrite the history of one of the most significant events of the postcoup period.

One thing the coup did was provide the Carter administration with an opportunity to develop in El Salvador a pluralistic but non-Marxist government that would control the armed forces. The administration squandered that opening. But if El Salvador is "lost" to a Marxist government—or if American troops have to be dispatched to prevent that from happening—the Reagan Administration will be as much to blame.

Both the Carter and Reagan administrations insisted that they were supporting a moderate, centrist government caught between the extremes of the right and the left. This was the catechism—stated repeatedly by policymakers in El Salvador and Washington, accepted by editorial writers, and reported by most journalists, including me.

There were indeed extremes on the right and left. But the Christian Democrat-military junta led by José Napoleón Duarte and later the elected government headed by Álvaro Magaña were not in the center. Pages of confidential documents reveal that Duarte had moved to the political right and was controlled by the armed forces within months after the coup, and there was further steady consolidation of the power of conservative elements within the military in the years that followed.

Successive military governments in El Salvador, going back nearly half a century, blamed all of the country's turmoil on the Communists. Priests who worked with the poor were Communists. Students who marched in the streets were Communists who had learned from Communist professors in the university. Peasants who demanded a piece of land, and workers who wanted to earn more than $1 a day were Communists.

In El Salvador "[A]ny idea or activity, based on social justice, whether it comes from political, social, or religious sectors, is immediately branded as Communist," Morales Ehrlich told U.S. congressional committees in 1977. "With this position of staunch anticommunism and antisubversion, the government is able to justify violations of human rights, even the right of life and liberty of persons who merely disagree with the government, or who seek a more just society, or who work to insure free elections and a democratic process."

The United States reinforced this view. "I suppose to a large extent it is our own fault, because we in the United States made such a big thing about communism as a real threat to Latin America for such a long period," President Ford's ambassador to El Salvador, Ignacio E. Lozano, Jr., told a congressional sub-committee four months later. "If you are against them, or if you disapprove of what they are doing, they label you a Communist."

A U.S. military man who paid a visit to El Salvador in the mid-1970's recalled later, "President Romero told me that they would have no problems here if there weren't any Communists. I knew then, this guy doesn't know more than a pig does about Sunday. You can't blame it on the Communists." The visitor had been John Waghelstein, who as a colonel became the commander of U.S. military advisers in El Salvador in 1982, when the Reagan administration was describing what was happening there as a "textbook case of indirect armed aggression by Communist powers through Cuba." It was not just the Soviet Union and Cuba that were being blamed.

"What would the human rights situation in the area be like if Nicaragua had a peaceful and democratic regime?" the assistant secretary of state for human rights and humanitarian affairs, Elliott Abrams, asked rhetorically during a congressional appearance in 1983. He provided his own answer: "The real increase in violence in El Salvador dates back to 1979 which was the time the Sandinistas took over in Nicaragua and began to increase their aid to the guerrillas in El Salvador and indeed the headquarters of the guerrillas in El Salvador was moved to Managua."

I T is an all too familiar truism that "Those who cannot remember the past are condemned to repeat it," as Santayana observed.

The past in El Salvador is one of bitter poverty and extreme repression, enforced by a tradition of ironclad military rule. These are the roots of the revolution. It might be easier to adopt a policy by ignoring or distorting history or, as both the Carter and Reagan administrations did, by ignoring the pleas of Salvadoran church leaders, but such a policy is almost certainly doomed to failure.

2

ROOTS OF THE
REVOLUTION

I IMAGINE the situation in El Salvador today is very much like France was before its revolution, Russia before its revolution and Mexico before its revolution," one visitor recorded. "A socialist or communistic revolution in El Salvador may be delayed for several years, ten or even twenty, but when it comes it will be a bloody one."

That was the warning not of a firebrand revolutionary but of the United States attaché for Central American military affairs, Major R. A. Harris. And the year was 1931. Castro was barely five years old, still running around barefoot and in shorts. Nicaragua's Sandinista leaders were not even born. The term "cold war" had not even been coined.

Major Harris's ominous prophecy was predicated on the disparities between the haves and the have-nots, the country's very few rich and the multitude of impoverished peasants. The major explained:

> About the first thing one observes when he goes to San Salvador is the number of expensive automobiles on the streets. There seems to be nothing but Packards and Pierce Arrows about. There appears to be nothing between these high priced cars and the ox cart with its bare-footed attendant. There is practically no middle class between the very rich and the very poor.
>
> From the people with whom I talked I learned that roughly ninety percent of the wealth of the country is held by about one half of one percent of the population. Thirty or forty families own nearly everything in the country. They live in almost regal splendor with many attendants, send their children to Europe or the United States to be educated, and spend money lavishly (on themselves). The rest of the population has practically nothing.

Not much changed during the decades that followed. In the late 1970's the wealthiest 5 percent of the country's families cornered 38 percent of the national income; the poorest 40 percent fought over 7.5 percent. It was the most unequal distribution of income in all Latin America. As recently as 1983 only 6 percent of the population earned more than $240 a month. A market basket of basic needs cost $344 per month.

The Packards and Pierce-Arrows are gone, of course, and there is now a larger middle class, primarily in San Salvador. They fill up their Volvos, Datsuns, and Toyotas at Esso and Shell stations, treat their families at McDonald's, pizza places, and ice cream parlors. The largest shopping center in Central America is in San Salvador—the modern, split-level Metrocentro, along the Boulevard los Héroes, where music blares from record shops and shoppers gaze through the plate glass at the images relayed from the selection of television sets arrayed among the beds and dinette sets. An escalator, which seems to have been installed to prove that the country is modern—the distance ascended is short, very short—leads to the lower-level Sears, specialty boutiques, a chocolate shop, and a veterinarian.

But a half century after Major Harris's observation the middle class, while growing, is still relatively small. Between 60 and 70 percent of El Salvador's people do not belong to the middle or even lower middle class; they are rural peasants, mired in poverty, as they have been for generations.

For the most part what social and economic progress the country has made has not filtered down to the peasants. Adult literacy, for example, increased from 49 percent in 1960 to 63 percent in 1978, but it was only 30 percent in rural areas. Functional illiteracy among the peasants approaches 90 percent. According to the World Bank, while access to primary education was "widespread in urban areas," only 8 percent of rural children from ages thirteen to fifteen years were in school in the late 1970's.

Medical care has also been focused upon urban dwellers. In the late 1970's there was only one doctor for every 3,592 Salvadorans, the lowest ratio in Central America, and of these few, fully two-thirds worked in the capital. In the provinces of Morazán and Chalatenango, where support for the revolution has been the strongest, there were only five doctors, or one for every 90,000 peasants.

Behind the cold statistics is the reality that has helped spawn a revolution. There are two worlds of El Salvador, the one of the middle class and rich and the far larger one of the poor. The chasm between those worlds was riveted in my mind each morning as I jogged on the south edge of the capital along the Autopista Sur, past the mighty Cuscatlán soccer stadium, in front of the gate to the Catholic university.* Just before the junction of the *autopista* and the Pan American Highway, an entrepreneur put in a go-cart track sometime in 1981. Adjacent to it a towering billboard advertises imported golf shirts. Under the billboard and across from the kids careening around the track, are the dirt-floor shacks—sticks, mud, and cardboard somehow kept together under rusting corrugated tin held in place by rocks.

Running on, I would come to the posh residential districts. On one side of the street are the expensive, modern houses, with swimming pools and well-tended gardens. On the other side are the ravines, which are the capital's veins. Into them are plunged shanties and shacks, where extended families share the dirt. From their porches or glassed-in dining rooms, the wealthy can gaze out across the city's expanse, across the top of the ravines. The misery beneath them is not visible. The capital is ringed by a belt of squalid, noisy, grimy neighborhoods— Mejicanos, Soyapango, San Antonio Abad—where merchants peddle their wares from ramshackle clapboard shops and women spread fruits and vegetables on the ground in open-air markets.

But the most glaring contrasts are outside the capital. A paved road leading south from the capital is for the convenience of those who can afford to go to the Pacific coast beaches, where the wealthy have their private clubs or second homes on cliffs with views that would be envied by Californians. A recently completed four-lane highway speeds businessmen some forty miles from the international airport to the Hotel Camino Real, across from Metrocentro. Another thoroughfare, divided by a pleasant boulevard and complete with toll booths, connects San Salvador with the western city of Santa Ana, the country's second largest city, boasting a theater for live productions and an ornate cathedral. Along the way, unhurried vistas of volcanoes and lush sugarcane fields and coffee groves are interrupted by billboards. A woman seductively promotes pantyhose. A victorious runner endorses a family shoe store chain. A Smirnoff's vodka bottle entices.

But get off the paved roads—as too few congressional delegations to El Salvador ever do—and you enter a semifeudal society. It's a time warp. It looks like Appalachia or the American West—in the 1800's.

Rural Salvadoran villages are built around a central square. The whitewashed Catholic church dominates one side. The other three sides are continuous rows of dull brown mud walls, with veneers of thin plaster, divided into family quarters, a pharmacy, a general store,

*The official name of the Catholic university is José Simeón Cañas University of Central America. It is also known as the Central America University and is usually referred to in El Salvador as UCA.

and the local Alcoholics Anonymous. Weeds grow out of the tiles over eaves that angle down over wooden walkways. Outside these villages are clusters of mud hovels, bisected by rutted dirt paths. Barefoot boys and men wearing chaps ride horses with bulky wood saddles. In the dry season the dirt, ground to a fine dust, is suffocating. During the rainy periods oozing mud makes each step an effort. Filthy naked children with painfully distended bellies, festering eyes, and open sores wander among grunting pigs, stinking garbage, scrawny dogs, and flies. Three out of every four Salvadoran peasant children suffer from malnutrition. Their mothers and sisters trudge for an hour or more to the nearest source of water to haul it in gourd-shaped plastic containers balanced on their heads. Only one-fourth of the rural populace has access to safe water, and a mere 17 percent has adequate means of waste disposal. Diarrhea, not cancer or heart disease, is the major cause of death.

In any country without any exportable resources and only a very small industrial base, land is the key—to wealth for the few who control it; to survival for the peasants. In the late 1970's a staggering 78 percent of El Salvador's arable land was in the hands of the top 10 percent of the landowners. The wealthy plant their fertile lands with coffee, cotton, and sugarcane—for export. They hire peasants at slave labor wages. Under the blazing sun, women walk in the newly planted cotton fields, spreading fertilizers by hand. In 1982 they earned about $25 for every two weeks' work. In another field a man guiding a crude wooden harrow drawn by two oxen earned $3 a day. Those wages, which are earned only two or three months a year during the planting and harvest seasons, won't buy the family groceries—cooking oil, milk, bread—for a week.

To survive, peasants coax corn, beans, and vegetables from the depleted soils of their plots, frequently situated on seemingly vertical hillsides. They don't own the land; they only work it as sharecroppers or renters. More than 90 percent of these parcels are smaller than twelve acres, but twenty-two acres are necessary to provide subsistence for a family of six, the average size of a Salvadoran family. But those with even tiny plots are fortunate; nearly half of all Salvadoran peasants have no access to any land.

With the country's farmland devoted overwhelmingly to export crops, it is not surprising that calorie intake in the country as a whole was 82 percent of daily requirements in 1977; this meant it was substantially lower for the peasants. It was the second lowest in Latin America, barely above that in Bolivia. Even Haitians ate better. And Cubans were getting 118 percent of their daily needs. Nutritional deficiencies account for half the deaths of rural Salvadoran children under five years old. One out of every ten peasant children dies before reaching his or her first birthday, an infant mortality rate four times higher than Cuba's.

It was a level of poverty that Europeans had almost forgotten, a shocked European ambassador remarked when he first arrived in El Salvador in 1977. But what disturbed him most was that the middle and upper classes seemed to ignore the poverty in their midst. It was not just the very rich, he noted. "What I mean," the European told the U.S. ambassador, "is the class of smaller and middle-class businessmen whose very lives and livelihoods have to be here. They seem to have a blind spot in respect to this subject and have no idea that this poverty surrounding them can mean their ruin."

In the 1970's El Salvador's haves were ignoring the peasant poverty. A century earlier they had caused it, primarily as the result of their lust for profits from the nineteenth-century equivalent of oil: coffee. In order to maximize their earnings, they needed land, lots of it. So they took it—from the country's Indians. Then they forced the Indians to work for them.

The Pipil Indians who settled what is modern El Salvador had migrated south from Mexico. In the early sixteenth century the Spanish conquistadors subjugated the Indians, placing them under the control of the captaincy general of Guatemala. It would be three centuries before El Salvador, along with Mexico and the other Central American provinces, declared its independence from Spain. A year later, in 1822, fearing that they were about to be subjugated by expansionist-minded Mexico, the Salvadorans petitioned Washington for statehood. There's no record of what happened to the request, and in 1839 El Salvador became an independent nation.

Until late into the eighteenth century the land tenure system was centered on communal lands, some owned by the municipalities, others by Indian communities. On these unfenced lands the Indians grazed their cattle and harvested their corn and beans. For export the Indians cultivated indigo, from which came blue dye. When the markets for that product disappeared, the Indians began cultivating coffee, again on their communal lands.

But as the international thirst accelerated so did the demands of private individuals for larger properties and capital. Above all, they wanted a labor force to be available at planting and harvest times. As long as there were communal lands, there was no pressure on the Indians to work for someone else. So, the government stepped in.

David Browning, the British scholar whose 1971 book *El Salvador: Landscape and Society* is the outstanding early history of El Salvador, described what transpired:

> In a series of decrees, passed over a short period, the government sought to dismantle an agrarian structure that had evolved gradually over four centuries and to replace it with a system based exclusively on individual private land ownership, and, more importantly [*sic*], on a concept that regarded the land and its inhabitants as capital resources that should be employed efficiently in order to maximize personal fortunes. Such a concept was totally alien to those cultivators whose attitude towards the land and towards the recurring cycle of planting and harvest still remained rooted in their Indian past. Meanwhile the speed of the land reform and the impatience with which it was enacted prohibited consideration of the complex character of the system being destroyed or the problems that were created by its destruction.

The individuals who established coffee fincas, as the large plantations are called, were those who had access to credit: doctors, merchants, priests, public employees, and artisans, according to a government report in 1879. Browning noted that "it was the big landowners and more wealthy members of society who developed the large and most important coffee fincas, with a larger group of people possessing more limited capital resources also taking part in the general speculation, but the majority of the population were [*sic*] excluded."

In one of its first measures to benefit the private coffee growers, the government in 1846 decreed that anyone who planted more than 5,000 coffee bushes was exempted from municipal taxes for ten years and would not be required to pay export duties for the first seven years of operation. The government went even further, transferring state-owned plantations to private coffee planters.

Now that the private individuals had land, they needed laborers. The government first tried the voluntary approach, exempting coffee workers from military obligation. But that wasn't a sufficient incentive. So in 1881 the government abolished communal lands, thus taking from the Indians their self-sufficiency and economic freedom. In the preamble to the abolition decree, the government declared: "The existence of lands under the ownership of the *Comunidades* impedes agricultural development, obstructs the circulation of wealth, and weakens family bonds and the independence of the individual. Their existence is contrary to the economic and social principles that the Republic has accepted." Having had their land taken from them, the

Indians asked that the coffee growers at least be required to provide them with subsistence plots. The coffee grower-controlled government refused.

Thus El Salvador's economic oligarchy was born; the seeds of the peasant revolution were planted. Protests against the conversion of communal lands to private estates and the government's intransigence in the face of peasant demands for subsistence plots led to five scattered and unsuccessful peasant uprisings before the end of the nineteenth century.

By 1930, when coffee accounted for a staggering 95 percent of the country's export earnings while its production was still controlled by a handful of families, the peasants had grown more restless. More important, they had a leader, the charismatic Agustín Farabundo Martí. The son of a landowner, Farabundo Martí found his revolutionary roots in the university, where he pored over the works of anarchists and Marxists. After being arrested during a student rally, he was exiled to Guatemala, where in 1925 he was a founder of the Central America Socialist party. Shortly thereafter he went to the United States to work with groups opposed to American intervention in Latin America. When the New York City police began chasing him down because of his activities with the Anti-Imperialist League, he fled to Nicaragua, to fight in the mountains with Augusto César Sandino against the United States Marines. Returning to El Salvador in 1930, he founded the Socorro Rojo Internacional, Red Aid Society, which was closely allied with the recently founded Salvadoran Communist party.

On May Day 1930 the Communists staged an 80,000-person demonstration through the streets of the capital, with workers and peasants demanding government action to alleviate the unemployment and a minimum wage for agricultural workers. Hundreds of opposition activists were rounded up and imprisoned, and the government responded with a decree prohibiting rallies and strikes and banning the printing and circulation of leftist leaflets. But Farabundo Martí and union leaders continued to organize, primarily among the peasant Indians in the western part of the country.

Farabundo Martí was arrested on several occasions, the last time on January 19, 1932. Three days later, on January 22, the peasants in the western section of the country, who had suffered the most from the loss of their lands to the coffee oligarchs, openly rebelled, seizing several towns and villages around Izalco in Sonsonate Province. On February 1 Farabundo Martí and two fellow organizers faced a firing squad. It took a bullet in his head while he lay writhing on the ground to end Farabundo Martí's life.

The uprising has been documented and graphically recounted by a United States historian, Thomas P. Anderson, in his book *Matanza: El Salvador's Communist Revolt of 1932*. Subsequent military governments, Anderson wrote, have "fostered a legend of bloodthirsty mobs butchering thousands of middle-class citizens, and of a heroic army that barely managed to turn back the barbarian wave." But the reality was the reverse.

Anderson, who interviewed survivors, concluded that the rebellious peasants, armed principally with machetes, killed about 100, including soldiers, and that the army had little trouble crushing the rebellion. Then General Maximiliano Hernández Martínez, who had seized power in a coup six weeks earlier, set about to ensure that there would not be another peasant protest. A worshiper of the occult, Hernández Martínez once declared, "It is a greater crime to kill an ant than a man, for when a man dies he becomes reincarnated, while an ant dies forever." The general extracted retribution at the rate of at least 100 to one. El Salvador's rich Indian language, dress, and culture were wiped out. While no one knows exactly how many Indians and peasants were murdered by Hernández Martínez's troops, some Salvadoran historians put the figure as high as 40,000. The most commonly used number is 30,000. A massacre of the same proportions in the United States would mean the death of 4.4 million.

Roadways and drainage ditches were littered with bodies, gnawed at by buzzards and pigs. Hotels were raided; individuals with blond hair were dragged out and killed as suspected Russians. Men were tied thumb to thumb, then executed, tumbling into mass graves they had first been forced to dig. General Hernández Martínez's name and methods have been venerated by one of the military death squads operating in El Salvador today.

Subsequent military governments in El Salvador have deliberately tried to erase from the country's history the brutality of 1932. The National Library has been purged of all records, including newspapers, that covered the period of the revolt. Government files have been destroyed. But for most Salvadorans and foreign historians, the modern history of El Salvador begins with the *matanza,* the Spanish word for "massacre." In the concluding paragraphs of his book Anderson wrote, "Memories of the uprising account for the almost paranoic fear of communism that has gripped the nation ever since. This fear is expressed in the continual labeling of even the most modest reform movements as communist or communist inspired."

José Napoleón Duarte, who was six years old at the time of the *matanza* and who was to become the leading civilian politician in the country a half century later, is among those who trace the roots of the current revolution to the events of 1932. Two days after Christmas 1980 I talked with him on the patio of his modern but not ostentatious home in San Salvador. It was early in the morning. He slouched in a wicker chair, unshaven, in a white T-shirt partially covered by a lightly checkered blue robe, shoes under a hammock that hung among the tropical flora. I asked him why the guerrillas were in the hills.

"Fifty years of lies, fifty years of injustice, fifty years of frustration," he answered, in almost a cadence, with the stress on each "fifty." "This is a history of people starving to death, living in misery. For fifty years the same people had all the power, all the money, all the jobs, all the education, all the opportunities." His response came as a surprise. I did not expect to hear him suggest there was any justification for the revolution. But what struck me more—over and over again, I played in my mind what he had said—was what he had not said. He had said nothing about Castro or Cuba. He had not mentioned the Sandinistas or Nicaragua. There was no talk of the cold war and the Soviet Union. (Duarte was to raise those themes later, when they reflected the views of the Reagan administration in Washington.) What Duarte was saying was that the revolution had been caused and fueled by the conditions in El Salvador. The "same people" who had the "all" were direct descendants of the families who had begun as the coffee oligarchs.

Los Catorce. "The Fourteen." The term, thought to have been coined by a *Time* magazine correspondent in 1958, became the metaphor for the tight grip that a few families have had on the Salvadoran economy. The actual number may be three or four times that. In 1963 Bert Quint of the *New York Herald Tribune* wrote that seventy-five individuals in 25 interrelated families controlled 90 percent of the wealth in El Salvador. Some put the number today at 200 families. But whatever the exact count, it is an infinitesimally small percentage of the population, which traces its lineage back to the families that had amassed personal coffee fortunes by the end of the nineteenth century. The economic and social register at that time was dominated by names such as Hill, Regalado, Palomo, Parker, Sol Meza, D'Aubuisson, De Sola. In the twentieth century, after the Depression, their economic empires grew, not by acquisitions so much as by mergers consummated with wedding vows. The intermarried-family groupings were not content with just growing coffee; they began processing and exporting it as well. By the 1970's, 23 of the largest 26 coffee-growing families were also the leading processors. In addition, these 26 family groups included twelve of the fourteen largest cultivators of cotton and nine of the ten top sugar growers. (Cotton has historically been the country's second export; sugarcane, the third.) It was an extraordinary concentration of wealth and economic power, and the government, far from unleashing eager trust busters, assisted the agriculturally based oligarchs. The first paved roads and rail lines in El Salvador were constructed by the government to connect the coffee-growing regions with the capital and ports. When the rich turned to cotton, grown principally along the coast, the government extended the roads into those regions.

But the oligarchy didn't rely solely on agriculture; they expanded and broadened their economic base as any well-managed conglomerate would. They set up banks. The Banco Salvadoreño, for example, was owned by the Guirola family, which was second in coffee exports, fifth in cotton, and among the top ten in sugar. The Dueñas, Regalado, and Álvarez clans, which together owned 100,000 acres of prime agricultural land, owned the Banco de Comercio. Credit went to those who already had, more than to those who needed. With loans from family or friends, often on the basis of paper assets, the country's economic elite moved beyond agriculture. The Dueñas clan started insurance companies; the Regalados got into insurance, investment finance, and utilities. The De Sola family went into real estate, construction and manufacturing.

In the 1960's El Salvador sought to diversify away from its over dependence on agriculture. The idea was to create a Latin version of Taiwan, relying on Salvadoran workers, who were not organized to demand reasonable wages—and the military governments would assure they wouldn't be. Salvadoran laborers are widely, and justifiably, considered the hardest-working in Central America. Encouraged by this, plus free trade zones and liberalized tax incentives, foreign investment nearly tripled in the decade after 1959, but it was still only about $114.6 million in 1969.

This industrialization drive was encouraged by the Alliance for Progress, which was President John F. Kennedy's antidote to Fidel Castro and Communist revolutions. In 1961 the United States provided the Salvadoran government with $25 million in economic assistance, which was about double the total extended in the prior fifteen years. It was one of the pitifully few times, until the current crisis, that the

United States paid any attention to El Salvador, aside from regular infusions of military aid and advisers.

To El Salvador, Kennedy dispatched Murat W. Williams, a Rhodes scholar and career diplomat who from 1947 to 1949 had been the number two man in the Salvadoran embassy. During his first tour of duty in El Salvador Williams had sounded a warning similar to Major Harris's seventeen years earlier. In a letter home he wrote, "[S]ince only a few of the people have any money and since 95% of the wage-earners earn less than a dollar a day there is generally a good deal of anxiety about the troubles that may some day come." Williams's tenure as ambassador from 1961 to 1964 presaged what Ambassador Robert White experienced twenty years later.

Williams believed passionately that economic and social reforms were more important in the campaign against communism than military programs. He tried to scale back the size of the military missions; upon his arrival he was horrified to discover that the United States had more air force personnel in the country than the Salvadorans had planes or pilots. But his efforts were thwarted by the Pentagon, which also dispatched a contingent of Green Berets, some of whom had been early advisers in Vietnam. One has to wonder what their mission was since there was no guerrilla activity in the country at the time.

Williams also found little support in the State Department. The head of the Latin American section, who had been Williams's predecessor in El Salvador, advised him, "Murat, you should work more closely with the big families. They have all the power." A member of one of the Fourteen families, Tomás Regalado, whose wealth was estimated at $60 million, told a *Washington Post* reporter in 1963 that "you Americans should stop building schools under the Alliance. Our economy is not strong enough yet to support such social projects." (Regalado meanwhile sent his own sons to expensive private schools in the United States.)

Nevertheless, Williams persisted, encouraging the Salvadoran government to overhaul its tax system—in 1961 only 8,000 Salvadorans admitted to making $2,400 a year, the level at which taxes started—and to enact a minimum wage for coffee workers, who were being paid 60 cents a day. The lanky, patrician-looking ambassador, who spoke fluent Spanish, loved to travel among the Salvadoran peasants, dedicating schools and health facilities built with Alliance for Progress funds. The wealthy called him a Communist and launched a "get Williams" campaign. "The Catorce are furious with you," Williams was sternly warned by a Salvadoran economist. "They have always depended on three supports: the army, the church and the

American legation. Since you came they have lost the legation."

Of course, the oligarchs outlasted Williams and the ideals of the Alliance for Progress. El Salvador remained an agriculture-based economy. Coffee was still king, bringing in some 60 percent of the country's foreign exchange each year throughout the 1970's, and was controlled by the elite as tightly as it had been a century earlier. In 1979, 4 percent of the country's estimated 40,800 coffee growers controlled 67 percent of all the coffee produced. At the bottom of the economic pyramid the country's peasants grew poorer. According to a United Nations study, the number of Salvadoran peasants without any land, even to rent or to work as sharecroppers, skyrocketed from 12 percent in 1960 to 40 percent in 1975. During the same period the average monthly wage of a landless laborer fell from 464 colones (about $185) in 1961 to 429 colones ($171) in 1975.

Most Latin American countries have been controlled by economic elites during the past couple of hundred years. But nowhere, with the possible exception of Guatemala, has their grip been as tight and long-reigning as in El Salvador. The Salvadoran wealthy survived, and grew richer, because they had formed an alliance with an ally far more powerful and reliable than the United States: the military. For fifty years, while the wealthy made money, the colonels and generals kept the peasants and workers in line.

3

NO DEMOCRACY HERE

THE woman, who spoke perfect English, sounded nervous. She was. She and her friends had made it a practice of avoiding the press, she stressed. "We aren't the oligarchy," she said early in the conversation. But would I like to meet some Salvadorans, who owned businesses and were trying to make a go of it, who hadn't fled the country with their capital? Of course! Getting anyone in El Salvador to talk, especially back then, January 1981, was not easy.

There were two Cabinet ministers, a couple of teachers from the American school, a woman who owned two hotel gift shops, and several successful businessmen, whose ventures ranged from real estate to granaries. It was a ranch-style brick house, hung with tastefully arranged modern art and some traditional works by Latin artists. Sliding glass doors opened onto a well-manicured lawn arranged with bright, sweet-smelling tropical flower beds. It was a Sunday brunch—in a tropical Beverly Hills. Over coffee and Bloody Marys we talked, of course, about the violence and turmoil. The president of a food company showed me the death threats he had received from one of the leftist organizations, threats to blow up his factory, threats to kill his workers. I listened and asked questions, lots of them, jotting their observations and opinions in my reporter's notebook.

They knew that the peasants had been treated poorly, that they lived in miserable poverty. But, they argued, poverty and wide chasms between the rich and poor exist in Mexico, in India—"even in your New York," said one. Yet there were no revolutions in those places. Why in El Salvador? they wondered.

What they were saying, in effect, was that revolutions don't erupt full-grown from slums, rural poverty, and skewed income distribution. They were right, of course. But there is another factor in El

Salvador's revolutionary equation: the absence of democracy. Mexico and India may not be—indeed, they are not—democracies in the pure Athenian sense. But there are democratic outlets for the impoverished peasants, angry workers, leftist politicians. They can vote. They can organize. They can demonstrate. Not in El Salvador. Salvadorans have been under the heel of the military boot for more consecutive years than the populace of any other Latin American country.

The country's last truly free presidential elections were in 1931, when Arturo Araújo, a European-educated engineer and lawyer, was elected. By Salvadoran standards of the time, he was a liberal, proposing tax reforms and a reduction in the military budget to offset the effects of the Depression. It was double heresy. He lasted for only a few months before being tossed out by a coup.

That marked the beginning of the era of generals and colonels shooting their way into the Presidential Palace or getting there through rigged elections. Occasional efforts to return the country to democracy were thwarted by hard-line conservatives within the military. The United States acquiesced, usually through inaction.

Araújo was replaced by General Hernández Martínez, architect of the *matanza.* Known as *el brujo*—the Witch Doctor—because of his occult practices, Hernández Martínez espoused fascism. He prohibited blacks, as well as Chinese, Arabs, and Hindus, from migrating into El Salvador. A great admirer of Benito Mussolini and Adolf Hitler, in June 1940 he declared it a national crime to express sympathy for the Allies. When Italy joined the war, 200 blackshirts marched triumphantly, and unmolestedly, through the streets of San Salvador. The oligarchy was quite pleased with Hernández Martínez's rule, especially with the way he controlled the peasants. He once told his subjects, "It is good that children go barefoot. That way they can better receive the beneficial effluvia of the planet, the vibrations of the earth. Plants and animals don't use shoes." The general held power longer than any Salvadoran ruler, until 1944, when in part because of pressure from the United States, he was forced to resign. His successor, also a general, called for immediate elections and allowed workers to organize. The former alarmed the military, the latter angered the oligarchy, and he was quickly tossed out, by Colonel Osmín Aguirre Salinas, whom Anderson described as "the personification of coffee-grower interests." Aguirre, who had been Hernández Martínez's chief of police during the *matanza,* cracked down on all political opposition. When some 10,000 supporters of a civilian presidential candidate rallied in Plaza Libertad, Aguirre had hundreds arrested. The elections were held, but Aguirre made sure his candidate won; the country's liberal leaders were forced into exile.

Concerned about another long Hernández Martínez-style dictatorship, a group of younger officers staged a coup in 1948. Their leader, Lieutenant Colonel Oscar Osorio, won the next election, again marked by fraud, in 1950. He allowed industrial workers, but not the country's peasants, to organize; that meant the right to organize was meaningless because there was virtually no industry in the country. Osorio's handpicked successor was nearly as cruel and dictatorial as Hernández Martínez had been. Again, a group of reform-minded junior officers staged a coup in 1960. The government they formed included a couple of civilians, including a university professor, Fabio Castillo Figueroa, who is today a leader of the Democratic Revolutionary Front (FDR), the political arm of the revolution. This government "marked another opportunity for a genuine process of democratic transition in El Salvador," said Enrique Baloyra, a professor of political science at the University of North Carolina and author of a comprehensive book about Salvadoran politics, *El Salvador in Transition,* published in 1983. If the government had succeeded, he said, the Salvadoran political system "probably would have stabilized at the center-right, not the right," and the moderate left could have been persuaded to participate in elections.

Once again it was not to be. Washington withheld its recognition of the junta apparently because the U.S. ambassador thought that some of the members admired Castro. The Salvadoran oligarchs were upset by the junta's reformist rhetoric, and when their conservative allies in the armed forces realized that this government was serious about holding free and honest elections, they replaced the civilian-military junta with a conservative colonel, Julio Adalberto Rivera. In Washington, with the Alliance for Progress in place, President Kennedy said of the Rivera government, which had civilians in some Cabinet posts, that "governments of the civil-military type in El Salvador are the most effective in containing communism in Latin America."

Rivera envisioned perpetuating military rule, not with coups but "legally," through a political party. The Partido Conciliación Nacional (PCN) was born, as the official government party. In the 1961 elections for delegates to draft a new constitution, only the official PCN candidates won any seats. In the following year's elections for president and seats in the unicameral legislature, the PCN was again the only party.

Not surprisingly the PCN candidate emerged on top in the 1967 presidential elections. This time, however, there was opposition. The moderate, leftist Authentic Revolutionary party, the presidential candidate of which was Fabio Castillo, received 14 percent of the vote, and the Christian Democrats 22 percent. The Christian Democrats had been on the scene for only a few years, and the party owed much of its success to the popularity of one of its founders, José Napoleón Duarte.

After graduating from a Catholic high school in San Salvador, Duarte, with scholarship in hand, like his older brother headed to the University of Notre Dame in South Bend, Indiana. He didn't know a word of English when he arrived in the United States. "I'll say this about Notre Dame—it taught you to have guts," Duarte told journalist and author Tom Buckley in 1981. At Notre Dame, Duarte said he rose at 5:00 A.M. and went to bed at midnight. He worked in the laundry and washed dishes while earning a degree in civil engineering. After returning to El Salvador in 1948, he married the woman who had actually been the girl next door. He went into business with his father-in-law; together they developed a successful construction business, erecting many of the modest number of high-rise buildings that extend above palm trees, giving the capital its modern look. Duarte became a founder of the Boy Scouts, the Antituberculosis League, and the Twenty-Thirty Club, which is a combination Kiwanis and Lions.

He was thirty-five years old before he became involved in politics. "One day there was a coup," Duarte recalled during a long evening of conversation in his home in December 1980. It was the coup in 1960, and Duarte remembered: "A man went on TV and said we have no program other than free elections. My brother and I looked at each other. We realized that the only alternative to the army was the Communist party. That would only mean more violence."

So Duarte began attending meetings with a small group, mostly lawyers who had studied political theory at the National University. They were reading and discussing the papal encyclicals, principally the *Rerum novarum,* which called upon Christians to build a more just society. Issued by Pope Leo XIII in 1891, it defended private property as a natural right but declared that it must be used in a socially just manner. The pope supported the rights of workers to organize and called for the establishment of agricultural cooperatives. Forty years later, in 1931, Pope Pius XI reiterated Leo's principles in *Quadragesimo anno.* These encyclicals are the theoretical underpinnings of the Christian Democratic party, which was a force in nearly every Latin American country by the early 1960's. "I didn't know what the encyclicals were," Duarte told me, "so I went to the library and started reading."

When the Salvadoran Christian Democrats became an official political party, Duarte was named secretary-general. In 1964 he was elected mayor of San Salvador and set about building a political machine and grass-roots support. Duarte acted like nothing the Salvadorans had ever seen, as if he were the mayor in a country that was serious about democracy. A short, stocky man, with a beaming grin and thick head of black hair, he was constantly talking with and listening to his constituents, mingling happily with them in sunny parks and teeming markets. He urged them to form community self-help groups, installed streetlights, and repaired potholes. They reelected him in 1966 by a two to one margin and gave him an even greater victory spread for his third term.

Duarte had a tremendous personal following, and the Christian Democrats had built a powerful political machine. But they were not yet strong enough to take on the military alone. For the 1972 presidential election, they joined in a coalition with the National Revolutionary Movement (MNR) and the Nationalist Democratic Union (UDN). The MNR had been formed by a group of moderate socialists from the university and was led by Guillermo Manuel Ungo, son of a founder of the Christian Democrats, and today the president of the Democratic Revolutionary Front. The UDN, headed by a former vice-president who had resigned because of the government's lack of concern for the peasants, was a surrogate for the Communist party, which had been outlawed after the *matanza*.

The coalition called itself the National Opposition Union (UNO). Duarte headed the ticket. His running mate was Ungo. When the early returns gave the lead to UNO, the government simply stopped announcing the count. To no one's surprise, when the results were announced, the PCN candidate, Colonel Arturo Armando Molina, had the most votes, 334,600, to 324,756 for Duarte and Ungo. No one seriously disputes that there was blatant fraud and that Duarte and Ungo had won the election.

A colonel who backed Duarte and UNO attempted a coup to stop Molina from taking power, but Duarte hesitated to call on his civilian supporters to back it. With some assistance from air strikes by the planes from Anastasio Somoza Debayle's Nicaragua and the military dictatorship in Guatemala, the government easily squelched the uprising, killing some 200 people, mostly civilians. Duarte was arrested by the army, beaten badly—his nose and cheekbones were shattered—and forced into exile.

"Where were all you guys ten years ago?" Duarte said a few days before the elections in 1982, when several hundred journalists and dozens of international observers descended on the tiny country. It was more a denunciation than a question. The 1972 elections had been virtually ignored. *The New York Times* had published a few stories, including an Associated Press account, which described Duarte as a "leftist candidate politician" and made no reference to the charges of fraud.

But even if the press had been there to expose the fraud, it seems unlikely that it would have made any difference. Some of the Salvadoran Christian Democrats, but not Duarte, did, in fact, make an informal appeal to Washington. But the Nixon administration, which was busily trying to overthrow the democratically elected leftist government in Chile, was unconcerned about a military government's fraudulently coming to power in Latin America.

I F the United States had acted in 1972, if it had insisted that Duarte and Ungo, not the military, be allowed to take power, it probably could have avoided the problems of today. The 1972 election is widely seen as the turning point, after which the march toward an armed revolution was inexorable. At the time of the election there was only one guerrilla organization, the Popular Forces of Liberation; it lacked any significant popular support or ability to carry out military or even isolated terrorist activities. The first kidnapping and assassination by a leftist guerrilla group was not to occur until five years later. But the fraud convinced many individuals, particularly professionals and university students, that there was no opportunity for peaceful, democratic change in El Salvador. They began to form other guerrilla organizations and, more important, to organize, with help from priests and labor leaders, workers and peasants who would demonstrate for change and eventually provide the popular support for the armed revolution. One of the first demonstrations was in 1975, against the government's spending at least $1 million for the Miss Universe Pageant. When 3,000 students marched through the streets of the capital, to protest the repression during two earlier demonstrations against the pageant, soldiers fired on them with machine guns and automatic rifles, killing at least 12. The government said the march was part of a "Communist plot." Colonel Molina had already sent troops to occupy the National University and deported more than 40 teachers who he charged were Communists.

The mounting repression moved the Salvadoran conference of Roman Catholic bishops, then, as today, a body dominated by conservatives, to denounce "the climate of violence, repression and lack of fundamental human rights" in the country. "The highest circles of our society do not escape this violation of human dignity," the bishops said, "but this anguish falls overwhelmingly on the most humble, weak and unprotected sectors of our people."

With much fanfare Molina's government, near the end of its five-year term, announced an agrarian reform program. It would have affected only 3.7 percent of the nation's arable land, for the benefit of about 20,000 peasant families. But even this was too much for the oligarchy. A presidential election was approaching, and the National Association of Private Enterprise (ANEP), a group that continues to wield tremendous power in the country, promised massive financing to the PCN candidate, Colonel Carlos Humberto Romero, in exchange for his promise to oppose the land reform. Both promises were kept. The land reform died.

The 1977 presidential election served only to reinforce the military's contempt for democracy and the rest of the population's growing frustration with the attempt to achieve change through peaceful, constitutional channels.

"We have discovered a big operation, directed by the National Electoral Council, to make possible that fraud," Guillermo Ungo, as general secretary of the MNR, wrote the Washington Office on Latin America shortly before the election about a plot to effect another fraud that the party had uncovered. He asked the organization to pass on the information "in order that the State Department does not depend on the official information which is the one the American Embassy will have and serve."

WOLA brought Duarte, from his exile in Venezuela, to the United States. But Duarte found that no one cared much about the reign of terror and political repression in El Salvador. The only senator to talk with Duarte was Edward Kennedy, the meeting urged by Kennedy's aide, Mark L. Schneider, who had met Duarte and become a close friend during Schneider's Peace Corps days in El Salvador. On the House side Duarte managed to see only Thomas Harkin, the Iowa Democrat who had just begun his second term and was to become one of the strongest human rights advocates in Congress. "The Republicans wouldn't talk to us at all," Duarte recalled several years later in his interview with Tom Buckley. WOLA arranged "doughnuts and coffee" for Senate and House aides, Duarte recalled to me. "Only two showed up!" A lunch for the press attracted five reporters. "It wasn't news," says Duarte.

For the 1977 elections the military had devised a more creative way to carry out the fraud. A shortwave network linked the PCN headquarters with the polling places. There were instructions to "put more sugar than coffee in the tank." "Sugar" was the code word for PCN votes, "coffee" for ballots for the opposition party, UNO, and "tank" for ballot boxes.

"The head of M-4 is buying the tamales" came a voice from one of the outlying provinces. "Tamales" was the code word for fraudulent votes.

Another voice: "Well, about the worry we had about the little bird, the ten little birds. I have to tell you that they are here at our headquarters in this district. . . . I am giving them lessons." The code for opposition party poll watchers was "little birds." "Giving lessons" meant using force.

Several thousand UNO backers gathered in the capital's Plaza Libertad to protest the fraud peacefully. They remained for three or four days, until soldiers and ORDEN forces moved in with armored personnel carriers at about two in the morning. As the soldiers encircled the square, the demonstrators sang the national anthem. Then, as they scurried for safety inside the Rosario Church—the priests had given them the keys—the soldiers opened fire. The government said that fewer than 10 persons were killed, but other accounts put the number at more than 200. The government used fire hoses to wash the blood from the square.

In Washington, human rights organizations were able to generate some interest in the fraud, now that Jimmy Carter had become President and was emphasizing human rights as a priority of United States foreign policy. The House subcommittees on International Organizations and on Inter-American Affairs held two days of hearings, apparently the first ever devoted exclusively to El Salvador. A leader of ANEP, Ernesto Rivas-Gallont, who was to become El Salvador's ambassador to the United States in 1981 and was still in that position in 1984, told the congressional subcommittees in 1977 that the demonstration had been part of a "plan of subversion" and that it had been broken up "without any violation of human rights."

But José Antonio Morales Ehrlich, the Christian Democrats' vice-presidential candidate in 1977, told the congressmen, "I saw many people fall from bullet wounds," and said that women and children had been among those killed. "American jeeps" had been used by the soldiers who attacked the demonstrators, he said. At the time of the attack ten U.S. military advisers were assigned to the headquarters of the Salvadoran Army, leading Morales Ehrlich, who was to serve with Duarte on the U.S.-backed junta from 1980 to 1982, to ask the congressmen for "a clearer understanding of the role of 10 U.S. military personnel in my country, especially when violations of human rights are increasing. Let me also add that the weapons and military equipment received by our armed forces from the United States are used mainly as an instrument of repression."

Two months before Morales Ehrlich testified, Jimmy Carter had been sworn in as the thirty-ninth President of the United States, and human rights, in his words, became "the soul of our foreign policy." Carter's concerns for human rights rested on more than his own personal ethical code. It also had a realistic strain, a belief that U.S. security interests were best served by stability and that stability would come about when there were democratic outlets for change. As Carter's secretary of state, Cyrus Vance, told an audience of the Foreign Policy Association, "These moves toward more democratic and open societies in Latin America are distinctly in our interest. The great strength of democracy is its flexibility and resilience. It opens opportunities for broadly based political and economic participation. By encouraging compromise and accommodation, it fosters evolutionary change." In short, evolution to democracy, not revolution to Marxism.

Carter's human rights policy had "a tremendously powerful impact" in Latin America, Morales Ehrlich told the congressmen. But he was clearly skeptical, understandably so in view of the long history of U.S. support for military regimes in El Salvador as well as throughout Latin America. "In my country," Morales Ehrlich said, "people are asking themselves the following questions: Is it really true that the United States is now going to demand that our governments respect human rights, especially when such rights are violated daily? Can it be that our military governments will no longer be able to rely on U.S. backing nor be able to continue their abuses?"

The answers were inconsistent at best, negative at worst. Much is made of the fact that U.S. military aid to El Salvador was suspended in 1977. But that wasn't directly the work of the Carter administration. The Salvadoran government rejected the aid rather than comply with congressionally mandated human rights standards. Moreover, the administration maintained a military mission in the country, and the United States embassy remained "closely identified with the military government" of General Romero, *The New York Times* correspondent Alan Riding reported in 1978.

For the most part, however, the Carter administration paid little attention to El Salvador until late 1979. This is not a criticism of the Carter administration as much as a reflection of the nature of U.S. foreign policy. Historically it has responded to crises rather than anticipated them. "The urgent preempts the important," Kissinger frequently told aides when he was secretary of state.

Because of the absence of any strong interest by the Pentagon and National Security Council in events in El Salvador during the early years of the Carter administration, it became a crucible for the human rights advocates within the State Department. Among them was Mark Schneider, who had developed a special interest in El Salvador while serving in the Peace Corps there from 1966 to 1968. After seven years as an aide to Senator Edward Kennedy, Schneider was appointed the senior deputy assistant secretary in the human rights bureau by President Carter. Schneider's boss, Patricia "Patt" Derian, thought El Salvador was "the kind of place where we really could have helped to make a difference." But "I don't think we have any successes to show in El Salvador," Derian concluded after she had left State when Reagan became President.

Although her self-criticism may be a bit harsh, it is clear that the Carter administration's actions did not match its human rights rhetoric, as illustrated most graphically by the U.S. position on El Salvador's request for a $90 million loan from the Inter-American Development Bank. The loan was for a hydroelectric project at San Lorenzo. Without U.S. backing the loan could not be approved.

Initially the Carter administration withheld its support for the San Lorenzo loan because of the appalling human rights situation. The Salvadoran episcopal conference, in March 1977, issued one of its strongest statements to that date, denouncing the escalating repression "against the peasants and all those who accompany them in their just cause." The bishops deplored the increase in "torture as a means of intimidation" and the mounting attacks on the church by the private businessmen's association, ANEP, and its allies in the armed forces. During the first months of 1977 two priests, including Rutilio Grande, were gunned down, and several others were tortured and expelled from the country. In May, in a operation dubbed Operation Rutilio, the army stormed Aguilares, the dusty, squalid village where Father Grande had worked with poor peasants. Tanks moved into the plaza, and helicopters buzzed overhead. "We were nervously ringing the bells [of the church] to call for help from the people when soldiers with rifles burst into the bell tower and shot one of the peasants," recalled a priest who was one of three inside the church when it was attacked. "Bullets sprayed the altar." At the police station the priests could hear "the beatings and cries of peasants." The church was ransacked, then converted to a barracks. When Archbishop Romero tried to go to Aguilares to remove the blessed sacrament from the church, the soldiers wouldn't let him pass. He sent the chaplain of the National Guard; the soldiers arrested him. Soldiers shot open the tabernacle and threw the hosts on the floor. At least fifty peasants were killed. Hundreds were dragged away. The soldiers tossed bodies into mass graves and prohibited family members from being present.

A few months later, over strong objections of the human rights bureau, the State Department decided to support the San Lorenzo loan, and it was approved. (During 1978 and 1979 the Carter administration voted for three World Bank loans to El Salvador and one other loan by the Inter-American Development Bank. On another IDB loan, it abstained; it voted against no loans.) The department's changed position was brought about in large part because of the vigorous lobbying by Carter's first ambassador to El Salvador, Frank J. Devine. Devine argued that the Salvadoran government "seriously intended to improve the human rights situation" and that the loan would be a way to "keep their feet to the fire." Even liberal and staunch human rights advocates in Congress, such as Senator Kennedy and Representative Harkin, the Iowa Democrat who had written the legislation that linked development bank loans to human rights performance, were persuaded by Devine not to raise objections to the loan.

As was to become the pattern in the 1980's, once the Salvadoran military had what it wanted from the United States, it went on with business as usual. Less than a month after the loan had been approved, the Salvadoran government enacted the Law for the Defense and Guarantee of the Public Order—known as the *Ley de Orden*—it was a Draconian measure, "practically a license to kill," said Professor Baloyra. The American Association for the International Commission of Jurists roundly condemned it, noting among other things that it made an "invidious distinction between crimes against, for example, businessmen and those against peasants." The law restricted all rights to organize, to strike, and even to express any opinions "through word of mouth, through writing or through any other means, that tend to destroy the social order." Three of the country's leading bishops, including the archbishop, attacked the law because it "leaves unprotected the greatest number of Salvadorans, the poor, the workers, and farmhands, for they are impeded from having recourse to the pressure of public opinion in their search for justice, while the rich and powerful are in fact well organized." The bishops went on to declare, as they had many times, that "permanent, institutionalized injustice that keeps the majority of our people in inhuman conditions is truly the root of violence."

Ambassador Devine defended the public order law. "We believe any government has the full right and obligation to use all legal means at its disposal to combat terrorism," he told the American Chamber of Commerce in a speech the day after the law was enacted.

Carter's appointment of Devine as his ambassador to El Salvador was one of the clearest signals to the Salvadoran military that it could ignore the administration's human rights pronouncements. To make room for Devine, Carter recalled Ignacio Lozano, Jr., President Ford's ambassador, who had been openly critical of the government repression. Lozano had opposed the San Lorenzo dam loan primarily because of the disappearance of an American.

The four Roman Catholic churchwomen murdered in December 1980 were not the first American victims of the military brutality in El Salvador. Four years earlier a twenty-four-year-old American black, Ronald J. Richardson, had disappeared. Lozano believed that he had been seized by the government, and he forcefully demanded an investigation. But as with the cases four years later of the four American churchwomen and two American land reform workers, the Salvadoran government ignored the diplomatic protests.

The State Department did not back Lozano's insistence on an investigation and accounting by the Salvadorans. "I was urging Washington to pursue the Richardson case and not let them off the hook on it," Lozano recalled. "The excuse not to pursue the Richardson case," he remembered, was that the Carter administration wanted "a more friendly relationship" with the new Salvadoran government. General Romero had been sworn in as president six months after Carter's inauguration, and the State Department, not wanting to offend a friendly country, accepted the promises for reform. Deputy Assistant Secretary for Inter-American Affairs Charles Bray III told Congress in July 1977 that General Romero had "indicated his intent to pursue socioeconomic reform. He has made conciliatory gestures toward the church." The general-president was also going to crack down on the death squads, the State Department assured Congress. None of this was to be, of course. Nor would there be any investigation in the Richardson case.

"They hung him up by the arms to some device like a mill which stretched his arms," reported a Salvadoran soldier who saw Richardson tortured in the National Guard headquarters. "They tied his arms and the chain stretched him. They covered his head with a hood which cut off his breath." He was also subjected to electrical shocks. Richardson, who was wearing blue jeans, a red shirt with black stripes and a beret, and carrying a backpack when he was captured, was led away, "bleeding at the nose and ears." He later died.

This firsthand account was given to the United States in March 1978. There was no follow-up, not by the State Department, not by the embassy in El Salvador, where Devine had replaced Lozano. Five years later the State Department was still covering up what happened. The State Department has said it has twenty-three documents in its files relating to the Richardson case. It has refused to release eight of them, under a Freedom of Information Act request, and there were substantial excisions in eleven of the fifteen it did release. Lozano said he "cannot think of any legitimate reason why they would not release" the cables relating to the Richardson case. They contain no information relating to national security, he said. One possible reason for not releasing the documents, he suggested, was "to protect some of the current actors." The current Salvadoran minister of defense, General Carlos Eugenio Vides Casanova, "had some fairly high-level job" at the time of Richardson's disappearance and murder, Lozano recalled.

When Carter first indicated that he was going to replace Lozano, the embassy staff in El Salvador, impressed by the ambassador's position on human rights, took the highly unusual step of sending a cable to Washington urging that he be retained. Even though this was six years ago, the State Department will not release the cable; State's response to the embassy staff's request was released, but with more than half of it excised.

From the perspective of the implementation of Carter's human rights policy, the appointment of Devine has to be viewed as a mistake. While he applauded Carter for "having championed human rights," Devine thought there was "a difference between doing this in one's own country and asserting the right or duty to impose our human rights standards upon other countries, which may or may not be ready for them." He did not think El Salvador was ready. He viewed visits by the department's human rights leaders Derian and Schneider as "causes of difficulty."

Devine's appointment reflected a number of convergent factors. After twenty-eight years in the diplomatic corps, most of it in Latin America, he was technically qualified for an ambassadorship, and El Salvador was an insignificant country. On the broader level it was a manifestation of Carter's respect for the Foreign Service. During the campaign, candidate Carter had promised that all diplomatic appointments would be made on merit, and after becoming President, he established an Advisory Board on Ambassadorial Appointments. On the twenty-four-member independent board were a significant number of minorities: women, blacks, Hispanics, and Asians. Since 1946, when the Foreign Service was formally established, political appointments by a President have averaged 36 percent. Only 27 percent of Carter's appointments were political, compared with 42 percent by Kennedy and 41 percent by Reagan. But what Carter apparently failed to appreciate was that taking appointments outside of politics took them outside his policy—that is, by not making political appointments, he had less control over the ambassadors.

At State there was constant tension between the human rights bureau and the five geographic or regional bureaus (Europe, Africa, East Asia and the Pacific, Inter-American, Near Eastern and South Asian). The bureau of human rights and humanitarian affairs grew out of a recommendation in 1968 by the Commission on the Observance of Human Rights Year that the President appoint an assistant for human rights. In 1971 President Nixon asked Congress to create a human rights bureau within State, but Congress did not act. After two more unsuccessful attempts, led by Representative Donald Fraser, Democrat of Minnesota, and Senator Kennedy, Congress in 1976 established such a bureau. The conflicts between the human rights bureau and the regional bureaus reflect the bureaucratic infighting found in all large agencies. In addition, the regional bureaus have a tendency to view foreign governments as clients and to look upon them favorably, whereas the human rights bureau, almost by its nature, is critical of them.

The first person to have the title of assistant secretary for the human rights bureau was Patricia Derian. Her commitment to human rights, and the tactics for achieving them, had been honed in the 1960's during the civil rights struggles in the South. She was a founder of the Mississippi Civil Liberties Union as well as an organizer of the biracial Loyalist Mississippi Democratic party, which successfully challenged the all-white Mississippi delegation for seating at the 1968 Democratic Convention in Chicago. In 1972 she worked on George McGovern's presidential campaign. When approached about actively supporting Carter, she said, "If he's not a sexist and not a racist, I'll help him." She decided he was neither of these and during the campaign worked with what she described as "liberals, intellectuals, and attitudes." After Carter's victory she was asked if she wanted to be chief of protocol. "I can't tap dance," she said with a laugh. Then she was offered the human rights job. "Do you have to win all the time?" asked Warren Christopher, deputy secretary of state, when interviewing her for the post. "No, but a lot," she replied. "I was being tough," she recalled. At State she didn't win many; most of her memorandums were not officially stamped as having been received in the secretary's office. Diplomatic Derian may not be; blunt, very. She told numerous dictators around the world what she thought of them, and Derian, who was without any previous government experience, wasn't much kinder to the State Department bureaucrats.

Derian's greatest problems were with the bureau of Inter-American Affairs, usually referred to within the department as ARA (American Republics Affairs). "It was not a happy relationship," Derian said. "ARA was very opposed to the human rights effort in Latin America. They thought we were punishing our friends, that there was too much emphasis on [human rights violations in] Latin America, that Latin America really wasn't any worse than anyplace else, that Americans had been omnipresent in Latin America, and that we were acting like imperialistic, ugly Americans."

In February 1978, the head of the Latin American bureau, Terence A. Todman, went public with his reservations about the human rights policy. "We must avoid holding entire countries up to public ridicule and embarrassment," he said in a widely reported speech. "We must avoid condemning an entire government for every negative act by one of its officials." The speech was heralded by Latin American dictators. In Paraguay, where one of the world's longest-reigning dictators, General Alfredo Stroessner, has ruled since 1954, Todman was publicly called "the wisest among the officials of Mr. Carter's government."

In El Salvador, however, Todman's speech further convinced religious and opposition leaders that Carter's human rights policy lacked any real teeth. "I feel greatly disappointed because we had hoped the U.S. policy on human rights would be more sincere," El Salvador's leading human rights voice, Archbishop Romero, told Alan Riding of *The New York Times*. "At first, Carter's policy raised great hope here, but now it's creating enormous frustration," lamented Guillermo Ungo.

As appalling as the repression had been under the previous military governments, it actually worsened, reaching "epidemic proportions" under General Romero, says Professor Baloyra. Political assassinations increased tenfold, and the number of "disappeared" doubled. (In El Salvador, as well as in much of Latin America, "disappeared" has become a noun describing those picked up by soldiers or police and never seen again.) The Inter-American Human Rights Commission of the Organization of American States (OAS) issued a chilling report in late 1978. An investigating mission that went to El Salvador found widespread instances of gruesome tortures, physical and psychological, carried out in secret detention cells. During just one month, May

1979, 115 were killed, and 30 more seized off the streets or dragged from their homes, never to be seen again. With the onset of the May downpours, which signal the advent of the rainy season, one writer at the Catholic university suggested that God was leaving the blood on the streets "to blend into the earth and the cement as a witness of the most tragic and bloodiest month in the last forty-seven years."

"The root of all violence is institutional violence," Archbishop Romero remarked. "The situation in the country is lamentable, particularly among peasants and slum dwellers. The rich are getting richer, the poor are getting poorer."

General Romero,* as had his predecessors, as would his successors, blamed the country's problems on outside interference, on the Communists.

In October 1979 General Romero was deposed in a bloodless coup. Like the participants in the coups in 1948 and in 1960, the officers who organized it had visions of social reforms and bringing democracy to their country. But these dreams, like those of the young officers before them, were quickly crushed, by conservative, hard-line officers. Today the Salvadoran Army is the most powerful political institution in the country, in control as it has been since 1931. It has allowed some democracy, but only limited amounts and only for the country's moderates and conservatives. There's no doubt who's in charge.

*General Romero and Archbishop Romero are not related.

4

THE ARMY: THE LAW
AND ABOVE THE LAW

YOU are going to kill them."

"My lieutenant, by myself?" the burly thirty-seven-year-old National Guard corporal asked respectfully. They were standing in the flickering shadows cast by broad deep green leaves onto the pavement in front of the modern Sheraton Hotel, tucked on the lower slope of a volcano in a fashionable residential neighborhood of San Salvador.

No, it was not a one-man job. The twenty-eight-year-old red-headed lieutenant walked over to another soldier, dressed in civilian clothes, who was guarding a white Toyota sedan and a Cherokee station wagon —they belonged to an army major and a wealthy right-wing businessman—and ordered him to participate also. The lieutenant pulled an Ingram .45 caliber submachine gun equipped with a silencer from a Chevrolet, and handed it to one of the guardsmen. An army captain gave him a khaki Windbreaker to conceal the gun.

The soldiers crossed the blacktop hotel parking lot. As they pushed open the hotel's glass doors, they were greeted with blasts of music from the recently opened roller disco, Copacabana. Guided by a prominent right-wing Salvadoran businessman, Hans Christ, they moved past the reception desk on their left, cut right to the end of the lobby foyer, then turned sharply left down the carpeted hall to the Salón de las Americas. A few feet inside the restaurant entrance they stopped, pulled out their submachine guns, and squeezed off nearly forty rounds. Calmly they retraced their steps, leaving behind, at the table where they had been having a late-night dinner meeting, the riddled bodies of the director of El Salvador's land reform agency, José Rodolfo Viera, forty-three, and two Americans: Michael Hammer, forty-two years old, and Mark Pearlman, thirty-six.

Prodded, not so gently by the United States, as is the case in the only

44

times murders are ever investigated in El Salvador, the Salvadorans eventually obtained confessions from the two killers. They identified the officers who had given them the orders and guns on that night in the street: Lieutenant Rodolfo Isidro López Sibrián, who was assigned to the intelligence section of the National Guard, and Captain Eduardo Ernesto Alfonso Ávila Ávila, who worked in the chief of staff's headquarters. The corporals even reenacted the events for the judge.

At the first court hearing in El Salvador, in October 1982—more than eighteen months after the killings—López Sibrián had dyed his hair black and shaved off his mustache to avoid being identified in a lineup; Ávila Ávila's uncle, a member of the Salvadoran Supreme Court, sat in the front row. The charges were dismissed. The U.S. embassy said it was "dismayed and incredulous." Washington was alarmed. The Reagan administration needed convictions or at least a trial; in order to continue supplying military aid to El Salvador, the administration had to "certify" every six months that progress was being made in bringing the killers of Hammer and Pearlman to justice.

General Wallace Nutting, the senior U.S. commander for all Latin America, was called in from his headquarters in Panama. "I figured if they won't take it seriously from me and the civilian side of America, maybe they ought to listen to General Nutting," Ambassador Hinton explained some months later. (Nutting has repeatedly denied to reporters that he ever made this visit.) Nutting met with the Salvadoran defense minister and other senior military commanders. He told them bluntly that they were seriously jeopardizing future military aid if they didn't bring López Sibrián to trial. The Salvadoran generals and colonels ignored him.

But more than just military aid was at stake for the Reagan administration. There were serious political ramifications to the case. The murdered Americans had worked for the American Institute for Free Labor Development (AIFLD), an arm of the AFL-CIO, which has a long history of being closely connected to U.S. foreign policy. Just as the AFL-CIO had been a staunch supporter of the U.S. policy in Vietnam so was it generally supportive of Reagan's hard-line policy in Central America. Letting López Sibrián go unpunished meant risking the loss of that support, which Reagan could not afford. There was an even greater concern: the 1984 presidential election. "The AFL-CIO has enough clout alone to make it an issue in the campaign," said a State Department officer who was involved in pushing the Salvadorans to act in the Hammer-Pearlman case.

So President Reagan himself got personally involved—with an unusual call and a questionable, if not unseemly, request. While an appellate court was considering the dismissal of the charges against López Sibrián in early 1983, Reagan called the president of El Salvador, Álvaro Magaña. "Look, you've got to help us on this thing, you just gotta help us" was how a U.S. diplomat* who was in El Salvador at the time characterized Reagan's message. In short, the chief executive of the United States was asking the chief executive of El Salvador to interfere in the judicial process.

The case of Lieutenant López Sibrián attests more succinctly to the impotence of the Reagan administration in El Salvador than all the vocal protests of human rights organizations. The Salvadorans ignored the U.S. ambassador, General Nutting, and the President of the United States himself. Not only were the charges dismissed, but López Sibrián was given command of troops in Chalatenango, a key military province. After later being removed from his command, López Sibrián was regularly seen driving around the capital in his red Mustang.†

"If they can't get that son of a bitch in jail, then fuck 'em, let's go home, we're wasting our time here," a military adviser in El Salvador shouted after the charges had been dismissed against Lieutenant López Sibrián. "You can rest assured that the government of El Salvador is in no doubt as to our views about this matter," a State Department spokesman said after the appellate court had upheld the dismissal of charges.

"[I]t is quite clear that future assistance would be very unlikely to be recommended by the administration in the absence of progress in this case," the assistant secretary of state for Inter-American affairs, Thomas Enders, assured the Senate Foreign Relations Committee in February 1983. "That is a very live issue for us, and it symbolizes really in one man what is wrong," he added about López Sibrián.

But the American military advisers didn't leave. Aid wasn't sus-

---

*All references to a "diplomat" or "Foreign Service officer" throughout this book are to U.S. diplomats and Foreign Service officers, unless otherwise indicated.
†Captain Ávila Ávila admitted his part in the assassinations to an American acquaintance, according to a story by Craig Pyes, an investigative reporter for the *Albuquerque Journal,* who was relying on the contents of a cable that was provided to him by U.S. government sources. The State Department refuses to release the cable in which the confession was relayed to Washington. When Ávila Ávila was finally detained by military authorities in December 1983, the State Department made much of it—as evidence that the Salvadoran government was acting against the death squads. But Ávila Ávila was only detained, not arrested, and the charges were for desertion. No charges had been brought against him for his involvement in the Hammer-Pearlman killings as of March 1984.

pended; more was recommended. And the President "certified" on four separate occasions that the Salvadorans were making progress in bringing to justice the murderers of Hammer and Pearlman. The weakness of U.S. power matched the weakness of will.

When it was first announced that López Sibrián and Ávila Ávila had been involved in the slayings, Roberto d'Aubuisson, the country's archconservative political leader and president of the national legislature at the time, went on television and declared, "They are my colleagues and my friends, just like those who through 20 years of military service I knew and lived with." Then he added, "I feel honored to be their friends and I know they are good soldiers." The State Department called the López Sibrián case a "crucial symbolic issue." It was for D'Aubuisson as well, but he knew where the power rested.

As much as the López Sibrián matter says about United States policy in El Salvador, it says more about the Salvadoran armed forces as an institution.

"Look at López Sibrián," began a Foreign Service officer who held a senior position at the U.S. embassy in El Salvador. "Why isn't López Sibrián in jail? Because everyone knows the terrorism statutes don't apply against officers. . . . It's the officer corps as a system. You know, you kick over one stone and how many more are going to be kicked over? Best let the stones lie. . . . It's a mentality that's built into these guys at the military school."

He went on. "I remember one of our guys from the MilGroup [U.S. Military Group] said to me the way to reform the officer corps in the long run was to take about six thousand pounds of TNT over to the military school and blow it away. By the time they get out of military school they know how to smuggle in cars without paying any duty. And the idea that they are creatures beyond the law is already in them."

It all begins at the Captain General Gerardo Barrios Military School, named for a corpulent, goateed general who was president of El Salvador from 1858 to 1863. Opened in 1867, it was the first service academy in Central America. Chilean officers, and a few German ones, provided most of the professional training during the first decades. But in 1948 the commandant of the military academy was a United States Army colonel, H. Grant Learnard. His deputy was a Salvadoran, Colonel Córdoba. Their relationship had some light moments.

"Have any of you fellows seen Córdoba?" Colonel Learnard grumbled to Murat Williams, the U.S. chargé d'affaires who had rushed to the roof of the embassy when the siesta hour was interrupted by machine-gun fire one day. "I told the s.o.b. to spread some manure on the parade ground this morning, but he practically thumbed his nose at me and began making a lot of phone calls. Before I could get him to do anything, he was taking shots of liquor out of his desk drawer and then dashed off in a jeep. I told the s.o.b. that if he didn't get that job done I would report him to the President."

A few hours later Williams and other foreign diplomats were called to the Presidential Palace—where they were greeted by Colonel Córdoba. He informed them that he had just taken over the government. One of the new government's first acts was to remove Colonel Learnard as head of the military academy.

Today the military school is a modest compound of low-slung cement buildings behind a towering wall on a noisy street in the capital. There has also been nothing particularly distinguished about the young cadets who enter. They take entrance exams, but it's not like West Point. El Salvador's star athletes and honor students usually head for universities in the United States if they are from wealthy families. The middle- and upper-middle-class parents send their youngsters to the National University—or did before it was closed in 1980—or the Catholic-administered University of Central America, which was founded by the country's wealthy who thought that there were too many "Communists" teaching at the state institution.

For a lower-middle-class Salvadoran male who is moderately intelligent and willing to exert himself physically, a military career offers what he could not otherwise obtain, having been born into a rigidly class-conscious society where status derives principally from inherited wealth. There is money—not from salaries, which are paltry ($840 a month for a colonel in 1979), but from graft. There is power—considerable and abused. And a chance to become president; not surprisingly cadets themselves refer to the military academy as the School of the Presidents.

"The people who go into the military," explained a U.S. embassy officer, "are not the oligarchs who are sort of riding herd on the Salvadoran society through their military role. We're talking about the Garcías of the world who are lower-middle-class, but somehow learned to read and write. . . . We may not like it, but there it is." José Guillermo García, the son of lower-middle-class parents, entered the military academy in 1953. He was one of those dubbed "presidential" by his classmates. After some twenty years of unremarkable service he was appointed by the military president to head ANTEL, the government-owned telephone company, a position coveted by officers on their way to the presidency. It is a post that offers money—rake-offs from the multimillion-dollar telecommunications contracts—and power: to bug and tap telephones and thus to acquire information about personal lives and political activities. In 1979 García became the minister of defense, and in spite of repeated attempts by the civilians in the government to oust him and numerous confrontations with U.S. congressional delegations—Senator Patrick J. Leahy, Democrat of Vermont, after politely listening to one of García's canned lectures in 1982, complete with pointer, wall maps, and protestations that the soldiers were not guilty of any human rights violations, said he felt like a young district attorney being shown a training film about the harmful effects of marijuana—García hung on and was generally considered the most powerful person in the country.

The legal minimum age for entering the military school is sixteen, but García's successor, General Vides Casanova, with help from his uncle, who was a career military man, enrolled when he was just fifteen years and three months. It is at that impressionable age that the cadets are first exposed to the armed forces' motto: "As long as the institution lives, the republic lives."

"I always thought they should add one more line: 'and even beyond,' " said a Foreign Service officer derisively. "I wish they had the same loyalty to the nation as they do to the institution." U.S. officials, civilian and military, who had to deal almost daily with the Salvadoran military, concluded that it was the officers' unwavering subservience to their institution that stood in the way of their ever doing anything to purge their ranks of the most violent, least democratic members. "They'd rather go it alone than give up the sovereignty of the military to some crazy congressman or policymaker who doesn't like the way they treat prisoners or something like that. Forget it!" said another diplomat, who had spent two years in El Salvador.

This attitude of being members of a superior class is drilled into cadets from the day they arrive. Upperclassmen harass plebes with taunts of "lice," "crabs," "cockroaches." But the most pejorative, the worst that a young cadet can be called is a civilian. That is the lowest form of life.

Some students of the Salvadoran officer corps argue that it doesn't have a political ideology, that the only ideology is the loyalty to the institution. Noting the peasant- and lower-middle-class background of most of the officers, even some Salvadoran leftists say that the officers are not rightist and anti-Communist by conviction but have taken on that political coloring because for generations the institution's savior was the oligarchy, and today it is the United States. If the Soviet Union were providing the aid to keep the armed forces from collapsing as an institution, the argument goes, the officers would be anti-U.S. and Communists. Perhaps, but today there are strong conservative, even fascist, strains running through the armed forces, most troubling among officers at the highest levels who proudly trace their political and military heritage back to General Hernández Martínez. "In this country, we're not prepared to live in a true democracy like the United States," Lieutenant Colonel Jorge Adalberto Cruz told Robert McCartney of *The Washington Post* in August 1983. "What we need here is a leader who dictates the policies that we should follow." Cruz at the time was a commander of troops in Morazán. "He's the epitome of what a lieutenant colonel should be in combat," said a U.S. military adviser.

Whatever the political ideology, it is the fealty to the institution that explains why officers are not punished: It would not only hurt the individual but besmirch the name of the armed forces. In spite of the claims by the Reagan administration, no Salvadoran officer has been punished for a human rights violation. The traditional "sanction" for an officer whose criminal activities or notorious behavior become an embarrassment for the army is to send him abroad to an embassy. An army major who raped a dozen women in the late 1970's was made an ambassador to a major country after his conduct had become public. Captain Ávila Ávila, the man who ordered the murders of Hammer and Pearlman, was sent to Costa Rica as military attaché. He was forced to leave that country after he had blown up a car which he said was being used to ship arms to the Salvadoran guerrillas.

"The armed forces are before the people, before the government, before the state," explains Lieutenant Colonel René Francisco Guerra y Guerra, an organizer of the 1979 coup. "The armed forces are before everything."

While at the military school, the cadets acquire another loyalty: to their *tanda,* which is what they call their class. The *tanda* is part fraternity, part family; "Mafia family" is the description routinely used by U.S. diplomats. The bond is forged by the punishing physical demands at the academy: Out of an entering class of 100 to 150, only 20 to 30 survive to graduation. They consider themselves elite. *Tanda*-mates serve as best men at each other's weddings, are godfathers to each other's children, pull and push each other along and up the career ladder. All that would be acceptable, albeit perhaps a bit bemusing and sophomoric, but what has infuriated the U.S. military advisers and hindered the successful prosecution of the war is that it is his *tanda,* not his military performance, that determines an officer's assignment. García, for example, named a *tanda*-mate, who had finished last in their academy class, commander of the navy; that meant that his primary responsibility was to patrol the Gulf of Fonseca, which separates Nicaragua from El Salvador. He was so incompetent that the military advisers simply ignored him, giving commands directly to more junior officers. Army commanders in key provinces were equally inept, but they were García's friends and so held on to their commands, while U.S. military advisers chafed at the guerrilla successes. In the armed forces' public relations office, García put two other *tanda*-mates, both ruddy-complexioned men who were so hopeless and helpless—as well as usually drunk or well on their way by 11:00 A.M.—that foreign correspondents found them totally useless, though sometimes unintentionally entertaining. The U.S. embassy, having enough trouble with its client's negative image around the world, took to doing most of the armed forces' work, telling the two colonels when to hold press conferences, then notifying reporters of the hour and subject. When Vides Casanova became defense minister, key positions went to officers who shared his conservative political views.

A U.S. diplomat with considerable experience in El Salvador compared the guerrillas' military system with the government's. "The guerrillas advance people according to merit. And that's very good," he said. "That's admirable. Now that's what the goddamn army's got to do. Here we have an ass-kickin' son of a bitch out here, and he knows what he's doing, promote him. What we'd like basically is a system that rewards merit. . . . It doesn't reward anything. All you've got to do is live for five years and you get promoted. There's only one criterion, and that's surviving. Live thirty years, and you're a colonel, you retire."

The ranks in the Salvadoran military, goes the standard joke among Salvadorans and U.S. diplomats, are lieutenant, captain, major, lieutenant colonel, colonel, millionaire. At the military academy one military professor was fond of telling cadets, "Seniority in the military was created to avoid mobs when milking the state." He would add, "The military career is hard and overwhelming, but eventually returns great rewards."

"The Salvadoran army is not held together by an ideology of anticommunism. It is held together by a vast network of corruption," Leonel Gómez told a House subcommittee in March 1981, a few weeks after he had narrowly escaped death. A burly man with a drooping mustache and bushy hair, Gómez looks a bit like Mark Pearlman and was the chief adviser to Viera, the head of the land reform agency who was murdered along with Pearlman and Hammer. Many, including

Gómez, believe that the assassins thought Gómez was one of those at the table.

Gómez said that Viera and he were the army's chief targets because they had been publicly complaining about corruption. When Viera and Gómez took over the Salvadoran Institute for Agrarian Transformation in late 1979, they discovered that the farms the government had acquired for conversion to peasant cooperatives had been overvalued by at least $40 million and that some properties had been purchased twice by the government. The agency, known by its Spanish acronym as ISTA, at the time was run by an army colonel. Gómez said that all of the $40 million didn't go to him, but that "rather he would have the kickbacks delivered to the office of the President who would spread the graft among his and allied tandas." Gómez and Viera took the evidence of corruption to Duarte and García, but they did nothing, so the two began making their charges on television. Not long thereafter Viera was murdered.

One of the most notorious cases of military corruption involved the army's chief of staff, Colonel Manuel Alfonso Rodríguez. In 1976 he was arrested by the FBI in New York while trying to purchase several thousand machine guns. He had claimed, on false documents submitted to the State Department, that they were to be used by the Salvadoran armed forces, but in fact, they were intended for the Mafia in the United States. In the United States he was convicted by a federal court and sentenced to ten years in prison. In El Salvador, where it was widely known that he had been acting in concert with the country's president and defense minister, nothing happened.

Asked by Congressman Lee H. Hamilton, Democrat of Indiana, to respond to Gómez's charges that the Salvadoran Army was corrupt, Secretary of State Haig's office wrote in May 1981 that it disagreed. "The corruption Mr. Gomez describes occurred before October 15, 1979."

But the corruption continues. Gómez told of an army colonel who was in charge of the garrison in Sonsonate. In 1980 the colonel ordered the peasant-owned dairy cooperatives to lower the price at which they sold milk to the sole milk processor and distributor in the area. In turn the commander got a kickback from the businessman, "as much as $1,000 some days," Gómez said. A U.S. embassy officer confirmed Gómez's account. "When we found out about that, we raised all hell," he said. What was the "punishment" for the colonel, whom the U.S. official called a lush? He was transferred out of Sonsonate, made the commander of the garrison in Chalatenango.

Corruption was still "extensive" in 1983, according to Shirley Christian, *Miami Herald* reporter who had received a Pulitzer Prize for her coverage of Central America. Christian, whose contacts within the ranks of the Salvadoran military were the envy of other reporters, wrote:

> Officers are routinely bought off or blackmailed by civilians seeking military influence. Some officers receive payoffs from men doing business in their territory; each provincial commander has the opportunity, for example, to make a profit on the monthly food budget for the 1,000 or so troops under his command. In some cases, it is difficult to draw the line between corruption and the granting of favors, such as the offering of bank directorships and jobs in private business after retirement. Some officers accept only what is dangled in front of them; others aggressively seek payoffs.

The war has provided another opportunity for profit. The Defense Ministry routinely filed false reports about the number of bullets that had been fired during a specific period or operation. The United States would provide funds to replenish the inflated numbers. The money, which wasn't needed, went into the pockets of senior officers. Often the bullets, which hadn't in fact been used, were sold to the local civil defense forces or even to the guerrillas.

Even the staunchest backers of a military solution to the problem in El Salvador have been appalled by the institutional corruption. F. Andrew Messing, Jr., a former Green Beret active in the American Conservative Union, said in 1983, after his fifth visit to El Salvador, that "El Salvador is corrupt from top to bottom." He reported that military officials were illegally selling military equipment and pocketing the proceeds and that they preferred large-scale operations because "you get a chance to scrape off some money or sell equipment."

Perhaps this explains why the U.S. military advisers enjoyed so little, if any, success in their relentless campaign to persuade Salvadoran commanders to abandon their love affairs with massive, 2,000- to 4,000-man operations and instead use the small-scale patrols and ambushes more suited for a counterinsurgency war. Small patrols need less food and equipment, and that means there is less available for sale.

"By the time you get to be a lieutenant colonel, people are offering you nice little business deals, or you're military attaché somewhere and smuggling like a champ," said a disgusted senior U.S. diplomat about the rampant corruption in the Salvadoran armed forces. "Look at Ochoa," he said, referring to Lieutenant Colonel Sigifredo Ochoa Pérez. "First time he went to Costa Rica as a military attaché, they had to take him out of there, he was smuggling everything he could get his hands on—TV's, goods, booze, you know the usual stuff." Ochoa would buy the merchandise in neighboring Panama, a duty-free port, then resell it "to make money" in Costa Rica, the diplomat explained.

That the diplomat singled out Ochoa as an example of the depth of the corruption was understandable. At the time Ochoa was the field commander probably most admired and respected by the U.S. military advisers as the officer who knew how to fight a guerrilla war. Rare was the briefing in which Colonel Waghelstein, the senior military adviser in El Salvador in 1982 and 1983, did not encourage, indeed push reporters to visit Ochoa at his base in the province of Cabañas. "We created Ochoa," Waghelstein offered during one briefing. In January 1983 Colonel Ochoa, a colorful sort given to wearing a military neck scarf and aviator sunglasses, became somewhat of an embarrassment to Colonel Waghelstein and the American embassy. Staging a minirebellion in his province, Ochoa refused to obey orders given by Defense Minister General García. He publicly called his commanding general "corrupt, arbitrary and capricious." Ochoa's "punishment" for his insubordination in time of war? "Gilded exile," as the embassy described it in a Secret cable. He was sent to the Salvadoran embassy in Washington.

THE Salvadoran military is generally described as consisting of two elements. There are the army, navy, and air force, which are responsible for the defense of El Salvador's sovereignty from foreign aggression. And there are what are commonly referred to as the security forces—the National Guard, National Police, and Treasury Police, which are in theory responsible for internal affairs.

The National Guard was set up by officers from the Spanish Civil Guard in 1912 to keep order in the countryside—that is, to keep peasants working for low wages for the landowners. Guardsmen today wear black leather leg guards and black helmets and sport big brass belt buckles. The Guard commander has his headquarters in a principal city, usually the provincial capital, and assigns units to surrounding rural villages. The National Police, which is the only one of the security forces that even remotely resembles anything like a "police" force, is the urban counterpart to the National Guard. The Treasury Police, or Hacienda Police as it is known by its formal name in El Salvador, was created to collect taxes from importers—i.e., to stop the rampant smuggling. But its most important mission was to chase the moonshiners who were supplying Indians with *chi-*

cha, the local version of corn liquor. The philosophy of all the security forces is found in the saying "Authority that does not abuse loses its prestige."

U.S. training of the Salvadoran security forces, as opposed to the regular army, dates back to at least 1957, when the Agency for International Development (AID) began providing money and personnel. American advisers stationed in El Salvador reorganized the police academy, wrote a textbook for the Treasury Police, and trained special riot control units in the National Police and National Guard. Some 450 Salvadoran "police" received training under the program, and with AID funds the Salvadoran government purchased 2,045 revolvers and carbines, 750,000 rounds of ammunition, 950 tear gas grenades, and a mélange of other paramilitary equipment, such as jeeps, trucks, mobile radio units, helmets, and handcuffs.

In 1974 AID concluded that the National Police had become "a well-disciplined, well-trained, and respected uniformed corps." The National Guard was described as "well-disciplined and well-respected." The glowing conclusions could be dismissed as the favorable gloss that any agency would put on an evaluation of its own programs if it were not that the contrary evidence was so chilling.

In January 1977 the Organization of American States dispatched a human rights investigating team to El Salvador. The delegation's 266-page report, which was adopted by the Inter-American Commission on Human Rights, contained case after case, often with the victim's name, of torture, brutality, barbarity, inflicted by the "well-disciplined" National Police and National Guard. Acting together, the two units seized a man at the Avis car rental agency, beating him savagely in order to get him into their vehicle. He was given electric shock; his head was submerged into a toilet bowl until he fainted. The OAS report described another man seized while on the way to lunch with his wife. He was "savagely tortured" and castrated. "A very poor woman whose business barely earned her enough for her family to survive" was raped by a National Guard chief "while his accomplices and servants stood guard." Here is one case in full—illustrative of the norm, not of the extreme:

> Case 2854. "Alfredo Acosta Días, a member of the Directing Council of the UPN Party [a center-left political party], was seized on May 11, 1977, at 6:30 in the morning; he was still in bed. Also taken were the son of his wife, seventeen years old, and a guest in the house. The three were taken away in chains.

The abductors immediately took them to a National Police station some 500 meters from where they had been captured. . . . [Later Días was taken to the] central barracks of the National Police. When he got out of the vehicle, he was blindfolded; in addition to the manacles, his thumbs were tied with a cord, and he was kept standing until three in the afternoon. . . . He was then taken to a storage room. He remained blindfolded and handcuffed until nine o'clock at night, when they came for him and took him to a room where, blindfolded and in chains, he was interrogated for the first time until three in the morning. He was not beaten; they merely threatened to kill him if he did not cooperate and they placed a pistol in his mouth.

On Friday, May 13, at four in the afternoon . . . they blindfolded him, put him in shackles and tied his thumbs together. . . . He was beaten in various parts of the body with an object that appeared to be a yataghan; of course, no marks were left on his body. The cruelest torture was the electric shocks to the head, with wires attached to his ears; at the same time, with his bare feet in a pool of water, they tortured his feet with an electric rod; they did the same to his stomach. After one half hour of interrogation, they made him drink a good amount of liquor. The torture lasted until around 8:30 P.M. The worst side effect of the torture was the bite marks on his tongue; when they became inflamed, he was unable to chew, so that he spent a number of days without eating the famous "yoyo," the only food that they give to prisoners, which is two small tortillas with mashed beans in the middle. . . .

He had to sign a release form which said that he had been taken to investigate his political activities, that all his personal belongings were returned to him and that he had not been mistreated in any way.

What political activities did they have to investigate and why did they have to keep him incarcerated for 52 days? His political activities are a matter of public record: in 1972 he was elected deputy by the Department of Santa Ana; in 1974 he was again elected alternate deputy. On the date of his capture, he was Secretary General of the Partido Unión Democrática Nacionalista (UDN-Nationalist Democratic Union Party). He had appeared on television a number of times. He made his political positions known in the public square, in the Legislative Assembly, and in any other place, but always in the open. His political activities have been and are public so that the reason given by the National Police that he had been taken "in order to investigate his political activities," cannot be accepted.

In the National Guard barracks the OAS team found a table on which there were devices used to apply electric shocks and a one-way mirror. They were told the room was used by a photographer, "a statement denied shortly thereafter by the photographer himself." They found secret cells, one meter by one meter, the walls of which were "covered with roaches." They were told these were used for drunks and to store explosives that had to be kept in darkness. Using a flashlight, the OAS investigators found carved in the walls the names and initials of prisoners.

THE security forces' *modus operandi* hasn't changed much, if at all, though U.S. diplomats sometimes disagree on which branch is the most ruthless, with the worst infamy usually awarded to the Treasury Police. But not always. "The National Guard was probably the worst because they killed casually and anybody that sort of crossed their paths," said one senior embassy officer. He contrasted the National Guard to the Treasury Police, "which was known for its hard-fistedness and its terrible cruelty, but I suspect that the people that they killed were people who, in fact, had been targeted after some sort of investigation, some sort of discussion."

After the coup in October 1979 García, as minister of defense, named his friend Colonel Francisco Morán to head the Treasury Police. When the Christian Democrats first joined the government in January 1980, one of the conditions was that Morán be removed from his post. Eleven months later, when he was still in his position, the Christian Democrats threatened to pull out of the government unless he was removed. The United States was insisting on the same. Morán was not to have been punished but, in the time-honored tradition of the Salvadoran military, just transferred to another position or retired with full rank and pay. Even so, neither the Salvadoran civilians nor the United States had the will or the power to implement their demands—to withdraw from the government or to withhold the military aid—if they weren't met. Morán wasn't removed until the armed forces decided he should be. When Vides Casanova replaced García as minister of defense, he turned to his *tanda*-mate Colonel Nicolás Carranza to head the Treasury Police. Carranza is considered one of the most rightist members of the high command. Getting him out of a command position was one of the accomplishments of the Carter administration; his "return to grace"—as the embassy characterized in a Secret cable—signaled another shift to the right for the Salvadoran military.

A consistent approach of the Carter and Reagan administrations has been to distinguish the security forces from the regular army and to claim that it was the former that was responsible for the indiscriminate violence.

"We try to distinguish the Army from the other security forces such as the police and National Guard," John Bushnell, Reagan's acting assistant secretary of state for Inter-American affairs, told the Senate Foreign Relations Committee in March 1981, when he was being questioned about the violence within the Salvadoran armed forces. Similarly, a few months later Thomas Enders, who by then had been named the head of the Inter-American affairs bureau, told another congressional committee that the United States military aid was "being given, incidentally, not to the Guardia Nacional, or to the police services, but to the army."

But the proverbial Martian landing in El Salvador would find it difficult to distinguish the members of the security forces from the army soldiers. They all wear military-style uniforms, albeit of differing designs. They all brandish automatic rifles. The officers of all the security forces, like the officers in the army, the air force, and the navy, are graduates of the Captain General Gerardo Barrios Military School. Above all, the security force commanders—that is, the head of the National Guard, the head of the National Police, and the head of the Treasury Police—all are under the command of the minister of defense.

What this says is what Washington officials have always known but never acknowledged publicly: that the security forces are as much a part of the war against the revolution as are the army, air force, and navy. In a Confidential cable in June 1981 the embassy in El Salvador reported that the Salvadoran government had "publicly declared its intent to reduce the size and role of the public security corps (National Guard—4,300, National Police—2,895, Treasury Police—1,527) to take on more specific non-military functions as it increases the strength of the Army." It was not a realistic plan, the embassy advised Washington, because "in practice the public security corps contains the most thoroughly trained and experienced veterans in the armed forces whose skills are considered by them to be essential to conducting the anti-guerrilla campaign." A year later, in May 1982, in another Confidential cable the embassy reiterated that "the public security forces (National Guard, National Police, Treasury Police) continue to be an integral part of the counter-insurgency effort."

The security forces, along with the regular army, are not, however, the only government units for quelling dissent and keeping peasants in line. In the 1960's General José Alberto Medrano, whose National Guard soldiers were already feared and hated in the rural villages, set up the Organización Democrática Nacionalista, known by its Spanish acronym as ORDEN. The military government called it a civic organization and viewed it as a means of organizing grass-roots, peasant support for its political party, the National Conciliation party (PCN). But the word "ORDEN" soon became, and remains, synonymous with unbridled brutality.

ORDEN's method of operating was similar to "the method that was used during the Nazi system to control the people directly," Duarte informed a U.S. congressional committee that held hearings following the Salvadoran electoral fraud in 1977. "They [the military governments] use ORDEN to intimidate people." Duarte told the congressmen how during the election campaign ORDEN members, "with their machetes in their hands," went into villages, ordering peasants to vote for the PCN and "not to gather to hear what we in the opposition had to say. These are the people who killed some of my people. In one little town they killed a chauffeur of mine, who was driving my car."

The 1977 vice-presidential candidate for the Christian Democrats, Morales Ehrlich, who was from 1980 to 1982 to serve on the U.S.-backed junta, told the same committee how, using the security forces, ORDEN, and the regular army, "the Government has created a reign of terror in the country-side and urban areas." He explained that "hundreds of security force personnel armed with war equipment occupy a given village, or agricultural area. . . . The objective of these operations is not crime prevention but rather to instigate terror in the population as a whole." He concluded: "It should not be forgotten that frequently U.S. military equipment is employed for internal repression."

Yet during the same hearings the director of security assistance operations in the U.S. Defense Department, Richard Violette, in response to a question from Representative Donald M. Fraser, said he did not know what ORDEN was and that he had never heard of it. The deputy assistant secretary for Inter-American affairs in the State Department, Charles Bray, interjected that he was aware of ORDEN, but he described it innocuously as being "responsive to the ruling party, the Party of National Conciliation."

Bray's portrayal of ORDEN as independent of the official government structure reflected the attitude within the State Department, an attitude that prevails today: that the violence in El Salvador is not institutional, that the government and its armed forces are not responsible for it.

"There were heated debates, primarily over whether the government was aware of the human rights abuses and was really trying to stop them, as they asserted, whether there was a difference between

ORDEN and the government, whether there was a renegade military involved, or whether it was the institutional structure of the security apparatus," said Mark Schneider, the senior deputy in Carter's human rights bureau until October 1979. "We had a major argument between ARA [the bureau of Inter-American affairs] and ourselves about some massacres. ARA said there was no evidence—that from the embassy there was no evidence—that the military troops had done this, that ORDEN had done this, it could have been the guerrillas themselves," Schneider recalled. "In this one I remember we had a shouting match, Bushnell and I, because he was talking about the National Guard in a way that was so totally absurd that I really got angry. He was talking about it as basically a security force that was highly professional, that there was no connection between the National Guard, the Hacienda Police, and ORDEN and that if there were any torture or killings, they were by individuals and without any knowledge of the higher-ups. And I said, 'You're talking about a bunch of goons and cutthroats,' and that they knew full well what was going on."

Warren Christopher, the deputy assistant secretary of state at the time, thought it was a good idea for State Department officers to gather firsthand information about the human rights situation in El Salvador. Schneider went, along with Sally Shelton, who was a deputy within the ARA and later ambassador to a group of Caribbean nations, including Grenada.

After traveling into the hot, dusty countryside, where they heard grim accounts of ORDEN's torturing and killing peasants, Schneider and Shelton returned to the Presidential Palace. They asked about ORDEN. The country's vice-president said that it was headquartered in the office of the presidency. He explained that its head was a senior military officer and that in each province a military officer was commander of the ORDEN forces. In its 1978 human rights report on El Salvador, the Organization of American States provided grisly details of ORDEN atrocities and recommended that it be abolished.

Yet in congressional testimony in late 1979 the State Department's Inter-American affairs bureau was still downplaying ORDEN and thus exonerating the Salvadoran government. ORDEN, the bureau said, was "ostensibly dedicated to civic education and law enforcement, but is *occasionally* used in political activity. Owing to its record of *alleged* human rights violations, ORDEN has become a major target of the government's critics at home and abroad [emphasis added]."

One of the first acts of the Salvadoran government after the coup in

October 1979 was to issue a decree abolishing ORDEN. "But someone forgot to tell its members, who continued to work closely with the security forces," Professor Anderson noted. In February 1980 General Medrano, ORDEN's founder, and Roberto d'Aubuisson, whose reputation for brutality was so notorious that he was forced out of the National Guard after the coup, quickly set up the ultraconservative Nationalist Democratic Front, which was ORDEN under a new name. More significant, ORDEN members, who numbered about 80,000, were incorporated into the government's civil defense forces.

In a Confidential cable sent in May 1982 the embassy reported that the security forces and civil defense forces provide "a vital function in static defense missions," in part relieving the armed forces of these missions. "The civil defense force in particular has borne a disproportionate share of casualties in the past year and requires further training." The civil defense forces are "just going to go out and pillage and plunder, as they always have," said a diplomat who worked closely with the Salvadoran military during the more than two years he was in El Salvador (ending in mid-1983), explaining that they are made up of ex-members of the National Guard and of ORDEN.

Some rare insight into how the civil defense forces operate is provided by a Secret CIA cable sent from El Salvador in October 1981. The cable was not released under the FOIA and bears a notation at the bottom restricting its distribution. It was based on information provided by a former civil defense officer.

Among the more astonishing revelations is that the civil defense forces were being paid "up to 100 United States (U.S.) dollars per month." As for how the forces earned their money, which presumably was coming from wealthy landowners or the U.S. government, the cable continued:

> The former officer had received reports from government supporters in the community on rebel sympathizers. These were passed on to the local National Guard commander and to the Army regional command; some attempt was made to check their authenticity, but the process was cursory and there was no doubt that many innocent people died falsely accused. Sometimes the summary execution of sympathizers was carried out by the anti-guerrilla unit and at other times by the National Guard, depending on who knew the victim best and the circumstances in which the execution was to be carried out. The National Guard often collaborated with the unit by sealing off villages to ensure no outside intervention.
> The attitude of the Civil Defense, National Guard, and Army to the execution of rebel sympathizers was that the courts were unreliable and

that they had to be bypassed in the current emergency. No attempt was made to restrain the zeal of the anti-guerrilla unit or National Guard patrols; captured rebels were shot out of hand after interrogation. The officer himself shot a fifteen-year old female guerrilla who was captured in fatigues while participating in a rebel patrol, to save her from a gang rape that would otherwise have preceded execution.

October 15, 1979, was a watershed day for U.S. policy toward El Salvador. That was the day a coup deposed General Romero. It has become a tenet of U.S. policy that this coup marked the beginning of a new Salvadoran military, one that didn't rape, pillage, and plunder, one that respected human rights, and consequently one that merited the millions of dollars in U.S. military aid and equipment.

The Salvadoran government "has made a good many efforts to purge itself of its most egregious and violent elements," Reagan's UN ambassador, Jeane Kirkpatrick, declared in February 1981. "It's gone a long way, right to the minimum of what's compatible with survival."

Or as Reagan himself assured Congress in January 1982:

> The Salvadoran government, since the overthrow of General Romero, has taken explicit actions to end human rights abuses. The paramilitary organization "ORDEN" has been outlawed, although some of its former members may still be active. A military code of conduct was adopted in October 1980 explicitly prohibiting any actions by military personnel injurious to human rights. . . . The military high command has instructed the officer corps to ensure that all soldiers adhere to the code of conduct. A number of officers sympathetic to the violent right have been removed from command positions or reassigned to positions less sensitive to the domestic situation.

In order to continue military aid to El Salvador, President Reagan had to certify every six months that the Salvadoran government "is achieving substantial control over all elements of its own armed forces, so as to bring an end to the indiscriminate torture and murder of Salvadoran citizens by these forces." President Reagan issued that certification four times, the last in mid-1983.

But the reality was that the Salvadoran military was the law and above the law, as much in 1983 and 1984 as it had been in 1932 and 1979. If anything, it was more ruthless and brutal after the coup. Between October 1979 and January 1984 at least 40,000 innocent civilians were murdered in El Salvador, according to the legal aid office of the Roman Catholic Church there. If a comparable proportion of the United States population had been murdered, the toll would be more than 1.5 million. Most of those killed in El Salvador were peasants, workers, old people, and children—males and females. More than 90 percent were murdered by the Salvadoran armed forces. On the economic side of the ledger—that is, support for the land reform and nationalization of banks and export trade that were begun after the coup—the reality is also different from the publicly painted landscape.

In March 1981 Bushnell said in response to questions from Senator John Glenn, Democrat of Ohio, that the "overwhelming bulk" of the Salvadoran officers supported the reforms. A few months later Enders declared that the Salvadoran military had been transformed "from an institution dedicated to the status quo to one that spearheads land reform and supports constitutional democracy."

A different and considerably more accurate profile of the Salvadoran officer corps is found in the May 1981 letter on behalf of Secretary of State Haig to Congressman Hamilton. After stating that eighty senior officers had been retired after the coup, the letter explained that of the remaining officers, "about 35 percent solidly support the reforms . . . perhaps 40 to 45 percent basically support the government and the general concept of the transition of democracy, though some question the wisdom and desirability of the economic reforms; and . . . perhaps 15 to 20 percent of the officer corps oppose the reforms and the transition to democracy." That there was this much opposition in the officer corps to the reforms was something neither the American public nor Congress—except for this letter—was ever told. And in the past three years opposition to the reforms has grown among the officers, who resent them as having been shoved on the country by Carter's human rights policy. Moreover, it is the senior commanders who are the most resistant to the reforms.

In the four years since the coup of October 1979 the United States has poured in nearly $300 million in military aid, trained four Salvadoran battalions, and brought about 500 cadets to the United States for officer training. The money and training were accompanied by promises to the American public that they were being used as leverage to induce the Salvadoran military to improve its human rights performance and by stern lectures and warnings to the Salvadoran military commanders that they put an end to the indiscriminate violence.

But in truth, not all the money, not all the public warnings, not all the stern private lectures, not, in short, all the might of the United States has had any significant impact on the Salvadoran military.

"Other than the training we've done to improve the performance of the troops in the field, which is something, we've made practically no dent in their observance of human rights," lamented a diplomat who served in El Salvador for Carter and Reagan. The preservation of the institution demands that guilty soldiers, especially officers, be protected and blocks the desires some officers might have to clean out the most violent, least democratic elements. "We're talking about a Mafia, we're talking about cold-blooded criminals," replied one diplomat, explaining why a cleanup of the armed forces is not likely or even possible. "It's Murder Incorporated," said another.

"This whole Mafia operates completely oblivious to our efforts, completely impervious, isolated from our efforts," said yet a third diplomat who served in El Salvador for Carter and Reagan.

The case of Hammer and Pearlman "shows the limits we're willing to go to," said a State Department officer who served in El Salvador. Within days of his personal phone call to Magaña, President Reagan announced an increase in military assistance. "What's the message?" the diplomat asked rhetorically. "I don't think the President did it with malice aforethought because he really had to do both things, really at the same time. But the Salvos, who *really don't* want to deal with López Sibrián, say, 'Well, oh, gee, we're going to get the military aid, so why bother?' "

THE subordination of the armed forces to the civilian government remains one of the most difficult fundamental problems for this young democracy to achieve," the embassy reported in August 1983 in a Secret cable. This one sentence, in a cable that the State Department refused to release under the Freedom of Information Act, runs counter to all the public statements by the Reagan administration at the time to the effect that the United States was backing a moderate, democratically elected civilian government.

And just how much power the military still has in El Salvador, and how it uses and abuses that power, are revealed in the classified State Department report completed in December 1983. "The military exerts a pervasive influence over the nation and, as will be documented herein, has sought to shield from justice even those who commit the most atrocious crimes," the report said in the summary section. The report was of the investigation into the murders of four American churchwomen.

There has been one Salvadoran institution willing to challenge the "pervasive influence" of the armed forces. The cost has been high.

5

THE CHURCH: PERSECUTION AND REVOLUTION

HE was on his way to offer a Saturday evening mass in El Paisnal, the listless farm village where he had been born. A teenage boy and a seventy-two-year-old peasant man accompanied him. As their white Volkswagen moved down the dusty road between flat fields of fragrant sugarcane, gunmen lying in ambush opened fire. Father Rutilio Grande was the target, but his friends died with him on the spot, on March 12, 1977. The archbishop demanded an investigation. The government did nothing. The country's president, Colonel Molina, said that Father Grande had been killed as part of an international Communist conspiracy to divide the church* and the government. (It is widely believed that the assassins were hired by local landowners.)

"I greatly fear that very soon the Bible and the Gospel will not be allowed within the confines of our country," Father Grande had said to the peasants in Apopo in one of his last homilies. "Only the bindings will arrive, nothing else, because all the pages are subversive—they are against sin. And if Jesus himself were to cross the border at Chalatenango, they would arrest him. They would take him to many courts and accuse him of being unconstitutional and subversive, a revolutionary, a foreign Jew, a concocter of strange and bizarre ideas contrary to democracy, that is to say, against the minority. They would crucify him again, because they prefer a Christ of the sacristy or the cemetery, a silent Christ with a muzzle on his mouth, a Christ made to our image and according to our selfish interests. This is not the Christ of the Gospels! This is not the young Christ who at thirty-three years of age died for the most noble cause of humanity."

*All references throughout this book to the church are to the Roman Catholic Church.

Two months after Grande's assassination, members of a military death squad that called itself the White Warriors Union forced their way into a parish house in the capital and killed Father Alfonso Navarro and a fifteen-year-old parishioner. The killers were taking revenge for the kidnapping and murder of the country's foreign minister, Mauricio Borgonovo Pohl, by the Popular Forces of Liberation (FPL), the most radical of the guerrilla groups.

During the first five months of 1977 five priests were tortured, eight expelled, and six denied reentry after leaving the country. There were continual threats against priests, along with bombings of their houses, the church radio station, YSAX, and the Jesuit-run high school. In the summer of 1977 pamphlets circulated throughout the country: "Be a Patriot! Kill a Priest!"*

This fear and loathing of priests by the wealthy and the military hadn't always been that way, of course. For centuries an unholy alliance of the church, the state, and the money ruled throughout Latin America. The sword and the cross were indistinguishable. The church was the moral voice, and an archconservative one, of the military authority. At the side of every dictator in uniform was a monsignor in the cloak. Priests exhorted the wealthy to give alms for the poor. The poor heard that their reward would come in heaven. "Poverty is the most certain road to felicity," a Peruvian bishop told his Indians.

But all that began to change, radically, in the 1960's. Pope John XXIII set the church on a new path with the issuance of his revolutionary encyclicals *Mater et magistra,* in 1961, and *Pacem in terris,* in 1963. In them he emphasized the right to political participation, education, and a humane standard of living. Then, in 1965, the Second Vatican Council, which had been convened in 1962, declared that the church was a community of equals, be they laity, priests, or bishops. Finally, Pope Paul VI, in his *Populorum progressio* (1967), further emphasized the economic, social, and political rights of humankind.

*There had been portents of this campaign of violence against the church. In 1970, when the national legislature decided to discuss agrarian reform—even though it would not do anything—the archdiocese's delegate, Father José Inocencio Alas, was kidnapped near the National Palace by soldiers in civilian clothes. Alas was beaten, forced to drink a quart of pure alcohol mixed with drugs, then tossed out, naked, on a mountainous ledge. Two years later the brutally dismembered body of the parish priest in Chalatenango was found a few days after he had been arrested by the National Guard. In 1975 national guardsmen hauled another priest into their headquarters in the capital. They snapped handcuffs on his wrists, jammed a hood over his head, then proceeded to beat him about his entire body while one of his torturers mockingly chanted, "I am excommunicated, I am excommunicated."

And he urged the Latin American bishops to hold a hemispheric conference to examine the conclusions of Vatican II in light of conditions in Latin America.

The bishops heeded their pope and convened in Medellín, Colombia, in 1968. Paul himself journeyed to the conference, becoming the first pope in history to visit Latin America. He told the huge throng that welcomed him in teeming mile-high Bogotá, "We wish to personify the Christ of a poor and hungry people." That was just what many of the priests, who had long observed the miserable conditions and oppression of the poor, wanted to hear. In their final documents the bishops at Medellín denounced "institutionalized violence" and the "international imperialism of money." They committed themselves to the "preferential option of the poor."

"Medellín produced the Magna Carta of today's persecuted, socially committed Church, and as such rates as one of the major events of the century," said Penny Lernoux, who researched the church in Latin America for her book *Cry of the People.* It is not an overstatement. The church was now committed to working with the poor, not just serving the rich.

Working with the doctrines expounded in the encyclicals, at Vatican II, and at Medellín, a group of young Latin priests developed what has become known as the theology of liberation.

"It's very simple," Jon Sobrino, a Spanish-born Jesuit in El Salvador, explained to Alan Riding. "You just read the Bible with the eyes of the poor. You read the same Bible, but suddenly you see different things. The theology of liberation thus becomes the theoretical and ecclesiastical basis for certain actions, but the theology is, of course, less important than the liberation."

The new teachings and activities centered on the *comunidades de base,* or base communities, the establishment of which became possible in light of Vatican II's declarations on equality within the church of laity and priests. Somewhat like the church of the catacombs of the early persecuted Christians, these *comunidades* sprang up all over Latin America; by the late 1970's there were about 100,000. In groups of from ten to fifteen, peasants and workers from the same urban slum or rural village met regularly to read and discuss the Bible. Priest-trained lay preachers, known as Delegates of the Word, guided the gathered groups, often illiterate. Biblical teachings were analyzed in light of the conditions facing the poor: What does the Bible say about the right of workers to organize? What does it say about the right of revolution? What does it say about the rights of parents to get a decent education and health care for their children?

Perhaps nowhere has the church's commitment to the poor—liberation theology—had a more profound, indeed cataclysmic impact on the economic, political, and social fiber of a society than in El Salvador, a country that is 98 percent Catholic. In Nicaragua priests aligned themselves with the guerrillas against Somoza, and several held high positions in the Sandinista government after Somoza had been toppled. But the Nicaraguan guerrillas were in the mountains years before Vatican II and Medellín. In El Salvador the revolution against the military dictatorships began after Medellín, and while it would be irresponsible to posit a direct causal link between the two, it is not difficult to argue that the revolution would not have advanced as rapidly as it did without the blessings of important church leaders. Priests, not Fidel Castro or Che Guevara, had the greater impact on the Salvadoran revolution.

After Medellín, what priests and nuns began to preach to their impoverished parishioners, as Father Grande explained in a letter to his superiors, was that "their hunger, their diseases, their infant mortality, their unemployment, their unpaid wages, were not the will of God, but the result of the greed of a few Salvadorans and their own passivism." To alter their impoverished, oppressed conditions, the peasants and workers were told they must organize and act. God would bless them, but they had to act.

Father Grande and three other Jesuits, faithful to the church's new commitment to the poor, worked and lived in Aguilares, a sugar-growing valley north of the capital where a few landowners owned the fertile land and about 30,000 peasants struggled to survive on what they could coax out of their tiny, often rocky plots—if they were fortunate enough to have any land. During the harvest season the peasants competed with one another for the opportunity to earn $3 a day cutting cane in the blistering sun. The priests moved from village to village, spending two to three weeks living with peasants, sleeping with them on dirt floors, subsisting on their diet of tortillas and beans. This was an astonishing new church for the peasants—priests and later sisters in dirty blue jeans working alongside them in the fields, not just in white vestments visible only during services.

Eight months after the priests had arrived in Aguilares, 1,600 workers at La Cabaña sugar mill staged a brief strike when the owners reneged on their oral promise to give them a raise. It was probably the first time that farm workers had stood up to their bosses. And they were successful.

Throughout the country priests encouraged peasants to join the Federation of Christian Peasants, known by its Spanish acronym

FECCAS, and the UTC, the initials for what in English would be called the farm workers' union. FECCAS had its roots in the efforts by the Christian Democrats to organize and gain support among workers in the early 1960's. Because of the repression, it had never achieved much influence. The UTC was founded under Christian leadership in 1974. By 1979 FECCAS and the UTC were providing the bulk of the membership of the Popular Revolutionary Bloc (BPR), with 60,000 to 80,000 members the largest of the popular organizations and allied with the FPL, the largest of the guerrilla organizations. The political ideology of the BPR and FPL was unequivocally Marxist; some of the leaders were Leninists.

Many catechists and Delegates of the Word joined coalitions that had formed in opposition to the government. "But to suggest that large numbers of catechists and delegates were going over to Marxism, and even Communism, was a gross exaggeration and distortion," wrote Father James R. Brockman in his book *The Word Remains: A Life of Oscar Romero.* A professor at Xavier University in Ohio who researched the activities of the Salvadoran church during the 1970's, Brockman added that "to assume that all contact with Marxists must be avoided was unrealistic to say the least, and not the teaching or practice of the church."

While priests and nuns encouraged young Salvadorans to join the revolutionary organizations, they didn't directly advocate violence. They were persecuted "because they have tried to speed the pace of social and economic reform and modernization," William Rogers, assistant secretary of state for Inter-American affairs in the Ford administration, told a 1977 congressional committee investigating religious persecution in El Salvador. "There is no evidence that they have worked in any way other than through the legitimate channels."

But church leaders, looking at the decades of unrelenting repression, the history replete with fraudulent elections, gave guarded approval to the taking up of arms.

"Christians are not afraid of combat; they know how to fight, but they prefer the language of peace," said Oscar Arnulfo Romero, archbishop of San Salvador. "However, when a dictatorship seriously violates human rights and attacks the common good of the nation, when it becomes unbearable and closes all channels of dialogue, when this happens, the Church speaks of the legitimate right of insurrectional violence."

The archbishop was on solid ecclesiastical ground. Pope Paul VI, in *Populorum progressio,* had cautiously recognized the legitimacy of revolution "where there is manifest long-standing tyranny which would do great damage to fundamental personal rights and dangerous harm to the common good of the country." Romero called this "the classical teaching of Catholic theology."

That Romero had arrived at the conclusion that armed revolution could be legitimate was as dramatic an indication as could exist about the desperate, if not hopeless, plight of the poor and of anyone seeking democratic change in El Salvador.

When Paul VI originally named Romero his senior prelate in El Salvador in February 1977, the country's military regime was heartened, and El Salvador's wealthy elite contributed generously to his extravagant ordination ceremony. But the priests and nuns who were practicing the teachings of Medellín and the concepts of liberation theology were despondent. Everything in the new archbishop's background indicated that he was conservative. When in 1971 he had been named editor of *Orientación,* the archdiocese newspaper, he immediately changed its focus—from social and political questions and the guidelines of Medellín to more traditional and less controversial subjects such as drugs, alcoholism, and pornography. In an editorial *Orientación* denounced the "demagogy and Marxism" found in "the pamphlets and literature, of known red origin" that were circulating at the Jesuit high school in San Salvador. As the bishop in Santiago de María, Romero had been reluctant to accept accounts from his priests that landowners were cheating peasants, paying less than the minimum wage, which was $1 a day. "They are good people," he said of the coffee growers he had known. Above all, as a bishop he had been critical of the "politicized priests" who spoke out against government repression. While other bishops publicly expressed outrage at the persecution of peasants, Romero preferred the quiet, diplomatic approach. In 1975 national guardsmen raided Tres Calles, a hamlet in Romero's diocese, and shot and hacked to death five peasants. Romero sent a letter of protest to President Molina; it was deferential and respectful, and he did not make it public. Romero believed it inappropriate for a church leader to criticize government officials publicly.

But Archbishop Oscar Arnulfo Romero, born in 1917 to simple parents in a mountainous village so isolated that it could be reached only by foot and horse trail until the dirt road arrived when he was twenty-three years old, became the leading voice against government repression. Named the country's spiritual leader by Rome, he became the country's de facto political leader by default. His voice was amplified by the surrounding silence. Opposition political leaders were murdered or exiled. The major newspapers were, and are, archconservative, the voices of the country's wealthy. The shy, reflective man of prayer, who lived in a small room at a cancer hospital, was revered by the poor and peasants, who mobbed him wherever he went.

It has been written, so often that it has acquired a life and truth of its own, that Romero's "conversion" was brought about by the assassination of Rutilio Grande, who had stood next to him during his ordination as archbishop and been murdered twenty-one days later. But Father Brockman said Romero didn't like the concept that he had been "converted." It implied a turning to God after a period of estrangement. Romero acknowledged, however, that the brutality and depth of the government repression had changed him. "I would say that I evolved rather than changed," Romero said after one year as archbishop. "The circumstances of the country led me to overcome my timidity and come closer to the people. . . . The spirit of God has led me to this."

The man who as a priest had used the church newspaper to criticize outspoken priests and defend the government used its pages as the archbishop to list the names of the persons who were picked up off the streets or dragged out of their homes by the government security forces and who then "disappeared."

His principal forum was the pulpit. To hear his Sunday masses, hundreds crowded into San Salvador's Metropolitan Cathedral, an ugly, cavernous shell in the center of the grimy downtown business district. Concrete-reinforcing rods protrude from unfinished cement walls, and green plastic jalousies, not beautiful stained glass, fill the towering spirals. Romero's predecessor had stopped work on the cathedral, believing that it was better to spend money on projects for the poor than on the churches where they worshiped. Romero agreed. It was here that simple peasant women, heads covered with white towels or pieces of cloth, and barefoot men received not only spiritual guidance but a litany of the latest acts of official brutality. "The root of all violence," Romero said repeatedly, "is institutional violence."

To overcome this institutional violence, he defended the rights of workers and peasants to join the grass-roots organizations of workers and slum dwellers, formed to demonstrate against the government's policies and repression. He called the popular organizations one of the "signs of the times" that Vatican II spoke of. He pointed out in a pastoral letter that the right of workers to organize was contained in the Universal Declaration of Human Rights and had been asserted in Pope John XXIII's *Pacem in terris* and by Vatican II. Moreover, he noted that businessmen and the wealthy in El Salvador could form and join any and all manner of organizations and spend whatever sums necessary to get the government to do what they wanted. On the other hand, the popular organizations were illegal, and when workers tried to strike or took over factories in efforts to obtain higher wages or better working conditions, soldiers evicted them with machine guns and small tanks.

Romero recognized the Marxist orientation of the popular organizations, and that troubled him. "Naturally, if by Marxism is meant that materialistic and atheistic ideology which envelops human existence and gives a false interpretation of religion, it is completely inadmissible for Christians," Romero wrote in his third pastoral letter. He accepted, however, the legitimate use of Marxism as a theoretical or, as the Marxists say, "scientific" tool of economic analysis. The line between the two is a delicate one, for Romero as well as for other priests and nuns in Latin America. Romero, citing church documents, pointed out: "The fear of Marxism keeps many from confronting the oppressive reality of liberal capitalism. Before the danger of a system clearly marked by sin, they forget to denounce and combat the reality implanted by another system equally marked by sin." He concluded: "The best way to gain ground on Marxism is to take seriously the preferential option of the poor."

Romero's outspoken opposition to the repressive government and his support of the popular organizations were not shared by the majority of the six bishops who constituted the country's bishops' conference, which was—and remains—dominated by conservatives. One was the chaplain for the armed forces. But the most outspoken was—and, again, still is—Bishop Pedro Arnoldo Aparicio y Quintanilla, about whom General Romero once observed, "He wags his tail when you give him something." While Archbishop Romero was defending the popular organizations, Aparicio, from his pulpit in the San Vicente Cathedral, was condemning FECCAS and the UTC as Communist organizations, charging that unnamed priests and nuns were following the "Communist line," and blaming the deaths of the four priests who had been murdered up to that date on the leftists, not the government, which he said was not persecuting the church. During one sermon in October 1980 Aparicio declared that "foreign priests should ask the most Holy Virgin to grant the grace that they return to their own countries there to find the hate and resentment they want to instill in people." A few weeks later he said that *Orientación* was run by a Communist. These attacks were followed, predictably, by murders and bombings.

THE persecution of the Catholic Church in Latin America following Medellín has been "unparalleled in modern history," said Penny Lernoux. And nowhere was it more ruthless than in El Salvador. In Argentina, which has nearly five times the population of El Salvador and where in the 1970's extreme brutality and repression were employed to wipe out an urban-based revolutionary movement, the total number of bishops, priests, and nuns murdered during the fourteen-year period from 1964 to 1978 was 15. And in Brazil, a country of 115 million, where the liberation theology had its beginning—there were 40,000 *comunidades de base*—four priests and one nun were killed from 1964 to 1978, a period of harsh military rule. In El Salvador, during just four years, from the murder of Father Grande to the assassinations of the four American Roman Catholic churchwomen in December 1980, 16 Catholic religious leaders were killed.

The government tried to cover up the killings, or blame the left, or charge that the priests were Communists—or all three. The first priest Romero had ordained, Octavio Ortiz, was murdered while on a retreat, called a "young people's Christian initiation gathering," in San Antonio Abad, a warren of mud huts and shacks a few blocks up the volcano from the Metrocentro shopping center. The soldiers rammed an armored vehicle through the metal gate of the building where Ortiz and others were sleeping. After it was over, they lugged four bodies to the roof and pressed pistols into their hands. "In official communiqués," Brockman noted, the retreat site "became a guerrilla training center, its guitars weapons, its songbooks subversive literature."

Priests and nuns were not the only targets, or perhaps even the primary ones, of the persecution. Indeed, the cloak and habit might have provided them with some protection, which was not available to the scores of catechists, lay leaders, and Delegates of the Word who were killed. The government's fear of these people rose in part from a lack of understanding of their evangelical mission. What scared military officers even more was that a lay leader in the church might transfer his leadership skills, helping peasants to form cooperatives and workers to form unions. Leaders are feared by dictators. Hundreds were persecuted in El Salvador. One lay deacon was forced by National Guard soldiers to put on a red cape and crown, then to drag a cross for two miles. A few weeks later they returned, stuffed mud mixed with urine into his mouth, then stomped on him with their boots. A Delegate of the Word, who was also a leader of the UTC, had his eyes plucked out and head cut off by National Guard soldiers.

The persecution of the church in El Salvador, the general repression that by 1980 was claiming nearly 200 lives a week, was still being pretty much ignored by most Americans until December 4, 1980.

A cluster of reporters waited tensely, along with the U.S. ambassador, Robert White, whose anguished face betrayed that he knew, dreaded what was going to be found. Rivulets of sweat dripped from his face, stained the shirt on his bulky torso, as the Reverend Paul Schindler, a diocesan priest from Cleveland who had experienced nearly a decade of Salvadoran brutality, shoveled away the sun-parched dirt.

In the crude mass grave, stacked on top of each other were the bodies of four women. The first hauled out of the hole was Jean Donovan, twenty-seven years old, a lay missionary from Cleveland. Her face had been blown away by a high-caliber bullet that had been fired into the back of her head. Her pants were unzipped; her underwear twisted around her ankles. When area peasants found her, she was nude from the waist down. They had tried to replace the garments before burial. Then came Dorothy Kazel, a forty-year-old Ursuline nun also from Cleveland. At the bottom of the pit were Maryknoll nuns Ita Ford, forty, and Maura Clarke, forty-nine, both from New York. All the women had been executed at close range. The peasants who found the women said that one had her underpants stuffed in her mouth; another's had been tied over her eyes. All had been raped. Peasants who heard the bursts of automatic rifles on the evening of December 2, when the women were killed, didn't hear any screams or cries for help.

"They were subversives," National Guard Sergeant Luis Antonio Colindres Alemán told the soldiers he had commanded in the rape-murder.

A few weeks before the women were executed, a warning had been tacked on the pale green wooden door of the parish house in Chalatenango where Sisters Ford and Clarke lived in tiny cubicles, each sparsely furnished with a hard bed and small table. The parish quarters also served as a warehouse, brimming with burlap bags of beans, sacks of powdered milk, cans of cooking oil, and boxes of medicine, which the sisters distributed to the peasants in nearby hamlets. Above the drawing of a knife plunged into a skull dripping blood was the message "In this house are Communists. Everyone who enters here will die. Try it and see." It was signed by the Mauricio Borgonovo Anti-Communist Brigade, named after the foreign minister assassinated by the FPL in 1977.

The belief that the nuns were "subversive" wasn't held just by anonymous Salvadorans. During a Cabinet meeting in the Presidential Palace Defense Minister García presented a ten-year-old boy. In response to García's questions the weeping lad said that the nuns and priests in Chalatenango were collaborating with the guerrillas. "We've got to take steps against the missionaries," García exclaimed.

Shortly after that meeting, on December 2, Kazel and Donovan drove their white Toyota van to El Salvador's international airport to pick up Ford and Clarke, who were returning from a conference in Nicaragua. As the four women exited from the airport, their van was stopped, and Colindres ordered a guardsman to drive it, following a National Guard jeep. When they reached an isolated spot on a twisting road fifteen miles from the airport, the guardsmen, who were wearing civilian clothes, ordered the women out of the van. "Men, don't you have wives?" one of the women pleaded as the soldiers began raping them.

After returning to their barracks at the airport, Colindres gave each of the soldiers 15 colones (the equivalent of $6), then passed around a bottle of J & B scotch and Tic-Tac, the Salvadoran counterpart of corn liquor. "Nothing is going to happen," he assured his nervous companions.

I would like to suggest to you that some of the investigations would lead one to believe that perhaps the vehicle that the nuns were riding in may have tried to run a roadblock or may have accidentally been perceived to have been doing so, and there may have been an exchange of gunfire," Alexander M. Haig, Jr., told the House Committee on Foreign Affairs a few weeks after he had become Reagan's secretary of state.

"Have you no sense of decency, sir, at long last? Have you no sense of decency?" demanded *The New York Times'* columnist Anthony Lewis, drawing on the outrage directed toward Senator Joseph McCarthy during his witch-hunt for Communists in the early 1950's. Haig sought to quiet the furor he had created by joking when he appeared before the Senate Foreign Relations Committee and was asked by Senator Claiborne Pell, Democrat of Rhode Island, if the secretary of state really believed the women had tried to run a roadblock. "Not at all, no, not at all," Haig said with a tone of amazement in his voice. "My heavens! The dear nuns who raised me in my parochial schooling would forever isolate me from their affections and respect." When Pell asked if Haig, when he had used the phrase "exchange of fire," thought the nuns had been shooting, Haig responded, "I haven't met any pistol-packing nuns in my day, Senator. What I meant was that if one fellow starts shooting, then the next thing you know they all panic." Haig didn't apologize to the families. A State Department spokesman in a letter to William Ford, the brother of Ita Ford, said that Secretary Haig's remarks had been "misinterpreted," that his suggestion that the women had been attempting to run a roadblock was "only one theory and not a fact."

In late 1981 Congress enacted legislation requiring the President, as a condition for further U.S. military aid to El Salvador, to certify every six months that the Salvadoran government was making good-faith efforts to bring to justice those responsible for the murders of the four women, as well as of Hammer and Pearlman, and that of John Sullivan, a free-lance journalist from New Jersey who was kidnapped in late December 1980. Five national guardsmen had been arrested in connection with the killing of the nuns in May 1981, but there was no movement in the case against them until two days before President Reagan had to present his first certification to Congress in January 1982, when General García assured everyone that there would be developments in the case "within a very few days." Sure enough, some days later the guardsmen were turned over to civilian authorities, something that could have occurred when they were arrested eight months earlier.

"Where there's a will, there's a way," Archbishop Arturo Rivera y Damas said in his homily the following Sunday. The convenient timing of this development prompted him to add, "I hope this isn't simply a gesture to please, to gain publicity in order to promote further United States aid." His skepticism was well founded. During the next two years action on the case would come, predictably, every six months, as the U.S. President certified that progress was being made. After the Reagan administration had issued its second certification in July 1982, Assistant Secretary of State Enders assured the Senate Foreign Relations Committee: "We expect a trial date to be set this fall." As of March 1984 the men still had not been brought to trial.

"If you investigate the murder of the American churchwomen, you are going to find that it was not the responsibility of four or six or eight enlisted men, but that it involved orders from responsible officers," Robert White, ambassador at the time the women were murdered, told a congressional subcommittee in July 1981. He wasn't the only one who held that view. "There is one thing that bothers me, and this is how a sergeant could give orders unless beforehand, at least in a general form, someone has not opened the way for decisions of this nature to be taken," Rivera y Damas said after a mass in early 1982.

White's successor, Deane Hinton, didn't share his view that higher-ups were involved. Shortly before departing as ambassador, he said in an interview, "As I read the evidence and as I understand the society, there's no reason for orders. Suspicious women coming in from Managua; one of the 'fellers' always thought that Jean Donovan was attractive; they had money. It just got out of control. You got a bunch of barbarians. I don't think they needed orders."

The State Department and other government agencies have refused to release cables and other documents that would prove or disprove whether or not the guardsmen were acting on their own.

"Over a year ago, I and other members began the process of asking the Department of State for copies of cable traffic dealing with the murders of the churchwomen in El Salvador," Gerry Studds, a liberal Democratic congressman from Massachusetts, said with undisguised irritation during congressional hearings in 1982. But he said he as well as the chairman of the committee had been provided with only some "highly expurgated" cables. Then he asked White, who was appearing as a witness, "Can you think of any reason the administration might be so singularly unenthusiastic about sharing that cable traffic with us?"

"Yes, sir, I certainly can," White responded. When the laughter subsided, White explained that the cables would show that there had been "no serious investigation" into the deaths of the churchwomen. He added, "I can think of no possible way in which the national security of the United States would be jeopardized by the release of entire traffic on the nuns."

A few months later, in May 1982, the State Department in a letter to Senator Strom Thurmond, Republican of South Carolina, declared, "We have offered to provide the family members all cable traffic between the State Department and the U.S. embassy in El Salvador that contains evidence, or potential evidence, about the crime."

But the families of the murdered churchwomen have not been provided with all the evidence. Represented by Michael Posner, executive director of the Lawyers Committee for International Human Rights, a nonprofit organization in New York, they filed a Freedom of Information Act request with the State Department in June 1981, seeking access to all cables, memorandums, reports, letters, or other records that related either to the deaths or to any investigations into those deaths. More than two years later they had been denied 116 documents. Of the 92 documents that were made available to the families, substantial portions had been deleted.

Similar FOIA requests to the FBI, CIA, and Defense Intelligence Agency (DIA) have been equally, if not more, unsuccessful. The CIA said that before it could conduct a search for the documents, it would need the churchwomen's full names, as well as dates and places of birth. "Without such information," the agency said, "it will be difficult if not impossible for us to distinguish between individuals with the same or similar names." Finally, the CIA said it would require "proof of death." The FBI said it had ten volumes of documents, containing 2,912 pages, pertaining to the churchwomen's case. It refused to release any of them, relying on a provision of the Freedom of Information Act that exempts from release "investigatory files compiled for law enforcement purposes, but only to the extent that the production of such records would . . . interfere with enforcement proceedings." In the first court ruling on the applicability of that exemption to a foreign investigation, a federal district court in New York, in February 1984, upheld the FBI's position regarding all but 162 documents, which the court ordered turned over to the families.

Under pressure from the Subcommittee on Foreign Operations of the Senate Appropriations Committee, the Reagan administration in 1983 commissioned Harold R. Tyler, a former deputy attorney general and retired federal judge, to investigate the murder of the church-women. Judge Tyler submitted his 103-page findings on December 2, 1983. The State Department classified the report Secret and, as of February 1984, refused to release it even to the families of the murdered women. The department offered to release the Tyler report to one member of each family, but only on the condition that the person first pass a security clearance and sign a sworn statement that he or she would not discuss the contents of the report with anyone else. "It's preposterous for me to read that report and not be able to discuss it with my mother," said William Ford, an attorney and brother of one of the slain women, in rejecting the department's proposal. "I would like every American to read that report," he added. (The department stuck to its position even after an account of the Tyler report, which was provided to me, appeared in The New York Times on February 16, 1984.)

"Having reviewed the report, I am unable to discover anything in it that would justify its classification," Representative Michael D. Barnes, Democrat of Maryland and chairman of the House Subcommittee on Western Hemisphere Affairs, wrote Secretary of State Shultz in December 1983. Shultz refused Barnes's request to declassify the report. The department argues that to declassify the report would prejudice the trial against the soldiers. "It is difficult to see how it could," Barnes wrote.* In addition, he wrote that "Judge Tyler has himself informed me through staff that he does not think release of the report now would affect the trial."

A more likely reason that the Reagan administration does not want to release the report publicly—it was provided to me in its entirety— is that it contains numerous findings that run counter to public statements by the administration about the Salvadoran military and government. Among these is the fact that the Salvadorans tried to cover up the crime from almost the day that it was committed. "The first reaction of the Salvadoran authorities to the murder was, tragically, to conceal the perpetrators from justice," the summary of the report said. "Evidence available to the United States . . . shows beyond question that Colindres Alemán confessed his involvement in the crime to ranking members of the National Guard within days of the murder. They responded by concealing this fact from the outside world, and ordering the transfer of the killers from their airport posts and the switching of their weapons to make detection more difficult."

In the section about the Salvadoran investigations the report said: "Within days of the murders, Salvadoran authorities commissioned two investigations, one public and one private, both with apparently the same objective: to create a written record absolving the Salvadoran security forces of responsibility for the murders." The private investigation was commissioned by the National Guard and headed by Major Lizandro Zepeda Velasco. Colindres Alemán confessed to Major Zepeda, whose investigation Judge Tyler calls "a sham."

Judge Tyler further concluded, "[I]t is quite possible that Colonel Carlos Eugenio Vides Casanova, then head of the National Guard and now a General and Minister of Defense, was aware of, and for a time acquiesced in, the cover-up." When Judge Tyler's investigating team interviewed Vides Casanova, "we found him evasive; he professed a disturbing lack of knowledge of Zepeda's investigation, despite evidence that he was aware of and received reports concerning Zepeda's

---

*It seems highly unlikely that the Salvadorans who might be called as jurors would ever have seen whatever newspaper accounts of the report might appear in the Salvadoran press—the trial is scheduled to be held in Zacatecoluca, which is some thirty-five miles from the capital. Surely in that city, or in whatever other city to which the trial might be moved, it would be possible to find five persons, the number on a Salvadoran jury, who had not seen accounts of the Tyler investigation. Moreover, any prejudicial damage to the defendants' receiving an impartial trial had already been done by Duarte, who when he was president of the junta had publicly stated that he was "morally certain" that the arrested guardsmen were guilty.

efforts throughout the investigation. In his answers to us, General Vides Casanova attempted to distance himself as completely as possible from all investigations of the crime."

On the issue of whether higher-ups ordered the killings, Judge Tyler's report was inconclusive. The issue "is a troubling one," Judge Tyler said. "To the extent the Salvadoran authorities have investigated this matter, their inquiry is not nearly as complete as we would have liked. There is some evidence suggesting the involvement of higher-ups," the report stated in the summary. "Although it is unlikely that a dispositive answer will ever be known, we record here our best judgment: on the basis of the evidence available to us, we believe that Colindres Alemán acted on his own initiative." Later in the report, however, in the section "Involvement of Higher Authorities," Judge Tyler said, "[T]he record from which we have had to work is not as complete as we would have liked, or as would have been assembled for a comparable murder investigation in the United States."

Robert White said that "Judge Tyler didn't fully investigate" the issue of involvement by higher-ups. "I just don't believe that those guys would have done this without some higher orders." According to White, two national guardsmen who might have been able to link higher-ranking officers to the murders of the nuns were killed "by military death squads," then were officially listed as missing or killed in action. "In my view," White said, to convict the guardsmen who have been charged "and say that it began and ended with them would be simply a device to satisfy U.S. public opinion and would not really serve the ends of justice."

THE churchwomen's case is more than just another example of the unwillingness of the U.S. government to be honest with the public and Congress and of its reluctance to challenge the Salvadoran military. Worse—at least from the perspective of making a sound policy—it reflects a lack of understanding about the role of the church. The day after the bodies had been pulled from the earth, Jeane Kirkpatrick told reporter John Hall, "The nuns were not just nuns. The nuns were also political activists. We ought to be a little more clear about this than we usually are. They were political activists on behalf of the Frente [FDR] and somebody who is using violence to oppose the Frente killed these nuns. I don't have any doubt about that." Asked if she thought the government had been involved, she responded, "The answer is unequivocal. No, I don't think the government was responsible."

At the time of her statement, Kirkpatrick was a foreign policy adviser to President-elect Reagan, later to become UN ambassador and a key architect of the administration's policy in Central America. She denied making the statement about the churchwomen after it had appeared in the *Tampa Tribune* on Christmas Day 1980. Several months later, however, in a letter to Senators Charles Percy and Claiborne Pell, the chairman and ranking minority member, respectively, of the Senate Foreign Relations Committee, she admitted to having made the accusation—but only implicitly. She told the senators that her comment had been "taken out of context of a broader discussion of the character of the struggle in El Salvador." (It had not been. The article was in the question and answer format, and her response was to a very specific question.) She added that she didn't believe there was anything "either very original or controversial" about what she had said.

Kirkpatrick closed her letter to the senators with a request that "someone in your office" forward a copy to Michael Donovan, brother of one of the slain women. She didn't have his address, she said. Yet Donovan had sent letters to Kirkpatrick; they had gone unanswered. He went to her UN office to make an appointment; he was turned away by an aide. Donovan described Kirkpatrick's comment as "quite clearly a vicious attack on four brave American women."

The Reagan administration was still at odds with the church over the U.S. policy in El Salvador in 1983. When Pope John Paul II visited the country in March, he called for "reconciliation and dialogue" to end the war. Ambassador Hinton rejected the pontiff's plea for negotiations, asserting that the elections were all the United States was willing to discuss. About the same time Vice President George Bush told a group of Latin American experts in a private meeting that he could not understand how priests were able to work with Marxist revolutionaries. The day before that Secretary of State George Shultz, near the conclusion of his testimony before the Senate Foreign Relations Committee, criticized "churchmen who want to see Soviet influence in El Salvador improved." Senator Patrick Leahy of Vermont, who had been to El Salvador and is a Roman Catholic, was taken aback by the outburst from the secretary of state. "I wonder if you might submit for the record, Mr. Secretary, the names of those churchmen who want to see Soviet influence increased in El Salvador," Leahy shot back, "because I certainly would want to be the first to write them and tell them I think that is a terrible idea."

Leahy, a Democrat, was already a critic of Reagan's policy in El Salvador. But the comments by Bush and Shultz lost the President the support of Republican Senator David Durenberger of Minnesota. In a lengthy letter to the President the senator said, "I find it astonishing that the Secretary of State and the Vice President have so little understanding of what is at stake in El Salvador and the role which the Catholic Church can play in advancing the enunciated goals of the administration. I find it outrageous that they would suggest that the Church would bolster the ends of Marxism, for it is the Church which has repeatedly and universally called attention to the dangers of atheistic Marxist-Leninism." He called their statements "especially inappropriate and harmful to the overriding goal of peace."

AFTER Archbishop Romero had been murdered, Pope John Paul II named Arturo Rivera y Damas as senior prelate, keeping him as the acting archbishop, or apostolic administrator, until early 1983, when he officially designated him archbishop. Reagan State Department officials have commended Rivera y Damas for what they consider his balanced criticisms of violence—by the guerrillas as well as by the government. "When we speak of violence, we cannot use a double standard as do those who seek to justify actions by one side and condemn those by the other," Rivera y Damas said, for example, during a Sunday homily in January 1983. "The violence is equally condemnable when it comes from those who kidnap, ambush armed forces patrols, dynamite installations that provide jobs, and provoke electricity stoppages that affect entire zones; or when the violence comes from security forces and paramilitary bands as they kidnap persons of the civilian populations late at night, and have them disappear or kill them." He added, however, that "the repressive violence directed at defenseless persons and violence carried out by those invested with authority—whose role it is to protect human rights—is the more condemnable."

But the Reagan administration has ignored the pleas by Rivera y Damas for negotiations and an end to military aid. And in El Salvador the influential don't appear to be any more pleased with Rivera y Damas than they were with Romero. They don't like his criticism of the government repression and his calls for negotiations. As with Romero, what Rivera y Damas has to say rings like a shout throughout El Salvador, where there has been no opposition press since *La Crónica* and *El Independiente* closed after repeated bombings of their facilities and attacks on reporters. The remaining newspapers refused to publish the letter from Pope John Paul II to the Salvadoran bishops when the pope visited El Salvador in March 1983; the archdiocese had to buy space. The papers, some months previously, had not been reluctant to publish an interview with Bishop Aparicio, who used the opportunity to charge that there was a danger of the "infiltration of Communism into the Catholic church."

THE persecution of the church in El Salvador has had a toll far more profound than, although not as visible as, just the number of priests, nuns, and lay workers who have been murdered. Tens of thousands of Salvadorans, principally peasants in rural areas, are without the spiritual guidance and teachings of the church. Their marriages are not blessed. Their children are not baptized. They die without final rites. In 1983 the number of Catholic clergy in El Salvador was 35 percent fewer than in 1977. Priests and nuns who have remained live with the understanding, and the fear, that they may be next. They often rotate their places of sleep; they have drastically curtailed their pastoral activities.

"It's not the guerrillas we fear," said an Irish Franciscan priest who had been preaching in El Salvador for more than a decade, "but that we'd be accused of being Communists, of helping what the government calls subversives." He and three other Irish priests of the same order, along with three Welsh nuns from the order of St. Clare, had remained working in Morazán Province in spite of repeated threats. They are among the most courageous people I have ever met. They lived in an L-shaped one-story house on the corner of the town square in San Francisco Gotera. Across the asphalt was the headquarters of an elite commando battalion, the soldiers of which trained by sprinting up the steps of the nineteenth-century Spanish-style cathedral. In the priests' quarters, on a wall that faced across the porch to a garden of bright tropical shrubs, was a map hand-drawn on cream-colored pieces of paper that had been patched together. It showed the villages the priests and nuns served—or once had. As we sat on the cement-floor porch—one rocking chair was missing an arm; the cane was ruptured in another—they explained they could no longer perform masses in many of the villages north of Gotera. And even in the few hamlets they still served, they were careful about what they preached and what songs they sang. They no longer trained catechists; too many had been killed. Even the church's newspapers were wrapped in brown paper before being delivered to the remote parishioners.

On Christmas Day 1980, during a bone-jarring trip over a boulder-strewn, rutted dirt road, Sister Anselm, a tall, angular woman with a powerful handshake and cheerful, infectious laugh, pointed past the low sisal plants to the valley below. Several years ago, she explained,

the church here in conjunction with Oxfam, the third world development organization in London, began a program with the area's subsistence farmers. "Instead of relying on the government," she explained, villagers were taught improved irrigation and soil
conservation techniques. "It just mushroomed. They built a road, got
a teacher for the school; then some women got interested in health and
hygiene. When they realized they couldn't read, they started their own
literacy program." But the National Guard and ORDEN forces began
killing the leaders, sometimes brutally hacking them to death with
machetes, leaving their bodies for all to see, as a warning. Soon all the
self-help projects were abandoned.

When we finally reached Cacaopera, a ridgeline village, the already
hot sun was climbing out of the valleys beyond; a full moon still hung
in the piercing blue sky. On the steps of the eighteenth-century Spanish colonial church, youngsters acted out the Christmas pageant. In
the grimy dirt plaza, under pieces of shredded plastic strung across
shaky poles, women fashioned tortillas and sold flashlight batteries,
shoelaces, and toothpaste, oblivious to the Three Wise Men offering
their gifts to a pudgy-cheeked infant cradled in the arms of a young
girl. By the time the children, garbed in homemade capes and cardboard angel's wings, were singing "The Little Drummer Boy," eight
menacing-looking soldiers had entered the plaza from below. They
were unshaved. Machetes sheathed in elaborately tooled leather scab-
bards hung from the waists of their disheveled green uniforms. They
carried pre-World War II Czechoslovakian-manufactured bolt-action
rifles, which is what the rural civil defense forces carried—before the
arrival of modern U.S.-supplied M-16's. They rounded up a few
drunken peasants and tossed them into the local jail, a dirt-floor room
constructed of planks cut not long ago from surrounding forests.

The green stucco of the church was sprayed with a revolutionary
tribute to a priest born in this village who had been killed by the
soldiers. His father, a lay leader in the church, took "the final step,"
said Sister Anselm; he was now in the mountains with the guerrillas.
Inside the church barefoot men and frail women with patterned hand-
kerchiefs and cotton towels covering their heads sat on crude wooden
benches. After the mass Christmas cookies, brought by Sister Anselm
in a wicker basket, and fruit-flavored punch were served to children
with runny noses, distended bellies, and open sores, who gathered
around a bright hibiscus. Father Gerry Moore baptized seventeen infants. As I talked with Sister Anselm, wearing her brown and white
habit, peasants meekly offered her five- and ten-centavo pieces, for her
fifty-second birthday, which was that day, December 25.

After returning to Gotera, we went to Christmas mass, celebrated at 8:00 P.M. "Silent Night" drifted through the arched windows cut in the thick walls, colliding in the muggy air with the music blaring from the barracks. Altar boys in white robes with red trim assisted in the mass. Outside, sixteen-year-old soldiers snapped the bolts on their automatic rifles.

EL Salvador, in the image of a popular metaphor, is a stool with four legs: the oligarchy, the military, the church, and the United States.

"What's missing in that?" asked a senior U.S. diplomat who served in El Salvador. "The people."

6

THE OPPOSITION

CHRISTIANS TO COMMUNISTS

First came the FPL, formed by dissidents within the PCS, then the ERP, out of which, after a brutal internecine dispute and the execution of a revolutionary poet, was born the FARN. There're FAL and FAPU, the BPR and LP-28, FENASTRAS, FUERSA, ANDES, and MER. And these are just a fraction of the seemingly endless and tortuously complex agglomeration of armed guerrilla forces, unions, outlawed political parties, and grass-roots organizations that make up the Salvadoran opposition on the political left.

The collage is a political Rubik's cube. "Tracing details of the complex schisms and affinities is like studying schematic diagrams through a kaleidoscope," Christopher Dickey of *The Washington Post* observed in his definitive piece about the Salvadoran left, written at the conclusion of his three years in Central America.

But a sound policy requires working through this complex of acronyms and abbreviations. Fundamental questions must be answered. Why are the people fighting? Are the leaders romantic revolutionaries? Nationalists? Communists? Hard-line Leninists? If a leftist government came to power in El Salvador, would it seek alignment with the Soviet Union? With Cuba? Even if there were such a political alignment, would the government allow the country to be a Soviet military base? Or would it be a socialist government, perhaps modeled on those European countries that are staunch anti-Soviet U.S. allies? Are there democratic elements within the leftist opposition? If there are, what can the United States do to ensure that they would have influence within a leftist government?

U.S. policymakers by and large didn't even try to answer these questions. The policy under both the Carter and the Reagan administrations was to keep a leftist government from coming to power in El Salvador. It was a policy better served by viewing the opposition in simplest black-and-white terms, by using labels such as terrorists, Marxist-Leninists, Marxist-led peasants, or Communist-led insurgents.*

"The amount known about the leftist leaders was very little," said Richard Feinberg, who was on the policy planning staff at State during the first three years of the Carter administration. "It usually consisted of, 'He was recruited when he was in high school, and, you know, he's a hard-line Marxist-Leninist, and he's in this faction, but used to be in that faction.' And that would sort of be about it. There would almost never be a discussion of the ideological issues involved, beyond possible labels like 'Trotskyite' or something like that," Feinberg explained. "It was basically labeling. The information from the CIA would basically be: These guys are Marxists. There wouldn't be a debate. I mean, in the memos or whatever, they would just be referred to as the Marxists, or Marxist revolutionaries, or Marxist-Leninists, or sometimes even terrorists, or pro-Cuban. But there would always be some giveaway adjective that immediately determines the whole debate."

"We didn't know shit about the left," said a senior member of the Carter administration.

During the Reagan administration there was a dramatic escalation in the number of CIA operatives roaming around El Salvador. In addition, the Intelligence Support Activity (ISA), a highly secret unit set up in the Defense Department, sent a team of men and women, civilians and soldiers, to El Salvador in 1982. But the CIA and ISA concentrated primarily, if not exclusively, on operations designed to achieve a military victory. An embassy officer who served in El Salvador until mid-1982 said that the U.S. embassy "knew very little about who exactly is out there in the hills. . . . We know that they receive arms through Nicaragua. But beyond that I don't think we know very much. If we knew more about them, we'd do well to make it public, to tell the people, to inform them better about the real nature of the threat, what kind of people we're dealing with." In late 1983 an editorial writer

---

*By contrast, Reagan administration officials, and most reporters, did not politically label as rightists the forces that the United States trained and equipped and that were trying to overthrow the Sandinista government in Nicaragua. They were usually referred to as simply guerrillas, rebels, insurgents, or counterrevolutionaries (often shortened to the Spanish *contras*). President Reagan called them freedom fighters.

with close connections to the Reagan administration suggested to some senior officials that they meet with Robert Leiken, an academic with considerable knowledge about the Salvadoran left, in order to gain a greater understanding of the opposition. The officials said they were not interested.

Robert White, who frequently used the phrase "Pol Pot left" to refer to the Salvadoran left when he was ambassador, was more charitable after he had left El Salvador and resigned from the Foreign Service. In what is probably the most concise overview of the leftist opposition in El Salvador, White told a congressional subcommittee: "The guerrilla groups, the revolutionary groups, almost without exception began as associations of teachers, associations of labor unions, campesino unions, or parish organizations which were organized for the definite purpose of getting a schoolhouse up on the market road. When they tried to use their power of association to gain their ends, first they were warned and then they were persecuted and tortured and shot." The U.S. response in the late 1970's, he noted, had been to "reaffirm support for the economic and military elites.

"So the leadership of the groups gradually became discouraged and, of course, the Soviet Union—at least Cuba was there to give them understanding and support. So it is true in my book that the large majority of the leaders of the Salvadoran guerrillas are Marxist or Marxist oriented. There is a substantial number who are not.

"I would also add that I do not really believe that the ideological roots of these people go all that deep. I think it is more a response to persecution than anything else.

"Now there are substantial numbers of people who are fighting only because they have no choice. The great majority of the people who are fighting, indeed some of the leaders, are fighting because their towns were attacked and they were driven into the countryside and they cannot give up, because if they would give up they would be killed."

No less than a U.S. citizen who represented El Salvador as vice-consul in the United States from 1966 to 1976 and now serves several major corporations as an adviser on Central America, Bennett Poor, wrote on the Op-Ed page of *The New York Times* in 1981: "The peasant guerrillas are not, as some superpatriots in the United States would have us think, a band of anarchist cut-throats blindly following an alien ideology to a lemming's end." Rather, he wrote: "The vast majority of the peasant guerrillas, whether philosophically Marxist or just plain frustrated with the social structure, is guided by a passion for change but does not propose an alternate government structure." (As for the other side of the political spectrum, Poor wrote: "In El Salvador, the oligarchy—that is, the landed aristocracy—is not a clandestine group of Simon Legrees who are seeking to undermine every advance in human rights since the signing of the Magna Carta. Rather, it is a class of educated, hard-working, taxpaying ranchers and businessmen who, either by effort or inheritance, have had to assume the responsibility of the preservation of capital and the economic stability required to survive during dozens of changes of government in this century.")

THE first guerrilla group was the Popular Forces of Liberation (FPL), formed in 1970 by about a dozen young Communists, workers and intellectuals, who were dissatisfied with the orthodox posture of the Communist party. Surprising as it may seem—at least to most Americans who hear from Washington that "Communists" are responsible for the turmoil—the Communist party had advocated the democratic path to power, participating in the 1972 elections as part of a coalition that backed Duarte and Ungo and again in the 1977 elections.* It was not until early 1980 that the Salvadoran Communist party accepted the need for an armed revolution. But its military arm, the Armed Forces of Liberation (FAL)—500 combatants in 1983—was the smallest of the five guerrilla groups. The party's strength within the FMLN resulted principally from the fact that its leader, Shafik Jorge Handal, had been active in Salvadoran politics longer than any of the guerrilla leaders. Handal, the son of Palestinian Christian immigrants from Bethlehem, joined the outlawed Communist party of El Salvador in 1950 after having been a student leader in law school. His studies were repeatedly interrupted because of his arrests for political activity, and he spent most of the 1950's and 1960's in jail, exile, or hiding, exhibiting accomplished oratorical skills when he did surface. In 1980 he traveled to Eastern Europe and Vietnam in a search for military support for the Salvadoran revolution; his name was on many of the

*The fear that Communists will participate in the electoral process explains in part why Henry Kissinger, when he was head of Nixon's National Security Council, tried to block the election of Salvador Allende Gossens in Chile in the early 1970's, Seymour Hersh suggested in his prizewinning book *The Price of Power: Kissinger in the Nixon White House.* While Kissinger told reporters, "I have yet to meet somebody who firmly believes that if Allende wins there is likely to be another free election in Chile," Hersh wrote: "His real fear, of course, was precisely the opposite: that Allende would work within the democratic process."

documents released by the Reagan administration in 1981 to support its charges in a white paper that the Salvadoran revolution was a textbook case of Communist aggression. But the Salvadoran Communist party still favors a political solution, a reflection of its strength in union organizing rather than in guerrilla warfare.

Disagreements with Handal about strategy led Salvador Cayetano Carpio, who had joined the Communist party in 1947, to found the Popular Forces of Liberation in 1970. Carpio was born into a poor family, dropped out of seminary school, and became a baker and union organizer. This led to repeated arrests, beatings, and sadistic tortures, which he described in his book, first published in 1954, *Secuestro y Capucha* ("Imprisonment and Hood" a reference to the suffocating cover placed over prisoners' heads during tortures). Carpio studied in the Soviet Union for two years in the mid-1950's. In a decade—starting with seven people, no money, and not a single pistol—he built the FPL into one of El Salvador's two strongest guerrilla groups, its force of 1,500 to 2,000 troops operating almost exclusively in Chalatenango Province, where it has the support of tens of thousands of peasants living in the mountainous villages. Carpio, whose daughter Guadalupe, also a Communist, was killed during a political demonstration in 1980, was the near-legendary hero of the revolution. In spite of his age—in his early sixties—and poor health, Carpio, whose *nom de guerre* was Marcial, once walked through the mountains for ten days before slipping through a pincers operation that had surrounded his forces. He narrowly escaped death on one occasion by scrambling into a deep hole seconds before a bomb exploded less than 100 yards away. Carpio was often referred to as the Ho Chi Minh of the Salvadoran revolution, an image he did not seek to dispel. When I interviewed him in Managua in 1982, he was wearing thick wire-rimmed glasses and sporting a scraggly goatee. A slight, frail man, he spoke very softly—mostly small talk and predictable statements about the eventual triumph of the revolution. For Carpio, the ideological hard-liner of the Salvadoran guerrilla leaders —many within the left feared he would be another Stalin—the model for the Salvadoran revolution was Vietnam, not Cuba or Nicaragua. He advocated the prolonged popular war, which meant staying in the mountains—for years or decades, if necessary—organizing support among the peasants until the government, and its American backers, were defeated militarily. He was not opposed to negotiations in principle, as has been usually asserted, but because he did not trust the ability of the other guerrilla leaders not to give away too much at the negotiating table.

The other major guerrilla organization is the People's Revolutionary Army (ERP), which was founded in 1972, in response to that year's fraudulent election. Its organizers were frustrated Christian Democrats and student revolutionaries who had been reading Mao. They, like the founders of the FPL, criticized the Soviet Union for its advocacy of a peaceful transition to socialism, but they disapproved of the FPL's alignment with Cuba. While the ERP was still little more than a movement, lacking enough structure to carry out any military actions, it splintered from within, culminating in the execution of Roque Dalton García, the country's revolutionary and probably most famous poet, essayist, and historian. Dalton, who had spent several years in Cuba and Europe before returning as a political leader in the ERP, was accused by other leftists of "antirevolutionary" conduct, including both being a CIA agent and working for Cuban interests. After a so-called trial he was shot. The executioner was Joaquín Villalobos, the son of a middle-class family who dropped out of the university where he was studying economics to join the revolution in the mid-1970's. The internecine feud led to one faction's breaking away to form the Armed Forces of National Resistance (FARN), with Eduardo Sancho Castañeda—almost always referred to by his *nom de guerre,* Fermán Cienfuegos—eventually emerging as its leader.

A few years later yet another guerrilla group appeared: the Revolutionary Party of Central American Workers (PRTC), which was founded on the premise that a revolution could not be successful in one country if it did not involve the entire region. Like the FAL (the armed force of the Communist party), the PRTC never developed into a significant armed force, and in early 1984 it was on the verge of disbanding, its fewer than 500 combatants to be folded into the other groups. The PRTC's leader was Roberto Roca, who—like Villalobos and Cienfuegos—had been a student leader. Many of the other guerrilla leaders had also been student activists at the university. In many ways they were like the student radicals at U.S. universities in the late 1960's and early 1970's. But while the American youth, after leaving the campuses, marches, and egg-throwing demonstrations, entered the mainstream of business and politics, the Salvadoran leftists had no such alternatives. Revolution was the only means for change.

By 1983 the ERP, FPL, and FARN had between 80 and 90 percent of the guerrillas in arms. These groups "all have anti-Soviet origins" and still harbor "suspicions of the Soviet Union,"* said Robert Leiken, the

---

*The three most important guerrilla groups have also held divergent views about Cuba and Nicaragua. ERP leaders have expressed disapproval of the

scholar of the Latin American left who holds strong anti-Soviet views. As a senior fellow and director of the Soviet-Latin American Project at the Georgetown University Center for Strategic and International Studies, Leiken wrote prolifically about the dangers of Soviet designs in Latin America. Even Jeane Kirkpatrick has said, "The Soviets don't have very much popular support in El Salvador."

In the mid-1970's the guerrilla leaders recognized that they could not achieve a revolutionary victory without the support of the populace. They formed mass-based organizations or entered into alliances with and eventually took control of already existing ones. The FARN joined the United Popular Action Front (FAPU), which was strong among urban workers, while the ERP developed the Popular Leagues —28th of February (LP-28), named for the date of the 1977 demonstration in the Plaza Libertad to protest the fraudulent election. Foremost among the popular organizations was the FPL's Popular Revolutionary Bloc (BPR), a loose coalition of the peasant unions FECCAS and the UTC, two student bodies, and an association of slum dwellers. The BPR was "organized by several priests after the killing of some university students during disturbances in July 1975," according to a State Department report to Congress. Within the BPR was the teachers' union, ANDES, one of the most powerful and militant unions in the country. To this day teachers are particular targets of the government repression.

"The success of the bloc is that it addresses itself to real needs and immediate issues rather than offering long-term solutions," a priest said in 1978. "It campaigns for increased wages or a lowering of the price of fertilizer or seeds. It's obviously a leftist organization, but it talks the language that the poor can understand." Nonviolent demonstrations and civil disobedience, such as occupying churches, embassies, and government buildings, were their main tactic.

In March 1978 the leaders of the BPR peasant unions sought a meeting with officials of the government's Agricultural and Livestock De-

---

number of Cuban teachers, doctors, and advisers in Nicaragua. The FARN is considered the most politically moderate of the three groups and the most committed to a policy of nonalignment. One FARN leader told Leiken that Nicaragua's press censorship was a serious error. "If they didn't like *La Prensa*, they should have created a better newspaper," he said.

"The difference between the Sandinistas and the guerrillas in El Salvador is that the guerrillas tend to be more nationalistic," Régis Debray, a close foreign policy adviser to French President François Mitterrand and longtime student of Latin American revolutionary movements, has told U.S. State Department officers. "They're very disturbed over what they see has happened to the Sandinista revolution and they vow that it won't happen to them."

velopment Bank to discuss peasant demands for lower interest rates on farm loans, decreased prices for fertilizer, and reduced land rents. When the government officials refused to meet with them, some 100 peasants marched through the streets of the capital. The police, opening fire, killed four and wounded more than 30. Five more peasants and a police officer were killed when a bus carrying peasant demonstrators fleeing the capital was stopped by a military roadblock. A few days later troops and ORDEN forces swept through San Pedro Perulapán, a stronghold of the BPR's peasant unions twenty-five miles east of the capital. Houses were looted and burned, and at least 15 peasants were shot or hacked to death with machetes. One FECCAS leader was decapitated. The soldiers hung his head from a tree above the body—a reminder to the others. The government charged that the peasants had provoked the incident, but Archbishop Romero, after conducting an investigation, accused the government of another massacre.

In spite of the repression, or maybe because of it, the bloc rapidly gained members, from an estimated 17,000 in 1978 to at least twice, if not four times, that number a year later. "It is as if violence and terror were less feared today than poverty and passivity," Alan Riding wrote in 1979. After soldiers had killed 14 bloc members, nearly 10,000 of their comrades turned out for the funeral, chanting, "State of siege, ha, ha, ha, state of siege,* ha, ha, ha." As for leaders of the popular organizations, since most were from the poor population and were not members of a Marxist elite or middle class, their arrest or death did not halt the movement because the leaders were quickly replaced.

In May 1979 some 150 BPR demonstrators occupied the Metropolitan Cathedral in San Salvador to demand the release of five of their leaders. After several days steel-helmeted troops began firing on the demonstrators, killing at least 22, some of whose bodies lay on the steps of the cathedral. The army spokesman, Luis Rafael Flores Lima, who was to become the army's chief of staff in 1981, charged that the demonstrators had fired first on a truckload of soldiers. But this time a number of foreign correspondents were in El Salvador—several embassies were being occupied, and that almost always ensured press coverage—and they reported that the soldiers opened fire at demonstrators sitting on the street and sidewalk in front of the cathedral. "They just mowed us down like chickens," said a twenty-three-year-old mechanic who was wounded in the leg. Another survivor, a medi-

*A state of siege suspends all constitutional freedoms, such as speech, assembly, habeas corpus. It is usually declared in effect for thirty days and often extended for an additional thirty days.

cal student, reported that he was beaten and tortured after being arrested by the Treasury Police. "I was hung up by my arms for several
hours and hit. I was then given electric shocks in the testicles. The
police thought that was very funny and kept laughing and telling me
I'd be impotent for life." He escaped death even though pushed off a
cliff and fired upon by soldiers.

To call international attention to the repression, the popular organizations regularly took over embassies. One of the few that weren't
occupied was the United States embassy, presumably not because of
any sympathy for Uncle Sam, but because the protesters knew they
were no match for the marine guards. Though the occupations were
usually peaceful, they added to the tension and caused nearly all embassies eventually to close, undermining the legitimacy of the government—precisely what the left wanted. There were some comical moments. While the Costa Rican embassy was being occupied by the
BPR, the ambassador invited his captors to dine with him by candle-
light. Picking up an empty wine bottle from the table, the gracious
host excused himself to obtain another bottle. He never returned.
When he reached the kitchen, he just kept on walking, out the back
door to safety.

Observing the takeover of the Spanish embassy in February 1980 on
my first trip to El Salvador, I found it hard to take the opposition
seriously, to believe that it presented any realistic threat to the Salvadoran government. The embassy was in a very modest two-story
house in a middle-class residential neighborhood, the street cool and
peaceful under a thick canopy of leafy trees. Across the front of the
stucco house the occupiers had strung their white banner, its hand-
formed block letters informing passersby that they were from the
LP-28 and that they were demanding the release of some of their
leaders. Inside, the scene was like the last days of a raucous fraternity
party. Yellow wrappers from Big Macs, empty cartons stained with
devoured cheese and sausage pizzas, beer cans and soda bottles, jars
of ketchup and mayonnaise littered the floors and overflowed trash
receptacles. In the den the hostages—embassy employees—watched
television and read popular magazines. Upstairs the ambassador, at-
tired in a green golf shirt, talked with reporters from his desk lined
with vials of Valium and other pills for his high blood pressure and
heart condition. He was released unharmed.

While the popular organizations were seizing embassies and government offices, the guerrilla groups, acting independently of each
other, launched more violent campaigns. During one five-month period the FPL killed more than fifty policemen. In 1977 the FPL assas-

sinated the foreign minister, Mauricio Borgonovo, following up with the executions of former President Colonel Osmín Aguirre, two senior military commanders, and Carlos Álfaro Castillo, a wealthy landowner who had been named rector of the National University. There were seemingly daily bombings of stores and factories, almost always after they were closed so that no one would be injured. But the sabotage, or fear of it, forced about fourscore businesses to abandon their investments.

The most popular tactic was kidnapping, with the FARN taking the lead. It burst into the international spotlight in 1978 with the killing of Israel's honorary consul, followed by a wave of kidnappings of Japanese, Dutch, Swedish, British, and other foreign managers of transnational corporations as well as of members of the Salvadoran oligarchy. A Japanese businessman, Fujio Matsumoto, was killed by his captors while trying to escape. But the motivation for these kidnappings was simple: money. And to that extent they were successful, spectacularly so. The Sol Meza family, one of the Fourteen, reportedly paid $4 million for the release of one of its members, the same amount that was paid for the release of another businessman, Victor Keilhauer. The president of the American Chamber of Commerce in El Salvador told a U.S. congressional committee in 1980 that the guerrilla groups had obtained $72 million in ransoms, a tidy war chest for purchasing weapons. The FARN passed some of the fruits of their crimes to the Sandinistas to help them against Somoza.

Whatever assistance the Salvadoran revolution was to receive from abroad in the 1980's, in the 1970's it was an internal affair, not even yet a revolution in the eyes of the State Department.

"Has there been a revolutionary movement in El Salvador?" Representative Benjamin Gilman, Republican of New York, asked during a congressional hearing following the electoral fraud in 1977.

"The short answer to your question is, 'No,'" answered Deputy Assistant Secretary of State for Inter-American Affairs Bray. "There is a group which calls itself the People's Revolutionary Army. We know very little about it."

"Mr. Bray, has there been any evidence of any influence from outside the country by any foreign powers?" Gilman asked.

"None to our knowledge," Bray answered, "but I'm not certain we understand the facts of the matter entirely, clearly."

After the coup in October 1979 the Carter administration quickly resumed military aid to El Salvador, which had been halted in 1977, and the United States soon became an active participant in the Salvadoran conflict. Faced with this, the guerrilla and popular organizations recognized that they must try to put aside their differences, that they must fight together or be defeated separately. Castro, who had been on the sidelines watching and cheering, was to play a role. But achieving unity proved more difficult than recognizing the need for it, and the historical divisions—based on ideological differences as well as on personal power struggles—surfaced periodically. They still exist.

The first unification was of the popular organizations. On January 11, 1980, leaders of the BPR, FAPU, LP-28, and two smaller groups held a press conference to announce the formation of the Revolutionary Coordinator of the Masses (CRM). As El Salvador's blue and white national flag was carried across the stage of the law school auditorium at the National University, a woman shouted, "The flag is not the property of the oligarchy," and the leftists sang the national anthem.

But the guerrilla units, which had yet to put together an effective military force, headed their separate ways—the FPL in Chalatenango, the ERP in Morazán, the FARN on Guazapa—while struggling to bury their ideological and personal differences. After a long holdout the ERP finally agreed to the formation of the Unified Revolutionary Directorate (DRU) in May 1980. But the divisions were too deep, too ingrained. In August the FARN called for a general strike. The others opposed it. It was a failure. The FARN was also advocating alliances with non-Marxist sectors of the populace and with moderate military officers. The others were strongly opposed, and in September 1980 the FARN stomped out of the DRU.

Earlier Fidel Castro had actively entered the picture. The Salvadoran guerrilla leaders, as had their Nicaraguan counterparts a few years earlier, gathered in Havana to discuss the problems confronting them. In a story that may be more apocryphal than true, but that accurately portrays Castro's tactical advice, he placed an M-16 rifle on the table. All the Salvadorans, to symbolize their unity, laid their hands on it. After the meeting the Farabundo Martí National Liberation Front, the FMLN, was born, encompassing the FPL, ERP, FARN, and much smaller PRTC and PCS. But the squabbling continued to plague the revolution's military effort. As 1980 was drawing to an end, the ERP and FARN were pushing for an insurrection to topple the government before Reagan took the oath of office. Carpio, the advocate of the prolonged popular war, told them the conditions weren't ripe, that they weren't prepared. Reluctantly, in the interest of unity, his FPL finally went along. But the old man of the revolution had been right. The people did not answer the call for insurrection. The guerrillas' "final offensive" in January 1981 failed. The guerrilla leaders and their backers later tried to downplay the January failure by saying it had been intended not as a "final" offensive but as a "general" offensive. That's simply not true.

Crippling differences continued. Prior to the "final offensive," the ERP refused to share arms coming from Cuba with the other guerrilla forces. In August 1981 the ERP forces seized Perquín, a moderate-size village at the end of the paved road in Morazán. It was the most significant military accomplishment by any of the guerrilla forces as of that date. It was to have been coordinated with FPL actions in Chalatenango, but the FPL units did nothing, allowing the army to send its elite units to Perquín, thus forcing the guerrillas to withdraw. There were also serious disagreements over how to respond to the elections in March 1982. The ERP advocated military actions to disrupt them. But Carpio dismissed the election as just another small and insignificant event in a long war, and he gave his troops a rest. A few weeks prior to the elections Carpio went to the Middle East to visit with Yasir Arafat, a trip that angered Nicaraguan and Salvadoran guerrilla leaders. Several months later the FPL launched an offensive in Chalatenango without telling the others.

The revolutionary leaders have tried their best not to air their differences in public but to present a unified face. Still, one internal squabble was so monumental and potentially cataclysmic—for U.S. policymakers as well as the guerrillas—that it burst onto the front pages around the world.

On April 12, 1983, in Managua, Nicaragua, Salvador Cayetano Carpio died. It was more than a week before the news seeped out. When it did, the FPL and the Nicaraguan government said that he had committed suicide. Few believed it. Hardened revolutionaries don't commit suicide. As reporters probed, they found that Carpio's death was linked to a bitter schism within the FPL—over the issues of a unified command and negotiations. He opposed both. Leading the desire for a more flexible approach was Melida Anaya Montes, known by her *nom de guerre* as Comandante Ana María.

It was in a one-level house in a middle-class neighborhood that I interviewed Ana María, in January 1980. She was flanked by two bodyguards, standing erect with automatic rifles. Their khaki shirts and blue jeans were immaculate, starched and pressed. They looked like college students—from the days before the sloppy look was "in." Ana María, a robust woman whose long black hair was pulled back tightly and whose face was partially covered with a bandanna sternly folded into a triangle, was old enough to be their mother. She had a doctorate in education, had taught high school, had been a professor at the university, and was a founder of the ANDES, the militant teachers' union, in 1964. Four years later she met Carpio and eventually rose to become second-in-command in his FPL, loyally adhering to his belief in the prolonged popular war. But after returning from a trip to Vietnam in 1981, she began to suggest a more flexible approach, one that might lead to a peaceful, negotiated settlement, and to stress the desirability of a unified command. By 1983 she had significant support within the FPL. But Carpio still had his loyalists, and on April 6, 1983, one of them, described as "like a son" to him, led a raid on the house in Managua where Ana María was staying after returning from Cuba. Ana María, fifty-four years old, was stabbed to death with knives and ice picks. Eight months after the events the FPL issued a communiqué saying that Carpio had ordered the murder of Ana María after becoming "blinded by his political ambitions and fanatic sense of self-importance."

At her funeral, Carpio delivered the eulogy. He had just returned from Libya, where he had sought weapons from Colonel Muammar al-Qaddafi. Reporters noted that he looked tired and ill, that he spoke haltingly, that in spite of the stifling heat, he wore a sweater and jacket. That was on April 9, the last day he was seen in public. The FPL said that he shot himself. The prevailing theory is that he was distraught that one of his most trusted followers had murdered his top lieutenant and longtime close personal friend; and because Castro and the Sandinista leaders were pressuring him to resign as leader of the FPL. But there are doubters and probably always will be. Did he take his life voluntarily? Or was he given a choice—and did he decide that suicide was more honorable than execution?

As they wrestled with internal dissension, the FPL during a few short weeks following the death of Ana María and Carpio carried out a number of operations that suggested the hard-liners were still in control. Foremost among these was the assassination of an American military adviser, Lieutenant Commander Albert Schaufelberger III, a thirty-three-year-old graduate of the Naval Academy who had once been an instructor in the SEALs, the naval counterpart of the Green Berets. In El Salvador one of Schaufelberger's assignments was counseling the American advisers on personal security measures. But he ignored for himself what he sought to impress on his comrades. When the air conditioning on his car malfunctioned, he removed the bullet-proof glass so that he could lower the windows. One evening, as Schaufelberger sat in his car waiting for his girlfriend at the modern tree-shaded campus of the Catholic university, an FPL gunman stuck a .22 Magnum through the open window and shot Schaufelberger in the head.

A few weeks later the FPL directed its violence on Salvadoran soldiers, executing some who had been captured in battle. Unlike massacres by Salvadoran government troops, which U.S. officials repeatedly sought to cover up, in this case it was the American military advisers in El Salvador who developed the evidence. The U.S. embassy in El Salvador and the State Department in Washington publicized it. In the embassy auditorium reporters were shown glossy eight-by-ten color photographs of corpses. The pictures had been taken by advisers. Colonel Waghelstein, the commander of the U.S. military group, offered them as evidence of what he said had been an "execution" of Salvadoran soldiers by FPL guerrillas near a bridge on the Pan American Highway known as Quebrada Seca. The guerrilla commander Joaquín Villalobos said over the main radio station of the revolution, Radio Venceremos, that the soldiers had died during an eight-hour battle. Some reporters angered Colonel Waghelstein and other embassy officials by raising doubts about the U.S. claims. While Waghelstein claimed that forty-two soldiers had been killed, Lydia Chavez of *The New York Times* reported only fifteen bodies in the photographs, many with chest wounds, suggesting they had been killed during battle. (But the United States won an important propaganda victory. Subsequently many journalists reported as a fact that forty-two soldiers had been executed at Quebrada Seca.) Acknowledging that the guerrilla policy had been to treat prisoners well, Colonel Waghelstein raised the possibility that the Quebrada Seca incident, which he said had been carried out by the FPL, might reflect a major break within the guerrilla factions.

But in the aftermath of Carpio's death the guerrillas achieved greater unity, with Villalobos emerging as the dominant guerrilla leader.* The former economics student and executioner of Roque Dalton was widely regarded in 1984 as the best military commander on either side of the war. One of his acts was to order the FPL to stop shooting prisoners, an order that was obeyed—with one result, as he

---

*In November 1983 a new guerrilla organization calling itself the Salvador Cayetano Carpio Revolutionary Workers Movement emerged. It pledged to follow Carpio's radical line, and other guerrilla leaders were disturbed by its existence. One of its units, the Clara Elizabeth Ramírez Metropolitan Comando, assassinated two members of the National Assembly in January and March 1984.

had hoped, being the willingness of more Salvadoran soldiers to surrender.

ON the political, as opposed to the military, side of the revolution is the Democratic Revolutionary Front (FDR), which was set up in April 1980. Loosely gathered under the FDR umbrella were hard-line Marxists, liberal priests, and dissident Christian Democrats, along with a mélange of professional and workers' organizations.

The FDR's first president was Enrique Álvarez Córdova. His life and death mirror the history of El Salvador, the forces that have polarized and radicalized, the causes that have forced democrats to unite with the armed revolution.

"He was the first wealthy man to die for his country," says Monsignor Ricardo Urioste, who had been Álvarez's parish priest for nearly twenty years. Born into the Fourteen, Álvarez was sent off to the Hackley Preparatory School in Tarrytown, New York, then studied economics at Rutgers University. He was El Salvador's "all-American boy." A boyhood friend's scrapbook contains a photograph—black and white, turning yellow—of Álvarez, a star on the Salvadoran national basketball team, in the old-fashioned two-handed set-shot position. Kiki, as everyone called him, was also a ranked tennis player and one of the most polished horse polo players in the country's history. "If you had watched him water-ski, you'd have thought you were at Cypress Gardens," a friend recalled. He dated a Miss Universe finalist and was a dazzling dancer.

Starting with his family's wealth—primarily from coffee—he applied his own considerable talents and energy to develop two cattle ranches, El Jobo and El Polvo, which were worth more than $2 million in 1980. Towering trophies and framed photographs with his prize-winning bulls fill the rough-paneled office at El Jobo. Featured in international agricultural journals, El Jobo was, in the mid-1970's, one of the two or three most productive dairy farms in the world, measured in volume of milk per acre of grazing land.

But Álvarez was one of the few of the country's wealthy people who saw the need for changes. He tried working within the system and became deputy minister of agriculture in 1968 and head of the agency a year later. Frequently getting no more than a couple of hours of sleep a night—"We don't have much time," he told friends—he set about to alter El Salvador's semifeudal land system. He began by proposing a limitation on the size of farms that received water from the government's irrigation system. And he encouraged his staff to draft a plan to limit the size of individual farms to 500 acres. Less than 2 percent of the nation's farmland would have been affected, but he was attacked by his millionaire friends, who used their influence and money to persuade the military government not to adopt the law. Frustrated, Álvarez returned to El Jobo. Two days after Christmas 1976 he called all his workers outside after lunch.

"I've been thinking for a long time about this," he began quietly, according to a later conversation I had with his friends. "I want my life to have some meaning. I'm not married. You are my family, my responsibility. I want to build a new type of organization in El Salvador, and I want you to be part of it." El Jobo became a cooperative, owned by the seventy-three permanent workers. Álvarez helped them buy their interests with loans.

After the coup in October 1979 Álvarez again became minister of agriculture, believing that the time had finally come for his agrarian reform plans. Ten weeks later he and all the civilians in the Cabinet resigned because of their inability to halt the repression by the army. He became president of the FDR in April 1980. His friends were shocked.

"We have exhausted all peaceful means," he explained to a *Newsweek* interviewer. "Many of us who are in the Front have tried to win the structural changes that our country so badly needs by working with past governments. Many of us even cooperated with the current junta. . . . We thought it was the last possibility for peaceful change. It did not work. We came to the conclusion that a change at the very center of power was necessary." He said the FDR-FMLN envisioned a government that was "anti-oligarchy," with a mixed economy, "one in which we can protect and develop small and medium-size enterprises. Finally, it will be a pluralistic government."

In November 1980 Álvarez and other FDR leaders were dragged from a Catholic high school, tortured, and executed.

Álvarez's successor was another man dedicated to bringing about change through the democratic process, Guillermo Manuel Ungo, the man who had been Duarte's running mate in the elections that the army stole in 1972. From an upper-middle class family, Ungo had been sent by his father to the Carnegie Institute of Technology in Pittsburgh with the understanding that he would take over the family's printing business. But he left after two years, returning to El Salvador to study law at the National University. It was there that he became involved in politics, as a member of a student movement known as Catholic Action. Along with other Social Democratic intellectuals and professionals, he founded a political party, the National Revolutionary

Movement (MNR), in the 1960's. He was exiled along with Duarte after the 1972 elections, though Ungo returned a few years before Duarte did.

"For a decade I stubbornly participated in elections in a country where democracy was considered subversive," he said when it was suggested that the FDR's alliance with the FMLN raised doubts about his commitment to democracy. "I doubt if many American democrats would have the endurance to do so when elections meant jail, persecution, fear, and fraud, when everyone said you were a fool to participate."

Like Enrique Álvarez, Ungo thought the October 1979 coup provided another opening for a democratic, civilian government. He was one of the three civilian members of the five-man junta. But he, too, resigned after the civilians' unsuccessful showdown with the armed forces' high command.

I can't understand why people like you who have democratic ideas can be in an alliance with guerrillas and Marxists," Everett Briggs, a deputy assistant secretary of state, said in greeting Rubén Ignacio Zamora, the FDR's man in charge of foreign relations during a meeting at the State Department in December 1981.*

Very briefly Zamora tried to explain to Briggs why the democratic process had not worked in El Salvador. He might have responded by sketching his own life's history. One of ten children in a devout Catholic family—"My parents were always telling us, 'Don't steal, don't tell lies, be kind to people' "—Zamora spent eight years in a seminary before the priests decided that he wasn't meant to be one of their number. "I was reading Camus, existentialists. They thought I was a

*The meeting, arranged by an American scholar well known and respected within the State Department and trusted by the Salvadoran left, was to have been private. Neither side was even to mention the fact of the meeting, let alone its substance. But Assistant Secretary of State Enders discussed it during congressional testimony the day after. Not only did he breach the confidentiality of the meeting, but he misrepresented it. Enders said that the State Department was talking with a representative of one of El Salvador's political factions to discuss its possible participation in the upcoming elections, a statement designed to show that there was support for the U.S. push for elections in El Salvador. But Zamora had made it clear prior to the meeting that he was representing the FDR, not his political party, and that the subject was the broader one of a negotiated settlement, not elections, which the FDR-FMLN consistently maintained it could not participate in because of fear that its members would be assassinated, as had Álvarez and so many others.

rebel." So he went to law school, where he was vice-president of the student association and active in the Social Christian Student Movement, the Christian Democratic party's source of energetic volunteers. Zamora was among the demonstrators at Plaza Libertad protesting the electoral fraud in 1977. A few days later, as he and his wife were walking home from the Catholic university, where he was a professor, they were picked up by the National Police. His wife was a Nicaraguan, and when the press there "raised hell," Zamora recalled, she was released a few days later. But he was held for six days, kept naked in a small, secret, windowless cell crawling with cockroaches and rats. He was injected with drugs and interrogated. Zamora, a big full-bearded man, laughed when he remembered that while he was being held, the conservative head of the university fired him for not appearing for his classes. While in prison, he slipped a note on a small piece of paper to his parents, telling them he was well and that they should be proud of him because he was practicing the Catholic values they had instilled in him. "Especially for my mother, that helped her a lot," he remembered. The government released him on the condition that he leave the country, and he did. With a grant from the Ford Foundation, he returned to Britain, where he had previously received a master's degree from Essex University. He remained in exile until after the coup in October 1979, when he was named minister of the presidency, a job akin to chief of staff.

However, believing that Duarte and the Christian Democrats had made too many compromises with the armed forces in order to remain in power and that they were unable to control the violence by the army, Zamora, and several others, resigned from the party in early 1980. Zamora had planned to remain in the country, working to build the Popular Social Christian Movement. In an interview three years later he remembered too well why he had to leave. It was because of what happened one evening a few days after Roberto d'Aubuisson, the archconservative political leader who is widely believed to have his own death squads, had publicly accused him and his brother, Mario, who was the country's attorney general, of being guerrillas. Rubén told the story flatly, without visible anger, taking off his glasses, rubbing his eyes, pressing his fingers together, lighting another long Rothschild.

Rubén and his brother lived next door to each other. One night about eleven, as Rubén arrived home after a long day of political meetings, Mario's wife called out, "We're having a party. Why don't you come?" Though tired, Rubén decided to join his friends, including José Antonio Morales Ehrlich, who had very recently become a member of the junta, and other leaders of the Christian Democratic party. After a couple of drinks Rubén excused himself. "If I continue to drink, I am going to get drunk. Better I go and sleep." They teased him.

The next thing Rubén remembered was being awakened by the screams of Mario's wife. "Where is my husband? Give me my husband!"

"Oh, my God, those people got drunk, and something is happening there," he recalled thinking at that moment. He jumped out of bed and headed next door.

"Stop! You don't know what is going on," his wife shouted. "Stop there!"

Rubén went to the telephone and dialed his brother's number. The line was dead.

The masked men had entered Mario's house by crawling across the roof and lowering themselves down to a center patio. They had forced everyone to lie facedown on the floor. Then they began demanding, "Which of you is Mario? Where's Mario?"

"I went to the house and found him lying in the bathroom," Rubén recalled, his eyes staring into nowhere as if he were recalling the body of his brother lying where he had been shot. For Rubén, then thirty-seven years old, it was the beginning of his third period in exile. This time he took his wife and three children, a fourth to come later, to Nicaragua.

Zamora traveled frequently to the United States, explaining the FDR-FMLN's position to church groups, universities, and editorial boards. He was effective, offering a view of the Salvadoran opposition that didn't accord with what Washington was saying. The Reagan administration denied him a visa in 1983.

Serving with Zamora and Ungo on the FDR's seven-person political-diplomatic commission, as they call it, are other prominent Salvadorans who tested the democratic system and found it nonexistent. Salvador Samayoa, once a professor of philosophy at the Catholic university, was barely twenty-nine years old when he joined the post-October 1979 coup government as minister of education. When he resigned, he went into the mountains with the FPL. Fabio Castillo, a medical doctor and onetime rector of the National University, was in the 1960's a member of a junta that held power for a few months—before being ousted by another coup. He was later president of the federal elections commission and a presidential candidate himself. He was in exile during most of the 1970's, returned briefly after the coup in October 1979, and is now in exile again.

The lone woman among the top leadership of the FDR is Ana Guadalupe Martínez, who, born in 1952, is also the youngest. When she was twenty-four years old, she was seized by the National Guard because of her guerrilla activities with the ERP. She says she was shackled hand and foot, blindfolded, and tossed naked on the floor, while electric shocks were administered through five electrodes, attached to both sides of her hips, her left hand, her vulva, and the lumbar region of her spinal column. "Here we have made men talk, not to speak of women," her torturers taunted. She was brutally raped by a sergeant. She was once a medical student at the university, and her "official" picture (the one distributed by the FDR) is of a demure woman with permanent-waved brown hair and a silk blouse closed at the neck with a knotted scarf tie. In real life she is a guerrilla commander in the ERP. Ana Guadalupe Martínez was expecting a child, her first, in April 1984.

The position of the Carter and Reagan administrations has been that the Ungos, the Zamoras, indeed the entire FDR are irrelevant to the revolution and that if the left came to power in El Salvador, these political types would be the first to go. They would be discarded by the guerrilla leaders, and the hard-liners would take over. Such charges are similar to what defense lawyers say about paternity—easy to charge; difficult, if not impossible, to defend against.

Ungo has recognized that the alliance of the FDR and FMLN is a "marriage of convenience" and that he doesn't control the guerrilla factions. "But they don't control me," he added. "I need them, and they need me."

"That's the question that's always asked," Zamora answered when asked what guarantees there were that either he or any of the other leaders of the FDR would have any power in a revolutionary government. "It's a very effective one. You say, 'Look, how can you give me assurance that if your side wins, you are not going to fall into the hands of the Soviet Union, you are not going to become a puppet of the Soviet Union? How can you assure me that you democratic people are going to be in control of the situation and not the radical Marxist people who now have the guns and are going to have the guns after the victory?'

"I think it's not easy to answer that," Zamora continued, "because the problem is that you are asking for an answer for the future, to prove that something is not going to happen in the future. I cannot give you proof about the future. The only thing I can tell you is: Look, at least give us the opportunity—and the fact is that right now there is no opportunity at all—to try to work out a pluralistic society. There is no opportunity now because the whole thing is being defined in terms of shooting and guns, and you cannot talk about pluralism, democratic exercise, and so on in the middle of a war. That is crazy. That is why we support a political settlement."

As any student of revolutions knows, one thing is certain: The longer the war continues, the less power the politicians will have in the end. The longer the guerrilla commanders remain in the hills, living under wretched conditions, constantly being bombed, the less charitable they will be about sharing power with civilians who have been jaunting around Europe, living comfortably, eating well. If in the end the guerrillas achieve a military defeat of the Salvadoran government, they won't need—though they might nevertheless accept—the civilians. If that is the outcome, the Reagan administration will have to share considerable responsibility because of its intransigent refusal to negotiate.

Ungo and Zamora, as well as others within the FDR, have been successful in convincing the guerrilla leaders, except for a few remaining hard-liners within the FPL, to accept a negotiated settlement. Should the FDR-FMLN come to power, some idea of what its government might look like can be found in one of its manifestos. It contains the predictable bombasts about "Yankee imperialism" and the "criminal political-military machine" that has ruled in El Salvador since 1932. But it is also specific in the political and economic programs, which would clearly be the foundation of a socialist government. It calls for the abolition of the secret police, ORDEN, the National Guard, and Treasury Police. (Even the Reagan administration has recognized the need to get rid of these forces, according to a Confidential cable that was leaked in 1982.) It commits El Salvador to become a member of the movement of nonaligned countries. On the economic front the government would nationalize the entire financial system, all foreign trade, and electrical production and distribution, and would establish a "system for effective planning of the national economy." The government would "create sufficient sources of jobs so as to eliminate unemployment in the briefest possible period of time," regulate wages in accordance with the cost of living, and reduce and control prices of basic goods and services. There are also plans for increases in social services for the "popular masses" and a literacy campaign.

While it seems likely that these promises would be enacted, there remain unanswered questions as to whether there would be restrictions on press and on political and religious freedom, as in Castro's Cuba. And in Nicaragua the Sandinistas have not delivered on the democratic rhetoric that preceded their seizing of power.

THE PEASANTS REVOLT

As the warm summer sun set into the hills, a short rectangular box was lowered into the earth on the edge of a field under a single sprawling tree. The recently sawed and hammered wood had been covered with a white cloth emblazoned in blue block letters: *FMLN*. Inside was the body of Luis Hernández Ramos, twelve years old.

He had been shot during a battle, running a message handwritten on a lined piece of paper from a child's school notebook. The communiqué was from one guerrilla commander to another. Luis was a *correo*—messenger—an honored responsibility for boys too young to serve as combatants in the revolutionary army. At the hero's farewell the assembled peasants—women in simple cotton dresses, children, strapping teenagers—heard Luis's name added to the roll call of martyrs.

"Compañero Luis," began a Roman Catholic priest, using the appellation, often shortened to compa, that Latin American revolutionaries use when addressing each other. "Remember, a seed has to be buried so that a tree grows."

Off to one side were four columns of Luis's schoolmates, most of them barefoot, in ragged, patched pants and soiled shirts. The smaller boys in the first row were barely visible over the top of the red banner with a white star and the black letters *FMLN* that they proudly stretched in front of them. Older boys held aloft El Salvador's blue and white national flag. On another large piece of cloth was hand-lettered: "The tomb was the Christmas gift that the genocidal junta and Reagan gave to the children of Morazán. Compañero Luis, your example will not be wasted and therefore you will always be present. FMLN."

From the ranks of the schoolchildren, a boy stepped forward and read a poem in honor of his friend:

Perhaps the people think that Reagan sent toys
to the children of northern Morazán.
But the bullets, the bombs, the mortars fell on
houses of our compañeros.
I don't understand how they can talk of progress

and social changes when the children of El Salvador
are starving.
And the enemy kills them like animals.

The dedication was composed by a fifteen-year-old who had attended only two years of school. Now learning to read and write in the rebels' school, he labored to print his name in my reporter's notebook: Yovanis Hernández. He hadn't seen his mother, brothers, and sisters in more than a year; he thought they were in a refugee camp in Honduras. His father worked in one of the production brigades, which are responsible for planting and gathering the harvests and for making clothes and other materials for the revolution.

"What do you want to be when you grow up?" I asked.

"I want to become a person who teaches the people," he said. "There are so many people who do not know how to read or write. We have to help them."

For two weeks in January 1982 I hiked with—always uphill, it seemed—talked with, and eventually accompanied into battle the peasants who were part of the revolutionary forces in the province of Morazán, situated in the eastern end of El Salvador, with a northern border on Honduras. At the time it was the zone where the revolution was the strongest militarily.

An opportunity to "go behind the lines," to meet those who were fighting to overthrow the U.S.-backed government was something nearly every foreign correspondent covering Central America longed for. We knew that the view from the modern capital, where early in the morning men and women in expensive outfits jogged through posh neighborhoods, was giving us a narrow and skewed perspective. We had frequent interviews with Salvadoran leaders. They branded the opposition subversives and Communists. The only thing that the Salvadoran leftists wanted, we were told at embassy briefings and in private conversations, was power. The Reagan administration, quickly after coming into office, had issued a white paper charging that the Salvadoran guerrillas were well armed by Cuba, Nicaragua, and other Communist-bloc countries. I believed much of what I heard, certainly that there were Cubans and Nicaraguans fighting with the guerrillas. How else could they be so successful against a much larger and better-equipped army?

I had been covering El Salvador off and on for nearly two years and was still searching for answers to questions about these people who were fighting against the government. Why had they taken up arms? What did they want?

I had been with the guerrillas once previously. On January 9, 1981, I was conducted from one clandestine rendezvous to the next until I found myself climbing the forested slopes of the 4,629-foot-high Guazapa Volcano, about fifteen miles north of the capital. I didn't really learn much during that excursion—except that the Salvadorans participating in the revolution didn't fit any stereotype. A cherubic lad, scrubbed so clean that he would have made any mother proud, and a middle-aged housewife, whom I could picture at home watching the afternoon soap operas, served as intermediaries until we were out of the city and riding in the back of a new pickup filled with green melons. When the Salvadorans, who looked like college students on the way to a frolic in the woods, began tossing the melons over the side, I struggled to keep them from splattering as they reached the ground. I couldn't understand why the others weren't concerned—until the truck was empty of melons. Hidden under them had been a few rifles, ammunition, a mortar tube, and some homemade green military jackets. At the front of the file moving up the narrow trail was a slightly overweight woman in her early twenties wearing a maroon sweat shirt with a rainbow sewn on the front, carrying a grenade launcher still covered with a protective grease coating. Another woman, clad in an olive green military jacket with hand grenades in the front pockets, led a horse bearing burlap bags of corn from which protruded a mortar tripod. At a distance that would save them from the sudden sweep of a machine-gun ambush came an accountant, a bank clerk, a printer, and a college student, swapping among them the heavy crates of grenades and ammunition. Stopping occasionally to chat quietly with peasants, who offered them oranges and "Godspeed," they hiked —up sharp inclines, through tunnels of trees, past clusters of mud huts. At the guerrillas' base camp an architectural student and his wife carefully traced on thin paper overlaid on a government map, their work to be used by the guerrilla commanders.

But that trip was cut short, after a restless night I spent shivering in the mountain cold and feeling anxious about what was to follow. The next day the guerrillas launched attacks throughout the country. Some of the leaders had boasted publicly that this would be their "final offensive," that they would topple the government before Reagan was inaugurated on January 20. If they were to make good on those boasts, I did not want to miss that story while sitting on a mountaintop. I persuaded my journalistic colleagues, including Ian Mates, a twenty-six-year-old cameraman for the London-based UPITN, to descend from the mountain so that I could get to a telex. A few days later we decided to return to the Guazapa region to observe how the guerrilla group we had been with was faring in its plans to take Suchitoto. As my colleagues were getting into their car in the driveway in front of the Camino Real hotel, I opted not to accompany them, for reasons that I do not recall. Driving down a dirt road, their car was struck by a remote-detonated land mine. A tiny piece of shrapnel pierced Ian's skull. He died a few days later.

It would be nearly a full year before I would have another opportunity to seek answers to my questions. With me was Susan Meiselas, a photographer who was awarded the prestigious Robert Capa Prize for her photojournalistic coverage of the Nicaraguan revolution.

There was a full moon as we quietly slipped into guerrilla territory.* We removed our trousers, then held our shoes above our heads while crossing a wide river. Under other circumstances it might have been romantic, a backpack trip in the California Sierras. But now I was scared. I flashed back to many years earlier, to when I had been in Vietnam and how patrols were ambushed at night. Our Salvadoran escorts were so poorly armed—with pistols and rifles that looked to me like antiques—that I knew they would be no match for an army patrol. With every noise I stiffened. At one point the guides motioned us to scurry over a wall and hide in a cornfield. (Not until months later did I learn that the Salvadoran Army commanders did not much care for night patrols.) We walked all night, stopping once for some hot beans, served by a man who seemed to have appeared out of nowhere.

In the area where we traveled with the revolution, the northern

---

*It has been frequently charged that the guerrillas arranged the trip to Morazán to coincide with the date that President Reagan would have to make a presentation to Congress in order to continue military aid to El Salvador. But the timing of my trip, which I have noted I had wanted to make for nearly a year, was the result of the fortuitous convergence of independent circumstances. After I had been hired by *The New York Times* in February 1981— prior to then I was working as a "stringer" for *The Times* and other magazines and radio stations, including *Newsweek, The Wall Street Journal,* CBS, and the Canadian Broadcasting Corporation—I was assigned to the Metropolitan Desk. It was not until November 1981 that the editors at *The Times* allowed me to remain in Central America long enough to undertake a lengthy trip into the mountains. The trip was originally scheduled for early December. It was canceled because the government launched what was until that time its largest search and destroy operation, in the very area of Morazán that I was to visit. When that operation ended and I was advised that it would be secure to make the trip, I was in New York for Christmas. From that point on the scheduling was done largely at my initiative, which had no relationship to any political activities in Washington.

third of Morazán, there is only one paved road—the black road, the peasants call it—connecting Perquín with the provincial capital of San Francisco Gotera. Northern Morazán is like much of rural El Salvador: low mountainous hills with patches of deciduous and pine forests; meadows; natural springs; rushing streams. There are a few small typical Salvadoran villages; the animals; the boys kicking soccer balls; the whitewashed, badly-in-need-of-attention Catholic church; the shops and mud-walled houses; the men whiling away time under eaves slanting down over walkway verandas.

But most of the Salvadoran peasants have not yet migrated to these villages. More often they live in isolated hovels at the edge of the family's tiny plot; or there will be two rows of maybe ten to twenty huts, on either side of a path rutted by yoked oxen drawing carts that ride on solid wooden wheels. Walls are either sticks and twigs jammed with mud between poles or adobe brick. The "modern" houses have thin layers of plaster over the mud.

From conversations with scores of peasants—grizzled old men who in the sweltering heat of day and dark of night lugged supplies over treacherous mountain paths, preadolescent boys who rushed scribbled messages between field commanders; guerrilla fighters whose clothes were soiled and tattered and whose weapons had usually once belonged to government soldiers; teenaged girls and middle-aged women who were perpetually slapping cornmeal between their palms to make tortillas—emerged a rough profile of the peasant revolutionary in Morazán: born and reared in the department and quite likely never traveled beyond it; only two years of formal education; at least one parent, child, or sibling murdered by the government soldiers, frequently after having been hacked with a machete; living family members part of the revolution.

It is, in short, a homegrown, predominantly peasant revolution. This is in marked contrast with the primarily urban-based armed uprisings in the 1960's, in Brazil, Argentina, Venezuela, and Uruguay. Nor were the peasants as organized or as involved in Nicaragua, where it was principally insurrections in the cities that contributed to the fall of General Somoza in July 1979.

"Because the United States has supported military governments and coups, you can't conceive that a popular revolution can exist without the international support of Moscow, or Cuba, or Nicaragua," began Eduardo, a thirty-year-old Mexican-born and -educated doctor working in Morazán. He was wearing blue jeans, light brown woodsman's boots, and a soft wide-brimmed hat that covered his thick hair. We were sitting in the cool and quiet of a cluster of banana trees outside the local hospital. Nearby the face of a woman sitting beside a natural spring showed the pain of the blisters on her legs, burned when a kettle in which she was boiling beans had toppled. A man who appeared to be in his forties picked shrapnel from his right calf. His crude crutch was propped against a rock.

"Because the revolution doesn't come from Washington, you think it must come from Moscow," Eduardo continued, the sharpness in his voice reflecting exasperation with my pestering questions about the help that the peasants were receiving from Cubans and Nicaraguans. "Well, listen, it's simply propaganda that we're satellites of Nicaragua or Cuba, that we're in the service of Cuba or Nicaragua. . . . The principal characteristics of this revolution are that it is popularly based, that it is nationalistic. . . . It's no secret that the leadership of the FMLN are Marxists. But the people are Christians."

This matches what Clifford Krauss, correspondent for the *Atlanta Constitution,* found in Chalatenango, a western province, where he spent three weeks behind rebel lines in January 1982. "I met few people who had not lost at least one relative at the hands of the army, national guard or the paramilitary Orden force," Krauss wrote. There was "petite 15-year-old" Irena, who had "struggled across the Sumpul River as Army troops cut down her parents and five sisters in a frenzy of gunfire and mortar shelling aimed at hundreds of refugees escaping Chalatenango province for Honduras." Irena told Krauss, "When I saw my entire family dead in the river, I decided I had to fight the enemy with a rifle in my hand." When Krauss talked with her, she was carrying an M-2 automatic carbine.

The Reverend Earl Gallagher, a Brooklyn-born Capuchin priest who was working in Honduras at the time of the massacre at the Sumpul River, said, "There were so many vultures picking at the bodies that it looked like a black carpet." According to an account of the massacre by the presbytery of the Copán Diocese, fleeing peasants were fired upon by helicopters, the Salvadoran National Guard, and ORDEN. "Women tortured before the finishing shot, infants thrown into the air for target practice, were some of the scenes of the criminal slaughter," the church reported. "The Salvadorans who crossed the river were returned by the Honduran soldiers to the area of the massacre. In mid-afternoon the genocide ended, leaving a minimum number of 600 corpses. . . . A Honduran fisherman found five small bodies of children in his fishtrap."

In northern Morazán, three weeks before I entered, soldiers from the Atlacatl Battalion, the elite fighting unit that was the first to be trained by the military advisers sent by President Reagan, had murdered nearly 1,000 peasants, primarily women, children, and old people, during a search and destroy operation supported by helicopter gunships and heavy artillery. "It was a great massacre," said a survivor, thirty-eight-year-old Rufina Amaya, whose four children and blind husband had been killed. "They left nothing."

The carnage was everywhere. I saw skulls, rib cages, femurs, tibias protruding from the rubble of cracked roofing tiles, charred beams, children's toys, crushed sewing machines, and kitchen utensils. Fourteen bodies lay in a heap at the edge of a cornfield, under the swooping green leaves of banana trees.

Some peasants had composed a song about the massacre: "It was in the month of December 1981. Conducted by the Yankees' Atlacatl Battalion. What a bitter Christmas for the children of my village; they don't get to play with toys, only the bullets and mortars. . . . They killed women, hundreds of children and old people. Today they talk of elections, in order to cleanse their hands."

"I want my wife and children to go to Honduras, but I am going to stay and fight," quietly explained Gumersindo Lucas, a thirty-nine-year-old peasant from La Joya, where the soldiers had killed his sixty-two-year-old mother as she lay ill in bed.

The massacre had also converted fifteen-year-old Julio. The soldiers had killed his mother, father, nine-year-old brother, and two sisters, ages seven and five. "I cry much because I lost my family," he said softly. Some days he performs chores, hauling water in plastic gourds from the canyon below or sweeping the dirt in front of the adobe. But often he just sits, his sad eyes gazing into the valley. He cannot read or write but hopes to attend the rebels' school. He is at ease sitting in the crude wooden saddle mounted on a powerful horse. But he fumbles clumsily with a rifle, which he has now decided he must learn to use.

Some 4,000 peasants in Morazán had escaped death, slipping through the government's pincers operation in long columns. "We found ourselves surrounded, the enemy was closing in on us," explained Nolvo, who looked at least a decade older than his twenty-nine years. Drawing in the dirt with a stick, he described the movements of the column of 1,100 peasants he had led. They had walked for eight days, usually at night. During the daylight hours they lay motionless as the helicopters buzzed overhead and the soldiers came so close their conversations could be heard. Most of those in the column were old men and women, many in their sixties—an old age in Latin America, where the average life expectancy is many years less—and children so small they had to be carried. They survived on water, sugarcane cut from the fields, and pieces of rationed corn tortillas. During the march one woman gave birth. In another fleeing column, led by Joe David Sanderson, an American adventurer, two women delivered children. One named her son Farabundo Martí; the other, her daughter, Victoria.

"No modern technology, no American adviser can admit that a woman will walk for days, give birth, then walk for ten more days," said one revolutionary leader. "That's our strongest weapon: the peasants. That's why we'll win. No planes, no bombs, no weapons can defeat that."

THE ceremony for Luis was the first community affair following the return of the fleeing peasants. After the final shovelfuls of light-colored dirt had covered Luis's casket, the senior guerrilla commander, Jorge Antonio Meléndez, *nom de guerre* Jonas, spoke. His voice rasped hoarsely when he concluded by reminding the children, "Now, if any of you don't understand, ask questions." He had been explaining the history of the revolution, how the peasants had been exploited economically and repressed. Then the festivities began. It was like a midwestern church social. Families and friends sat chatting in small circles on the ground. Tiny children crawled in the prickly weeds. Young boys kicked a ball. Adolescent girls giggled. Teenagers danced—a mixture of jig, square dance, and rock 'n' roll. Music, if it could be called that, was provided by the Torogozes Cultural Brigade, named for a colorful bird. There were two battered guitars, a violin, and a bulky bass fiddle, the strings of which were just that—strings: three strands of twine, frayed to varying degrees. Rhythm was kept by a man who tapped on an animal skin stretched across the opening of what looked like a barrel, painted yellow and supported by three narrow pieces of wood that had been nailed to the bulging midsection.

The director of the seven-member cultural group was Andreas Barreda. His pregnant wife and five small children had been killed by soldiers when they swept through Guaycamaya several months earlier. "They burned houses, everything," Barreda told me in a controlled tone. But he had found an outlet for his emotions, in the songs he had composed and scrawled onto the wide lines of a notebook that schoolchildren use throughout rural El Salvador. Many of the words are misspelled; Barreda had been only to the second grade. Among the twenty-three songs were "Burned Houses," "We Are Revolutionaries," "Ambition of Reagan" ("He wants to be ruler of the entire world; but it's not to be here"), and "Taking of Perquín," a tribute to the guerrillas' seizure of that village in August 1981, their major military accomplishment to that date.

Entering the crumbling adobe, which was serving as the cultural group's headquarters, I heard a tape recorder playing a song written and recorded to the memory of Archbishop Romero.

"I bet you never expected to see me here," reflected the grinning expression on Gaspar's face. For two days Gaspar, a short, jolly twenty-one-year-old, had led us across rivers and up and down mountain trails, burdened with, but not slowed by, supplies he carried in a knapsack that had only one strap. Now he was practicing on his battered guitar.

When he was thirteen, Gaspar picked coffee beans and cut sugarcane for a man who paid him $55 every two weeks during the short harvest seasons, a sum that made him wealthy by the standards of a Salvadoran peasant. Eventually his family saved enough money to buy a small plot. Encouraged by some priests, several peasant families began to work their lands cooperatively. "The priests introduced us to a new form of cultivation; they called it conservation," Gaspar explained as we leaned against some rocks during one rest break. Generations of Salvadoran peasants have eked out a subsistence of corn, beans, tomatoes, and other vegetables in a cycle of plant, harvest, burn, plant. The soil is soon depleted. By working together, the priests explained, the peasants could leave sections of land idle, while growing enough on the other parcels to feed several families. "The priests told us God would bless our harvests, but that we had to do the work. The army said we were Communists, subversives, that we were feeding the guerrillas," Gaspar recalled. Finally, after several of his neighbors had been murdered, Gaspar and his four brothers went into the mountains with the guerrillas. His parents, wife, and thirteen-month-old daughter were in a refugee camp in Honduras.

THE sun was retiring, the day's heat giving way to the evening warmth and stillness familiar to a midwestern boy. From the hills wafted strong scents of trees and grass. The day's-end chores were being done. Boys came over the ridge, bearing gourds filled with water from the stream bed below. A guerrilla whose rifle was awkwardly slung over his shoulder stooped to sweep the dirt with a broom hand-fashioned from reeds tied in a bundle. Inside a small adobe hut, powerful peasant hands curled around a black-flecked gray cylindrical stone which they forced across a rectangular, concave slab as the women ground corn into meal, the process for making tortillas first used by Indians centuries ago. Sitting on a roughhewn log in front of the adobe, Father Rogelio Ponseele, a Belgian-born Roman Catholic priest, talked about the revolution. "I believe that God is here, with these humble people. The immense majority of them are Christians. They are motivated by their Christian faith."

Father Rogelio reminded me that I had previously seen him at the funeral mass that he had concelebrated for the leaders of the FDR who had been tortured and killed in November 1980. He was bulky then. Now, after nearly a year in the mountains, his clothes drooped on his lanky frame. Father Rogelio had come to El Salvador in 1970 and had worked in the capital slums until his parish house was destroyed by a bomb. The bombing had been preceded by anonymous telephone threats to kill all "Communist priests."

"I had either to leave the country or to work with the people of El Salvador in their fight," he recalled. "I opted to come here." On Christmas Day 1980 Father Rogelio left the capital and began his journey into the mountains. It was not a snap decision. At first, he said, "We had faith in the junta," referring to the civilian-military government that came to power after the coup in October 1979. "But the process begun in October 1979 has failed. The junta had good intentions." He was silent for several moments, recalling to himself and then aloud the land reform program, which never reached the announced goals, and the promises to end the repression, to control the military violence. "But the fact is it is a failure. What is important is not what the intentions are but what the facts are, what has happened—the power within the junta, the army, is an obstacle to the reign of God."

How can a priest justify working with an armed revolution? I asked. It was not just a journalistic question but one that troubled me personally.

"To bring a Christian perspective," he replied. "It's a people so oppressed, so humiliated that it has the right to take up arms."

Father Rogelio had trained some twenty-five catechists, some of them combatants. His Sunday masses were well attended and broadcast over Radio Venceremos. During his year with the revolution he had baptized some 200 newborns and performed ten to fifteen marriage ceremonies. "I don't encourage marriages," he added. "We are in a war. I tell them one of them may die tomorrow."

I pressed him about the political orientation of the revolution and whether the leaders were Marxists.

"Yes, the comandantes have studied Marx, but they aren't orthodox Marxists," he said. "What to me is impressive is the humanity of the leaders. They respect the individual and the Christian faith. There is a very sincere respect for the church."

I asked him about all the peasants who were following the Marxist leaders. "A peasant understands perfectly that the harvest is the fruit of his labor," he explained. "As a Christian he knows that it is also the blessing of God. The victory of the revolution will be the same—the fruit of the peasants' labor and also of God's blessing."

WHY are you fighting? Why are you part of the revolution?"

It is difficult to turn more than two or three pages in my yellow pocket-size reporter's notebooks without discovering an answer to that line of inquiry, which I directed at every man, woman, and child— whether he or she was cook or combatant, teacher or farmer—whom I met during my two weeks in Morazán.

"Because of the repression," answered Cruz. He was sixty-one years old. His trousers could be described not as having been patched but, more accurately, as patches held together by strips of what had been his trousers. He offered nothing further. So I asked about his family. Government soldiers had killed one son several years ago, he said. After that another son had gone into the mountains with the guerrillas and had recently been killed in combat.

We were resting, after climbing up a switchback trail. A principal role for old men in the revolution is as members of human packtrains. They walk for hours, often barefoot or wearing the remnants of shoes that offer scant support, in files of five to ten, crossing rivers and ascending out of V-shaped gorges, stooped forward under the burden of supplies that are not only heavy but awkwardly packed in sacks and boxes that don't balance naturally on a man's shoulder. I turned to his companion, sitting in the dirt on the other side of me, with the same question.

"For a better Christmas," said Herbert Chica, sixty-six years old. His three daughters and two sons all were in the mountains with the revolution. The old men's hands were powerful and gnarled, the deeply tanned skin on their faces cracked and creased like a baseball player's first glove, the legacy of a lifetime of laboring in the fields under the unrelenting sun. But those labors had also endowed them with incredible stamina.

Thirteen-year-old Jesús Castro, wearing a green baseball-style hat with the letters *FMLN* crookedly scrawled with a ball-point pen above the visor, had spread a piece of cloth on the dirt and field-stripped his carbine, the rusty parts of which he was trying to clean, ignoring most of my questions with an air of one who can't be bothered when he has more serious tasks. So I turned to a girl who was sitting passively at a table beneath the adobe overhang. Three strands of imitation white pearls glistened at the open neck of her khaki shirt, which looked as if it had actually been pressed. Her blue jeans were clean. She had yet to lose her adolescent chunkiness. This girl is still too shy to be concerned with boys, I thought. What on earth was she doing here? I asked her.

In a timid, barely audible voice, she told me that her fifty-five-year-old father and fifty-three-year-old mother, who had fled with her three younger brothers and sisters to a refugee camp in Honduras, had urged her to remain in the combat zone. Her twenty-one- and twenty-three-year-old brothers were combatants.

"How old are you?"

"I will celebrate my fifteenth birthday in six days." A flat answer. Nothing in her voice or expressionless face suggested she felt the thrill that most teenagers would on approaching that year.

"How are you going to celebrate?"

"With this radio," she replied in the same emotionless tone, patting her small black Japanese-made two-way radio, which had been issued to her because she is a part of the guerrillas' communications network.

"Why are you fighting?"

"For a new society," she replied shyly.

Her answer was, like those I heard from scores of peasants, so simple, with nothing about "Yankee imperialism" or "exploitation" by the Salvadoran oligarchy.

In the "hospital," thatched banana tree fronds, held up by hewn poles —the Twenty-third Psalm was tacked onto one—four peasants queued to get aspirins, counted out by Sonia, a fourteen-year-old who had learned rudimentary health care at the rebels' health school in the mountains. Another *brigadista,* as the health workers are called, attended to a day-old girl lying on a cot fashioned of rope so thin and frayed that it seemed not to have the strength to hold the tot. The child had been named Victoria. The previous day, I had seen the baby's seventeen-year-old mother being carried down a hilly path, in a sling tied to a single pole resting on the shoulders of a man at each end.

Nearby twelve-year-old Juan lay still in a hammock, his left arm below the elbow wrapped in white gauze. He had lost three fingers when a contact bomb—the guerrillas' homemade grenade—exploded. He said he didn't know where his parents were or even if they were alive. Shortly before Christmas his village had been bombed. His body began to tremble.

There was a chronic shortage of medicines, in spite of whatever medical supplies guerrillas were receiving from Cuba and Nicaragua. To treat iron-deficiency anemia, an American doctor, Charles Clements, who spent a year with the rebels on Guazapa Volcano, taught the peasants to place a nail in a glass of water for twenty-four hours before drinking the water. Dr. Clements, a graduate of the U.S. Air Force Academy who had flown missions in Vietnam, combated malaria by instructing the peasants in how to make a medicine from tree bark, as the early Spaniards did. The peasants at first called him the "gringo who tried to get everybody to eat rabbit food" because he told them to eat the leaves of yucca, papaya, and radishes to compensate for the lack of vitamins.

SOME children knelt in the dirt. Others sat on rows of crude benches. Most were barefoot and seemed to be partial to wearing some kind of cap, on which those who could write had scrawled "FMLN." Heads rested on an arm bent at the elbow, with the hand of the other arm holding a pencil which slowly moved across the lined pages, copying the day's lesson.

"How much is three times three?" asked Carmelo, the school's twenty-five-year-old instructor who himself had only two years of formal education.

"Nine," the students chimed in unison.

This was the Luis Hernández Ramos School for Children, named in honor of the fallen messenger, who had been a student here. Actually the place where Luis had been taught was completely demolished by the government's soldiers during a recent operation. This stucco-covered adobe had been only partially destroyed; the students had swept shattered red roofing tiles into a pile to make room for the benches and desks.

The students, ranging in age from nine to fifteen years, slept on the ground or on hard platforms, under leaves laid over sticks, held up by short poles. They had also dug a bomb shelter, about eight feet deep, with a two- or three-foot layer of dirt on the tops of logs. Thursdays were for washing clothes. On Sunday the students visited their families—if they were alive. One out of every ten students was an orphan, a few had parents in the refugee camps, but most were the sons of men and women who worked in the production brigades.

The director of the school was Alan Caballero, thirty-four years old, a 1969 graduate of the prestigious Pan American Agricultural School in Honduras. Started by the United Fruit Company in the 1940's and the recipient of funds from the U.S. Agency for International Development, the school proudly notes the number of its graduates who have gone on to become ministers of agriculture and wealthy coffee and banana growers throughout Latin America.

Caballero had owned a ninety-acre farm, which he had turned over to the guerrillas. He first became involved in antigovernment politics after the military had stolen the election in 1972. He had more formal education than anyone I met during my time in Morazán. He said that he had never been to Cuba or Nicaragua but that he had read some of the works by Marx and Lenin. "I'm not a Marxist-Leninist," he insisted, describing himself as a democratic socialist.

Sitting in a hammock, M-16 next to him, he explained that the school's curriculum was divided into three general categories: basic courses in reading, writing, and arithmetic; the national political situation; and physical fitness. There are also special courses, taught when the military condition demands: in first aid, communications, and being a messenger.

"We are trying to develop a different mentality," he said. "If a student in the government's school brings a soda or candy, he keeps it for himself. Here a student who brings an orange shares it." In the third row a fifteen-year-old-boy wearing a khaki-colored safari shirt with a U.S. flag on the left pocket craned his neck around a heavy log holding up the tile roof for a better view of the chalkboard. It was writing class, and he formed the words with his lips as he formed the letters in his notebook: "To Compañero Nolvo I give three oranges. To my sister I give three bananas." (Nolvo had been the leader of the column that safely eluded the government's pincers operation.) He had never attended school before and had learned to read and write in the past five months. Two of his brothers were "combatants," he said. "I want to serve my country," he told me, first as a *correo,* then as a combatant himself.

In the "classroom" Carmelo wrote that day's hygiene lesson on a green chalkboard:

Wash with soap.
Trim your fingernails.
Cook food well.
Clean cooking utensils.

"Why is it important to wash with soap?" Carmelo asked.
In the front row a shirtless tyke thought about offering an answer.

He started to raise his hand but stopped to play with the visor of his floppy red and black cap. Finally, overcoming his shyness, he extended his arm. Carmelo recognized him, and he answered, "Washing with soap takes the germs from the skin."

O NE evening, a few days after the ceremony for Luis, the peasants gathered again, this time in a field about 120 yards long and 50 yards deep. A waist-high rock wall, the kind familiar to New Englanders, formed the perimeter. This was a military ceremony, and some 120 guerrillas stood in formation.

Masking tape and string secured the stocks of their Korean War M-1 carbines and pre-World War II Czechoslovakian-made bolt-action rifles. A few had more modern German-made G-3 automatic rifles, the stenciled numbers on the butts indicating that they had once been issued to government soldiers. They were slung over their shoulders with twine and frayed belts. Bullets spilled from homemade pouches. The only thing uniform about their mufti was that it was tattered and soiled. Shoes were not designed for lasting long in the rugged mountains. Soles were split from uppers.*

As they stood erect, these guerrillas looked like Appalachian hillbillies, like a reinforced McCoy family about to go into battle with the Hatfields. But in a few days I was to witness how militarily disciplined they were.

T HE line snaked through the trees, down a squat slope to a stream. With rifles slung over their shoulders, the guerrillas moved through the partly demolished adobe hut where young girls and older men served each of them two tortillas sprinkled with salt, a couple of squares of meat, and coffee—hot and strong! Few words were spoken. Then they gathered in the mountain clearing, where the commanders gave the final orders, including the passwords and a caution: During the last operation a soldier, after shouting that he was surrendering, had opened fire, killing several guerrillas who approached him. They

---

*Reporters who visited other guerrilla zones came away with similar impressions. During his three weeks in Chalatenango, Clifford Krauss reported: "I saw no Cuban or Nicaraguan advisers, no planeloads of guns and ammunition and no abundance of supplies." The guerrilla units were, he wrote, "poorly equipped but highly disciplined. Hundreds of young militia fighters had nothing more than pistols and machetes with which to fight, against an army equipped with U.S.-leased helicopters and artillery."

milled around in small groups, smoking and whispering.

The command was given to move out. It was dark. Only the stars made it possible to see anything. Yet the long column moved steadily and confidently for three tense hours—fording streams, crossing clearings, and climbing mountain trails. There were four platoons of rebel soldiers; with each was a communications person, usually a young woman, carrying a small black Japanese-made walkie-talkie. There was also a squad of about a dozen medics.

No one spoke. But the snapping of twigs and rustle of leaves underfoot reverberated in my ears like elephants in a stampede. I was sure that the government troops defending the guerrilla objective could hear us coming and would be waiting with their rifles set on full automatic.

By 11:00 P.M. the moon was full. It was too risky to continue. The command was given to stop. No one moved off the narrow path. The guerrillas dropped on the spot and fell asleep on the damp, cold ground, without the protection of a bedroll or ground cloth. At 3:00 A.M. the commanders got everyone up. They advanced for another hour until in place for the attack. The mission was the government's fortified positions defending Jocoaitique, a village of some 3,000 people that rests on a small plateau, enclosed on three sides by hills.

After the main force units had been positioned, an elite contingent of confident guerrillas, led by Goya, the *nom de guerre* for a tough-looking commander who had acquired his basic military skills in the Salvadoran Army, continued to advance. Through the open field below the village, they belly-crawled nearly 400 yards, over rocks and prickly weeds, at one point crawling within a few feet of government soldiers inside a bunker.

A pistol shot cracked the silence. I looked at my watch. Five o'clock straight up. It was the exact minute the commanders had set for the attack. The morning stillness erupted with the explosion of grenades, followed instantly by splintering bursts from automatic rifles.

The government forces defended from at least four strategically placed bunkers, which were built of rocks piled five to six feet high. They fired through the space between the tops of the rocks and the tile roofs. It was through these apertures that the guerrillas tried to throw their contact bombs. But the openings were too small. So the guerrillas heaved small boulders onto the tile roofs, and through the holes these made tossed their grenades.

Two rebels attacking one bunker were killed. Later, as their comrades passed by their sprawling bodies, they stopped. One of the dead was wearing combat boots, a luxury for the guerrillas. A rebel started to remove them. He paused and turned away. Then he leaned over his dead friend and continued tugging.

"I'm sorry, compa, I'm sorry," he said, choking.

Three hours into the fierce battle I asked with amazement why the government's helicopters had not arrived. "The pilots are still sleeping. They won't come before nine," explained a rebel crouched next to me below a low embankment as the bullets flew overhead. At nine-thirty, two helicopter gunships began spraying the area with machine-gun fire. They departed and returned several times, but not a single guerrilla was hit. One time, as they appeared suddenly over the hill, several guerrillas along with Susan and me were caught in a clearing. Some of the rebels dived in a ditch. Remembering the advice someone had once given me, I dashed for a tree and moved around it, keeping the trunk as the shield from the helicopter's line of fire. But the only tree Meiselas and I could get to quickly was infested with thousands of nasty gnatlike flies that swarmed into our hair and clothes and stung viciously.

Shortly before noon two unarmed peasant men and a young boy approached the raging battle zone along a dirt road. They were leading two grayish white donkeys, bulging white cloths tossed over them like saddlebags. Wrapped in them were stacks of tortillas and kettles of beans—the guerrillas' lunch—and a resupply of contact bombs. From a hilltop position, government soldiers fired on the rebels who sprinted across an open area, carrying the food and supplies to the frontline fighters.

Seven hours after the attack had been launched, government soldiers who had surrendered or been captured were gathered in an open clearing. A burly sergeant, one of the biggest men I ever saw in El Salvador, lay in the weeds with a gaping bullet wound in his chest and a bloody, shredded hand. Although he was a member of the National Guard, the armed forces unit most hated and feared by the peasants, the guerrillas shouted for a medic and water. However, the efforts to save his life failed.

Once the government defenders had surrendered, fled, or been killed, the guerrillas moved into the village. One rebel climbed to the roof of the church, the whitewashed stucco exterior of which needed painting and a patch job, and began to dismantle the towering antenna attached to one of the bell towers. It had been mounted by the national guardsmen, to give them communications contact with San Salvador. Now it would be used for Radio Venceremos.

In front of the San Lucas Pharmacy, twelve black National Guard helmets rolled back and forth, top sides down, on the cobblestone street. The pharmacy had been taken over by the Guard for its headquarters. Inside were several metal-frame spring cots, painted military green. Sitting on one, next to a National Guard manual, a guerrilla who appeared to be about fifteen years old winced as a *brigadista* attended to a bloody hole on his neck just below his left ear, where a bullet had grazed him. Outside, the guerrillas filled four army duffel bags and several large cardboard cartons with gauze, bandages, and other medicines. Other rebels rummaged through suitcases containing the guardsmen's personal possessions. One found a flowered shirt he liked. Another tried on a pair of brown dress boots, too large, but sturdier than the street shoes he left behind.

A Salvadoran newspaper reported that "the terrorists ransacked and destroyed several houses, and also dragged several children from their houses, presumably to some camp." But while I was in the village, which was until the last guerrillas left shortly before dusk, I witnessed no destruction of property. The guerrillas entered homes when invited. Women served them tortillas; children gave them bananas.

Standing on a cement bench in the central plaza, pleasantly crowded with towering palm trees, evergreens and red and yellow flowers springing from tropical bushes, a rebel reporter, using a small radio, filed an on-the-scene dispatch for Radio Venceremos.

UNITED States and Salvadoran officials insist that Radio Venceremos is located in Nicaragua. That is what most journalists have reported.*

"Welcome to Nicaragua," said Mariposa, a vivacious twenty-three-year-old, with a laugh. Sitting in front of two silver microphones, a lanky fellow with curly black hair rehearsed the next broadcast, reading from a script that had just been pulled out of a beat-up typewriter. On a long plank were several tape recorders, equipment for mixing recorded sounds, even a tiny television set. The previous day's newspapers had already arrived deep into rebel territory, another indication of the network that supports the guerrillas.

A couple of hundred yards away was the recording booth, a six-foot-

---

*After my journey into Morazán I told a U.S. diplomat in San Salvador that I could assure him the radio station was not in Nicaragua. He didn't believe me. But, I said, I had been with a reporter when he filed a dispatch. The diplomat was still not convinced. He insisted that the reporter had staged the whole thing for my benefit, so that I would report the station was in El Salvador. According to Lawrence Pezzullo, the U.S. ambassador to Nicaragua until mid-1981, the station had operated in Nicaragua for a brief period in January 1981 but had been moved after protests from the United States.

deep hole. Beneath the massive logs covered with two to three feet of dirt were generators, amplifiers, and equipment the flickering needles of which monitored the sound levels. A microphone hung from a string attached to the logs. Aboveground the station's technician, a thirty-one-year-old university-educated engineer, searched among the wires and jumble of other scrap materials in a footlocker. The station, which is operated as a collective, had an archivist and scriptwriter in addition to two broadcasters, one of whom was Mariposa, a law student who had dropped out to go into the mountains. Her parents were also part of the revolution; her father was a tailor who made uniforms, while her mother bought supplies and medicines.

Radio Venceremos is the primary means by which the rebels can convey their views to Salvadorans, especially to the peasants. There is international news, usually only that which is favorable to the revolution, lessons in how to make simple weapons and erect barricades, periodic warnings to truck drivers to stay off highways because the guerrillas plan to burn their vehicles—part of the campaign to disrupt the economy. Captured government soldiers are interviewed on the station, and guerrilla leaders make long speeches. In addition to the customary shouting of revolutionary slogans, there is sometimes a lighter side. When Ambassador Deane Hinton married a wealthy young Salvadoran woman, the station delighted in reporting the event, with the observation "What the oligarchy could not win in the diplomatic struggle, it will achieve in the marriage bed."

Government soldiers have desperately tried to locate and destroy the station. It's not surprising they never found it. It is frequently moved. And when I was in Morazán, the adobe hut out of which it was operating had been abandoned for so many years before it was used for the revolution's radio station that it was barely possible to make out the path that had once been used by whoever had lived here. It was so overgrown with weeds and forest that one had to be practically inside the place before being aware of its existence. Having been unsuccessful in destroying the station, the government tried jamming the frequency. The rebels countered by operating on at least two frequencies, switching from one to the other as the jamming devices zeroed in.

The U.S. embassy regularly monitors the programs, for although the station is long on revolutionary rhetoric, it is also largely accurate when reporting on events in the countryside. After the attack on Jocoaitique, for example, the Radio Venceremos correspondent pressed the guerrilla commanders for an exact count of the number of weapons captured and casualties on both sides. With the commanders concerned about more urgent military matters, he was unable to get an exact number, so I asked why he didn't report the "approximate" numbers and label it as such. He could not do that, he said. "If we report that we took twenty rifles, and the soldiers know it was only fifteen, or that four compas were killed, and it was six, they won't believe our other reports." Inaccurate reports were bad for morale, he said.

The final tally from the Jocoaitique mission, which the Radio Venceremos reporter listed for me on a piece of paper, was eighteen G-3 automatic rifles, fourteen older-model rifles, twenty-three pairs of military trousers, fourteen army shirts, twelve knapsacks, and ten batteries for combat radios. In addition, the guerrillas carried away a heavy cloth bag filled with so many rifle bullets that it required two of them to carry it. The guerrilla leaders have consistently maintained that missions such as these, not Cuba or Nicaragua, constitute the principal source of their weapons. During the ten days preceding the attack on Jocoaitique the same guerrilla forces seized forty-seven automatic rifles, a ninety millimeter cannon, and thousands of bullets in attacks on six government outposts. (Clifford Krauss, the *Atlanta Constitution* correspondent, reported that after an operation in which the guerrillas had marched forty miles in two days, "baby-faced guerrillas and tough veterans came back with lots of loot on their backs: 31 automatic rifles, two .30-caliber machine guns, 20 pistols, two radios, 20 uniforms and one typewriter.")

One of the guerrillas' most effective and lethal weapons is the contact bomb. At the guerrillas' "bomb factory" in northern Morazán, an adobe hut at the edge of a stream, peasants placed a small bag of corn kernels on one side of a crude, hand-fashioned pendulum balance. The weight of this bag, they had learned from trial and error, had to be matched by yellow and silver powdered chemicals that they mixed in the other side. Nearby another peasant produced tiny pieces of jagged-edged metal by splintering a sewing machine that had been found in a house demolished by government troops during a recent sweep. The shrapnel and measured amounts of chemicals were then poured into small transparent plastic bags. The plastic bags had been collected from trails where they had been discarded by the government soldiers, who first emptied them of their fruit-flavored drinks.

The filled bags were then wrapped in newspaper, which was in turn covered with masking tape. The finished product looks like a baseball with the cover torn off and then repaired by a child. When the materials are available, the guerrillas can assemble 75 to 100 contact bombs a day.

"We utilize everything we have," explained Polo, the thirty-one-year-old father of a year-old son and the holder of an engineering degree from El Salvador's National University. "The enemy uses what the United States gives it."

But much of what the United States gives the Salvadoran Army quickly finds its way into guerrilla hands. The guerrillas have adopted and successfully implemented a policy of encouraging soldiers to surrender.

During the attack on Jocoaitique twenty-six members of the rural civil defense force surrendered. They looked very much like the rebels: teenagers wearing civilian clothes that were soiled and torn. Their rifles were bolt-action. One seventeen-year-old among them said they had been forced by the national guardsmen to help defend the village.

"They are not our enemies," said Licho, the commander of the operation, as he recorded the prisoners' names and ages. Between occasional bursts of rifle fire that sent the group sprawling on the ground, Licho, who was wearing a green camouflage baseball type of hat and carrying a G-3 he had recovered in an earlier battle, said they would be released after a few days.

The rebel commanders have insisted that prisoners be treated well, a policy that has not been easy for many of the guerrillas to understand.

"We wanted to kill all of the enemy because they have killed so many of us," explained one young guerrilla. "But the comandantes said no. Now we understand that if we kill prisoners, no one else will surrender and present us their weapons. If we respect them and guarantee them their rights, others will surrender. So we will have more weapons."

There is another pragmatic reason for treating the prisoners well and releasing them: a desire that after they have returned to their units, they will tell other soldiers that the guerrillas are fellow Salvadorans, probably someone they knew, perhaps a neighbor, and that there aren't any Cubans or Nicaraguans in the mountains.

"We thought we'd be tortured. That's what we were told in the barracks," said twenty-five-year-old Sergeant Manuel Antonio Rosales, one of five prisoners I interviewed in Morazán. "But it is the opposite. We have been treated well." He said that Salvadoran Army officers also told their troops that "Cubans, Nicaraguans, Russians, and Chinese" were fighting with the guerrillas. "But we've seen only Salvadorans," he added, glancing at the guerrilla guards carelessly lounging under a tree about thirty feet away.

The youngest of the prisoners said that he had been dragged off the street in his village and pressed into the army; the officials had written on his induction papers that he was eighteen years old. He was only fifteen. He said that he was thinking about remaining with the rebels. "I don't want to fight, but there are different roles. I can be a *correo* or cut firewood."

While I was skeptical of what I heard from soldiers who were under the physical control of the guerrillas, I was subsequently told by senior U.S. military officials in El Salvador that it was guerrilla policy to treat prisoners well and to release those who chose not to remain in the mountains. It was a policy that has worked well for the guerrillas and created serious problems for the Salvadoran armed forces, with entire small units sometimes surrendering. When guerrillas attacked a patrol of soldiers in Zacatecoluca, in the east-central province of La Paz, 69 soldiers and one officer surrendered along with more than seventy M-16 rifles. A few months later 133 soldiers and two officers surrendered en masse. They were disarmed and turned over to the International Red Cross. More than 500 government soldiers were captured and released during the last six months of 1983, according to guerrilla leaders.

FOUR plasma bottles were suspended on strings attached to overhead log beams. On one hard table moaned a guerrilla who had caught several automatic-rifle rounds in the stomach, rupturing his intestines in five places. He, along with the other guerrillas wounded during the battle at Jocoaitique, were carried on stretchers—rope woven between two long poles—for two hours up and down the mountain trails to a one-room mud-brick hovel that had been converted to a field hospital.

It was two o'clock in the morning. Peasant women held flashlights to provide illumination as Dr. Eduardo sewed up the ruptured intestines, pushing them back inside the man's stomach before beginning to close him up. During the seven hours that he was hunched over the table, Eduardo periodically arched his shirtless torso, seeking at least momentary relief from the fatigue and tension. At one point he turned to me, by then practically asleep standing up, and asked, "Who's going to win the Super Bowl?"

As his fingers drew needles and threads through the ruptures, he softly explained what he was doing to the peasants, among them two *brigadistas,* neither of whom had completed more than five years of school. One of them was thirteen-year-old Araseli, who had a stethoscope draped around her neck. With the confidence of an experienced nurse, she wrapped a gray belt around the arm of a wounded guerrilla, squeezed the bulb, and recorded his blood pressure. Then she moved quickly to another injured man to replace his serum bottle just before it ran dry. Calmly she injected pain-killers.

Araseli had acquired her skills only after the leaders of the refugee camp where she was living in Honduras had insisted that everyone assume some responsibility. She decided to join the health team. Eventually her parents, giving her some clothes and money, urged her to return to El Salvador to take part in the revolution along with her two older brothers, both combatants.

THE guerrilla commanders had thought it would take them two or three days to overrun Jocoaitique. But eight hours after launching the attack, they were moving through the rutted cobblestone streets, as squealing pigs and scrawny dogs dodged children rolling hoops. They had suffered only four killed and a few more wounded.

The obvious question is how did these peasants learn to fight so well.

"We have learned from experience, from our failures as much as our successes," answered Jonas, the senior military commander in Morazán. He was twenty-eight years old.

His real name is Jorge Antonio Meléndez. One of the founders of the People's Revolutionary Army (ERP), he had once been a university drama student. In the mountains he looked as if he were playing the role of a man who had fled the frenetic city life for the more tranquil existence in the Maine woods. He was solidly built, like a college halfback, with heavy eyebrows, a full black beard, and thick, shaggy hair, usually covered with a Tyrolean hat. He wore brown woodsman's boots and broad suspenders. Both his mother and father were part of the revolution, working clandestinely in the capital. His wife was seized on January 11, 1981, the day after the rebels launched what they had hoped would be their final offensive.

(About six months after my trip with the peasants in Morazán, I went to the women's prison in San Salvador to do a story. After talking for about thirty minutes with a petite brown-haired woman prisoner who had become a leader inside the prison, I told her that I had been in Morazán and had met a guerrilla commander whose wife was in the prison. "What's her name?" she asked, the tone in her soft voice and look in her eyes saying that she was not sure that she believed me, that she could trust me. I told her I did not know her name—and I thought, as I spoke, the lapse of memory would increase her suspicions —but that the commander's name was Jonas. There was silence. Then very softly she said, "I am she." I thought I noticed that her eyes moistened a bit. But she inquired no further about her husband. In June 1983, as part of the government's amnesty, she was released from prison and reportedly left the country immediately.)

"Jonas has all the characteristics of revolutionary leader," said Eduardo, the Mexican doctor. "He lives with the people, senses their needs. He knows how to communicate with the peasants, who understand and respect him." Jonas mingled and laughed with the peasant fighters as one of them, not as an educated city boy who had come to tell them how to do it. When he approached his troops, whether they were listening to the radio, chatting among themselves, or simply resting, they did not spring to attention as young soldiers do when even a junior officer enters the range of salute.

Jonas used his drama training well. He was a polished orator. I heard him deliver two hourlong discourses to large gatherings of peasants. With his hat in his hand and without the benefit of notes, he reminded children about their responsibilities, recited military successes. He sounded like a professor as he recounted the history of electoral fraud in El Salvador and how efforts to protest the fraud and economic inequality in the country had been crushed. "When we organized, they killed our leaders," he said. "When we demonstrated, they met us with bullets and tanks."

Turning to the combat units, he said forcefully and unequivocally that when the guerrillas were victorious, they would have to share the government with the civilians of the FDR. "It is just," he asserted. U.S. officials have repeatedly stated that the FDR has no power in the revolution, that the armed guerrillas, not the civilian politicians, would have all the power if the revolutionary forces were brought into the government.

During an interview, which began at about 5:00 A.M., I pressed Jonas about the political orientation of the revolutionary government, if it were triumphant.

He insisted: "The ideology of the government is not important." As he sat eating beans and tortillas in morning chill, he went on. "Regardless of their ideology, we need the participation of all those sectors— industrialists, technicians, businessmen—who want to help build the country."

I shook my head from side to side, with a look that said, "Yeah, sure, that's what you tell an American reporter, but I don't believe you."

He might sincerely have held that view, as might other guerrilla leaders. The unknown is whether those leaders would have any meaningful power if the revolution succeeded or whether the hard-line military commanders would be in control.

Jonas also expressed strong favorable opinions about Duarte, who at the time was president of the junta, and several other high-level Cabinet officials. He said the major problem was that they did not control the armed forces. But even then, he said, "the majority" of the government's army officers "are democratic—they do not want to participate in the massacres." The problem, he said, was that the most conservative elements of the armed forces were in control.

One of the obstacles to a negotiated settlement in El Salvador has been the fear on the part of Salvadoran military leaders and the Reagan administration that the rebels want a complete dismantling of the government army. But Jonas said that it was "very important" to have integrated armed forces—that is, that the guerrilla forces be folded into the regular Salvadoran Army. Other guerrilla commanders expressed the same desire for integrated armed forces.

"The officers who want to remain in the army won't lose their rank as long as they serve to defend the sovereignty of our country and not to repress the people," said the zone's political commander, José Leoncio Pichinte. Pichinte, twenty-nine years old, had been a rank-and-file labor organizer in the capital for many years. His wife was killed during a shoot-out in one of the capital's slum-belt barrios in August 1980. Three months later he miraculously escaped death. Had he not been delayed in traffic, he would have been at the meeting with Álvarez and the other FDR leaders when they were seized, then killed in November 1980.

One morning while in Morazán, I arose early, even before the women had started hauling water and grinding corn for tortillas, and hiked to a field where I was told I could observe the guerrillas going through their daily military exercises. Some 120 guerrillas, organized into platoons, were practicing close-order drill. Why, I asked, was a guerrilla army being taught how to march in formation and other parade ground drills? "After the victory we will be in the army," answered the company commander barking out the commands.

Nearly all the combat commanders, at the squad, platoon, and company level, whom I met in Morazán, had been born and reared in that department and had learned basic military skills in the Salvadoran Army.

Licho, who could read and write "only a very little," had entered the army in 1977, when he was fifteen years old. "The military instruction is good, but the ideology is bad because it's against the people. They don't teach you to respect the human rights," he said above the music blasting from the combination tape deck-transistor radio that he was lugging as he strolled across a field, returning from the successful attack on Jocoaitique, which he had commanded.

At his side was Goya, the *nom de guerre* for twenty-four-year-old Maximilio Vásquez Vigil, a Morazán native who had also completed only two years of formal schooling. He had been a government soldier for twenty months from 1976 to 1977. Asked what rank he was when he was discharged, he said, "A sad soldier." In 1978 Salvadoran soldiers killed his mother, his father, a sister who was eight months pregnant, and his brothers' children, one and two years old, he said.

With his light green beret, black mustache, jungle combat boots—taken from a government soldier killed in a previous battle—and a military swagger, he was the caricature of a tough guerrilla fighter. He had been a platoon commander when the rebels seized Perquín in August 1981. Because of the guerrilla policy of promotions based on performance—exactly what the American military advisers wish the Salvadoran armed forces would do—Goya had been promoted to company commander.

Another company commander was Manuel de Jesús Rodríquez, who had taken the *nom de guerre* of Che. He had been in the Salvadoran Army in 1972. Missing several front teeth, Che was one of the better-educated guerrillas I met, having reached the sixth grade. His two younger brothers were guerrilla fighters, and his father worked in a production brigade. His wife and two infant daughters went to a refugee camp in Honduras in December 1980. At twenty-nine Che was an "old man" of the guerrilla forces. Few of the peasants who made up the combat units in Morazán were older than twenty-four or twenty-five; a substantial majority of them were eighteen years old and younger.

I asked Jonas, Licho, Goya, Che, and scores of other guerrillas with whom I talked during my two weeks in Morazán if they had ever been to Cuba or Nicaragua for training. All said no. I didn't believe them then. But it seems possible that they were telling the truth. Jonas, as senior, would most likely have been trained there. However, a profile of Jonas prepared by one of the U.S. intelligence agencies makes no mention of his having been to Cuba, a frequent assertion in other profiles by the same agency.

The only foreigners I met or heard about with the guerrillas in Morazán were Rogelio, the Belgian priest; Eduardo, the Mexican doctor; and three other doctors, including a German woman. The only foreigner I met who participated in combat was a thirty-nine-year-old American, Joe David Sanderson. A free-lance adventurer who had gone to Vietnam after the war, worked with the Red Cross in Africa, and lived with the peasants in Bolivia, Sanderson, who had adopted the *nom de guerre* Lucas, told me that his main reason for being in Morazán was to write a history of the revolution in the manner of John Reed and the Russian Revolution. In April 1982 Sanderson was killed in combat.

WHEN the bearded twenty-three-year-old instructor shouted, "About face," four columns of twenty-four bewildered peasants, whose heads had been shaved, bumped into each other as they responded to the simple but strange military command. But their faces were taut with seriousness when they crawled on their bellies through the weeds, then turned somersaults with their rifles as fulcrums, and bounded into firing crouches on the rocky field. This was the guerrillas' military school. In the class was an eighteen-year-old former government soldier, captured when the guerrillas seized Perquín. He said that he had been given the opportunity to return to the army but that he had decided to fight with the revolution.

The revolution's military school in Morazán—approximately 300 peasants, including some 20 women, received rudimentary military instruction in the mountains there during 1981—seeks to consolidate the peasants' political, ideological, and military thinking, explained Orlando Rodríquez, the school's director. Rodríquez, a thirty-one-year-old Salvadoran, had gained considerable combat experience fighting in Nicaragua during the war against Somoza.

In the rebels' military manuals, handwritten in children's notebooks, were course titles: "Democratic Centralism," "Strategy of the Revolutionary War and the Taking of Power," and "Bourgeois Ideology." The notebooks also contained definitions of socialism ("the means of production are held collectively and the political power is in the hands of the workers"), feudalism ("man is in the service of the landholder"), and capitalism ("the owner of the land, owner of the factory, and owner of the workers' effort sells the workers' product").

During one class, with the students sitting on crude wooden benches under the tiles slanting down over the porch of a building that had once belonged to a dairy farmer, Rodríquez used a stick to point to the inverted pyramid he had drawn on a green chalkboard. At the apex were the names of several of El Salvador's wealthiest families, grouped under the category "oligarchy." About two-thirds of the way down the pyramid were the "rich peasants" ("those who own cars and cows," Rodríquez had written), followed by "workers" and "poor peasants." On the bottom were the "daily farm workers."

WHEN the guerrillas entered Jocoaitique, most of them headed for the general store. A seventeen-year-old laid her G-3 automatic rifle on the glass-top counter as she took out her money to pay for a tube of Colgate toothpaste. The owner refused to accept her money. Nor would he accept any money from the hungry guerrillas who wanted to pay for bread, bananas, small plastic packages of snack foods, as well as cigarettes, soap, and flashlight batteries.

I thought the store owner had probably acted more out of fear than of support for the guerrillas. So, when he and his family were alone in the store, I returned and asked why he had not allowed the rebels to pay. He may also have distrusted me, but his answer sounded sincere.

"It's my satisfaction," he said. "They're fighting for us."

HOW MUCH POPULAR SUPPORT

How much popular support within El Salvador do the guerrillas have? It is probably the most frequently asked question. It is also one of the most difficult to answer. No Salvadoran is going to pledge publicly his or her allegiance to the revolution—unless he or she is in the mountains with a gun in hand or standing next to someone who has one. Thousands of Salvadorans who were merely perceived as being no more than sympathetic to the left have been snatched off the streets, dragged from their homes, had acid poured on them, their skin peeled back, their genitals or breasts hacked off, then been tossed into a ravine or garbage dump.

While I was in El Salvador, I used to wonder who might appear in the streets to celebrate if the guerrillas ever won. I'd sometimes look at the grease-covered kid who put gas into my rental car, and the women who rented it to me, and wonder if they weren't quiet guerrilla supporters. After meeting some guerrilla leaders in Morazán who told me that their parents provided logistical support for the revolution, I would look at the man who owned the little stationery store in the shopping center, where I bought my reporter's notebooks, and wonder, Now is he . . . maybe . . . ? And after an executive-looking type in a three-piece suit escorted me to the clandestine interview with Comandante Ana María, and that middle-class housewife served as a contact for my rendezvous with the guerrillas on Guazapa, I concluded that it was really impossible to judge anyone's political views by appearance, job, profession, or public comment.

Though U.S. policymakers continually assert that the guerrillas do not enjoy appreciable popular support, it is largely an irrelevant issue for them. The U.S. policy is based not on what the Salvadorans want or even on what might be best for the country, but on what would be best for the United States. "I'm here to advance the interests of the United States," Ambassador Hinton explained candidly during a long evening's discussion at his residence. "I'm not here to solve all the problems of El Salvador."

During a press conference at the conclusion of a fact-finding tour by a congressional delegation in June 1982, Ambassador Hinton asserted that the Salvadoran peasants feared a victory by the left if the United States withdrew military assistance. But one member of the delegation was irritated by Hinton's characterization. He said the congressmen had heard no expressions of fear of the left from the groups with which they had met. (The meetings had been arranged by the embassy, which wasn't in the habit of exposing delegations to persons who were opposed to the U.S. policy.) The man who challenged Hinton was not a liberal Democrat, but rather Mickey Edwards, a conservative Republican Congressman from Oklahoma.

The heated debate over the question of how much popular support the FDR-FMLN has among the Salvadoran people has true believers on both sides. To Jeane Kirkpatrick, "it's quite clear, I think, to anyone who has studied the recent history of El Salvador, that the guerrilla movement in any of its embodiments—and it has many embodiments—has little popular support." Barely pausing, she went even further, declaring to a luncheon audience of the Members of Congress for Peace Through Law in February 1981, that "there has been no popular support for the guerrillas at any point since the struggle polarized. ... [T]hey don't have any popular support to back their military cause." On the other side are those—most vociferous, it often seems, are the ones who have never been to El Salvador—who claim that virtually the entire peasant population of El Salvador is ready to rise up in support of the revolution.

The FMLN claims to have up to 1 million sympathizers, including some 100,000 "militias" who provide supplies, such as food, batteries, medicine, and clothes; deliver the mail; and provide the guerrillas with intelligence about the locations of military units. On its face the claim seems absurd. One million people is approximately 20 percent of the Salvadoran population. But the claim was supported, at least in a general sense, by a U.S. diplomat who concluded at the end of his tour in mid-1983 that the support for the guerrillas is "a lot more than the administration says" and that "the political left would be a strong representative force if allowed to exist." Duarte himself, after the 1982 Constituent Assembly elections, told me that if the left had participated, its candidates might have received as much as 20 to 30 percent of the vote, which would have meant a second-place finish, after the Christian Democrats.

The peak of support for the revolution probably occurred in early 1980. To the extent that it has declined since then, a number of factors can be cited. On the positive side the land reform has wooed away many peasants. The government repression, however, has taken even more adherents: Tens of thousands have been brutally killed; many times more have concluded that opposition is not worth the risk. But the guerrillas are also responsible for the waning of some of their support—in part because of their inability to deliver a victory, in part because of the tactics used to try to achieve one.

After the failure of the "final offensive" in January 1981—one strong indication that the guerrillas did not enjoy the level of popular support they thought they had for an insurrection—the guerrillas vigorously began to attack the country's infrastructure. This strategy was aimed at causing a collapse of the economy, and with it the fall of the government, and at convincing the populace that the government was not in control and did not therefore deserve to be supported. The guerrillas blew up bridges, including the country's major one, the Puente de Oro (Golden Bridge), a lengthy expanse over the Río Lempa. They attacked the country's electrical grid, dynamiting power stations and sundering electrical pylons. For weeks at a time the entire eastern third of the country was without power. And they burned buses, some 1,300, or nearly one-third of the country's fleet. Peasants complained bitterly when there were no buses or the roads were blocked, aggravating their efforts to reach markets, to buy or sell. But it seems unlikely that these sabotage efforts cost the guerrillas as much support as U.S. and Salvadoran officials contend. Most of the country's peasants, and certainly those who support the revolution, had long lived in abject poverty, without amenities such as electricity, water, or medical care. One bus driver whose bus was burned by guerrillas directed his anger at Washington, not at the guerrillas. "In place of bullets, the government of the United States ought to send us buses," he told *The Washington Post*'s Christopher Dickey.

The war has also taken a considerable toll on El Salvador's agriculturally based economy but, again, with little effect on the country's peasants. Between 1979 and 1982 about $235 million in agricultural production was lost because of the fighting. But virtually none of the loss was in the staples of the Salvadoran poor: corn, beans, and rice.

While it is plausible to argue that the revolution has lost support, there is evidence to suggest the contrary. Charles Clements, the former U.S. Air Force pilot turned rebel doctor, said that during the year that he attended to the revolutionaries in Guazapa (1982–83), the size of the peasant population aligned with the guerrillas there increased by 20 percent. Statements by U.S. officials also demonstrated an increase in guerrilla strength. At the time of the "final offensive" the U.S. embassy was saying there were about 2,000 well-armed fighters. Six months later, according to a Confidential cable, the number had grown to 4,000. And when Colonel Waghelstein left in mid-1983, he said there were 6,000 guerrilla combatants. The significance of these increases is underscored by the fact that the guerrillas had undoubtedly lost hundreds of combatants during the two years of steady fighting. Thus they had replaced their losses, and then some.*

One means of trying to assess the level of popular support is to examine the military situation. "In order to conduct a successful revolutionary war popular support must be achieved," Colonel Waghelstein wrote in his master's thesis for Cornell University. Or to paraphrase Mao, guerrillas are fish that swim in peasant waters.† Without peasant support the guerrillas would die—especially in El Salvador, a tiny country with no jungle.

Nonetheless, the Salvadoran guerrillas not only have survived but have steadily grown stronger. In July 1982 Colonel Waghelstein said that the guerrillas would be "reduced to banditry within two years."

*In February 1984 the embassy in El Salvador was saying that there were 9,000 to 12,000 guerrillas. It seems likely that the total was inflated to justify more U.S. military aid. But if not, if the guerrillas were, in fact, able nearly to double their size in six months, it was another strong indication that they had a deep reservoir of support.

†It is this concept that drives military commanders—not only in El Salvador but in any country where there is a peasant-based insurgency—to believe that it is not a human rights violation to bomb villages and kill unarmed peasants living in areas where the guerrillas operate. They argue it is a necessary part of the war, to empty the waters where the guerrillas swim. One difficulty with the military theory, aside from any questions of morality or rules of war, is that it would justify the guerrillas' killing hundreds of thousands of people who implicitly support the government by living in government-controlled areas, such as the capital, or who continue in their jobs, thus supporting the economy the guerrillas, as part of their military strategy, are trying to disrupt.

But as 1983 ended, guerrilla forces overran the military base in El Paraíso, which was designed by Americans and was one of the most important bases in the country. More than 100 government soldiers were killed—they were buried by a bulldozer in a mass grave—in the greatest single loss during the war. Then, less than seventy-two hours later, on January 1, 1984, the guerrillas destroyed the quarter-mile-long Cuscatlán bridge, the last suspension bridge open to motorists traveling between the eastern and western parts of the country. By 1984 the guerrillas controlled more areas of the country than ever: the northern thirds of four provinces—Morazán and La Unión in the east, Chalatenango and Cabañas in the west—as well as smaller portions of valuable real estate around Guazapa and along the southeastern coast. In February 1982 I visited Jucuarán, which is in Usulután Province about ninety miles from the capital. It was firmly in government control. Soldiers mingled in the square with peasants waiting to receive the food and supplies that were loaded on huge military trucks. In January 1984 Stephen Kinzer of *The New York Times* wrote from Jucuarán that the guerrillas "appear to have established firm control over this town and an area of about 60 square miles around it, giving them free access to the Pacific coast and authority over rich coffee and cotton plantations."

And the guerrilla military successes came in the face of a tripling of the size of the Salvadoran Army—from about 10,000 in early 1981 to more than 35,000 by early 1984. The United States trained four battalions of Salvadoran soldiers. Some 500 officers were put through the U.S. Army school at Fort Benning, Georgia. C-130 cargo planes bulging with rifles, machine guns, mortars, combat boots, and uniforms set down regularly at Ilopango Air Base in San Salvador. U.S.-supplied trucks and helicopters ferried the soldiers into battle. U.S. jets provided overhead air support and bombed villages. Incendiary bombs burned the rebels' fields. U.S. planes from Panama, loaded with sophisticated electronic gear, flew overhead at night to detect the guerrilla locations and movements. Regardless of the weapons the guerrillas received from Cuba, Nicaragua, or elsewhere—which were more than they acknowledged but far less than the Reagan administration contended—they still had no helicopters, no tanks, no jets, no sophisticated equipment.

"It's not for a lack of weapons, not for a lack of vehicles, not for a lack of airplanes, not for a lack of ammunition" that the Salvadoran Army hasn't defeated the revolution, a senior Mexican diplomat observed in 1982. "There's one simple reason: They have no support of the people. The people support the revolution." A U.S. diplomat agreed: "Obviously they [the guerrillas] have tremendous popular support or they couldn't do what they are doing."

Other U.S. leaders disagree. "The vast majority of the population want something other than the armed violence that the guerrillas are offering, but that doesn't say they support the government," Colonel Waghelstein told reporters in 1982. Or, as one senior embassy officer put it in a private conversation, "They don't like the guerrillas, and they don't like the army; they don't know what the hell to do."

Historically and culturally Latin American peasants have been stoically passive. Their main objective is to survive. They have been subjugated by Spanish conquistadors, European immigrants, and Americans. While some Salvadoran peasants are fighting in the revolution, most are resigned to the fact that they will have little to say about the outcome.

But the neutrality of the Salvadoran peasants is fatal for the government. Unless the government and army have the active support of the peasants, they cannot expect to defeat the guerrillas. "A government's continuity in power is just as dependent on popular support as is the insurgent," Waghelstein concluded in the final paragraph of his thesis. The Salvadoran government's continuity in power has been maintained by the United States since 1979.

"I get a lot of mail asking me to examine my conscience and every so often I do examine it," Hinton said one evening near the end of his two years as ambassador.

"And what do you find?" he was asked.

"The alternative would be worse."

There is no doubt that Hinton sincerely believed that, as did most diplomats who served in El Salvador, and maybe it would be. But according to reports by the archdiocese's legal aid office, the FMLN forces were responsible for the deaths of 63 civilians during the fourteen-month period ending in July 1983. During the same period, the number of civilians killed by the government forces was 4,867. It's not that the guerrillas are reluctant to kill. But as a priest who did not support the armed revolution—two of his catechists had been killed by the guerrillas because they were also members of ORDEN—explained, the guerrillas killed selectively: soldiers; policemen; members of ORDEN. The government forces, he said, killed randomly. "Maybe they'll kill ten, and one guy was a guerrilla."

Several U.S. diplomats, whose time in El Salvador covered from early 1980 to late 1983, said in separate interviews that they were not aware of any massacres by the guerrillas. "That's a very interesting question," responded one senior diplomat when asked if there had been any guerrilla massacres. "You mean, did they come into an area and indiscriminately kill everybody they saw, left, right and center, young and old, as the army and security forces have done? No, they didn't, they did not, not that I know of." Another diplomat, after first saying no, there had been no guerrilla massacres, paused and then told about an incident in Santa Elena, a picturesque valley town, "something out of a Velázquez painting," as he described it. One night, according to what the town's mayor told a team from the U.S. embassy that had gone to investigate in response to reports of a guerrilla massacre, a group of men who he thought were guerrillas had placed a dynamite charge in a little store that sold beer, sodas, and sundries. Twenty people were killed.

Seeking guerrilla sympathizers three days later, the mayor said, soldiers from the Atonal Battalion had come into the village. A man with a mask over his face began pointing out people—a typical *modus operandi*—whom the soldiers then marched out of town. They all turned up dead along the main road leading from Santa Elena to Usulután.*

In spite of the record, which shows that the FMLN guerrillas have by and large respected human rights—abiding by the Geneva Conven-

---

*The Salvadoran armed forces, with eager assistance from the local press, have tried to counteract reports of massacres by government soldiers with charges of guerrilla massacres. Within days after the stories appeared, in late January 1982, about the government's massacre of nearly 1,000 in Mozote and surrounding villages, the armed forces claimed that guerrillas killed between 150 and 200 civilians in the town of Nueva Trinidad, in the province of Chalatenango. *El Diario de Hoy* ran a screaming banner headline 400 MURDERS BY TERRORISTS. El Salvador's other major newspaper, *La Prensa Gráfica,* put the number at 150. The army, which regularly refused to take reporters anywhere, made two helicopters available to take some to Nueva Trinidad. The reporters found that the government's story didn't hold up. They found 16 bodies. One was a guerrilla; 10 were members of the civil guard. There was no evidence that any of them, or the five civilians, had died other than during the fighting and not as result of an execution afterward. Military personnel showed them what they said was a mass grave with 150 bodies. But the "grave" was unopened, and the reporters said it was not large enough to hold more than a few bodies. It is interesting to note that this story ran on the front page of *The Washington Post.* Similarly, in 1983, a story by Sam Dillon, a reporter for the *Miami Herald,* about the guerrillas' executing 18 soldiers after they had surrendered was prominently played on the front page of the *Post,* even though a story he had written a few days earlier about the government's killing 10 civilians and leaving their bodies in a garbage dump did not appear at all. Some would argue that this reflects a bias on the part of the *Post.* I am inclined to believe that it reflects how rare guerrilla massacres were. When they happened, they were front-page news; government killings were so common that they were not.

tion with respect to the treatment of prisoners, for example, as the Salvadoran government does not—U.S. diplomats, even those who are numbed by the government's brutality, believe that it would be worse if the FDR-FMLN were victorious. "I don't think they'd kill half a million people or something like that or turn half the population of San Salvador out to the woods to be farmers or anything like that, but they'd probably take their toll," said one. Would the brutality and human rights situation be more terrifying than it is under the government that the United States backs? "Not in terms of actually taking people's lives, no. They couldn't possibly kill more than these guys are killing now. But there's a human right to live in freedom and a human right to live without the person next door informing on you to the neighborhood committee. There's a human right to travel; there's a human right to vote. Granted they haven't always been respected by past governments, but one would hope that maybe someday they would be."

An article about the Salvadoran left by a Mexican writer and social critic, Gabriel Zaid, so impressed the U.S. embassy in El Salvador that it distributed it to reporters. The article, written for *Dissent* magazine in February 1982, was titled "Enemy Colleagues," and embassy officials liked the negative things that Zaid wrote about the Salvadoran left, especially its propensity for internal violence. But Zaid also offered a solution: Purge the left of its most violent elements as part of a negotiated settlement that would also purge the army of the officers most responsible for the brutality. Opportunities to achieve that moderate solution have been available, first to the Carter administration in the first weeks following the coup in October 1979, later to the Reagan administration when the "final offensive" had been defeated and the FDR-FMLN was willing to negotiate. The opportunities were squandered.

PART TWO

7

THE COUP: A LOST
OPPORTUNITY

THE U.S. embassy had been alerted so many times that it would happen within twenty-four hours that when it received "terribly good information" that it would come during the weekend of October 12, the embassy officers asked each other, "Well, is this it? Or is it another false alarm, another weekly notice?"

"By the time we awoke Monday morning, it had happened," recalled Ambassador Devine.

At 6:30 A.M. lieutenants and captains in barracks throughout the country began locking up their commanding officers. A few hours later General Romero received a call in the Presidential Palace informing him that his term as president had been prematurely terminated. The fifty-three-year-old general thought he could hold on, but after calling various commands, he was forced to accept his fate. Less than twelve hours after it all had begun, Romero was on his way to Guatemala, aboard a plane that had been sent for him by that country's dictator, General Romeo Lucas García.

"The finest hour that El Salvador had in its memorable history was that coup of October 15, 1979," Devine recalled four years later. It also was, or could have been, the finest hour for the United States. The postcoup government wanted everything that the Carter administration professed to want: land reform; elections; civilian control of the military; elimination of corrupt, brutal officers; respect for human rights. Above all, it was a pluralistic government. Of the thirty-four Cabinet ministers and deputy ministers, sixteen were from the political left, eleven from the right, and seven were considered centrists. Thus it offered a meaningful option for the impoverished peasants and frustrated politicians who were being lured by the revolutionary siren. The new government "represents the last chance of staving off a takeover by the far left," Devine advised Washington in a Confidential cable a few days after the coup.

The coup, and the weeks that followed, were a "golden, last opportunity," said Richard Feinberg, a senior member of the State Department's policy planning staff at the time. But it became a lost opportunity. The Carter administration may be faulted both for failing to act and, when it did, for shoring up the conservatives in the armed forces, at the expense of the moderate officers and civilians in the government. The administration ignored the Salvadoran church and Archbishop Romero, who played an important advisory role to the coup plotters.

After a long history of neglect toward El Salvador the United States began to display a bit more interest after the fall of Somoza in Nicaragua in July 1979. The Sandinistas' victory had caught the administration by surprise. It was still hoping to negotiate a settlement, one that would have given the Sandinistas positions in the government but not complete control—and, more important, one that would have preserved the Nicaraguan Army by integrating the guerrillas into it— when the Sandinistas marched into Managua and took it all. One of their first acts was to disband Somoza's army. The Carter administration didn't want this scenario repeated in El Salvador. As much as it recoiled at the abuses by the Salvadoran Army, it wanted to preserve the military institution, a reflection of the historical reverence the United States has toward the army, at least in countries friendly to it.

After Somoza's fall Viron P. Vaky, assistant secretary of state for Latin America, and his deputy, William Bowdler, who had played a key role in Nicaragua, made secret trips to El Salvador. They were the first visits by high-level American officials in years. They tried to persuade General Romero to advance the date of elections, which weren't scheduled until 1982, and to commit himself and the armed forces to ensuring that they were free ones. Vaky and Bowdler, during their separate visits, met with church leaders and Christian Democratic politicians; but they made no effort to talk with the political left.

After his visit Vaky told a congressional subcommittee that El Salvador was "perhaps the most volatile" situation in Central America. But the State Department was still slow to react to events in the tiny country. In September Devine sent a cable alerting State to the likelihood of a coup. The response was a "thunderous silence," said Devine. When the reply finally arrived several weeks later, Devine was instructed to meet with the church, opposition political parties, and the armed forces in an effort to gain their commitment to elections. It was too late.

The coup of October 15, 1979, like many cataclysmic events in history, has been distorted by misconceptions piled upon myths, perpetuated by the personal ambitions and political interests—liberal or conservative—they serve. In El Salvador, both rightists and leftists have charged, for example, that the coup was generated in Washington and executed by the CIA. Both the Carter and Reagan administrations have used the coup to justify their subsequent actions in El Salvador. But the policymakers have tailored their version of events to fit the policy, paying tribute to the coup, while ignoring or recasting the machinations and developments that followed.

Rarely does a U.S. policymaker, whether asking Congress for more money or the public for support, fail to invoke the coup. The essence of the argument is always the same: The coup ushered in a new era. The military's alliance with the wealthy was severed. The armed forces made a commitment to democracy and respect for human rights. The soldiers were no longer led by corrupt, brutal officers.

The coup was certainly intended to be the prelude to all that—and more. Those who plotted and executed it were so determined to get the armed forces out of politics that they initially proposed that no officers serve on the postcoup junta. They were so desirous of opening the political process to everyone, thereby lancing the pressure for an armed revolution, that they proposed the leader of the BPR as a member of the junta. They had plans to nationalize all of the nation's financial institutions and to distribute all farms larger than 247 acres. They even intended to arrest and put on trial the officers who were engaged in corruption, headed the death squads, and had ordered or executed the killings of peasants, workers, teachers, and demonstrators.

But such dreams were not to be realized. The young, progressive officers who carefully plotted the coup lost control of it as swiftly as they had executed it. Their ideals and objectives were subverted by senior, more conservative officers who had the backing of Devine and the U.S. embassy in El Salvador and key Carter administration officials in Washington. These senior officers were not about to surrender their unfettered sovereignty to civilians. They recoiled at the prospect of having criminal charges lodged against any of their colleagues. They blocked the implementation of the economic reforms. And they continued to use excessive force against dissent: More people were killed in the three weeks following the coup than in any three-week period during the Romero regime.

Change the place and the date—and some details—and the Salvadoran coup of October 1979 resembles numerous other coups throughout Latin America in this century: Bolivia, Guatemala, Peru, Ecuador. Most Latin American armies are divided—between officers who think the country is best run by generals and other officers, usually in the minority, who want the military out of politics. Coups are frequently followed by countercoups. Sometimes the coups are executed by officers who want to effect major social changes; more often, by colonels and generals who want power for their own personal ends.

As for the Salvadoran coup of 1979, it is part of the cataclysm that it was spawned by the Sandinistas' overthrow of Somoza's army on July 19, 1979: The Salvadoran officers did not want to suffer the same ignominious fate as their Nicaraguan counterparts, who had been jailed or forced to flee after their defeat. They decided to get rid of Romero, the litany goes, before they and their cherished institution fell with him. While it is likely that some officers supported the October 15 coup for that reason, the coup's genesis reaches back a decade, to a chance meeting of two Salvadorans in Columbus, Ohio.

René Francisco Guerra y Guerra was reared as one of eleven children in an upper-middle-class, politically conscious family. His father, a successful furniture maker, was arrested and condemned to death in 1945 because of his opposition to the military dictatorship. He was freed after the regime had been deposed by a coup. After René's father had died, his mother squandered the family's wealth. It was not only the free education but the possibility of scholarships for advanced study abroad that attracted René to the military academy, which he entered when he was fourteen years old. After being graduated second in his class and quickly advancing to the rank of captain, he received the scholarship he coveted, and in 1970 he set off for Ohio State University to pursue a master's degree in electrical engineering.

It was on one of his first days in Columbus, while searching for an apartment, that Guerra y Guerra met Guillermo Quiñónez, a doctor who had acquired Marxist political ideas as a student at the National University in El Salvador. Guerra y Guerra wasn't a Marxist and never became one, but he agreed on the need for drastic changes in the Salvadoran economic and political structure. Together the two young men set down a long-range plan. They would return to El Salvador and organize cells of like-minded individuals. Quiñónez would recruit civilians; Guerra y Guerra, officers. The leaders of the cells would infiltrate themselves, and their ideas, into important positions in the country's economic, political, and military institutions.

Quiñónez returned to El Salvador first, in 1973, and established a small civilian coordinating committee. As a cover for its plotting, it established an engineering society. Among the participants were two of Guerra y Guerra's brothers, Rodrigo and Hugo, both of whom, as the master plan called for, became active in the National Conciliation party (PCN), the army's political party. As the PCN candidate Hugo was elected mayor of San Salvador in 1978. (In that capacity he was to call Ambassador Devine on the day of the coup.) Quiñónez became the general secretary of the General Assembly of the National University. Another member of the civilian coordinating group was a professor at the Catholic university. The fifth member was a prominent economist, now with an international development bank, whose task was to recruit other economists and to draft the land reform and nationalization programs.

After finishing at Ohio State, Guerra y Guerra studied in Japan for another year. He returned to El Salvador in 1976, probably with more education than any officer in the history of the Salvadoran Army. Before he could begin recruiting, he had to get to know the members of several *tandas* that had been graduated during his absence. He spotted a captain, a commander in the artillery regiment, whom he knew to be honest and whom he had good reason to believe had been exposed to the need for social changes. One day in November 1978 there was shooting in the street; Guerra y Guerra suggested to this captain that it would not be safe to venture out, so why not have lunch together in the Presidential Palace, where Guerra y Guerra, now a lieutenant colonel, was assigned as an aide to General-President Romero. While they were eating, the president came by their table and informed them that during a shoot-out between the National Police and the FPL, a priest, Ernesto Barrera, had been killed. Guerra y Guerra's luncheon guest was Captain Román Barrera, the priest's cousin. The captain managed to keep a poker face, but as soon as the general walked away, Guerra y Guerra and Barrera hastily retreated to Guerra y Guerra's office.

In El Salvador's small, tightly knit society, everyone appears to know everyone; the interrelationships are almost incestuous, it seems. Guerra y Guerra's cousin was also a priest, and it was from him that he had learned about the activities of Father Barrera in the FPL. Lieutenant Colonel Guerra y Guerra now explained this to Captain Barrera and then proceeded to lay out his program for change. He had his first recruit. Eventually added to the military coordinating group were Álvaro Salazar Brenes, an air force major, and an army captain, Francisco Mena Sandoval. Mena Sandoval had been expelled from the military academy for allegedly being a Communist, but he had remained in the army, working his way up through the ranks. At the time he joined the Quiñónez-Guerra y Guerra cabal, in addition to being an active-duty captain, he was in charge of security for the Hill family, one of the country's wealthiest. He was to betray the coup plotters to senior officers; later, however, in a move that suggested his political bearings had never been fixed, he went into the hills with the guerrillas.

Initially all the plotters thought that it would be possible to effect change from within. Guerra y Guerra was one of General Romero's senior aides, and they had long talks about the need for reform. But like the Carter administration, the committee members had to accept the fact that Romero was incorrigible, that he wasn't about to clean up the corruption or control the violence. So, in December 1978, the civilian and military committees agreed there would have to be a coup. The young, physically fit officers shinnied up ropes to clandestine second-story barracks sessions above the heads of their superior officers. By the summer of 1979 there were thirty-seven primary cells, each headed by a lieutenant or captain, and scores of subcells. The thirty-seven were represented on the military coordinating committee by seven officers.

On October 5 the civilian and military coordinating committees, in a tiring session that lasted into the early-morning hours of the next day, began to discuss the makeup of the postcoup government. The first impasse: Should there be military men on the junta? Paradoxically the officers argued against the military's participation; the civilians insisted on it. Unable to resolve their differences, they sent a delegation to consult Archbishop Romero. He advised the officers it would be okay to have one of their own on the junta. Back at the meeting, it was decided to have a five-member junta. A new disagreement arose. The military coordinating committee wanted one officer; the civilians argued for two. Another visit to the archbishop. He said two.

For one of the civilian representatives, everyone agreed on Ramón Mayorga Quiros, the thirty-seven-year-old rector of the Catholic university. The officers then proposed twenty-three-year-old Juan Chacón for the second civilian slot. It was a profound manifestation of their commitment to pluralism. From a peasant family in Chalatenango, Chacón had left the fields in 1975 to become a factory worker in the capital. He soon joined the Popular Revolutionary Bloc (BPR). Not long thereafter his father, a lay preacher in the Catholic Church, was killed and dismembered by the National Guard. In 1979 Chacón had been elected secretary-general of the BPR. The civilian coordinating committee rejected Chacón.

On October 6, the day after the civilian and military coordinating committees decided on a junta of five, the military coordinating committee convened at Xanadu, a beach resort on the Pacific, to elect the officers who would serve on the junta. Colonel Adolfo Arnoldo Majano, forty-one years old, was elected unanimously. A small, bespectacled man, Majano, who had won a gold medal in the 400 meters in the 1958 national youth games, was extremely popular with the country's young officers, most of whom he had taught while a professor at the military academy, where he was the assistant director at the time of the coup. But the selection of Majano proved to be a mistake, at least from the perspective of the desire of the young officers to rein in the conservatives in the military. Majano's loyalty to the institution made him reluctant to challenge his superiors, even though he knew they were corrupt and brutal, and he was not a dynamic leader. A chess aficionado—he was the country's national champion in the late 1960's—he faced decisions, during his year on the junta, that called for swift and forceful action. But he was cautious, approaching each decision as he would a well-thought-out move of a knight or queen.

Then came the vote for the other military position on the junta. Guerra y Guerra finished first with seventeen votes, followed by Colonel García, who was commander of an insignificant garrison at the time, with seven. Had the junta included Majano and Guerra y Guerra, both liberals and honest, the Salvadoran history would almost certainly have been completely different. But that was not the end.

It has been reported that the United States embassy, concerned that Guerra y Guerra was too much of a leftist, stepped in at this point to block his becoming a member of the junta. It's possible, but on the basis of the available evidence and considering that the CIA had only a token operation in El Salvador at the time, I don't believe so. Even Guerra y Guerra does not blame the United States. He says that Colonels García and Jaime Abdul Gutiérrez, in collaboration with Mena Sandoval, conspired against him.

Gutiérrez, who had an undistinguished military career—his biographical sheet was barely half of a page, the shortest of anyone serving on the junta from 1980 to 1982—learned about the coup plotting from Mena Sandoval in August. He asked to become a member of the military coordinating committee. Guerra y Guerra was opposed. Gutiérrez's participation would mean that Guerra y Guerra, a lieutenant colonel, would no longer be the senior officer among the coup plotters. Moreover, Guerra y Guerra thought Gutiérrez was corrupt. Gutiérrez had been general manager of the state communications system, ANTEL, during the Molina period. Guerra y Guerra had been the acting general manager of ANTEL for a brief period before the coup.

(His second day on the job, while he was attending a funeral, Guerra y Guerra was approached by the undersecretary of justice, who offered him an $80,000 bribe. The Cabinet official was also a lawyer for a European company that was bidding on a communications equipment contract. A few days later he upped the offer to $120,000. Guerra y Guerra told President Romero about the bribe. Romero responded by dismissing not the justice minister but Guerra y Guerra.) In the ANTEL files Guerra y Guerra found between $12 million and $18 million in fictitious invoices relating to an earth satellite station that had been built while Gutiérrez was general manager. How this money was divided among Molina, Gutiérrez, and García (president of ANTEL at the time) isn't known, but a U.S. diplomat familiar with the ANTEL case said about Gutiérrez, "You're entitled to your piece of plunder, but not to that magnitude."

In order to be brought into the coup, Gutiérrez asked two of Archbishop Romero's doctors, who were also Gutiérrez's personal friends, to intercede for him with the archbishop. The senior prelate advised Guerra y Guerra to accept Gutiérrez, in part to ensure that he did not work against the coup. Guerra y Guerra's fears proved well founded. Mena Sandoval and Major Salazar Brenes regularly voted with Gutiérrez, leaving Guerra y Guerra and Barrera in the minority.

Gutiérrez wanted García brought in on the coup; they were close friends from their days together at ANTEL. Mena Sandoval sided with Gutiérrez, but Guerra y Guerra, once again after consulting with Archbishop Romero, held firm. This time a compromise was reached: García would be an adviser to the coordinating committee but would not be a member. But García was tough and wily. As the coup plotting escalated, he tried to gain control. On one occasion he called a group of junior officers to a meeting when Guerra y Guerra was away from the capital—or so García thought. But Guerra y Guerra had been alerted to the meeting and barged in on it, leading García to abandon his plans prematurely.

The day after the meeting in which Guerra y Guerra had been elected to the junta, Gutiérrez and García demanded a new vote, arguing that the prior vote was invalid because only thirty of the thirty-seven delegates to the coup movement had been present for the first vote. On the second secret ballot Guerra y Guerra retained his seventeen votes, but García's support jumped from seven to fourteen. The argument was made that because Guerra y Guerra didn't have a majority, only a plurality, he shouldn't serve on the junta. Mena Sandoval proposed that Gutiérrez be named to the junta. Gutiérrez had received only one vote. Mena Sandoval's bizarre "logic" was that since Gutiérrez had the fewest votes, he would be the least divisive of the candidates. The others agreed. The tack on which Guerra y Guerra had plotted the Salvadoran ship of state had not just been changed, but been reversed nearly 180 degrees, although that would not become fully apparent for several months.

THE long-simmering coup was now rumbling like one of the country's volcanoes about to erupt. Although Gutiérrez and García had joined with the young officers, they were also discussing their own coup with Colonels Vides Casanova and Flores Lima, a top aide to General Romero. And Romero himself, realizing the precariousness of his hold on the presidency, sought to organize a preemptive coup. The ingenious young officers leaked those plans to BBC television, thereby throwing it into disarray.

The favored days for Latin American coups are Thursday and Friday, allowing the coup makers time to bring the country to some normality and calm over the weekend. Salvadorans waited, expectantly, tensely, especially on Friday night, which was being openly discussed as the time the coup would come. But those rumors had been purposely planted by Guerra y Guerra's group to confuse the officers who supported Romero. The tension escalated as Sunday arrived, and the order was given to launch at 7:00 P.M. A countermanding order was given two hours before, because the coup plotters thought they had been discovered. Then a coded message, scribbled on colones, the country's banknotes, ordered the trusted officers who received them to swing into action the following morning.

The carefully laid plans called for the young officers to take control of their barracks between 6:30 and 8:30 A.M., the hours that the senior officers and sergeants opposed to the coup would be seated unarmed at their breakfast mess. A crop-dusting plane had been rented and was standing by to take the plotters to Nicaragua if the coup collapsed.

There were a lot of jittery officers as the sun rose on the morning of October 15. Their best-laid plans were going astray.

It has been widely reported, and accepted, that Colonels Gutiérrez and Majano were the leaders of the coup. It is an interpretation of events perpetuated by U.S. policymakers in order to enhance the colonels' stature and thereby bolster the policy of supporting the junta. But it is another myth.

Gutiérrez and Majano even failed to appear at the designated command post at the designated hour of 5:00 A.M. Guerra y Guerra thought, on the basis of what some of his officers had told him, that the delay was purposeful, to give Salazar Brenes time to assassinate him. Guerra y Guerra never turned his back on Salazar, and he kept the safety off on his German-made MP-5. Majano never showed up. When Gutiérrez finally arrived, more than an hour late, he was dressed in civilian clothes, his small machine gun in a briefcase he was carrying, and he told Guerra y Guerra the coup had failed.

This further convinced Guerra y Guerra that Gutiérrez was working against him, and he rushed to his jeep. During September, while general manager at ANTEL, he had used the opportunity to secretly install a secure telephone in the First Brigade headquarters. Support of the First Brigade, located in the capital, had always been deemed essential for a successful coup. Now, from the mobile phone in his jeep, Guerra y Guerra phoned the secure number.

"Colonel, where the hell are you?" came the nervously excited voice on the other end of the line. "We have been looking for you. We've had this thing under control since a quarter to seven, as ordered—all the barracks, but some small ones, are under control already."

His effort to subvert the coup having been thwarted, Gutiérrez quickly changed into his military uniform, then called General Romero with the news of the coup and asked him to resign. Romero refused. At about 11:00 A.M. Guerra y Guerra, who had not previously talked with anyone in the U.S. embassy about the coup, sought a meeting with Ambassador Devine, to ask the United States to bring pressure on Romero to resign peacefully in order to avoid bloodshed. Devine declined to meet with him. At 3:00 P.M. the U.S. ambassador received another call. "Apparently feeling that it would be more secure against eavesdropping, he spoke to me in English," Devine said about the caller, whom he declined to identify. It was Hugo Guerra y Guerra, the mayor of San Salvador and René's brother. Devine told the mayor that he would not take any action, except to inform Washington.

Devine insisted that the United States was not involved in the coup, that he was under "strictest instructions not to provide any encouragement" for it. Robert Pastor, the person on Carter's National Security Council responsible for Latin America, also denied any U.S. involvement. "One of the things that I was determined not to repeat was a Chilean episode, not to get involved in the business of overthrowing governments," Pastor said after he and the Carter administration were out of power. In 1973 the Nixon administration, with Henry Kissinger playing a leading role, had been actively involved in efforts to overthrow the leftist Chilean government of democratically elected

Salvador Allende. Before that, there had been the CIA's toppling of the Guatemalan government of Jacobo Arbenz Guzmán in 1954. Those events, bolstered by the somewhat arrogant belief that nothing can happen in any Latin American country without foreign intervention, have helped generate the widely held belief that the United States was behind Romero's ouster.

The embassy in El Salvador was well aware that a coup or coups were being plotted. And specific details of the Guerra y Guerra plot were provided to the embassy by Gutiérrez. But though I am prepared for the possibility that in twenty or thirty years, when documents are declassified, the case for U.S. involvement will be established, I believe now, on the basis of a wide range of interviews and the available documents, that the United States, while it welcomed Romero's ouster, did not directly participate in it. Further support for the conclusion that the United States did not actively support the coup comes from the observation of Richard Feinberg that "the United States typically hesitates to oust conservative pro-U.S. figures—that is, President Romero. . . . You know, there's some sense that 'good God, this guy's a friend, we've influenced him all these years.' Plus there's the concern, 'can you control the process? This guy may not be too good, but what's going to happen next?'" As for the Salvadoran coup, moreover, Guerra y Guerra said emphatically that he never sought, and would not have accepted, U.S. help. Both he and Mayorga said they never even discussed it with Ambassador Devine because they considered him too conservative a man, one who would not be in agreement with their political objectives.

In any case, U.S. intervention wasn't needed. Two hours after Hugo Guerra y Guerra's phone call to Ambassador Devine, Romero climbed aboard the presidential helicopter waiting for him in the hillside park facing the Presidential Palace. He was flown to Ilopango Air Base and from there to Guatemala.

Guerra y Guerra was furious that Romero had been allowed to leave the country. He wanted to place the general on trial, to answer for the corruption and killing. But Guerra y Guerra was overruled by Gutiérrez. The *coup de grâce* to the young officers' coup was soon to follow.

Shortly before midnight on Monday, after the coup makers had read their proclamation to the nation, Guerra y Guerra, who hadn't slept for nearly three days, dropped into a bed. When he was awakened by an officer loyal to him, he found his nemesis, García, sitting at a table. While Guerra y Guerra had been sleeping, Gutiérrez, without consulting the other members of the junta—at the time Mayorga and Majano —had named his friend García minister of defense. Although Majano hadn't been consulted, he did not protest.

One of García's first acts was to order the release of the senior officers who had been arrested and who, according to the plan of the military coordinating committee, were to be brought to the military school, where they would be held until they could be given trials on charges of corruption, torture, and murder. Among them were Major Roberto d'Aubuisson, one of the most notorious torturers, and Álvaro Magaña. (After the elections insisted upon by the United States in 1982, D'Aubuisson and Magaña became the president of the National Assembly and the provisional president of the country, respectively.) The young officers wanted to try Magaña because as head of the National Mortgage Bank he had made illegal loans to military officers. But there were to be no trials. Most of the officers who had been arrested were assigned new positions of command; others were sent to attaché posts in Salvadoran embassies abroad.

There was a housecleaning, but it missed most of the dirt. Between 80 and 100 officers were dismissed from the service, but most were colonels and generals who were near retirement anyway. Moreover, many officers who ran the death squads and torture chambers weren't touched, and by 1984 they were in positions of power.

During those early-morning hours after he had been made minister of defense, García gave the orders for military units to attack two seedy working-class barrios in the capital that had been taken over by the ERP. In Mejicanos the ERP guerrillas had tossed rifles to residents, expecting them to rise up in insurrection. They hadn't. Archbishop Romero criticized the ERP's actions as "irresponsible and precipitate," while he castigated the army for using unnecessary violence. Between 30 and 40 people had been killed. Some were certainly guerrillas; most were persons suspected of being sympathetic to the revolution; none were soldiers or policemen. The day after the coup, soldiers stormed four factories that workers were occupying to press their demands for higher wages and improved working conditions. At least nine were killed. Nevertheless, the national mood ran from euphoric relief—that the dictator was gone—to cautious hope—that it was not merely a change of faces. After the months and years of violence, hope was all that remained. In his homily the day before the coup, Archbishop Romero noted that 580 persons had been killed for "political reasons" during the first nine months of 1979—four times more than in all of the previous year. After mentioning specific cases of the dead, captured, and disappeared, during the previous week, he cited the plea of a nine-year-old boy whose mother had been seized: "Please let her go!" The archbishop added, "In this suffering land, even freedom must be begged."

On the Friday following the coup, Ambassador Devine invited Archbishop Romero, Monsignor Ricardo Urioste, the vicar-general, and another priest to lunch on the patio at his residence. "Seldom in my time there had I seen people sitting around so relieved. It was as if they were saying, 'God's back in heaven,'" Devine recalled.

The left's response to the coup was predictably divided. What U.S. officials fail to mention is that the Communist party openly embraced it, with several of its members becoming ministers or deputy ministers in the new Cabinet. The ERP called for an insurrection. The FPL criticized the ERP's actions as "suicidal" but denounced the coup as having been engineered in Washington to defeat the Salvadoran people. Ten days after the coup, members of the BPR seized the ministries of Labor, Economics, and Education, demanding the release of all political prisoners, an increase in the $3-a-day minimum wage, and a freeze on food prices. After a few days the protesters abandoned the buildings, releasing their hostages unharmed.

At the urging of Mayorga and Archbishop Romero, the revolutionary organizations then agreed to suspend for thirty days all demonstrations, military attacks, and other disruptive actions, to give the new government an opportunity to demonstrate its bona fides.

On the other end of the political spectrum many of the Salvadoran business elite feared precisely what the left hoped: that the new government's actions might indeed match its rhetoric. Many of them were as convinced as were the leftists that the coup had been sponsored by the Carter administration, but the rightists charged that the country was being delivered to communism. To register their dissent, in the posh residential neighborhoods, there was organized "bullet throwing," as one junta member described it. At 6:00 P.M. the wealthy would step out onto their manicured lawns and squeeze off a few rounds to show their disapproval of the junta. They undermined the economy, taking hundreds of millions of dollars, some say billions, out of the country. They would not give the new government a chance. They did not want it to survive. They began buying officers, to oppose the junta and the progressives within the military. The two major newspapers, both stridently conservative in editorial content and reporting, blistered the junta.

Trying to hold the country together in this near anarchy was a junta that would have had difficulty governing in the best of times. The young officers who had so skillfully executed the coup had not been as careful in selecting the postcoup junta. Little, if any, consideration had been given to whether the junta members, as well as many within the Cabinet, had the political or administrative skills needed to run a country or to how, or if, they would be able to work together.

Mayorga, who, as noted, had been the unanimous choice of the coup plotters, was an engineer and professor. He had never even been involved with any political parties, as had so many of his university colleagues. When he was approached by the young officers about serving on the junta, he had said no. The morning after the coup he was still undecided and consulted Archbishop Romero. The archbishop agreed that the prospects for avoiding a civil war were bleak, but he told Mayorga that he had a Christian obligation to try to make a difference. Mayorga knelt to receive the archbishop's blessing.

The second civilian on the junta was Guillermo Manuel Ungo, his appointment a reflection of the effort to bring the left into the government. A Social Democrat, Ungo had been nominated for the position by the Foro Popular, a coalition of moderate to left labor unions and political organizations such as the Christian Democrats and the National Revolutionary Movement (MNR), which was Ungo's party.

Two days after the coup the new government announced a press conference without even knowing who the fifth junta member would be. Mario Antonio Andino, a prominent forty-three-year-old business leader, stumbled into the post. The sequence of events, as Andino recalled three years later, began when Colonel Majano called the Chamber of Commerce, seeking the support of the private sector for the new government. Nothing was said about allowing the businessmen to name a member of the junta. When a small group of business leaders went to the appointed meeting with Majano at the San Carlos barracks, he wasn't there. Colonel Gutiérrez told the group he knew nothing about the meeting. "What are you doing here?" he asked sharply. "You are the causes of our problems."

Andino countered, "It's a funny thing you think the private sector has ruined the country; in our concept, it is you, the army." As the businessmen were leaving the barracks, Andino joked to his colleagues, "We weren't invited to this party." Several hours later Andino received a frantic call from the Presidential Palace urging him to get there as soon as possible because he had been selected for the junta. As he rushed into the room where the press was waiting, someone announced, "And here is the fifth member of the junta." Andino didn't even know who the other members were.

Andino, a European-educated engineer, was the manager of the Phelps Dodge factory in San Salvador at the time he was named to the junta. American reporters usually referred to Andino as a liberal, and perhaps among Salvadoran businessmen he was, but he was opposed to the nationalization of the banks and the export trade as well as to parts of the land reform program.

The day after the coup Archbishop Romero prepared a message that was read over the country's radio stations at noon. He called on the country's wealthy elite, "who have been guilty of so much evil and violence," to listen to the needs and demands of the poor. He admonished the revolutionary leaders to demonstrate "true political maturity, flexibility, and capacity for dialogue." Then he cautioned the new government that it must demonstrate that its "beautiful promises are not dead letters."

The promises were contained in the armed forces' Proclamation of the 15th of October, drafted initially by the coordinating committees, with some last-minute inputs from Mayorga and some of Jesuit priests at the Catholic university. Archbishop Romero had approved it. It was a stirring promise of liberty, justice, and equality—economic as well as political—for all. Along with a few specifics—abolition of ORDEN, the right of peasants and workers to organize—were large doses of economic and social theory. The proclamation called for measures "that bring about an equitable distribution of the national wealth, while at the same time rapidly increasing the gross national product." There would be an agrarian reform, "reforms in the country's financial sector, taxes and foreign trade" in order to provide more "economic opportunities," and "measures to protect the consumer so as to counteract the effects of inflation."

Long after the original coup plotters and their lofty objectives had been crushed, officials in Washington and in El Salvador continued to pay tribute to the proclamation. But in reality the "beautiful promises" were "dead letters" almost before the airwaves that carried the news of them reached the not so distant corners of the tiny country.

The new government called itself the Revolutionary Governing Junta. But it was not very revolutionary, and it was even less a government. The government was, as it always had been, the armed forces.

A few days after the junta was announced, Colonels García and Nicolás Carranza, the archconservative vice-minister of defense, who was also appointed by Gutiérrez, called a meeting to introduce the civilians on the junta to the country's key military men. When the civilians arrived, they were stunned and disappointed to discover that the twenty-five to thirty military officers present were not the young officers who had planned and executed the coup but senior officers who had been placed in command positions by García.

The situation was tense. Mayorga and Ungo argued that it was necessary not only to effect structural changes in the economy but to begin a process of democratization. They tried explaining to the officers that the society had been repressed for so long that demonstrations, both from the right and from the left, were inevitable. "We told them, 'This is healthy, this is good, let them,' " recalled Mayorga. The military men called it chaos and said it would lead to a Communist takeover. Nevertheless, Mayorga and Ungo asked the commanders for a "quota of sacrifice," meaning they wanted the army to avoid using guns and tanks to break up demonstrations. García countered that some of the demonstrators were armed. The civilians protested that all they were asking was that the soldiers not fire first and that they use the restraint necessary to apprehend those who were armed, usually only with pistols, since it was hard to conceal automatic rifles. García and his subordinates bristled at the idea of taking orders from civilians.

A few weeks later, during another stormy session between the civilians and the officers, the former argued that if the massacres didn't stop and if the reforms weren't implemented, there was going to be a terrible bloodbath. Colonel Vides Casanova, commander of the National Guard, stood up. He reminded those present that in 1932 the country had survived the killing of 30,000 peasants. "Today, the armed forces are prepared to kill 200,000—300,000, if that's what it takes to stop a Communist takeover." Carranza spoke in agreement. García nodded approvingly. Majano was silent.

"In a word, we wanted restraint from the military, and in a word, they wanted bullets," said Mayorga, succinctly explaining the differences between the civilians and the armed forces. Bullets it was to be.

During one street demonstration the security forces killed 24 antigovernment protesters. When peasants occupied two ranches and a slaughterhouse, demanding wage increases and improved working conditions, soldiers stormed the properties, killing 35. The next day some 500 bloc members marched to protest the killings; troops opened fire.

The military was also intransigent on the proposed structural changes in the economy promised in the proclamation, especially the land redistribution program. Álvarez, the minister of agriculture, had drafted a decree freezing all transfers of properties larger than 90 hectares (222 acres) until the government had drafted the details of the agrarian law: what size properties would be affected; how compensation would be calculated; who would receive the expropriated lands. The decree was designed to prevent large landowners from making paper sales of their properties to family members and friends, thereby bringing the amount of the property in their individual names below the limit of any new law. The junta, since it had deposed the old government, held all the executive and legislative power and therefore had the authority to enact the decree with a stroke of the pen. But Gutiérrez and Andino balked, and García, who wielded considerable power even though he was not a member of the junta, insisted that it be approved by the Permanent Council of the Armed Forces (COPEFA). COPEFA had been established by the young officers who prepared the coup, as an advisory council to the government, to serve as an intermediary between the junta and the armed forces' high command. García never discussed the decree with COPEFA. But he did send it to the Supreme Court for its review—not only a delaying tactic but also highly improper since the court would have to rule later on the constitutionality of the decree.

In mid-December the decree was enacted, but by then it was too late. The issue that most publicly exposed the civilians' impotence and the army's omnipotence related to the whereabouts of the country's political prisoners and disappeared. No one knew the exact number of political prisoners and disappeared during the Romero regime, but it was several hundred. The junta named a special commission to investigate. Colonel Majano declared, "The gates of the country's jails will be open for them to look where they want to." Look, they did. Find more than a few, they didn't. "They were dead and gone," said Devine. "The army had thoughtfully destroyed the evidence." The families of the missing, backed by the archbishop and civilians in the new government, demanded that those responsible for the disappearances be held accountable. But the military was not about to permit that to happen.

In late December the moderates and leftists in the government threatened to resign unless the armed forces agreed to certain measures. Foremost among these was a reactivation of the young officers' council, COPEFA, which García had effectively neutralized. They also demanded that the armed forces stop intervening in labor disputes, that there be a dialogue with the revolutionary organizations, and that the armed forces acknowledge that the constitution had been suspended on October 15. (One of the first acts in any coup is suspension of the nation's constitution.) But the armed forces continued to claim certain privileges in the suspended constitution, and the businessmen's organization, ANEP, and other rightist groups argued, correctly, that the land redistribution and other economic restructuring that the new government was proposing were prohibited by the constitution. Above all, those threatening to resign wanted García ousted as the minister of defense.

The showdown came on December 27. The junta, the Cabinet, García, Vides Casanova, and several other senior military commanders convened in the Presidential Palace. "It was a rough session," Andino recalled.

Colonel Vides Casanova informed the civilians, "Colonel García is the man from whom we take orders, not the junta." He went on: "We have put you into the position where you are, and for the things that are needed here, we don't need you. We have been running this country for 50 years, and we are quite prepared to keep on running it." ´

The beleaguered civilians left the meeting knowing that it was all over. But Archbishop Romero asked them to postpone their final decisions until the armed forces formally replied. On January 3 the archbishop chaired a formal mediation session between the civilians and the military.

The armed forces rejected the civilians' demands.

Ungo, Mayorga, and at least thirty-seven of the highest-ranking government officials, including the heads of all the independent government agencies, resigned. The next day, January 4, Andino joined them, charging that the colonels in the army had capitulated to "rightist tendencies." Archbishop Romero, in his Sunday homily, praised those who had resigned for what they had tried to do for their country. And repeating an earlier plea he had made in person, the archbishop called on Colonel García to resign "out of honesty and as a sign that he seeks the genuine good." García ignored the plea. He was the only one of the eleven Cabinet ministers who did not resign.

The grand dreams of democracy, pluralism, respect for human rights, and structural changes in the economy were being crushed by Salvadoran reality. The armed forces were not about to turn the country over to civilians.

Frustrated by its inability to bring about immediate change or to end the rightist violence participated in by the security forces and, to a lesser extent, the army, the civilian members of the cabinet and junta resigned after two and a half months in office," the embassy noted in a Confidential cable on the first anniversary of the coup. It was an honest account. But that is not the way it has been presented publicly by the State Department, which has even rewritten the history of the collapse of the first junta.

Each February the State Department submits to Congress its thick report on human rights practices in countries throughout the world. The report dated February 2, 1981—prepared by the outgoing Carter administration—stated: "Unable to act effectively and frustrated by their own inability to agree on promised reforms and to control the security forces, the civilian members of the first post-October 15 government resigned after ten weeks." While the report conveniently omitted any reference to violence by the army—since the United States was backing the army, it did not want it tainted—it was markedly more honest than the report submitted in February 1982. That one was prepared by Reagan's team at State: Elliott Abrams, head of the human rights bureau, and Thomas Enders, assistant secretary for Latin America.

"The junta gradually disintegrated. Its civilian members, unable to act effectively and frustrated by their inability to agree on promised reforms, resigned after ten weeks," the report stated. Not only did Abrams and Enders omit any mention of the government violence as the cause of the collapse of the first junta, but they made no mention whatsoever of the violence by the army and the security forces.

The next year, the State Department reported: "In early 1980, the leftist participants abandoned this junta to join the extreme left in a situation of mounting civil strife," the report said. This was simply not accurate.

In fact, Andino, who could hardly be considered a leftist, resigned because the United States forced him to. He had intended to remain on the junta after the others had resigned. But then he was summoned to the embassy, where, he recalled, Devine and James Cheek, about to become deputy assistant secretary for Latin America, told him it would be "for the good of the country" and a "great sacrifice" if he resigned. Moreover, after resigning, he didn't join the "extreme left." He became president and director of four affiliates of Phelps Dodge in Central America. Nor did Mayorga, whom Devine described as "a very decent human being, he really cares about social justice," join the "extreme left." The engineering graduate of the Massachusetts Institute of Technology took his family to Washington, D.C., where he worked at the Inter-American Development Bank. Among the other so-called leftists who resigned: Manuel Enrique Hinds, minister of the economy, who became a leader in the National Association of Private Enterprise (ANEP), the country's most powerful, and conservative, business association; the vice-president of the Central Bank, who went to work for the World Bank; the vice-minister of planning, who went on to Harvard; the minister of planning, related by marriage to one of the Fourteen, who also went to the World Bank.

Not surprisingly, the Carter administration had welcomed the coup. At last Romero was gone, and State Department spokesman Hodding Carter III described the new government as "centrist and moderate." But Washington did little to help it survive. Devine, on a trip to Washington, prevailed on President Carter to send a letter of encouragement to the junta, which the Ambassador hand-delivered upon his return. But beyond that, "we sat on our hands," recalled Patt Derian, then the head of the human rights bureau. It's an assessment shared by many others who held high-level government positions at the time. "Nobody saw this as a major problem for which major decisions had to be made," explained a senior State Department official who was then in the Latin American bureau. There were no interagency or National Security Council (NSC) meetings convened to discuss how the United States should respond to events in this tiny, insignificant country. Nicaragua was still the most pressing issue in Latin America, and even it took a distant second place to the crisis in Iran, where the hostages had been seized on November 4, 1979.

The first junta probably could have been saved if the Carter administration had acted decisively—if, for example, it had insisted on the implementation of the land reform in November or December, instead of a few months later; if it had made it clear to the Salvadoran military that aid was dependent on its submitting to civilian control; if it had insisted on a thorough purge of all the officers closely linked to the violence; if it had reached out to Ungo, Mayorga, Andino, and the moderate military officers. But it did none of these things; indeed, in some cases it did the opposite.

There were reasons, other than just a lack of interest and concern, that the Carter administration was reluctant to back the new government forcefully. Intelligence reports from El Salvador referred to Mayorga, Ungo, and even Majano as leftists. The CIA station chief at the time, who had been there for about two years, had an "incorrigible bent to the right," said Robert White, who dismissed him soon after arriving as ambassador. But the damage had been done. "In the State Department, if you use the word 'leftists,' that's like one big black mark next to your name. That's a flashword," said policy planner Richard Feinberg.

These reports caused even more alarm at the Pentagon and NSC, which were arguing for military aid to the new government. The NSC was headed by Zbigniew Brzezinski, whose "hard-line anticommunism was just beginning to show itself about this time," said a senior Carter administration official. The embassy in El Salvador fed the hard-liners' fears with cables raising doubts about the ability of the

Salvadoran Army to control the insurgency. In fact, the guerrilla groups were not a serious threat at the time. In September 1979 the State Department reported to Congress that the largest of the Salvadoran guerrilla groups, the FPL, had a membership of 800, followed by the FARN with some 600. The ERP, according to State, was the "smallest terrorist group." No one was suggesting that they had received any arms or training from outside the country.

Nevertheless, two weeks after the coup, on October 30, the Carter administration publicly let it be known that it was planning to provide the new government with "significant" military assistance, principally tear gas, gas masks, and chest protectors. At State, the human rights bureau opposed the military aid. Derian argued that it was still too early to judge whether the new government was going to be any different from the previous ones, whether the civilians would be able to control the armed forces and bring about a meaningful reduction in the violence. The human rights advocates lost. The State Department endorsed the military assistance.

In El Salvador Archbishop Romero denounced the proposed military aid. "Even if it is only providing tear gas and protective jackets," he said during a Sunday homily after the announcement in Washington, "this will mean more confident repression of the people." He urged the United States "to condition its aid to purification of the security forces, a satisfactory resolution of the problem of the disappeared and punishment of those guilty." The Carter administration ignored the archbishop, as it had the human rights bureau. Not only was the aid not conditional, but it was sent even though the government of El Salvador had not requested it.

The amount involved was piddling, only $300,000. But its symbolic value, especially in view of the fact that it was disclosed the day after the Salvadoran security forces had killed at least twenty-four leftist demonstrators, was worth a marine division. It was a message—to García, to Vides Casanova, to Carranza, to the other hard-line military commanders—that they could ignore the civilians in the government because they had an ally in Washington. The message was reinforced a few days later. Six U.S. military advisers arrived in El Salvador. The civilian members of the junta had not even been consulted.

But Devine had discussed the military aid with Majano and Gutiérrez at a meeting in the Presidential Palace to which the civilians had not been invited. Devine liked the two colonels and frequently invited them to Saturday morning Danish and hot coffee on the patio of his residence. He shared their concerns that the situation was becoming chaotic, that force was needed to impose law and order, that the military institution had to be preserved. In late December Devine met with the young officers who had prepared the coup. He listened as they expressed their anger that the senior colonels were thwarting their plans for democracy and for armed forces that didn't brutalize their own citizens. Their view was that Gutiérrez and García were serving at their sufferance and that if they continued to issue unacceptable orders, they, the young officers, would remove them just as they had Romero. "You had to be impressed with these guys," Devine recalled. But he cautioned them that their attitude, especially their unwillingness to obey their superiors, bore the "seeds of destruction" of the armed forces as an institution. Devine spoke "the same kind of language that you could hear from the right, from García, Vides Casanova, and not the language of the young officers and not the language of the civilians in the government," recalled Mayorga.*

With the situation in El Salvador beginning to alarm the Carter administration, the State Department realized that Devine had to be replaced. It had already decided to send Robert White, but the rapidly escalating chaos—and the fear that a leftist government might emerge—demanded immediate attention of someone experienced. Carter summoned James Cheek, a career diplomat who had earned the esteem of many of his colleagues for speaking out against U.S. support of General Somoza in Nicaragua years before his overthrow. Cheek arrived in El Salvador during the final week of December, in the midst of the showdown between the civilians and the armed forces.

Cheek met with Ungo and Deputy Foreign Minister Héctor Oqueli to ask them to keep their moderate socialist MNR party in the government. They replied that they could participate in the government only if there were assurances that it would have control over the armed forces, that senior military commanders, including García, were removed, and that there would be a dialogue with the revolutionary organizations. Cheek could make no such assurances. "It was a deaf dialogue," Oqueli said of the conversation with Cheek.

*The United States may have helped García gain control in another way. According to a Salvadoran banker, a few weeks after the coup García deposited about $50,000 in his account, saying that it had come from the United States. In addition, García's deputy, Colonel Carranza, was being paid $90,000 a year by the CIA at the time of the coup, according to a report by Walter Cronkite on CBS, on March 21, 1984, and by Philip Taubman in *The New York Times* the next day. Presumably García and Carranza used the money to buy the loyalty of the officers they could not influence with their rank and personality. If so, it would follow a pattern that the CIA had employed in Chile. In his book about Kissinger, Seymour Hersh reported that the CIA "passed thousands of dollars" to military officers opposed to Allende.

The Carter administration's last chance to save the reformist-minded junta came when the civilians presented their ultimatum to the armed forces. But instead of declaring that future aid would be granted only if the armed forces agreed to submit to civilian control, the administration contributed to the collapse of the junta by providing the military with an alternative: the Christian Democrats.

As a condition for joining with the armed forces, the Christian Democrats wanted García out as minister of defense, Carranza out as vice-minister, and Colonel Francisco Morán relieved of command of the Treasury Police. The armed forces promised to meet these conditions. After the Christian Democrats had joined the government, the armed forces reneged, but the Christian Democrats didn't walk out, a pattern that was repeated frequently in the next three years.

The Christian Democrats had another condition: no one from the private sector on the junta. This meant Andino had to go. Cheek and Devine, as noted earlier, delivered the message. Andino was told that there was "great enthusiasm in Washington for the Christian Democrats—including Bob Pastor." Pastor, Brzezinski's Latin America expert at the NSC, was to play an active role in the next year in getting military aid for the Christian Democrat-military government.

The full extent of the U.S. activity in El Salvador following the coup is still unknown. In response to my FOIA request for all cables sent by Devine and Cheek between October 13, 1979, and March 11, 1980, the State Department refused to release sixteen. It is certain, however, that the task of getting the Christian Democrats and the military to agree to rule together was not an easy one for Devine and Cheek. The Christian Democrats and the armed forces detested each other then, and still do. "We were walking hip-deep through a swamp," recalled Devine. "It was like getting lions and tigers to forget each other's claws." García and the other commanders were told that if they tried to rule without the civilians, it would look like a continuation of the status quo since 1932. U.S. assistance would be jeopardized; favorable world opinion would be lost.

The lions and tigers might have been brought together, but the United States was now in the swamp. It had a government, but one that was "less broadly based than the previous junta," the State Department advised all diplomatic posts in a Secret cable in early January 1980. It was a government without support. The United States would have to supply that as well as the military aid that Archbishop Romero begged it not to send.

8

A PLEA IGNORED

BECAUSE you are a Christian and because you have spoken of your desire to defend human rights, I should like to express my pastoral point of view regarding what I have read and make a concrete request," Archbishop Romero began his letter to President Carter. The Carter administration had announced that it was sending $5.7 million in military assistance to El Salvador, a quantum shift, in both the size —eleven times the average amount of military assistance for each of the preceding thirty-three years—and the nature of the policy. The archbishop was passionately opposed to the aid. Military aid from the United States, he wrote, "instead of promoting greater justice and peace in El Salvador will surely increase injustice here and sharpen the repression that has been unleashed against the people's organizations fighting to defend their most fundamental human rights."

Romero read a draft of the letter during his Sunday homily. The worshipers applauded. Romero sent it on February 17.

The archbishop advised President Carter, "The present government junta and above all the Army and security forces unfortunately have not shown themselves capable of solving the country's problems, either by political moves or by creating adequate structures. In general they have only resorted to repressive violence, amassing a total of dead and wounded far higher than in the previous military regimes, whose systematic violation of human rights was denounced by the Inter-American Human Rights Commission."

Romero explained to Carter that "neither the junta nor the Christian Democrats govern the country. Political power is in the hands of the armed forces. They use their power unscrupulously. They know only how to repress the people and defend the interests of the Salvadoran oligarchy."

The junta that was forged in January, with the United States acting as broker between the Christian Democrats and the armed forces, retained Gutiérrez and Majano as the military representatives. On the civilian side were two Christian Democrats, José Antonio Morales Ehrlich and Héctor Dada Hirezi, and Dr. José Ramón Avalos Navarrete, an independent whose appointment caught almost everyone by surprise because no one in political circles had heard of him. A cardiovascular surgeon, he was to remain a virtual nonentity even though he served until the elections in March 1982. Héctor Dada had been the minister of foreign affairs in the first junta. Morales Ehrlich, a lawyer, was the secretary-general of the Christian Democrats and had been a vice-presidential candidate in the elections that the army stole in 1977. He had not given up on the possibility of democratic change, but two of his sons were members of revolutionary organizations.* Duarte, who had returned from seven years in exile in Venezuela after the coup in October, was not made a member of the junta, in large measure because he wanted to save himself for the elections, which he thought would be called within a matter of months.

Both the industrialists' association and the powerful business association, ANEP, railed against the new junta, charging that private enterprise was not represented on it. With their military allies, they, too, plotted a coup. Unequivocal statements by Acting Ambassador James Cheek that the United States was opposed prevented it.

The leftist organizations also condemned the junta and called on their members to prepare for an insurrection. The Communist party, after the collapse of the first junta, now supported the armed revolution. It was beginning to appear that the left might have enough popular support to topple the U.S.-backed government.

Early in the morning of January 22, the date chosen to commemorate the anniversary of the peasant uprising of 1932, crowds began to gather—in the center of the capital at Cuscatlán Park; to the north at the National University; on the west at an intersection shared by a bigger-than-life-size statue of El Salvador del Mundo. Poisonous

*"The extent to which El Salvador is a country at war with itself is reflected in the experiences of the Morales family," Warren Hoge of *The New York Times* wrote in a poignant article in which he contrasted their life-styles. "Mr. Morales spends his days in the presidential palace in a chandeliered office with beige taffeta curtains, champagne-colored carpeting and period furniture." His twenty-two-year-old son Antonio, who was a political prisoner, "occupies the upper berth of a bunk bed in the old high-ceilinged prison."

chemicals were sprayed on them from an airplane. But they weren't deterred. Peasants, factory workers, government employees, students, professionals; men, women, children; teenagers, old people—all had come to demonstrate against the government. Estimates of their number varied, ranging up to 200,000, but it was almost certainly the largest demonstration in El Salvador's history. As one column passed the U.S. embassy, there were chants of *"Cuba sí, yanqui no!"* They poured steadily down the Avenida Roosevelt, past gas stations, restaurants, Rosales Hospital, and the Hotel Alameda (where European journalists usually stayed), into the downtown business district, where department store walls were spray-painted with endless revolutionary graffiti. Banners identified the various popular organizations. Hand-lettered placards waved overhead demanded "Peace," "Justice," "Stop the repression!"

The atmosphere was festive and peaceful—until the marchers reached the center of downtown, where the low gray National Palace, badly in need of cleaning, fronts on a cement plaza-*cum*-parking lot, bordered on the north side by the ugly Metropolitan Cathedral. Snipers opened fire. All radio stations were taken over by the government for forty-eight hours, so that only the official version of events could be broadcast. Initially the government said the demonstrators fired first; later it blamed unknown civilians. Archbishop Romero said that the National Guard had fired from inside the National Palace. At least 21 demonstrators were killed; some 120 were wounded. The archbishop condemned the "irrational massacre."

The Carter administration defended its proposed military assistance with the argument that it was for "nonlethal" equipment. "Keep in mind what we are talking about is trucks, communications equipment, not weapons, in the usual sense, such as guns," the deputy assistant secretary of state for Latin America, John Bushnell, told the House subcommittee, which held hearings on the request. According to Defense Department documents, the equipment also included "night vision sights and image intensifiers"—perfected in Vietnam. More important, the argument that aid is "nonlethal" is disingenuous. For example, two-and-a-half-ton cargo trucks, which were part of the $5.7 million package, are used to transport soldiers into combat or to break up demonstrations. It was a "nonlethal" jeep, though not necessarily one supplied by the Carter administration, in which the national guardsmen drove to the spot where they raped and murdered the four American churchwomen. As for the three communications-monitoring sets, worth about $38,000 each, which were part of the "nonlethal" aid, they are "perfect for use against guerrillas and insurgents," a U.S. Army aide told Cynthia Arnson, who closely monitored U.S. aid to El Salvador.

ARCHBISHOP Romero's letter to Carter was greeted with "jubilation" in the human rights bureau at State, Patt Derian recalled, "but the general attitude was that he was interfering and trying to embarrass the President." Carter did not himself respond to the archbishop's plea; he had Secretary of State Vance do so. "We are as concerned as you that any assistance we provide not be used in a repressive manner," Vance wrote. The equipment and training from the United States, Vance sought to assure the archbishop, "will be designed to enhance the professionalism of the armed forces so they can fulfill their essential role of maintaining order with a minimum of lethal force."

When Bushnell read this portion of Vance's letter to the appropriations subcommittee, Representative Clarence D. Long, Democrat of Maryland, who had been in Congress for seventeen years, observed, "I have never heard us justify sending military arms to any country except on the highest moral principles. We have been doing it for a long, long time. That does not really satisfy me to hear bland assurances."

The Carter administration requested the military aid even though the problem in El Salvador was not seen as being caused by Cuba or Nicaragua. Bushnell told the subcommittee that "we don't have anything to suggest large-scale support from the Sandinistas for the left wing in El Salvador." Other State Department officials "acknowledge that there is little evidence to support allegations of a heavy supply of arms from Cuba," wrote *Washington Post* reporter Michael Getler in April 1980. One month later Ambassador Robert White told reporters there was "no evidence" that Nicaragua, Cuba, or any other foreign powers were helping "the enemies of the Salvadoran Government."

Archbishop Romero knew how the military aid would be used. In his letter to Carter the archbishop took note of the $200,000 worth of gas masks, bulletproof vests, and other "nonlethal" equipment that had been sent the previous November, along with six military advisers, who were to provide instruction in riot control. "You must be informed that since then the security forces, with their increased personal protection and efficiency, have been repressing the people even more violently. They do not hesitate to use their weapons and they shoot to kill."

The repression, which had caused the Carter administration to distance itself from the regime of General Romero, had only intensified under the Christian Democrat-military government that it was now vigorously backing. During the first three months of 1980 some 900 civilians were killed by the government forces, according to the church, exceeding the total for all 1979. "Ten bullet-ridden bodies of people who have 'disappeared' are found daily on city streets or provincial highways, while the armed forces are increasingly attacking protest groups they describe as 'subversive,' " *The Times'* Alan Riding reported from San Salvador in early March. In the space of a few days, the bodies of 11 union leaders from Santa Ana were found throughout the countryside. In San Salvador a twenty-seven-year-old leftist politician, Roberto Castellaños, and his twenty-three-year-old Danish wife, Annette Matthiessen, were picked up by the National Police. Their tortured bodies were found on a roadside forty miles from the capital. At another spot, two farm workers, ages twenty-five and forty, were found along with four unidentified bodies. During the weekend 11 students were killed by soldiers in San Miguel. When workers went on strike at Beckman, an electronics manufacturing firm owned by a California-based company, security forces stormed the building. The soldiers took three workers to a separate room, shot them in the head, then attacked a woman with a machete.

"I think there is some misperception by those who follow the press that the government is itself repressive in El Salvador," Bushnell told the House appropriations subcommittee. He asserted that the violence was "from the extreme right and the extreme left." It was during this testimony that he provided his grossly distorted picture of the violence in El Salvador and his conclusion that "the smallest part" of it was caused by the government security forces and army.

But during the last nine days of January, 162 persons were killed and 42 captured or disappeared by government forces, according to the Salvadoran commission on human rights. The commission reported that 38 had been killed when the army swept through Aguilares; 23, during a military operation in Coatepeque; 11, in Santa Ana. The embassy forwarded the commission's reports to Washington as "another indication of the level of violence in El Salvador." A report by Amnesty International to the Inter-American Commission on Human Rights, dated March 21, 1980, contains seven pages of incidents in which security forces, army units, or ORDEN killed unarmed civilians, usually peasants, around the country.

As it fueled the opposition, the repression sundered the Christian Democrats and the government from within. Less than two months after he had joined the junta, Héctor Dada resigned because "we have not been able to stop the repression, and those committing acts of repression disrespectful of the authority of the Junta go unpunished." He added, in his letter of resignation, that "the promised dialogue with the popular organizations fails to materialize." Three weeks later the mounting repression convinced three more high-level Cabinet officials that they could not in good conscience continue to serve in the government. The minister of economy, Oscar Menjivar, the minister of education, Eduardo Colindres, and the undersecretary of agriculture, Jorge Villacorta, all resigned. In explaining why, Villacorta said, "This war, whose dead are in the majority peasants and militants of the popular organizations, reflects who the security forces and the Army consider their principal enemies."

Within the Christian Democratic party there had been heated discussions about whether or not to join the government after the collapse of the first junta. In the interest of unity, the party reached a compromise whereby it would enter the government, but only on the understanding that the civilians be given control over the armed forces in order to halt the repression. That control never came; there was even an increase in assassinations of Christian Democratic mayors and party leaders, including Mario Zamora, the country's attorney general. In March the party was again split by the question of whether to remain or to withdraw. At its convention Duarte argued that the party should remain in the government and that he should replace Dada. There was considerable opposition to Duarte. Colonel Majano said that the young officers were opposed to him, and Morales Ehrlich also spoke against him. But Duarte had handpicked most of the delegates, and they supported him.

On the second day of the convention one-fifth of the delegates withdrew from the party, declaring that the Christian Democrats "should not participate in a regime which has unleashed the bloodiest repression ever experienced by the Salvadoran people." On the same day Héctor Dada, Rubén Zamora, Alberto Arene, who was the head of the government's peasant development agency, and Roberto Lara Velado, a party founder, resigned from the party. In their resignation statement the departing Christian Democrats said, "Respect for human rights is incompatible with the exacerbated and growing repression exercised against the popular organizations and against the people in general." Then, in reference to the land redistribution and nationalization of the banks and export trade, which had been announced a few days earlier, the resigning members said that "a program of reform with repression runs contrary to the fundamentals of Christian Democracy."

Archbishop Romero then called on the Christian Democrats to withdraw from the junta, arguing that their presence helped legitimize the repression. They ignored his plea, just as the Carter administration did.

In his letter the archbishop begged Carter, "assuming you truly want to defend human rights," to prohibit "all military assistance to the Salvadoran government" and to "guarantee that your government will not intervene, directly or indirectly, by means of military, economic, diplomatic, or other pressures, to influence the direction of the destiny of the Salvadoran people." He told Carter that "the people's organizations are the only social force capable of resolving the crisis. It would be totally wrong and deplorable if the Salvadoran people were to be frustrated, repressed, or in anyway impeded from deciding for itself the economic and political future of our country by intervention on the part of a foreign power."

He concluded the letter: "I hope that your religious sentiments and your desire for the defense of human rights will move you to accept my petition and thereby avoid any intensification of bloodshed in this tormented land."

Within the Carter administration, Patt Derian and the human rights bureau opposed the $5.7 million in military assistance. Derian argued that sending the aid was in violation of the provision of a 1974 amendment to the Foreign Assistance Act that prohibits military assistance "to any country the government of which engages in a consistent pattern of gross violations of internationally recognized human rights." El Salvador was surely such a country, Derian thought. In addition, she argued for the stick, not the carrot, as the approaches to aid were widely viewed. "I think you get nowhere bribing people, which is an unpleasant way to put it, I guess, but is kind of the way I see this whole carrot approach," she said later. "The only way you made an impact on those guys was to hit 'em with a board and have them understand that if you're going to get anything from us, you're going to have to clean up your act in very specific ways."

There was virtually no opposition in Congress to the $5.7 million in military assistance, even though it was a marked departure in U.S. policy toward El Salvador. Democratic Senators Edward Kennedy of Massachusetts and Edward Zorinsky of Nebraska registered public opposition, as did twenty-six members of the House, in letters to President Carter or in public statements. The $5.7 million was what is called reprogrammed money—that is, taken from money already authorized by Congress. The President could reprogram it—in this case for El Salvador—unless the House or Senate committees with jurisdiction voted against the reprogramming. Senator Daniel Inouye, Demo-

crat of Hawaii and chairman of the Subcommittee on Foreign Operations of the Senate Appropriations Committee, in a private poll of
subcommittee members found majority support for the administration's proposal, so he did not hold hearings. The Subcommittee on
Foreign Operations of the House Appropriations Committee held
hearings, at which Bushnell and Cheek presented the State Department's case. The Pentagon, which also sent witnesses, assured the
subcommittee that the assistance would enable the Salvadoran government "to more effectively counter subversion and terrorism from
the extreme left and right." It was an argument that was to become
routine during the Reagan administration. The reality, however, was
that the assistance would be used by the very people—that is, the
armed forces—who were responsible for most of the "terrorism." And
it was never used against the right.

A very important backer of the $5.7 million grant was Robert Pastor,
who was responsible for Latin American and Caribbean affairs at the
NSC during the Carter administration. Pastor's appointment and conduct irritated many people in the State Department. Traditionally
someone from the department had been appointed to the post. Not
only did Pastor lack diplomatic and government experience, but he
was young—barely thirty years old when he arrived at the NSC the day
after he had finished his examination for a Ph.D. at Harvard. "He
began making demands on ARA [the Inter-American affairs bureau at
State]," recalled Devine. The head of the bureau at the time, Terence
Todman, quickly told his staff "to treat his [Pastor's] memos as requests, not instructions." Derian described Pastor as a "a real roadblock" to the efforts of the human rights bureau in El Salvador.* Pastor's defenders say that he was reflecting the views and attitudes of his
boss, Zbigniew Brzezinski, a hard-line anti-Communist.

*After Carter had been defeated and Pastor left the NSC, he wrote prolifically
about El Salvador. His feature piece in *The Atlantic* contains one of the most
cogent analyses of the U.S. interests in El Salvador, concluding that even a
hostile regime there would not alter the "global strategic balance" or threaten
our *vital* interests as the Reagan administration contends. In *The New Republic,* the Op-Ed page of *The New York Times,* and scholarly journals, he argued
that the United States must seek to limit the political role of Latin American
militaries and criticized the Reagan administration for giving military aid too
freely to El Salvador. While at the NSC, Pastor referred to the Salvadoran
opposition as the Pol Pot left and terrorists; in his writings he has recognized
the need for negotiations with democratic elements within the Salvadoran left.
"It's almost as though when he came out of the White House, he became a new
personality," said Derian. "The things he's written since he left are sturdy,
sensible, reasonable."

Pastor viewed the $5.7 million in military assistance as the carrot to induce the Salvadoran military to go along with the Carter administration's push for land and economic reforms and respect for human rights. When Pastor learned that Murat Williams intended to testify in Congress against the military assistance, he called Williams at his farm in Virginia, where the former ambassador to El Salvador lived in retirement. Williams was shocked. He had never met Pastor. He listened politely as Pastor asked him not to testify against the aid. Williams replied that his opposition was consistent with that of Archbishop Romero. "Archbishop Romero is naïve," Pastor replied.*

Archbishop Romero's unceasing condemnations of the government repression and, directly or indirectly, the U.S. policy of backing the junta caused serious problems for the Carter administration. Not only was the archbishop beloved at home, but his voice rang throughout the world. He had been nominated for the Nobel Peace Prize in 1978 by 118 members of the British Parliament. Eighteen United States congressmen had endorsed the nomination.

But among high-level policymakers in the Carter administration, "there was a fear that he [Archbishop Romero] was a little too far over to the left," recalled Robert F. Wagner, presidential envoy to the Holy See for Carter. On two occasions after the coup Carter dispatched Wagner, former New York City mayor and eminent Catholic layman, to Rome in an effort to mute Romero's criticisms of the junta and to gain his backing of the U.S. policy. Wagner's last effort was in January 1980, when the State Department realized that the new junta could not survive without Romero's support. Pope John Paul II passed on the Americans' concerns and desires in a private audience with Romero, who had been summoned to Rome. The pope cautioned Romero "to be careful of ideologies that can seep into the defense of human rights and in the long run produce dictatorships and violations of human rights," Father Brockman wrote in his book about Romero's life. Romero responded respectfully, "But Holy Father, in my country it is very dangerous to speak of anti-Communism, because anti-Communism is what the right preaches, not out of love for Christian sentiments but out of a selfish concern to preserve its own interests."

In El Salvador Cheek met frequently with Romero, as Devine had

---

*After the telephone conversation Williams twice wrote to Pastor without receiving any reply. Many months later, when Williams mentioned Pastor's comment in a speech, Pastor finally replied. He did not deny calling Romero naïve, but he wrote that it did not reflect his "greatest admiration" for Romero. He also protested to Williams that he had thought it was a private comment. But when Pastor called Williams, he had identified himself as being with the NSC.

rarely done. In a Secret cable Cheek advised Washington that Romero's "consultations in Rome might have had at least some moderating effect." He noted that the archbishop had expressed his opposition to a Marxist takeover, that he had expressed "strong criticism of the extreme left" during a recent homily, and that he had adopted a "generally more benign attitude toward the PDC [Christian Democrats]."

After another meeting with U.S. officials, who had expressed concern about Romero's discussion of the political program of the popular organizations, Romero noted in his diary that it wasn't his desire to please the Americans, but to do what was best for El Salvador.

Archbishop Romero would not, could not, according to the dictates of his faith and conscience, remain silent about what was going on.

On Sunday, March 23, 1980, the cavernous cathedral was occupied, as it had been on many occasions during the past two years, by popular organizations demanding release of political prisoners and an end to repression. The protesters also had seventeen bodies they wanted to bury in the cathedral because they were afraid of being shot if they left to go to the cemetery. Romero disapproved of the occupation of churches, so he celebrated mass from the basilica—even though a suitcase with twenty-two sticks of dynamite had been found in the basilica two weeks earlier.

The mass was broadcast over YSAX, the church radio station, back on the air after the latest bombing. Romero began with an appeal to the popular organizations not to use churches as places of "political indoctrination, much less for military training." A few days earlier a policeman had been beaten and tortured by one of the popular organizations holding the cathedral. "We do not at all approve anything so cruel," the archbishop said.

Then he turned his attention to the other side, the government. The last week had been "tremendously tragic," with twenty-seven peasants killed in three military operations. He read from a report by Amnesty International charging that eighty-three persons had been killed between March 10 and 14. In La Laguna soldiers had killed a man and a woman and their thirteen- and seven-year-old children, along with eleven others; in Plan de Ocotes they had killed four peasants, including two children.

As he neared the end of his homily, the archbishop's voice sounded tired. "I would like to make an appeal in a special way to the men of the army, and in particular to the ranks of the National Guard, of the police, to those in the barracks. Brothers, you are part of our people. You kill your own peasant brothers and sisters. And before an order to kill that a man may give, the law of God must prevail that says: Thou shalt not kill! No soldier is obliged to obey an order against the law of God. No one has to fulfill an immoral law."

The worshipers interrupted him with applause. He seemed to gather strength, his voice rising. "In the name of God, and in the name of this suffering people whose laments rise to heaven each day more tumultuous, I beg you, I ask you, I order you in the name of God: Stop the repression!"

More applause. Prolonged yet dignified. By frail women in simple cotton dresses, by hunched men with wrinkled faces, by parents whose sons and daughters had disappeared.

It was the archbishop's last appeal.

A few days earlier, in a private home, Roberto d'Aubuisson had presided over a meeting of active-duty military personnel. They drew straws for the "privilege" of killing the archbishop, according to investigative reporters Laurie Becklund and Craig Pyes, relying on State Department cables and interviews with embassy officers. (The department has refused to release the cables.)*

After the mass on March 23, which had lasted nearly four hours, including his customary question-and-answer session with foreign journalists, Romero was more exhausted than usual. At a friend's house he took off his shoes and put his feet up in front of the television. Instead of his usual Campari, he had a scotch on the rocks. He watched a sad story about an old clown. "It's true," he said. "When one gets old, he's not good for anything."

The next day he went to his confessor. "I want to feel clean in the presence of the Lord," Romero told him. Then he began to prepare for the anniversary mass he was to celebrate for the mother of Jorge Pinto, whose weekly newspaper, *El Independiente,* had been bombed two weeks before. The mass had been announced in the newspapers,

---

*In February 1984, nearly a year after the Pyes-Becklund stories had run, former Ambassador Robert White told the House Subcommittee on Western Hemisphere Affairs that "beyond any reasonable doubt" D'Aubuisson had "planned and ordered the assassination of Archbishop Oscar Arnulfo Romero." White described the meeting in more detail. He said that D'Aubuisson had "summoned a group of about twelve men to a safe house" where the lots were drawn for the "honor" of assassinating the archbishop. A military officer who had not won the draw, and who was to become the embassy's informant many months later, was disappointed, so he gave bullets from his gun to the officer selected "in order that he might participate vicariously in the murder of the Archbishop." The man who carried out the execution was himself later executed during a soccer game, on orders from D'Aubuisson, who feared that he could not be trusted, White testified.

as had the fact that Romero would celebrate it. Some of his friends urged him not to do so. The threats on his life had been increasing. The Vatican had sent warnings. Romero had begun shifting the places where he slept. He admitted to sleepless nights, fearing a bombing or kidnapping.

But Romero went ahead with the mass, in the chapel of the cancer hospital run by sisters. He read from the Twenty-third Psalm. "The Lord is my shepherd. . . . Though I walk in the valley of the shadow of death, I fear no evil."

As he finished the final words of the short homily, a single shot rang out. Romero may have glimpsed his assassin at the rear door of the chapel and started to flinch. The bullet entered the left side of his chest, hit his heart, and lodged in his lung. He slumped to the mosaic stone floor behind the altar, at the foot of the large crucifix. Blood ran from his mouth and nose. He was rushed to a hospital, where he died. But before lapsing into unconsciousness, he uttered his final words: "May God have mercy on the assassins."

The next night terror seized the village near Ciudad Barrios where Romero had begun his life. Six young peasant men were dragged from their homes by National Guard soldiers. Ignoring family pleas, the soldiers bound and gagged the men, threw them into a pickup truck, then took them down the road and shot them. Another peasant was hacked to death outside his house.

In Washington, sixteen hours after Romero had been assassinated, the House subcommittee began hearings on the $5.7 million in military aid that the archbishop had so strongly opposed. Several congressmen wanted to postpone the hearing, out of respect. But the Carter administration was anxious to get the military equipment off to El Salvador as rapidly as possible. "We do not think at this point that the event should cause us to deviate from the course which we have embarked on in the government," Bushnell told the subcommittee as the hearings began on schedule. At the conclusion of the morning and afternoon hearings of witnesses, the subcommittee chairman, Clarence Long, suggested that the least consideration for the archbishop dictated deferring the vote. The next day, Wednesday, was the funeral, Thursday and Friday Congress would not be in session, and Monday, Long noted, was "always an awkward day to get any sizable group together for a vote." He suggested that the vote be taken the following Tuesday.

"Tuesday is a long time off," responded Bushnell. Long was irritated and reminded Bushnell that it had taken the State Department two and a half weeks to get the subcommittee the information it needed.

Representatives Jack F. Kemp (Republican, New York), David R. Obey (Democrat, Wisconsin), and Charles Wilson (Democrat, Texas) urged an immediate vote on the aid, but they were overruled by a majority of the subcommittee. When the vote did come, the military assistance was approved 6–3, with Democratic Congressmen Long, Julian Dixon (California), and Sidney Yates (Illinois) voting against it. Kemp and Obey voted for the aid, along with William Lehman (Democrat, Florida), Matthew McHugh (Democrat, New York), Virginia Smith (Republican, Nebraska), and C. W. Bill Young (Republican, Florida).

WHEN Vance's reply to the archbishop's plea not to send military aid arrived in El Salvador, Romero read it during his Sunday homily, on March 16. In his letter, Vance had assured the archbishop, "The United States will not interfere in the internal affairs of El Salvador." Romero told the gathered, "We hope that the events will speak better than the words." Among those attending mass that day was Robert White, who had arrived in El Salvador eight days earlier.

9

SEARCH FOR AN
ELUSIVE CENTER

EL Salvador was now a priority among United States concerns, at least in Latin America. To try to salvage what was beginning to look more and more like a hopeless situation, the Carter administration turned to Robert E. White, a career diplomat who seemed almost fond of taking on tyrants. In the State Department, and at the NSC, there was the familiar concern about dominoes. Nicaragua had "fallen" to the Sandinistas. The administration did not want another leftist government coming to power so close to the United States. But it also couldn't stomach the Salvadoran right. White's burden was to find a political center.

"While theoretically you may be an ambassador and buried in the bureaucracy, you are a proconsul, so far as we are concerned, because this needs it." It was not some jingoist with imperialistic designs who gave White this mission, but Senator Jacob Javits, the New York Republican respected for his distinguished moderation. During White's confirmation hearings, Javits continued: "You are going down there and work as an ambassador. If you only do that, the United States will not be well served. You really have to be an activist and take a chance with your career. If not, this just isn't going to go." But while Javits welcomed White's appointment, another Republican senator, the conservative Jesse A. Helms of North Carolina, was appalled. To Helms, White was an "extreme leftist," and his appointment as ambassador to El Salvador was "like a torch tossed in a pool of oil."

How prophetic both senators were. White's tenure in El Salvador was incendiary, at least in the view of the country's powerful rightists, who picketed his residence with placards calling him a Communist and telling him to go to Cuba. On one occasion, after D'Aubuisson had been arrested for plotting a coup, a pistol-packing crowd of chanting rightists kept White a captive in his own residence until he and his deputy drove through the gate in an armored Cadillac while marine guards dispersed the vigilantes with tear gas. Moreover, his outspoken criticisms of human rights abuses and his support of the land redistribution program earned him the tag of "social reformer" from the Reagan administration. Upon becoming secretary of state, Haig wasted no time in firing White.

White was a rarity among diplomats, especially those in delicate posts: He almost always expressed his views on the record. He called D'Aubuisson a thug—on the record. That was the quintessential Bob White, speaking his mind. At a briefing at the embassy White, just under six feet tall, walked into the small auditorium looking very diplomatic in his pinstripe suit. As he positioned himself behind a low table with a few microphones and tape recorders, the press officer, Howard Lane, began to explain the ground rules. "This is for background purposes. You can attribute it to a 'foreign diplomat' or—"

White interrupted. "Hell, no—what I have to say is on the record! You can attribute it to me."

"Brash." "Flamboyant." "Demonstrative." "Emotional." Such are the adjectives most frequently applied to White. His concept of social justice had developed during his Catholic upbringing. Descended from what he calls an Irish "two-boater" family—the poorest of the potato famine poor who needed two generations and two boat trips to get everyone to the United States—he was born in Stoneham, Massachusetts, in 1926. He enlisted in the navy when he was eighteen, served in the Pacific, then was forced to work for two years—his father had died—before entering and graduating from St. Michael's College in Vermont. White received a master's degree from the Fletcher School of Law and Diplomacy and studied in England as a Fulbright scholar. In 1955 he embarked on a Foreign Service career that was checkered by confrontations with Latin American dictators. In Nicaragua as the number two in the embassy in the early 1970's, he so angered General Somoza that the dictator demanded his recall. As a representative to the OAS meeting in Santiago, Chile, in 1976, White criticized the lack of press freedom under General Augusto Pinochet Ugarte. That riled Secretary of State Kissinger; a letter of reprimand went into White's personnel file. White stormed to Washington, threatening to resign if it wasn't expunged. It was. In Paraguay, where he was ambassador before being called upon for duty in El Salvador, White earned the animosity of that country's dictator, General Stroessner, because of his defense of labor leaders.

When White departed Washington for El Salvador, the CIA, Pentagon, and senior Latin hands at State didn't think much of his chances of survival; they told him he'd be back in two or three months—after the government had fallen. A thick CIA report predicted a leftist triumph. White, on his arrival, thought the greatest threat was from the right. Cheek had already prevented one rightist coup. Another was being plotted. In short, the U.S.-backed junta had little popular support within El Salvador. The business community thought Duarte and the Christian Democrats were Communists; the left thought the junta was too rightist. The church, even after the assassination of Archbishop Romero, continued to criticize the government because of its inability to control the violence. The junta members distrusted one another. Almost from the moment he joined the junta, Duarte wanted to be more than just a member. He wanted to be president. Majano opposed Duarte's aspirations. Meanwhile, Gutiérrez and García detested Majano. They didn't like his moderate to liberal views and feared that he was too popular, that he had the potential of becoming a populist leader like General Omar Torrijos in Panama.

Into this caldron plunged White, becoming the proconsul Javits had urged. During 1980 "the United States acted as the junta's foreign ministry, close domestic political counselor and propagandist, arbiter of internal disputes, liaison with business interests, consultant on agrarian reform and labor organizations, and, increasingly, military adviser," noted Richard Feinberg. In a real sense, it was Robert White who was all these things.

White had remarkable latitude in implementing and to a large degree even fashioning U.S. policy in El Salvador. Indeed, it would not be an overstatement to argue that there wasn't a Carter or U.S. policy, but a White policy. In Jimmy Carter's presidential memoirs El Salvador appears only once in the index, and likewise only once in Vance's account of his years as secretary of state under Carter. There is no index reference to El Salvador in Brzezinski's memoirs of his four years as Carter's national security adviser. During White's year as ambassador in El Salvador the Carter administration was preoccupied with the hostage crisis in Iran. White's freedom to operate was enhanced by the fact that Brzezinski's first deputy was David Aaron. White had been Aaron's boss in Guayaquil, Ecuador, when the latter was also in the Foreign Service. Aaron had complete trust in White's decisions and judgment. It was because of this relationship that White was able to end-run Pastor, whose support for the Pentagon's desires for large amounts of military assistance to El Salvador ran counter to White's policy.

After Carter had lost and White had been ousted, White became one of the harshest critics of the Reagan administration's policy toward El Salvador and as such a darling of the country's liberals. But White had no desire to see a left-of-center government in power in El Salvador. "He's a liberal, but he's antileftist," said an admirer. While he was ambassador, White described Ungo, Álvarez, and the other political leaders of the leftist opposition as "irrelevant fronts" for the guerrilla groups, which he, and others, lumped together as the "Pol Pot left." All the leftists wanted, he said repeatedly, was power for the sake of power. If he thought they were committed to improving the lot of the country's peasants and poor and of being more respectful of human rights than the government, he didn't say so, either publicly or privately. And he was not above interpreting events to denigrate the left. A prime example was the funeral of Archbishop Romero.

Tens of thousands jammed into the cathedral and the surrounding square and streets to pay tribute to the martyred archbishop. In what Christopher Dickey of *The Washington Post* described as "a panic-driven hell" at least forty were killed, many trampled to death as the suffocating waves of humanity fought for safety when shooting began. In a cable to the State Department, White said that "armed terrorists of the ultra left sowed panic among the masses and did all they could to provoke the security forces into returning fire. But the discipline of the armed forces held." That was also the version provided by the Salvadoran government. But twenty-three church leaders who were present, including bishops from Mexico, Ecuador, France, Brazil, Panama, Britain, and Ireland, signed a statement in which they declared that the panic began after a bomb had been thrown from the National Palace. That was followed by machine-gun bursts and shots, "which several of the priests present are sure came from the second floor of the National Palace," the bishops said.

The U.S. embassy obtained a copy of the church leaders' statement before it was published. In forwarding it to Washington, in a Confidential cable, White added that the embassy "along with all of the American press" found the account to be "severely distorted" and that the "strong weight of opinion, including international media reps, is that security forces did not start or participate in shooting." But the accounts by Dickey and by Joseph Treaster, who covered the funeral for *The New York Times,* do not show that the bishops' statement was "severely distorted." Nor do they support White's unequivocal conclusion that the extreme left had started the shooting and that the security forces had shown restraint. Treaster made no mention of who started the shooting, but he reported that a Mexican newspaper correspondent said he saw snipers firing from the windows of the National

Palace. Dickey concluded that there was not "any certainty about who started today's violence" and that "eyewitnesses who had taken different vantage points on balconies surrounding the plaza gave differing accounts on how it began." He reported that the leftists burned cars, which the bishops also noted in their statement, and that they were armed with pistols and contact bombs.

The point isn't so much who started the panic as the fact that the U.S. embassy promulgated the interpretation of events which fitted the policy. And the bottom line of White's policy was the same as Reagan's was to be: Stop a leftist government from coming to power in El Salvador. Their differences were on the means, not on the end. As White himself wrote in 1982: "Reagan is right to concern himself with denying communism a new foothold in the Western Hemisphere. He is wrong only in his methods." Reagan was to push for a military defeat of the left. From the beginning White had to fight Washington's desires to send advisers and military aid to El Salvador. White did, however, support the $5.7 million in aid in early 1980, much to the disappointment of Derian in State's human rights bureau. In a cable sent soon after arriving in El Salvador, White argued that the "modest amounts of communication and transportation equipment will not move us toward a military solution to a political problem but toward a political solution backed up by a competent, professional and restrained military establishment." He argued that the aid was "nonlethal" and that it was a "carrot" to induce the military to support economic and political reforms. Above all, as he explained later, "I'm a realist. I had to work with the Pentagon. To make enemies over $5 million in junk, of trucks, communications gear just wasn't worth it." Similarly, White let the Pentagon send in some three- and four-man mobile training teams (MTTs)—the government euphemism for military advisers. "You have to do something to keep them from going wild at you," White said in his own defense.

Many in the Carter administration wanted a military defeat of the left. But White had another approach. "If you don't want to go along with the revolution, then the only way to beat the extreme left is to alienate the extreme right," White explained. "You can't take on two armies at once. First, you break with the oligarchy and get the social reforms. Then you break with a faction of the military."

White, whose appointment was delayed by Senator Helms, wasted no time in becoming the activist Senator Javits had wanted and the torch in the pool of oil Helms had feared. Eight days after his arrival in El Salvador, on March 16, White attended a mass celebrated by Archbishop Romero. He attended the next week—Romero's final Sunday mass—as well. Though he was a devout Catholic, White's presence among the worshipers was as much a political as a religious statement. It was a clear, and frightening, message to the Salvadoran right. Lest there be any doubt, before he had been in El Salvador one month, White let the conservative business community know that it was no longer business as usual. In a speech to the Chamber of Commerce he assured his hosts that it was "very important that the armed leftist extreme not be victorious in El Salvador" and that the United States would do everything necessary to prevent that. This was just what the businessmen wanted to hear. But not what followed. "There is also, unfortunately, what you might describe as 'the enemy within,' and this would be the excesses of the security forces of this country and the inability to bring about order." There was more. He accused wealthy Salvadoran businessmen of financing the death squads and said that there "rests a heavy responsibility on the officer corps of the armed forces to put an end to the abuses." The die was cast: El Salvador's powerful and wealthy could no longer count on the unwavering support of the United States. (White said later that the Chamber of Commerce speech was also for "internal purposes"—to let the embassy officers know exactly what his policy was.)

He drove home the new U.S. position in early May, when D'Aubuisson, who had fled the country after the coup in October, returned with a well-developed plot to take over the country. D'Aubuisson had presented his views to conservative members of Congress, during a trip to the United States that was sponsored by the American Security Council. He told his receptive audiences that the Christian Democrats were Communists and that the U.S. policy was going to result in El Salvador's becoming another Cuba or Nicaragua. Upon entering El Salvador, he went from barracks to barracks with a videotape in which he displayed documents which he said showed that Majano had been a member of the Communist party of Mexico, a patently fraudulent charge. When the embassy learned of D'Aubuisson's plot, White told García, Gutiérrez, and anyone else in the military who would listen that if there were a coup, the United States would cut off aid. White was still enough of an unknown that the military commanders thought he might just be serious. The coup was thwarted.

When White arrived in El Salvador, he had found that the greatest threat to the survival of the junta was not the armed revolutionary left but the extreme right—the wealthy and their allies in the armed forces, such as D'Aubuisson, Carranza, and Vides Casanova. With his speeches and his success in derailing another coup, White had defused that threat—at least for the moment.

As for defeating the left, White frequently told reporters, "We'd have a revolution here even if there were no Cuba or Nicaragua." Therefore, his antidote would be what he was fond of describing as a "peaceful revolution that is non-Marxist and pro-democratic." For that to be successful, massive alterations in the country's economic system were necessary, so that the wealth was not so severely concentrated and the poor not so miserably poor. Poverty was a shrill siren of the revolution. Ameliorating it would lower the pitch. And since in El Salvador land was the measure of wealth, land redistribution became the linchpin of the economic restructuring, which also included nationalization of agricultural exports and government control of banks.

THE picture of the Regalado brother, a member of one of the Fourteen, hung crookedly on the washed-out bluish green wall, over the slatted shutters that swung open to a sweeping vista of palm trees and the lush green volcanic slopes. Lounging outside around a broken-down tractor, listless men, machetes dangling from the waists of their soiled trousers, explained that Regalado had owned the 1,500 acres of pasture where 900 head of dairy and beef cattle had once grazed. Now these men were the owners, along with the other peasants who had worked for Regalado, who had never lived on the farm. Asked how their present lives compared with their lot when Regalado was their boss, most of the men answered flatly, "The same." Then, as now, the men earned the equivalent of $36 every two weeks. "But we have faith," said the cooperative's president. "The land is rich."

San Cayetano was expropriated from Regalado and converted to a peasant cooperative as part of Phase I of the government's land redistribution program. During a visit I made to San Cayetano in 1982, the milking sheds were barren. Anticipating implementation of the land reform program, Regalado had slaughtered most of his beef herd and driven the rest to Guatemala, where he also took his farm machinery. Most other large landowners circumvented the new law, at least in part, in the same manner. A few miles from San Cayetano, at the 1,675-acre San Rafael el Provenir cooperative, only three pieces of farm machinery were parked under the corrugated tin roof of the machinery shed. Five small tractors, two combines, four trucks, and 1,200 head of cattle had been sold by the prior owner before the government acted.

There were three phases to the land reform* program, which was begun in March 1980 by the Christian Democrat-military junta. Under Phase I, farms larger than 1,235 acres were expropriated, with compensation, and converted to peasant cooperatives. Phase II was drafted to affect farms between 247 and 1,235 acres. Then there was Phase III, better known as the land-to-the-tiller law, whereby peasants were given the right to buy the tiny plots they had been working as tenant farmers or sharecroppers.

In an effort to transform the country's economy further, the government nationalized the banks. They were to be 51 percent owned by the government, with 20 percent of the stock to be sold to bank employees and the rest to private individuals. The third major provision of the economic restructuring program was the nationalization of the export of coffee, cotton, and sugarcane, which together amounted to about 75 percent of the country's foreign exchange earnings. These two measures were crucial if there was to be a meaningful assault on El Salvador's skewed income distribution. But they languished almost from the day they were announced, receiving only tepid support from the Carter administration and staunch opposition from Reagan.

The nationalizations did not accomplish the planned economic restructuring. They failed to bring important improvements in the economic lives of the intended beneficiaries and generated profits for the very class of wealthy individuals who were supposed to have shouldered the burdens of the economic changes, according to the economics department at the Catholic university in San Salvador. The U.S. embassy in El Salvador described the university as "academically credible," but the report, which was the only comprehensive analysis of the three economic programs, has been largely ignored since it was released in the summer of 1982—much to the relief of U.S. officials, who were trying to promote the appearance of significant economic change in El Salvador.

The university researchers found, for example, that in 1981, as in 1978, 19.4 percent of the banks' loans went to producers of the country's export crops, while the small growers of corn, beans, and other peasant staples received slightly less than 3 percent in both years. Similarly, after the bank nationalization, as before, some 4 percent of the borrowers received nearly half the loaned amounts. As for the

*There are often objections to the use of the word "reform" because it implies something positive. But the Salvadoran program is called land reform even by the Salvadorans bitterly opposed to it. Thus the land redistribution effort will be called land reform, without any value judgment intended.

nationalization of the coffee trade, it redounded principally to the benefit of the country's large private processors. Eight family-owned companies that processed 52 percent of the coffee before the nationalization processed 62 percent the year after. Furthermore, as a result of decisions by the state-run coffee-exporting agency, the private coffee-processing companies operated at 65 percent of capacity, while the processing plants owned by the government-created peasant cooperatives operated at only 31 percent of capacity.

"The most revolutionary land reform in Latin American history": That was the exclamation by Ambassador White, his successor, Deane Hinton, and nearly every other U.S. official in El Salvador and Washington during the Carter and Reagan administrations. "It broke the back of the oligarchy" was another popular cry. "Sweeping" and "radical" were among the more restrained adjectives.

Such superlatives are fine—to describe the land reform as it was written. But the reality falls far short. Many U.S. diplomats knew that the land reform wasn't all it was touted to be, that there were serious negatives, but they didn't say so publicly. "I don't think anyone who felt it was a mistake—and a lot of us did—ever spoke out because it was so basic to our policy that there would have been no point in speaking out," said a Foreign Service officer who held a senior position in the embassy in El Salvador. "It had become an American article of faith. It was a symbol for good-willed, decent, liberal Americans who want something good to happen in societies."

In a cable in January 1981 William Hallman, the embassy's political officer, wrote: "Land reform will prove illusory as a means either of producing greater national wealth or better distributing it." As for Phase I, he concluded that it has "resulted in the creation of government owned cooperatives which promise more of boondoggles and mismanagement than greater riches, although access of these cooperatives to the national budget, the nationalized credit institutions and U.S. assistance may improve the lot of those country people fortunate enough to be integrated into the system." Because Hallman's views ran counter to the glowing statements about the land reform from the Carter administration at the time, he had to send his cable through the Dissent Channel, a State Department procedure, rarely used, that is designed for those who cannot remain silent when their opinions are not acceptable to their superiors. The State Department refused to release any part of Hallman's cable under the Freedom of Information Act.

The department is covering up other negative reports about the land reform. A Confidential memorandum, written in 1982, noted that an evaluation of the land reform by the Agency for International Development, the agency responsible for the U.S. involvement in the effort, was "considerably more optimistic" than was warranted. Of the two-page memorandum, only two paragraphs, both devoid of any substantive comments, were released under a Freedom of Information Act request.

Like the coup of October 15, 1979, the land reform is shrouded in myths and misperceptions advanced by those whose political interests are thus served. Both conservatives bitterly opposed to the land redistribution and liberals who see it as another unwelcome example of heavy-handed Yankee imperialism charge that the Salvadoran program has a bold "made in the U.S.A." label stamped on it. In contrast, American officials have sought to portray their involvement as minimal. "The land reform now being implemented in El Salvador is a program developed by the Salvadorans, not by the United States," the State Department declared a few days after the program had been announced. "We understand that the Salvadoran Government has received the advice of private agrarian reform experts from several countries including the United States. This technical assistance was arranged entirely by the Salvadorans. The United States Government was not involved in planning the programs." This statement is disingenuous at best.

It is true that the basic provisions of Phases I and II were drafted by Salvadorans—principally Enrique Álvarez and his aides before the first junta collapsed. But the United States was involved, and it provided more than mere "technical" assistance. The American Institute for Free Labor Development's (AIFLD) man in El Salvador in early 1980 was Roy Prosterman, a law professor from the University of Washington. Prosterman, who speaks no Spanish, was asked by AIFLD to work on the Salvadoran program primarily because he had been a principal architect of the land reform program imposed by the United States in Vietnam. According to a "United States Government Memorandum," three days before the land reform was announced in El Salvador, Prosterman met with junta member Colonel Gutiérrez "and reached an agreement on two of Prosterman's proposed three changes to the ag reform law." Then, the memorandum continued, "Prosterman met with Archbishop Romero for two hours, went over the land reform, and the Archbishop said he would support the decree if the junta adopted it this week."

Ostensibly AIFLD is an independent labor organization affiliated with the AFL-CIO. But it has been, and remains today, as much an agency for the implementation of U.S. foreign policy as the agencies listed in the State Department directory. In the past, and possibly still today, AIFLD has been a cover for the CIA. Former CIA officer

Philip Agee, in his book *Inside the Company: CIA Diary,* described it as a "CIA-controlled labor center financed through AID." Agee operated in South America in the 1960's, when, he wrote in his diary, AIFLD's "first priority is to establish in all Latin America countries training institutes which will take over and expand the courses already being given in many countries by AID. Although these training institutes will nominally and administratively be controlled by AIFLD in Washington, it is planned that as many as possible will be headed by salaried CIA agents with operational control exercised by the stations." A key CIA agent who worked under the AIFLD cover was William C. Doherty, Jr., according to Agee. Doherty is today the executive director of AIFLD. He denies any past or present connection with the CIA.

An analysis of Agee's book by the CIA right after its publication in 1975 affirmed his reporting without exception and repeatedly referred to it as "complete" and "accurate," specifically including the parts about the AFL-CIO institutes such as AIFLD, according to Jonathan Kwitny, who provides a detailed look at AIFLD in his book *Endless Enemies.* Six former CIA operatives, in interviews with Kwitny, corroborated Agee's assertions about the connection between AIFLD and the CIA. Several of them said that the CIA funneled money to AIFLD through AID.

One or both of the AIFLD employees who were gunned down in the coffee shop of the Sheraton Hotel in San Salvador in January 1981, Michael Hammer and Mark Pearlman, may also have been CIA agents.

"Just recently two Americans have been killed in Salvador. Apparently they were some kinds of undercover persons, working under the cover of a labor organization," the U.S. solicitor general, Wade H. McCree, Jr., blurted out during a Supreme Court argument two weeks after the men had been killed. The suggestion came in response to questions from the justices during a case involving the authority of the U.S. government to revoke Philip Agee's passport. After his stunning statement had sent reporters scurrying for more information about the men's activities, McCree said that his remarks had been misunderstood and were intended to be hypothetical. The CIA declined to comment. AIFLD said it had "no knowledge" about whether or not Hammer and Pearlman had any relationship to the CIA.

There are other indications, albeit circumstantial, that Hammer had some connection with the intelligence agency. Since his student days at the Georgetown University School of Foreign Service in the early 1960's, he had been working for AIFLD, his service covering the years when the links between the institute and the CIA are least in doubt. After his murder the State Department, according to classified documents, made an unusual effort to ensure that highest-level Carter administration officials appeared and made remarks at his funeral. No similar effort was made on behalf of Pearlman or the four American churchwomen who had been killed in El Salvador one month earlier. Finally, Hammer was given a hero's burial in Arlington National Cemetery on specific authorization of President Carter.

AIFLD grew out of the Alliance for Progress, funded initially by the AFL-CIO and many of America's largest corporations, including Pan American World Airways, ITT, Kennecott, and Anaconda, all of which had extensive Latin American operations. Its stated purpose is to train labor leaders in Latin America, leaders who will be anti-Communist, antileftist, and pro-U.S. Similar AFL-CIO institutes operate in Asia (Asian-American Free Labor Institute) and Africa (African-American Labor Center). Over the years AIFLD began to rely more and more on the U.S. government for its funds. In 1967 the Senate Foreign Relations Committee inquired into AIFLD's activities. A report by committee staffer Robert Dockery, today a legislative aide to Senator Christopher Dodd, Democrat of Connecticut, noted that AIFLD had "de facto quasi-official status in the formulation and implementation" of U.S. policy in Latin America. Senator J. William Fulbright, Democrat of Arkansas, once snapped that "the price we paid" for the AFL-CIO's support of the war in Vietnam was AID's funding of AIFLD.

Today AIFLD could not exist without AID funding, which represented more than 95 percent of the organization's $10 million budget in 1983. AID has given AIFLD $5 million for its program in El Salvador. "It is a small country but our largest program," said AIFLD spokesman John J. Heberle. In return, AIFLD has provided crucial support for the U.S. policy, even to the extent of backing off some from its insistence that the killers of its two employees be brought to justice. In 1983 Representative Long added to the foreign aid appropriations legislation a condition that 30 percent of the $64.8 million requested for El Salvador would be suspended unless the Salvadoran government brought to trial the killers of the four American churchwomen and the two AIFLD employees. Although the Reagan administration was opposed to the condition, it said it could live with the proviso relating to the women, but not to the AIFLD workers. The administration knew that the highest levels of the Salvadoran military, and Roberto d'Aubuisson, were linked to the slayings of Hammer and Pearlman. One congressional aide sent two memos and made five calls to Doherty to ask for AIFLD's support for Long's condition. The calls

were not returned. AIFLD did nothing to ensure that the proviso relating to the men remained in the legislation, and it was removed before
the bill was passed by Congress. AIFLD, which has lobbyists who work
Congress, said its inaction was due to a "lack of human resources."
(The Roman Catholic Church leadership in the United States lobbied
heavily for the provision relating to the women.)

AIFLD, which was expelled from El Salvador in 1973 but returned
after the coup in 1979, has demonstrated in other ways that it is more
concerned about U.S. policy than about the interests of Salvadoran
peasants. It tried to subvert the land reform program that was being
considered by the first junta. AIFLD was opposed to taking land from
all the largest landowners, arguing instead that only one or two farms
be expropriated and converted to peasant cooperatives, "as pilot projects," said Leonel Gómez, deputy director of the Salvadoran Institute
for Agrarian Transformation (ISTA) at the time. The AIFLD representatives also tried to persuade José Rodolfo Viera not to take the job
as head of ISTA, offering him a position with AIFLD at $1,000 a month.
But after consulting with Archbishop Romero, Viera, a peasant with
only three years of formal schooling, became the ISTA director. At that
point AIFLD rented him a suite at the Sheraton, "for no reason at all,"
said Gómez. "They were just trying to buy him. But they couldn't."

AIFLD did, however, effectively buy the largest Salvadoran peasant
union, known by its Spanish initials as the UCS, and the Democratic
Popular Unity (UPD), an umbrella organization for four labor groups.
Peasant unions were banned from 1932 until the late 1960's, when the
government set up the UCS with assistance from AIFLD. It was about
that time that Michael Hammer first worked in El Salvador. When
AIFLD became involved with the UCS again in 1980, it paid some 400
UCS members salaries of $160 a month—a hefty amount for a peasant
—to work as promoters, going into the countryside to explain the law
and seek new members. Each peasant paid 25 centavos (about 60
cents) a month to be a member of the UCS; the rest of the organization's annual budget of nearly $2 million came from AIFLD. The UCS
has become little more than an alter ego for AIFLD and the U.S. policy.

During one crucial period when President Reagan had to certify
that progress was being made in the land reform program in order to
continue military aid to El Salvador, the UCS complained in a letter
to Duarte that "the failure of the agrarian reform process is an immediate and imminent danger." Just three days after that negative letter
had been made public, in a front-page story by Karen De Young in *The
Washington Post,* AIFLD released another letter purportedly written
by UCS leaders, this time praising the Duarte government's efforts in

behalf of peasants. This letter was the basis of a front-page story in *The New York Times* under the headline SALVADOR PEASANTS PRAISE LAND POLICY.

The letter was dated January 25 and purportedly written in El Salvador. AIFLD made it public with a press release on January 28. But mail does not arrive from El Salvador in three days, and the name of one of the UCS leaders, Samuel Maldonado, who supposedly signed the letter, was misspelled. In fact, the letter was written by AIFLD in Washington.

AIFLD has used the UCS and its leaders on other occasions, flying them to Washington to testify before congressional committees skeptical about continuing aid to El Salvador. But AIFLD leaders have never allowed them to say publicly what they voice in private, such as their support for negotiations to end the war.

When it comes to Phase III of the Salvadoran land reform, the land-to-the-tiller law, there can be no doubt that it was a U.S. program, in spite of State's insistence that the United States provided only technical assistance. Phase III, also called 207—the number of the government decree enacting it—"had to be shoved down their throats," said a diplomat noting the nearly universal Salvadoran government, civilian and military, opposition to it. An internal AID document described Phase III as having been "designed virtually in its entirety by Americans, and slipped into legislation without their [the Salvadoran government's] being consulted. The fact is known and resented."

The land-to-the-tiller law was Prosterman's idea. It was one of the changes in the program that he had pressured Gutiérrez to accept at their meeting in early March. Prosterman argues: "Douglas MacArthur pushed through the sweeping land reform in Japan after World War II, transforming the tenants into small family farmers, which effectively destroyed the communists as a political force, and helped set the stage for the economic miracle in that country. Chiang Kai-shek, with U.S. support, carried out an equally sweeping land reform in Taiwan after losing the mainland, with equally positive results, as did South Korea, just before the North invaded in 1950 (which is a key reason why there was never any 'behind the lines' problems in that conflict)." These land reform programs, Prosterman insisted, are a "strikingly better model for other Latin American countries" than what had been tried in Chile and Peru.

"The Salvadorans used to get amused at Prosterman sometimes," recalled White. "His frequent allusions to Taiwan, Japan, Vietnam. That's not Central America. He didn't know anything about Latin America." But Prosterman knew how to stop a leftist revolution—or thought he did. To a hostile audience of Salvadoran businessmen he argued that the land-to-the-tiller law would "breed capitalists like rabbits" and that there was no one more conservative than a landowner. And even though White said he didn't think Prosterman knew much about Latin America, he, too, was enthusiastic about land to the tiller. "It was going to build a middle class, a group of people who had a stake in society," he said.

But there was opposition to the law, even among Salvadorans and American officials who recognized the need for Phases I and II. They pointed out that a considerable number of Phase III parcels—all plots smaller than seventeen acres were affected by the law, but most of them were only two or three acres—were owned not by wealthy individuals but by schoolteachers, shopkeepers, widows, and others who had managed to save enough money over the years to buy a plot of land, which uninterested in farming themselves, they rented. Phase III, because it was hastily drafted to thwart the leftists' appeal, did not take into account any hardship cases.

There were also serious economic and agricultural deficiencies in the program. In a comprehensive report on the Salvadoran land reform program, Oxfam America, the Boston-based humanitarian and development organization, noted that the law altered the peasant practice of crop rotation. Under the renting system, a peasant moved to a new plot every couple of years, allowing the soil of his former field to lie fallow and regenerate. But when a peasant owns a tiny plot, he is forced to plant every available inch every year in order to feed his family. The soil is quickly depleted. From an agricultural and economic perspective, it would have been wiser to combine the small plots into cooperatives owned by several peasant families. Economies of scale would have operated, and while the farmers had grown enough corn or beans in one area to feed everyone, another section could have been left fallow.

Gómez and Viera, the ISTA officers, were also opposed to the land-to-the-tiller program—not because of the concept but for the practical reason that the government did not have the resources to implement it while it was also trying to carry out Phases I and II. Prosterman countered that land to the tiller was self-executing, that a peasant need only present proof that he had been working the parcel as a tenant for the prescribed period and title would automatically be issued to him.

In later months and years American diplomats and AID officials realized that the opponents had been right on many counts. The land to the tiller's "bequests upon the landless will be largely at the expense of small investors and those whose lives were improved by the chance of inheritance," Hallman, the embassy political officer, wrote in his January 1981 Dissent Channel cable. "This is not a political net plus." An AID report noted: "If campesinos were to cultivate a single plot with poor soil on a steep slope for three years in succession, it would be converted to a sterile desert." And the law was hardly self-executing. "It is abundantly clear that Decree 207 is not, by any stretch of the imagination, 'self-executing,' " said another AID report. When 207 was enacted, the government said some 150,000 rural families would be beneficiaries; three and a half years later, as of November 1983, only 4,767 definitive titles, and 53,401 provisional ones, had been issued.

But in the spring of 1980 the Americans didn't think they had time to examine all these concerns. Land reform was hastily enacted because something had to be done to counter the growing strength of the left. "It was rushed through more for its political impact than its social impact," White said. "The left fears land reform," Prosterman assured the Salvadoran businessmen. "It deprives them of their most valuable weapon in implementing revolution because they can no longer appeal to the landless." He even went so far as to declare that "the leftist onslaught will be effectively eliminated by the end of 1980."

Of all the myths generated by the land reform, this is one of the most pervasive: that it took the banner from the left. It was a "logical conclusion," said one diplomat, but "no one ever offered us any proof—and the press never questioned it."

The land reform probably did take some of the wind out of the revolutionary sails, but not nearly to the extent that American and Salvadoran officials proclaim. For one thing, the program just didn't benefit that many people. "The overall numbers of people benefited [under Phase I] are relatively small," noted a Confidential State Department memorandum written two years after the program had begun. Only about 30,000 peasant families have become cooperative members under Phase I, the one phase most fully implemented. Even if all three phases were completed, there would still be 1.8 million Salvadoran peasants without land. More important, giving a peasant title to a plot of land won't bring the schools, water, electricity, and health care that have more meaning for the daily lives of peasant parents and their children than a piece of paper that bestows certain legal rights. It is also debatable whether peasants will be better off as the owners of the cooperatives than they were when they were working for an absentee landlord. "Many of the people working on the [Phase I] cooperatives may not be really aware of much change," noted a Confidential State Department memorandum in March 1982. "Some of them are even being managed by the same people who were formerly the agents of the large land-owners, so the net impact is lessened."

A significant reason that the real benefits of the land reform program did not match the rhetoric was that Phase II was never implemented. The Carter administration was ambivalent about Phase II—Pastor, at the NSC, thought it was a mistake—and the Reagan administration was unequivocally opposed. But the Salvadoran peasants desperately wanted it. Maldonado, the head of the UCS, said in an interview in mid-1982 that U.S. aid should be conditional on the implementation of Phase II, an opinion that AIFLD did not have him make publicly in any letters or congressional appearances.

If the purpose of the land reform is to effect a meaningful distribution of the wealth, as opposed to being primarily a political tactic to stop the revolution, then Phase II is essential. Many wealthy landowners avoided losing their lands under Phase I by subdividing them among family members into farms that were within the Phase II size —247 to 1,235 acres. Moreover, under a fully implemented Phase I, there would be some 325 cooperatives, affecting only 15 percent of the nation's farmland and benefiting 34,658 families, or 7.2 percent of the total farm families. Phase II, on the other hand, would have affected some 1,700 farms, covering 18.5 percent of the farmland and 50,000, or 10.5 percent, of rural families. From the perspective of redistribution of the wealth, only 13 percent of the nation's coffee is cultivated on Phase I properties, at least 30 percent on Phase II-size farms.

The Salvadoran land reform was designed to prevent a revolution. This is in contrast with the land reform in Nicaragua, which was designed to implement one. It is beyond the scope of this book to examine the Nicaraguan reform in any detail, but Lawrence Simon of Oxfam America, who has studied both countries' land reform efforts, described the Nicaraguan project as "more democratic and sweeping." It is more democratic in that the Salvadoran program was "imposed from abroad or above"—as Archbishop Romero said—while Nicaragua's was designed with considerable input from the peasants, who at one point marched on Managua to demand, successfully, that the Sandinista government expropriate and distribute more lands. But though the Nicaraguan program is more sweeping—affecting a greater percentage of farmland and rural families—it is also less radical in some respects than El Salvador's. While the Sandinistas took some lands for political reasons—from people who had fled the country and from those who joined the counterrevolutionary forces—productivity, not size, was the principal criterion used by the Sandinistas in deciding which farms to expropriate. One 44,000-acre privately held sugarcane plantation, for example, was not touched by the Nicaraguans.

There is another, and perhaps more significant, reason why the Salvadoran land reform didn't silence the revolutionary surge or generate more converts to the government: The repression continued unabated.

O N July 18 [1980], in a surprise move at night, the Army surrounded the Hacienda, which is called San Lorenzo, obliging its members that were on watch to lie face downward, then with their hands against the wall accusing them of being Communists, and tying up cooperative member Pedro Antonio Mijango. They took him away and the next day he was found dead near the road to Santiago de María."

Thus did the members of the Santa Catalina Agricultural Production Cooperative Association describe their plight in a plea to Archbishop Rivera y Damas. After this raid, they wrote, "all the cooperative members were terrified and did not go to town that night. Eight days later when they went to work they found the storehouse and part of the roof burned, with all the fertilizers completely destroyed, all the irrigation equipment, furnishings, agricultural containers, etc." The army returned again one month later, in August. "The Army put all the cooperative members and other workers face downward in the cultivated areas on top of ants' nests, tied up several of them." This time two members of the cooperative were seized by the soldiers, "taken to the edge of the Hacienda and publicly assassinated in a ravine." After that "no one came to work, much less to do guard work, and we lost in crops 80 manzanas [about 136 acres] of corn, 60 [102 acres] of millet, 2 [3.4 acres] of tomatoes, 1 [1.7 acre] of chile, the small projects of onions, peppers, jicama fruit and 8 manzanas [13.6 acres] of coffee, and things of lesser value such as wire, wood, tools, etc." The peasants concluded their letter to the archbishop: "We hope you will forgive us for having to add one more problem to your many concerns but after having reflected on who we might turn to, we decided that you were the most appropriate."

Another of the myths fostered by U.S. officials is that the land reform demonstrates that the Salvadoran military is no longer in service to the country's oligarchy, that after the coup it was transformed "from an institution dedicated to the status quo to one that spearheads land reform," as the head of State's Latin American bureau, Thomas Enders, proclaimed in 1982. In a similar vein, when the Subcommittee on Foreign Operations of the House Appropriations Committee was considering the Carter administration's request for $5.7 million in "nonlethal" aid in early 1980, the State Department's John Bushnell argued that the aid would be a "symbol" to those military officers who are "committed to reform." Moreover, he assured the congressmen, the military aid was needed so that the armed forces could "provide security to these farmers who have received land. To do that they need transport and communications equipment so they can respond when there is an incident and provide security in the countryside."

But about the only evidence that the military was supporting the reforms came on the day they were announced, when army units surrounded the banks and occupied many of the Phase I properties to prevent any interference with the expropriations. What happened after that, U.S. policymakers didn't bother to tell Congress and the American public. Salvadoran officers used the American trucks and communications equipment not to spearhead reform but to thwart it by continuing to repress the peasants, as they always had.

"How can this present process succeed if the peasants are repressed on a daily basis merely for organizing themselves?" Christian Democrat Héctor Dada asked rhetorically in his resignation letter submitted when he left the junta a few days before the land program was announced. "How can this process hope to reach fruition when the organizations representing thousands of peasants have not even been consulted while, to the contrary, the daily and growing repression against those organizations renders impossible any dialogue with them? How can this process serve democracy if, far from the democratic framework in which the Party envisioned it taking place, it is carried out under a state of siege?"

The state of siege was declared on the day the reforms were announced. It was to be in effect for thirty days. Ritually, every thirty days, except for one very brief period in early 1982, it has been extended for another thirty days.

"In reality, from the first moment that the implementation of the agrarian reform began, what we saw was a sharp increase in official violence against the very peasants who were the supposed 'beneficiaries' of the process," the deputy agricultural minister, Jorge Villacorta, wrote in his resignation letter, submitted a few weeks after the reforms had been announced.

It was reform with repression.

It was barely light when the soldiers pushed through the creaky gate into El Peñón, a farm near the Pacific. A few days earlier the peasants had elected the leaders of their cooperative. The soldiers had a list of the names. From the lines of peasants going into the fields for the day's work, they pulled out eight, took them down a dusty road, past the oxen lugging carts, lined them up against a dirt bank, and executed them.

At San Francisco Guajoyo, the largest original UCS cooperative, the assassins arrived at about three-thirty in the morning, while the 160 families were sleeping. They were dressed in military uniforms; a small armored personnel carrier was brought along in case things got out of hand. The men went from door to door, rounding up peasants whose names were on a list. ISTA employees showed their identification. To no avail. Fourteen peasants were shot, as the other members of the cooperative were forced to watch. Junta members Morales Ehrlich and Colonel Gutiérrez told AID officials that the perpetrators of the massacre were guerrillas who had dressed in army uniforms and stolen the small tank. But one person had survived. When Leonel Gómez, the ISTA deputy director, and an AID official found him in the Santa Ana hospital, they spirited him away, knowing that survivors are often hunted down and killed in their hospital beds. He was laid on a mattress in the back of a pickup truck, with the AID man holding his plasma bottle. The survivor provided the details: The killings had been carried out by the National Guard. Concerned AID officials visited Guajoyo after the incident. A few days later, according to a classified "Memorandum to File," the Guard returned and killed more peasants.

El Peñón, San Francisco Guajoyo, Santa Catalina weren't random or isolated incidents. They were part of a pattern. According to an AIFLD memorandum, 184 peasants, government employees, and others associated with the land reform were "killed violently" during the eight months after the reforms had been enacted. Gómez, who tracked the repression for ISTA, testified before the House Subcommittee on Inter-American Affairs that between March and December 1980, 240 leaders of cooperatives were killed. AIFLD and Gómez blamed the government for most of the killings.

The land reforms "have been attacked very strongly, from both the Right, so-called, and the Left, so-called," Jeane Kirkpatrick declared soon after becoming Reagan's ambassador to the United Nations. In one quick stroke she had absolved the government from any responsibility and accused the left. She was wrong, on both counts. But she was not alone in that assessment.

The obverse of the myth that the Salvadoran armed forces respected the land reform was that the left attacked it. Bushnell, when he was arguing for the $5.7 million in military aid, told the congressional

The foyer of the Christian Democratic party headquarters, February 1980. Ignoring requests from Christian Democrats in the government not to use military force, the Salvadoran military deployed small tanks and soldiers with automatic rifles to dislodge the members of one of the "popular" organizations who were occupying the headquarters to protest the repression. After the protesters had abandoned the building, military officers sorted out the leaders, took them back inside, and murdered them. The State Department commended the Salvadoran military, during a congressional appearance, for having kept the situation "under control."

Etienne Montes/GAMMA

United Press International Inc.

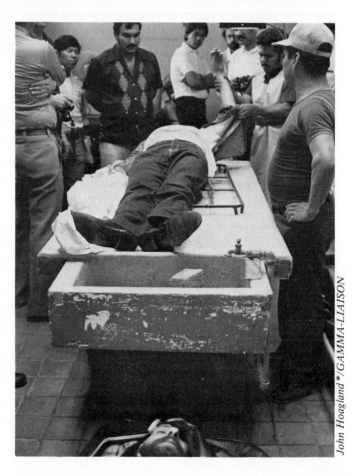

Above: Left to right, Carlos Eugenio Vides Casanova, José Guillermo García, José Antonio Morales Ehrlich, and José Napoleón Duarte.

Right: The bodies of American land reform workers Michael Hammer and Mark Pearlman in the morgue hours after being gunned down in the Sheraton Hotel, January 1981.

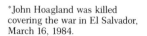

*John Hoagland was killed covering the war in El Salvador, March 16, 1984.

John Hoagland*/GAMMA-LIAISON

© Susan Meiselas/Magnum Photos, Inc.

Left, top: The site of the crude grave at the time the bodies of four American churchwomen were found, December 4, 1980.

Left, below: Robert E. White (U.S. ambassador, March 1980–January 1981) talking with a Salvadoran peasant and Father Paul Schindler at the grave site.

John Hoagland/GAMMA-LIAISON

Mattison/LIAISON Agency

James Nachtwon/Black Star

Left: Deane R. Hinton—President Reagan's first ambassador to El Salvador, 1981–1983. *Right:* Colonel John David Waghelstein—senior U.S. military adviser in El Salvador, 1982–1983.

Below: A U.S. adviser instructing young Salvadoran soldiers.

John Hoagland/GAMMA-LIAISON

Below, top: Left to right, guerrilla commander Ana Guadalupe Martínez; president of the Democratic Revolutionary Front (FDR) Guillermo Manuel Ungo; and a member of the FDR's political-diplomatic commission, Rubén Zamora, at a news conference in Mexico City in February 1984.

Below: Peasant members of the guerrilla forces in northern Morazán, where the author traveled in January 1982.

Below, top: Father Rogelio Ponselee at the funeral for twelve-year-old Luis, a messenger who was killed during a battle, in guerrilla-controlled northern Morazán, January 1982.

Below: Military commanders in Morazán, January 1982. At the far left is Jorge Meléndez, the senior commander in the zone. The short man with a beard is Leoncio Pichinte, who barely escaped death when government forces killed Enrique Álvarez and other FDR leaders in November 1980.

Raymond Bonner

United Press International Inc.

Above: Victims of the massacre at Mozote, January 1982.

Left: Assistant Secretary of State for Inter-American Affairs Thomas O. Enders and Deputy Assistant Secretary for Human Rights Elliott Abrams, testifying before the Senate Foreign Relations Committee a few days after the Mozote massacre stories appeared. Both said there was no evidence to support the massacre charges as reported in *The New York Times* and *The Washington Post.*

Raymond Bonner

Above: El Playón, a popular dumping ground used by the military death squads.

Right: Roberto d'Aubuisson, leader of the far-right Nationalist Republican Alliance (ARENA).

United Press International Inc.

subcommittee that the guerrillas were attacking the cooperatives because "it is clear to them that if this government reform program
succeeds, they will be very badly set back." He added that the guerrillas were moving onto cooperatives and evicting peasants who had
been given the land by the government. The belief that the left was
attacking the reforms was reinforced by most reporters, including this
one, who heard that line used repeatedly by U.S. officials, in El Salvador and Washington, and who did not have access to classified government reports that showed the contrary. The author of one Confidential
embassy memorandum, for example, reported being told by the manager of cotton lands that were expropriated under Phase I that "twenty
tractors were burned during the expropriation, not by the guerrillas
but by the Christian Democrats."

There was never "a concentrated plan of attack on the land reform
from the left," an AIFLD official said in an interview as late as mid-
1983. Internal government documents support what he said, presenting a far different picture of the attacks on the land reform from that
presented publicly by Kirkpatrick, Bushnell, Enders, and other officials.

"While innocent campesinos are being hit from both sides of the
political spectrum, there is a good deal of evidence that much of the
violence is being carried out by Government Security Forces," according to an AID evaluation of the land reform prepared in August 1980.
AIFLD's director in El Salvador, Richard V. Oulahan, in a memorandum dated November 12, 1980, wrote that of the 184 land reform-
related killings, "[m]ilitary forces, police, para-military forces and a
right-wing terrorist group with links into the Treasury Police" were
allegedly responsible for 133 deaths. The other 51 persons were killed
by "unknown sources," he noted, "probably a collection of those military and para-military groups already mentioned, plus leftist guerrillas and common bandits." Then he added, "Very few, if any, of these
deaths have or will be investigated and the authors brought to trial,
especially where police and military were involved. Government has
not been willing to stop actions by the right-wing 'Death Squad.'"

In another memorandum Oulahan summarized the reactions of the
military to the land-to-the-tiller law. In the province of Cabañas, he
reported, a local commander, "in collusion with the Guardia Nacional,
is responsible for the death of two promoters and almost had a UCS
lawyer assassinated for investigating the same." In San Miguel, Oulahan informed Washington, the army major in charge ordered his
subordinates not to allow UCS promoters to talk with peasants about
the land-to-the-tiller law and the benefits of joining the UCS. In sev-

eral provinces, Oulahan noted, UCS promoters were being harassed by the canton patrols, the rural civil defense forces. "In all cases the Canton Patrols and ORDEN are the same!" (This was one year after the coup, which American officials continued to insist had resulted in the abolition of ORDEN.)

Similarly, in his congressional appearance Gómez testified that of the 240 peasants killed, 80 percent "died at hands of the Army and security forces." Two had been killed by guerrillas, he said. The killers of the others were unknown. He also provided the subcommittee with the names and circumstances surrounding the deaths of the UCS and ISTA employees, individuals, Gómez said, who "had been paid with U.S. money." There was Edith Matamoros, a member of the San Jacintena cooperative, pulled from his home and "cruelly killed" by soldiers from the Third Infantry Brigade in San Miguel. There was Juan Francisco Velásquez, a UCS promoter, pulled from a bus by soldiers near Comalapa and later assassinated. There was Mario Ramírez, the UCS departmental secretary, who was captured in Ahuachapán, forced into a vehicle, and later found dead. And so on. There were 92 government or UCS workers on the list. Telling the subcommittee that 47 had been killed by the army and 13 by the security forces, Gómez noted, "This is very significant because there is a widespread myth in the United States that the security forces, National Guard, National Police, and Treasury Police, with connections to the local oligarchy, commit most of the human rights violations. The Army, made up of conscripts, it is claimed, is cleaner and able to resist the pressures of the local landlords. The truth," Gómez declared, "is different."

Very different also was the state of the Salvadoran nation portrayed in public by officials in Washington and the reality revealed by confidential documents. The Carter administration insisted that it was backing a "reform government" that was caught between the "extreme right and the extreme left" and "was attempting to control abuses committed by elements of its security forces."

That is how the State Department presented the policy in a letter to Representative Matthew F. McHugh, a New York Democrat who was beginning to have doubts about the wisdom, and the legality, of continued U.S. military assistance to El Salvador. Section 502(b) of the Foreign Assistance Act prohibits military aid to a country guilty of "gross violations of internationally recognized human rights." McHugh had written to Secretary of State Edmund S. Muskie suggesting that El Salvador was such a country. Replying for the secretary, J. Brian Atwood, assistant secretary for congressional relations, adhered to the same line that the administration had taken when it sought the aid six months earlier: that while there was violence, most of it was perpetrated by the guerrillas, followed by "right-wing extremists" and only incidentally by "some elements of El Salvador's security forces." Moreover, he asserted, the "nonlethal" equipment that the United States had supplied should result in "better discipline and less unwarranted violence against the civilian population.

"Tear gas and protective masks have already been used effectively for crowd control," Atwood wrote. "Previously, some public demonstrations ended in tragedy when security forces responded to violence by using firearms. Tear gas allows them a more humane and effective means of reacting to demonstrations when they become violent."

What the State Department was telling McHugh, and other members of Congress who received the same letter, bore very little resemblance to reality in El Salvador. The letter was dated October 22, 1980, one year after the coup. Confidential cables and documents prepared at the same time reveal that El Salvador's political landscape was almost indistinguishable from that before the coup: The armed forces ruled, employing the same repressive methods they had in 1932, in 1948, in 1972, in 1979. Even White had said as much in a lengthy Confidential cable, the subject of which was "El Salvador, One Year After the Coup." White advised Washington: "Plainly put, the military have the power; no government can exist without their approval." He allowed that the colonels were permitting civilians to have some share in the government. "But the price for the military's support of the JRG [junta of the revolutionary government] has been high. Members of the security corps and, to a lesser extent, of the Army have continued to hunt down and kill suspected leftist subversives, often on the basis of flimsy evidence."

Only about half of White's six-page cable was released under the Freedom of Information Act. The withheld portions almost certainly provide an even more dire look at the Salvadoran reality.

Foremost among the documents that shed an entirely different light on the Salvadoran government from that publicized by the United States is a memorandum prepared by the AIFLD director in El Salvador, Oulahan. Written on October 16, 1980, a year and one day after the coup, Oulahan began: "Government here operates with no real popular support." No one in Washington was telling Congress or the American people this. Moreover, he flatly debunked the myth that Duarte and the government were centrists. "In the past several months, Duarte and company have sided with the conservative military (perhaps because this group holds the key to power now), which has hurt their image among the population." Oulahan noted that "the conservative officials who look to a military solution are very much in control." As for the moderate young officers and their leader, Colonel Majano, they were concerned that the military remain united, "and this is the reason why," Oulahan wrote, "they have acquiesced in the swing to the right . . . as they lose more and more control."

It was a devastating but accurate analysis.

Majano had been sidelined because "Gutiérrez and García hated him," said White. The first public showdown came in May 1980, after the D'Aubuisson coup plotting had been uncovered. Majano ordered the plotters arrested. When the soldiers arrived to raid a farm near Santa Tecla, they were surprised to find D'Aubuisson himself. They also found documents linking him to the murder of Archbishop Romero, arms trafficking, and death squads. Some young officers loyal to Majano wanted D'Aubuisson shot for treason. Duarte and the Christian Democrats threatened to pull out of the government if D'Aubuisson and the other coup plotters arrested along with him were not brought to trial.

Within the military, there was widespread outrage—not at D'Aubuisson but at Majano for arresting him. Gutiérrez appointed as the military judge to handle the case a major who was a member of D'Aubuisson's *tanda*. To no one's surprise, he ordered D'Aubuisson and his cohorts released for lack of evidence.

The Christian Democratic threat had been an empty one, as had been previous threats, as would be subsequent ones. The military moderates lost more power when Gutiérrez was named the sole commander in chief, a position he had shared with Majano. Another blow to Majano's power was delivered a few months later, when García transferred all the officers loyal to Majano to insignificant posts or dispatched them abroad. García had no authority to order the transfers —Majano as a member of the junta was García's superior—but Majano did not protest. He, as noted earlier, was not a forceful leader, and he gave in when White presented a plan to bolster his stature. White wanted to send him to Washington. Pictures of him with Carter would have been another and very important signal that the United States was backing the moderates. But García and Gutiérrez persuaded Majano not to make the trip, telling him it was more important for him to remain in El Salvador for a military ceremony.

While the State Department was rosily declaring that the U.S. "nonlethal" assistance had made the Salvadoran Army more disciplined and less violent, Oulahan bluntly reported one year after the coup, "A U.S. military training program is taking place in Panama and while the reasons behind it are quite logical, the simple fact is that military inspired violence is much worse now than before." The State Department wrote to McHugh that "the Government has a training program to reorient and sensitize officers and enlisted men to human rights." Oulahan reported: "The armed forces have been operating with the list system here: if your name happens to be on the list and you are taken prisoner your future life expectancy is about one hour. Young people from 16 to 20 are indiscriminate victims of the security forces as those look upon most students as potential enemies." He noted that the U.S. embassy "continues to pressure the Junta and the Military for actions which will slow down and eventually stop official repression. Unfortunately, they do not seem to have had the desired impact."

The repression in 1980 reached a magnitude surpassed only by the *matanza* and was far worse than anything imagined under General Romero. During the first six months the archbishop's legal aid office documented 2,065 cases of persons killed by the security forces, army, or paramilitary bands. By the end of the year the number had reached at least 9,000. Every day mutilated bodies, missing arms or heads, were found: behind shopping centers; stuffed into burlap bags and left on dusty rural roads; hurled over cliffs into ravines. During just one week, in April 1980, the following were but a few of the incidents recorded by the archdiocese's legal aid office: National guardsmen and Treasury Police set fire to a house in the capital, killing Eugenio Esquivel Hernández (forty-four years old), Manuel García (twenty-two), and Fernando Arevalo (twenty). In San Pedro Perulapán, masked men decapitated Eligio Díaz (twenty-four), Miguel Hernández (thirty), and Teresita Díaz (fifteen), whose father had been killed by guardsmen three weeks earlier; they removed the skin of Antonio Hernández (nineteen) and Teodoro Hernández (twenty-six). All were catechists. In El Clavario, Tecoluca, the body of a peasant was found, the head and arms cut off and stuffed in a sewage pipe some forty meters from the rest of the body. The bodies of five young people who had been kidnapped several days earlier were found in Ayutuxtepeque, near San Salvador. One man had acid burns on his genitals; his right arm was broken; he had needle pins through his lips and burns on the back of his feet. In his clothes a note was found on a piece of cigarette paper: "Mother, they're keeping me in San Carlos prison and they're torturing me." Next to his body was a calling card with the initials E. M.— Spanish for *escuadrón de muerte* ("death squad"). On the Pan American Highway to San Miguel two bodies were found, hanged and riddled with bullets. At kilometer 96 on the road to Ahuachapán, the bodies of three teachers, a tailor, and a mechanic were found a few days after they had been kidnapped by security forces. Nelson Antonio

Carbajal (nineteen) was machine-gunned while exercising on a soccer field in Suchitoto.

Professionals became particular targets for the repression. "Death squads and uniformed forces have repeatedly entered hospitals and clinics and shot down patients, doctors, nurses and medical students in cold blood," reported a medical commission sponsored by the American Public Health Association and the American Friends Service Committee after a visit to El Salvador in the summer of 1980. "These assassinations are frequently preceded by the cruelest forms of dismemberment and brutality." In one instance, soldiers entered the home of a doctor and his wife, a nurse, which they said was a clandestine clinic for treating guerrillas. Two medical students and two relatives were visiting. Hearing the commotion, another doctor went to inquire. The soldiers killed all seven, blowing away their heads with high-powered weapons. In another case, according to the archbishop's legal aid office, ten men entered a hospital in Santa Tecla and riddled the body of a patient who was recovering from wounds inflicted the previous day by ORDEN forces.

In July government troops stormed the National University, killing at least fifty. The university was closed and remains so four years later. The National Guard, headed by Colonel Vides Casanova, then proceeded to strip the place of everything that could be unscrewed and carried away. "It's gutted over there," said a diplomat, referring to the high-rise buildings that look a bit like a middle-income housing project. The Guard officers sold off the entire contents: microscopes; books; chairs; desks. (The president of one of the many mini-universities that sprang up after the National University was closed bragged about how he'd got a "super deal," equipping his institution with inexpensively priced but high-quality goods he purchased from the National Guard.)

At least ninety primary schoolteachers were killed between January and October 1980, according to a report by Amnesty International. Vladimir Barrios, the thirty-two-year-old director of a school in Tecapán, Usulután, was gunned down in front of his students during a National Guard operation. A schoolgirl, Blanca Lidia Orellana, was seriously wounded.

The country's small opposition newspapers, *El Independiente* and *La Crónica,* were repeatedly bombed. *La Crónica'*s editor in chief, Jaime Suárez, and a photojournalist, César Najarro, were seized midday while sitting in a downtown coffee shop. Their bodies, hacked to pieces by machetes, were found a few days later.

The spokeswoman for the human rights commission, María Magdalena Henríquez, was kidnapped while shopping with her young son; her body was found a few days later. Two weeks after that the director of the commission, Ramón Valladares, was assassinated. Soldiers regularly sacked the archdiocese's legal aid office, during one raid removing the files pertaining to the archbishop's murder. The church radio station, YSAX, was bombed periodically. (In the letter to McHugh, the State Department had charged that the station "advocates leftist causes.") Churches were regularly sprayed with machine-gun fire. Security forces blasted the church in Zacatecoluca, then entered, killing ten peasants who had sought refuge there. They seized twenty-six others and later assassinated them. The perpetrators left their "E. M." calling cards, as did those who raided the church in San Miguel on the same day, killing five persons. More catechists and priests were killed. A seminarian in Platanares, Cuscatlán, was shot, then had his head destroyed with a machete. Father Cosme Spezzotto, a fifty-seven-year-old Franciscan from Italy, was assassinated while saying prayers in his church in San Juan Nonualco. A thirty-five-year-old priest, Manuel Antonio Reyes Monico, was picked up by government troops, and later shot.

During his homily on October 26, 1980, Archbishop Rivera y Damas condemned the armed forces' "war of extermination and genocide against a defenseless civilian population." The next week he criticized the leftists for their "reprisals" and "executions," then added that "the government's selective repression must also be condemned." Referring to the murder of human rights director Ramón Valladares and the assassination of university rector Felix Ulloa, who was shot and killed along with his driver, the archbishop said that "like the deaths of thousands of other Salvadorans, these deaths are not the result of confrontations, but of selective repression that subjects El Salvador to a continuous All Souls Day."

But the State Department assured Congressman McHugh, "We are convinced that the Government is attempting to control abuses committed by elements of its security forces as well as those of the extreme right and left." It then cited a report by Subsecretary of Defense Nicolás Carranza that 110 national guardsmen had been discharged for "grave faults" and that 405 other army personnel had been disciplined for other violations. It is tragic that the State Department would accept, let alone repeat, an assertion by Carranza, an officer whose links to the rightist violence were so notorious that getting rid of him was a primary objective of White, Pastor at the NSC, and the Christian Democrats. Moreover, State's declaration was contrary to what White reported in his Confidential cable summarizing the situation one year after the coup. "The Ministry of Defense has yet to punish anyone, civilian or military, for killing a leftist," White wrote.

The failure of the Carter administration to bring about any significant diminution in the violence by the government forces, if indeed any reduction at all, is attributable to a number of factors. "Part of it was the ambivalence of the President," said one of his senior aides. "He was a little wishy-washy, always reluctant to come down hard on the Pentagon and their insistence on more military aid." White's position was considerably weakened because the Pentagon dealt directly with the Salvadoran military. "We would deal with Duarte, but our military would deal with their military, and this undermined Duarte's strength—and White's," recalled one senior State Department official.

By October 1980 Pastor was again asking for a reconsideration of the still-existing ban on "lethal equipment" to El Salvador, according to a State Department memorandum. And the Pentagon in October sent in another small group of advisers. Their presence was kept a secret until December. When reports that there was a mobile training team in the country began to surface, Howard Lane, the press officer—who did not volunteer adverse information but wouldn't lie when asked a direct question—confirmed the presence of the advisers. "I don't know how they thought they could hide these guys in this tiny country," he snapped in exasperation. The story was that the advisers were there as part of Operation Golden Harvest, to help the Salvadorans protect the harvests from attacks by the guerrillas. The Defense Department, pursuant to a Freedom of Information Act request for documents relating to Operation Golden Harvest, said it had no records of any such operation. But documents it did supply—the only ones I received from DOD in response to my FOIA requests—showed that a mobile training team had entered the country in October and remained until December. Its mission, according to the documents, was to help the Salvadoran Army fight a war against the guerrillas.

Another reason that the Carter administration was largely ineffective in controlling the violent excesses of the Salvadoran armed forces is that it was fearful of weakening the military as an institution. That the Salvadoran Army was "corrupt, lazy, mostly a bunch of no-goods" was accepted at the highest levels of the administration, said a senior Carter official, "but it was important that it not be disintegrated." White agreed. "The primary purpose of the foreign policy," he said one month after leaving El Salvador, "was to preserve the military as an institution."

But preserving the Salvadoran military as an institution and at the same time reforming it is a Sisyphean task. It is the same policy cul-de-sac in which the United States finds itself, as it has in the past and will in the future, whenever it backs armed forces trying to keep a leftist government from coming to power. Rare is the military that is going to purge its ranks, to reform itself, except in order to survive as an institution. It is not inevitable that reforming the Salvadoran Army would lead to its total disintegration, but there is a possibility that it might. The Carter administration was not willing to take that risk. Perhaps no American administration would be, but it should be asked why El Salvador, if the present conflict ends, even needs an army. Costa Rica hasn't had an army since the revolution there in 1948; not coincidentally, it is the only Central American country that has been spared the coups and violence of its neighbors.

In El Salvador, White thought, if military aid were used as a carrot, it would eventually be possible to purge the army of its most repressive elements and remake the institution into one that defended against outside enemies but did not brutalize its own citizens. In October 1980, for example, White promised Defense Minister García two helicopters in exchange for the dismissal of Colonel Francisco Morán, the head of the Treasury Police, widely considered the most brutal of the security forces. (García agreed but never delivered, stalling until Reagan promised aid, and the helicopters came, without any conditions being set.)

Not long after he had arrived in El Salvador, White told reporters that the Carter administration would be successful if the Christian Democrat-military junta could "carry out the reforms, stay in power and control the violence." At the end of October the reforms were going forward, albeit shakily. The junta was still in power, but only because it had moved to the right politically and surrendered meaningful power to the armed forces. There was no effective control over the violence.

White did think he scored at least one major success: diminishing popular support for the left, primarily because of the reforms. To prove his case, he noted that a general strike called by the leftists in August 1980 went largely unheeded. Nearly all businesses stayed open, and most people went to work. White contrasted this with the unity celebration on January 22, 1980, and with Archbishop Romero's funeral in March. On both occasions tens of thousands of Salvadorans sympathetic to the left had turned out. While the premises were accurate, his conclusion—that the failure of the August strike demonstrated a weakening of support for the left—was questionable, failing to take into consideration numerous other factors. For one thing, to defeat the call for a general strike, the business community put aside its hatred of the junta and worked with it. Employers threatened to fire anyone who did not show up for work, a serious threat in a country where unemployment was at least 30 percent. The government put thousands of troops in the streets to block efforts to close businesses. The strike's failure also reflected discord among the leftists. Some of the major guerrilla groups were opposed to it. Noting the number of demonstrators killed in January and March, they argued that they could no longer ask their unarmed backers to serve as cannon fodder. Finally, unmentioned by White, as well as others who insist that the reforms stole support from the left, was the fact of ongoing repression. Thousands of Salvadorans suspected of being sympathetic to the revolution had already been tortured and murdered. To appear in support of the general strike would have been tantamount to signing one's own death warrant.

It would be unfair to reach a conclusive judgment about White's policy and efforts. He had, effectively, only seven and a half months in which to try to implement them—from his arrival in mid-March until November 4.

10

TRANSITION

THE Avenida la Revolución is a broad, leafy boulevard, slightly inclined upward to a towering cut stone monument bearing a mosaic figure of a man with outsize hands. Tonight the street was lined with armor-reinforced Cherokees and sedans with bulletproof glass. More vehicles were neatly arranged between the white lines in the spaces of the underground parking garage. Men in civilian clothes, brandishing Magnum pistols, automatic rifles, shotguns, and submachine guns with collapsible stocks, leaned against them. Inside the Presidente, a low, modern government-owned hotel—where Sunday brunch is enjoyed at the edge of the amoeba-shaped swimming pool—a ballroom was decorated with red and white balloons, bunting, and the Stars and Stripes. Blackboards were conveniently placed for easy viewing, to record the announcements coming over the Voice of America.

It was November 4, 1980, election night in the United States. A reason for a party in U.S. embassies around the world. In San Salvador, "The Americans were celebrating the fact that we are a democratic country, and golly, folks, if you could just do it the way we do it, wouldn't everybody be happy," recalled a diplomat. "And the Salvadorans were out for their own purposes, to find out if they were condemned to four more years of Carter-style government—which they perceived as giving away the store to the leftists—or maybe the Americans would come in with a new kind of government that would turn things around."

Several embassy officers had delayed their arrival, believing that they would have to stay awake at the hotel until two or three in the morning, waiting for the outcome. But Carter conceded early. Reagan won in a landslide, and what had been intended as an election night coverage party was transformed into a wild and enthusiastic celebration by the 250 Salvadorans present. In the posh residential neighborhoods of Escalón and San Benito, homeowners stepped onto manicured lawns and squeezed off a few rounds from their automatic rifles to register their joy. "They felt somehow vindicated by Reagan's victory," recalled another diplomat, "that 'we've held out against these pious, idealistic human rights policies of Carter. Now we can get down to some serious killing.' "

"Nobody talks about the fact—and it's not just coincidence—that within a month, well, maybe it was two months after Reagan was elected came the killing of the FDR leaders, an event that nobody even talks about up here—[plus] the nuns [churchwomen], Hammer and Pearlman, Sullivan,"* observed a troubled Foreign Service officer who had been in El Salvador during the slaughter. "Reagan certainly wouldn't have condoned the killing of anybody, but they, the rightists, the government, felt vindicated." The murders of the FDR politicians were "apparently part of a right-wing offensive throughout Central America aimed at dealing a severe blow before President-elect Ronald Reagan reaches the White House," *The Times'* Alan Riding wrote in a dispatch based on interviews with conservative businessmen, politicians, and military officers in Managua. One Guatemalan official told Riding that "the idea is to present him with a fait accompli. It also means that Reagan need not be associated with the bloodbath."

More church blood flowed in El Salvador. A day or two before the churchwomen were murdered, a Salvadoran priest, Marcial Serrano, was killed by an army sergeant and National Guard corporal. His body, with rocks tied to the feet, was tossed into Lake Ilopango. Two weeks after Reagan's triumph, troops stormed into the archdiocese's building, where they ransacked the offices of the church newspaper, *Orientación,* and destroyed the facilities of the radio station, YSAX.

"We hold the security forces and ultra-rightist groups responsible for the persecution against the Church and specifically for the assassination of priests and lay pastoral workers," Archbishop Rivera y Damas said in early December. "We therefore also hold responsible the Government Junta, which given its ultimate authority over the Armed Forces is responsible for actions by members of the military."

The transition period, the eleven weeks between Reagan's victory and his inauguration, were exhaustingly tumultuous in El Salvador.

*During the last week of December 1980, John Sullivan, a free-lance journalist, disappeared almost immediately after checking into the Sheraton Hotel; his badly mutilated body would not be found for more than two years. It is widely believed that he was killed by security force soldiers who mistook him for a priest sympathetic to the revolution.

Front-page political maneuvering cascaded over front-page mayhem. The situation became "so delicate" that White, for the first time since becoming ambassador, put all his remarks off the record in a press briefing on December 2. The Salvadoran government was restructured. Colonel Majano was forced out, a few weeks after he had barely escaped death from a powerful bomb that exploded just after his vehicle passed in front of the government's land reform agency. The guerrillas quietly ordered the "final offensive," then publicly boasted that the situation would become "red hot" and Reagan would find a revolutionary government in El Salvador when he took over the White House. For the outgoing Carter administration, the period offered another opportunity, as had November and December a year earlier, to try to bring the Salvadoran military to heel. But the administration wavered. It suspended all aid, but quickly reinstated economic assistance. Then, in an abrupt about-face, the Carter administration altered the entire complexion of U.S.-Salvadoran relations by sending in military advisers along with the first "lethal" military aid since 1977. The military aid was justified in part by a claim about a landing of boats from Nicaragua, a landing that may well have been fabricated.

ELEVEN-twenty Thursday morning, November 27, 1980, Thanksgiving Day in the United States. One hundred heavily armed men, their military boots showing beneath their civilian trousers, arrived at the Catholic San José High School, a few blocks from the American embassy. After piling out of a red Datsun pickup, a large blue truck, and other vehicles, several squads took up blocking positions on the street. Another unit, of twenty to thirty masked men, barged into the school, ordering teachers, students, parents, and members of the Socorro Jurídico, the archdiocese's legal aid office, to lie facedown. Twenty minutes later Enrique Álvarez, president of the FDR; Juan Chacón, leader of the BPR; and three other members of the FDR's executive committee, including two university students, were dragged away. The raiding party had been told six FDR leaders would be meeting. But Leoncio Pichinte, a laborer, had been delayed. When he got near the school and saw the armed men, he fled quickly, as he explained from his mountain hideout in Morazán, where I interviewed him in January 1982. The sixth person kidnapped on November 27 was another laborer who had come to the legal aid office for assistance.

The mutilated, bullet-ridden bodies were found on a road along the western shores of placid Lake Ilopango, where in better times the wealthy water-skied against the tranquil backdrop of volcanic cones.

Chacón's face had been hideously disfigured. His clenched left fist was extended above his blood-covered body, a final proud and defiant salute by the twenty-three-year-old peasant who had come close to being named a member of the first junta. Álvarez's left arm had been severed. (Álvarez had been out of the country most of the time since becoming president of the FDR in April 1980. He had returned against the advice of his colleagues.)

The United States, including the embassy in El Salvador, had to bear some of the moral responsibility for the assassinations, as a distraught senior diplomat in the embassy remarked privately the day of the men's funeral. "We were constantly criticizing Álvarez for fronting for 'terrorists' on the left, for adding respectability to murders by the left," a diplomat who was in El Salvador said at the time. Now, he added, all the opposition was being "systematically" eliminated. "If Reagan wants to back this government, that is for him to shoulder." But the Carter administration would also continue backing it for the duration of its term.

The Maximiliano Hernández Martínez Anti-Communist Brigade took credit for the murders, in communiqués in which the group said the FDR men had been "materially and intellectually responsible for thousands of assassinations of innocent people who did not want to be Communists. We also warn the priests who have an affinity for the terrorist Marxist bands that they will have the same fate if they insist in their sermons on poisoning the minds of Salvadoran youth. The brigade will continue the just executions of the traitors to our country." Two weeks earlier the death squad had announced a campaign to eliminate all "Communist thieves and prostitutes."

The public claim of responsibility by the death squad served Washington policymakers well, allowing them to maintain the fiction that right-wing vigilantes, not the government, were responsible for the deaths. But a CIA report stated that the executions of the FDR leaders "were the work of the security forces." (The report added, "Summary execution of prisoners is a standard practice.")

When White's bodyguards brought him the news about the FDR leaders, the ambassador slumped in his chair. "Who am I going to talk to now?" he muttered, a voice more troubled than angered. The chances for a peaceful settlement had been dealt a severe blow. A month earlier White had persuaded the military to allow the church to act as mediator in a possible negotiated settlement. The church had agreed, but the left rejected the offer. Leftist leaders say they didn't have faith in the bishops' conference, which was dominated by conservatives. What they don't admit, but what seems equally true, is that they thought a military victory was possible. In any event, it was believed, at least by White and others at the embassy, that the leftists had now decided to negotiate. Jeane Kirkpatrick, a member of Reagan's transition team, rejected that idea. In a round-table discussion with *The New York Times* ten days after the murders, she said, "A great many people suggest that their murder prevented them from accepting mediation and that is myth-making and we're watching the making of that myth right now." Robert Pastor later said it was "bullshit" that the FDR was willing to negotiate. Whether or not they were discussing negotiations will probably never be known. But it is also largely unimportant. In El Salvador, perceptions—about what Washington is or isn't going to do, about what the left is or isn't going to do, about any range of matters—are often more important than reality. Crucial to any explanation of the killings of the FDR leaders is that the military officers, and their civilian allies, who ordered them, might have perceived that the FDR was willing to negotiate , and they feared that Ambassador White might advance that solution to the civil war during his final weeks as ambassador.

White's new President would favor what he called "quiet diplomacy" when it came to human rights abuses, but White was still serving Jimmy Carter, was still his own man, and was still outspoken. He reacted to the assassinations in characteristic manner. For symbolic value, White went to the San José High School to deliver his message, "to express my feeling of horror and repugnance for the unspeakable crime perpetrated here." Directing his comments to the members of the Socorro Jurídico and the staff of the high school, he continued, "If this slaughter doesn't stop, if those guilty of this crime are not brought to justice, it will be another serious, perhaps irreversible, setback for the cause of peace and justice." Of course, there never was any government investigation; there couldn't be, since the government was culpable.

White condemned "these terrible crimes being committed by insane extremists on both ends of the political spectrum," implying again the myth that the Duarte government was in the center and not responsible for the violence. White's statement was noticeably lacking in any criticism of the Salvadoran government and the armed forces. Yet White had reported to Washington that the government security forces were involved.

"In various conversations I have had with diplomats, American citizens, and Salvadorans, I have yet to find anyone who does not believe that the security forces were responsible for the attack," White wrote in a Confidential cable sent on the same day that he spoke at the high school. One "well-connected" person, whose identity was deleted from the cable released under the Freedom of Information Act, "told me that the security forces had made a total mess of the situation. It was one thing, he said, to have the FDR bodies disappear in a quiet and efficient manner, but this clumsy, obvious, and brutal assassination would give the left a new cause among the people. He speculated that some of the security forces may have deliberately engineered the kidnapping and assassination in this obvious way in order to ensure an armed confrontation with the left."

White concluded his cable with the alert to Washington that the killing of the FDR leaders had generated "the most serious crisis since the assassination of Archbishop Romero." It would quickly be eclipsed by new horrors. From an American perspective, it was one thing for some 9,000 Salvadorans to be killed during 1980, most by government forces. Even the murders of the FDR leaders "fell on deaf ears" in Washington, as one State Department officer recalled. But the killing of Americans, especially when they were women and some were nuns —that was a horror for the front page and the evening news. It could not be ignored.

Within twenty-four hours after the bodies of the four American churchwomen had been pulled from the crude dirt grave in an isolated part of El Salvador, the Carter administration announced that it was suspending all economic and military aid to El Salvador. What most bothered the State Department policymakers was not the loss of the women's lives but that their assassinations would make it more difficult for the United States to continue backing the Duarte government. That seemingly cynical and callous assessment is supported by numerous confidential cables sent during December and by State Department conduct. When the brother of one of the slain women called the State Department a few days after his sister's body had been found, an employee shouted over the phone, "Will you people please get off our backs!" Then, as reported in a *New York Times* column by John Oakes, former senior editor of the paper, the department proceeded to inform the family it would have to reimburse the United States $3,500 for shipping the victim's body home.

A similar lack of concern was reflected in the failure of any high-level person in the administration to express regrets to the women's families until three weeks after their murders. Even then that action came only after the omission had been discovered by Patt Derian in the human rights bureau. She was horrified and immediately wrote four letters of condolence to be signed and sent by Secretary of State

Muskie. (By contrast, as noted, when the AIFLD employees were murdered, the State Department swung into action immediately to ensure that the highest-level administration officials would attend one of the funerals.)

In addition to suspending aid, Carter hurriedly dispatched a high-level bipartisan commission to El Salvador, a last-ditch effort to salvage something from the situation before he retired to Plains, Georgia. The mission was headed by William D. Rogers, a Washington lawyer, who had been Kissinger's assistant secretary of state for Inter-American affairs; William G. Bowdler, the assistant secretary for Latin America at the time and a former ambassador to El Salvador; and Bowdler's deputy, Luigi Einaudi.

The delegation's stated and widely reported mission was to conduct a preliminary inquiry into the deaths of the churchwomen and to insist that the Salvadoran government undertake a thorough investigation as a condition for restoration of aid. But the women's case was "secondary" on the list of the mission's real objectives, according to one member. A series of Confidential and Secret cables show that it was, in fact, third on the list of what the United States was demanding before aid would be restored. The first two conditions were, in general terms, a restructuring of the Salvadoran government, including the transfer of military officers most closely linked to the violence, and a reduction in violence by the security forces.

But the Carter administration, and, above all, White, were playing with a weak hand when it came to dealing with the Salvadoran government. Salvadoran leaders, especially in the military, had every reason to believe that if they could just hold on until January 20, they would receive all the military aid they needed—free of any conditions. In late November representatives of the Productive Alliance, a conservative Salvadoran business association, had met in Washington with three of President-elect Reagan's foreign policy advisers: Jeane Kirkpatrick; Roger Fontaine, then of the conservative American Enterprise Institute and later on Reagan's NSC; and James Theberge, who as ambassador to Nicaragua from 1975 to 1977 had been a strong backer of General Somoza. The Salvadorans were assured that the new administration would increase military aid, which would include combat equipment. Kirkpatrick sent another powerful message to the Salvadoran rightists when she said publicly after the FDR leaders were killed, "I must say that I found myself thinking that it's a reminder that people who choose to live by the sword can expect to die by it."

A few days later any doubt that the incoming administration would adopt a hard line in El Salvador was dispelled when the report of Reagan's State Department transition team was leaked to *The New York Times*. The report, written on stationery from the office of the President-elect, was based on interviews with "the top officers in the Bureau of Inter-American Affairs." Public statements about human rights abuses by Latin American governments had "conveyed a stridency that was frequently counterproductive," the transition team said. As for Robert White, the report branded him and other ambassadors "social reformers and advocates of new theories of social change with latitude to experiment within the country to which they are accredited." The report was pointedly critical of White for having supported the land reform as well as the nationalization of banks and export trade. Another transition team paper put White's name, along with some sixty other ambassadors, including many Foreign Service officers, on a "hit list" to be quickly replaced by Reagan.

Conservative Salvadoran leaders were further encouraged to hold on for the new era when Cleto DiGiovanni, Jr., paid them a visit in early December. DiGiovanni, a former CIA agent in Latin America, had written for *The Washington Quarterly*: "A pro-U.S. military government in El Salvador which had been economically viable has been replaced by a center-left government supported by the U.S. embassy. That government, having brought the country to near economic ruin by desperate and sweeping reforms, might fall to Marxist guerrillas." It was, in effect, an endorsement of the regime of General Romero and an attack on the Duarte government.

White, not one to remain silent in the face of adversity, summoned Christopher Dickey and me to the embassy. Not knowing what he wanted, I went excitedly with a mental line of inquiry. But White had his own agenda. He wanted a forum to blast the attacks of the Reagan administration for "undercutting my effectiveness" and "my ability to influence events and policy," especially his efforts to keep the government from moving farther to the right. The transition team papers and DiGiovanni's visit, he said, have "struck a heavy blow at the Christian Democrats and moderate military officers." Visibly angry, he declared, "When civil war breaks out in this country, I hope they get their chance to serve."

In Washington the incoming administration sought to quell the furor, saying that the hit list and other transition team papers were not official policy and that DiGiovanni had not been sent as an official emissary. But most of the transition team's recommendations, including the ouster of White, were adopted, and DiGiovanni on the plane to El Salvador had told an embassy staff member, who by chance was on the same flight, that his visit to El Salvador was an official one. DiGiovanni made the same representations in Nicaragua. "For the Reagan people to say now that 'these guys don't speak for us' is kind of lame," Lawrence Pezzullo, ambassador to Nicaragua, whose name was also on the hit list, said at the time to Dickey. "I don't buy that for a second."

In El Salvador the restructuring of the government began on December 7, when Majano was ousted. The Carter administration did nothing to keep the liberal colonel on the junta. His removal, reportedly approved, 300–4, by the army officers, was little more than the public recognition that the conservatives, bolstered by Reagan's victory, were in control and that White, who had never disguised his partiality toward Majano, was truly a lame-duck ambassador.

The Salvadoran political air was charged with rumors and speculation about what would follow. Sitting on the roof terrace of the Christian Democratic party headquarters, Duarte, on the afternoon that Majano was ousted, said that the Christian Democrats would withdraw from the government unless the "military in all ranks accept complete control of the military by the government."

With Majano out of the way, Duarte also began pushing his desire to be president. In this pursuit he had the support of the Rogers delegation. In his diary on December 11, Carter wrote that the delegation had met with Duarte, "(who is likely to be the new president to replace the five-person junta). . . ."

White was being undermined not only by the incoming administration but by the one he was still serving. The Rogers delegation did not tell him that one of its objectives was to make Duarte president. Duarte and the Rogers team also agreed on the desirability of removing García as minister of defense, another objective about which White was kept in the dark. Had White been apprised of these objectives, he might have been able to assist.*

The full extent of U.S. participation in the restructuring is being kept secret by the State Department. In response to my FOIA request for "all records pertaining to the restructuring of the Salvadoran Government during December 1980," the department withheld ten documents.

When the new government was announced, on December 13, Duarte was president. But not of the country—only of the junta, now reduced to four. Colonel Gutiérrez, Morales Ehrlich, and Dr. Avalos Navarrete

---

*Duarte did not have the full backing of his party. Within the Christian Democrats, there was support for Fidel Chávez Mena, the foreign minister, to become president; he also would have been acceptable to the United States.

remained along with Duarte. The armed forces had again called the Christian Democrats' bluff and won. It was clear who was in charge. "We have finally given you your presidency," Colonel Gutiérrez told Duarte when the agreement was reached. García remained as minister of defense, and Gutiérrez, rather than Duarte as president, became commander in chief of the armed forces. "The only reason I am in this position is because I have the support of the army," Duarte told me with unusual candor a few days later.

"Duarte made an expensive compromise to realize his dream of becoming president," a Mexican diplomat in El Salvador observed at the time. "If García is minister of defense and Gutiérrez is commander in chief, then Mr. Duarte is an adornment. . . . The military has been left in control of the military, and that is the country's problem." He added: "Only the United States is keeping the junta alive. The rich are against it; the upper-middle class doesn't support it but is afraid of the others; the middle class is divided. The lower class is absolutely against it."

The armed forces' leaders did promise to transfer about a dozen senior military commanders most involved with the violence. The United States offered to assist in the transfers by making some spots available in the prestigious Army Command and Staff College, and the Naval Staff College. "The officers transferred for excessive violence" were being "rewarded," Patt Derian protested in an internal State Department memorandum. But even that reward wasn't enough. In the end only a few of the officers were actually transferred. Colonel Morán, who was near the top of the Christian Democrat and U.S. list of those who had to go, held on to his post as head of the ruthless Treasury Police. One who was transferred was archconservative Nicolás Carranza, from vice-minister of defense to head of the state communications company, hardly a demotion when one considers that being head of ANTEL was a position coveted by military officers.

The effect of the reshuffling was a victory for the rightist forces within the military. Duarte and the civilians in the government had been allowed to remain "to preserve appearances," the Mexican diplomat in El Salvador remarked then. His conclusion was shared by U.S. diplomats, who explained in off-the-record discussions that the restructuring had been a de facto coup. Had the changes been accomplished with guns and tanks, as most coups are, the repercussions would have made it difficult for the Carter administration to find public or congressional support for backing the Salvadoran government.

The crisis following the murder of the churchwomen offered the Carter administration another opportunity, like the one it had squandered after the 1979 coup. Had Washington remained firm in dealing with the military conservatives, it might have been able to bring about some meaningful change in El Salvador. But neither happened.

Four days after the restructuring of the government, which was worse than just a change of faces since it gave considerably more power to the right, the Carter administration announced that it was resuming economic aid, citing the Salvadoran government's "commitment to a thorough, professional and expeditious investigation of the killings" of the American women. In an additional show of support for the Salvadoran government, the administration voted the next day in favor of a $45.5 million Inter-American Development Bank loan to El Salvador. But there never had been any serious investigation into the killing of the American churchwomen, and the administration well knew that there hadn't been. In a Secret cable to the embassy in El Salvador on December 27, Secretary of State Muskie pointed out that the Salvadorans had not contacted six Canadian missionaries who had seen the women at the airport shortly before they were abducted. "The [investigating] Commission does not appear to be meeting regularly, and we have impression investigation not as rapid as would be expected," Muskie wrote. Regarding Duarte, Muskie declared: "We do not see him active in pressuring investigation."

Although the administration had given away whatever leverage it had with the economic aid, it still had a stronger card to play: military aid. The Salvadoran military was still vulnerable to pressures from Washington, worried as it was that the guerrillas might be able to achieve a military victory. But the administration wavered. Even the suspension of military aid had not been all that it was publicly declared. The administration had continued to deliver military equipment, such as trucks, in the pipeline. Now it went further, relinquishing whatever clout it still had.

In a Secret cable sent the day after Washington had resumed economic aid—"Instructions for Ambassador" was the subject—Secretary of State Muskie instructed White to advise Duarte that military aid would be resumed "contingent upon demonstrable progress in the following areas of concern:" Subparagraph C is "that the investigation of the murders of the American churchwomen progress as rapidly as possible with full cooperation from the security forces." The cable was released under the Freedom of Information Act in early 1983, but subparagraphs A and B, the first two conditions for the restoration of aid, were blacked out. Those conditions, according to several diplomats who read them and from references to them in other documents, were a reduction in the level of violence by the security forces and the transfer of the most ruthless military commanders. None of the three conditions was completely fulfilled.

The Carter administration waited until January 14, 1981, before announcing that it was resuming military aid, thus making it appear that it had waited for evidence that its conditions had been met. But in fact, according to Secret cables and other internal State Department documents, the decision had been reached at least two weeks earlier. In a Secret cable on January 2, the State Department instructed the embassy to advise the Salvadoran government that the United States was prepared to send military equipment "on [an] expedited basis," and would immediately "deploy to San Salvador" two groups of advisers—one for helicopter maintenance; the other "to deal with guerrilla warfare."

On the final day of 1980 the State Department, under increasing pressure from the NSC and the Pentagon, had agreed to resume military aid. The human rights bureau had been excluded from the meeting, causing Patt Derian to express "my profound disappointment" in a strong memorandum to the secretary of state's office.

"Clearly the conditions upon which the phased resumption of military assistance was to be authorized have not been met," Derian wrote. She noted that the security forces were not cooperating with the investigation of the churchwomen's case, refusing even to provide the Salvadoran investigatory commission with lists of units in the area at the time the women were murdered. As for the transfers of military officers "responsible for excessive violence" and a "reduction in the level of violence originating from the security forces"—the other conditions precedent to the resumption of aid—she wrote:

> The current resumption is neither linked nor phased and in effect represents a decision to resume military assistance immediately and without conditions. . . .
> . . . Duarte seems to fear that the introduction into El Salvador of several thousand Cuban volunteers is imminent and that a general leftist offensive may begin shortly. However, our intelligence has no evidence of any large scale Cuban personnel movements and confirms that within El Salvador the Government remains in effective control of the country. There is, therefore, no military exigency which requires us to resume military assistance now.

Then she went further. "There are however compelling reasons to maintain the suspension." Foremost among these was that resumption of aid would "imply" U.S. government "exoneration of security force involvement" in the killing of the women, "thereby prejudicing the outcome of the investigation." She noted that one high-ranking Salvadoran government official had already told U.S. embassy officials that "our decision to resume economic assistance served to exonerate the military of responsibility for the nuns' death." Moreover, resumption of military aid "will render Duarte irrelevant. His standing with the military is a function of his general ability to obtain US assistance. Once he delivers such assistance there will be no further incentive for the military to cooperate or even tolerate him, to work with the PDC [Christian Democratic party], to bring the security forces under control, or to cooperate with the work of the investigatory commission."

Duarte had already been undermined in Washington, along with White. Duarte had told White that he didn't want any U.S. military advisers. White had conveyed this objection to Washington. U.S. military officials had leaked this to the Salvadoran military. The message was clear: White and Duarte could be ignored. Moreover, the decision to resume military aid had been taken while White was on his Christmas vacation in Florida. He was not consulted.

Derian was right on all counts, including her conclusion that to resume aid when the conditions had not been met "demonstrates a clear lack of resolve on the part of the outgoing Administration. This will be evident to the Government and to the military of El Salvador as well."

The decision to provide military assistance also ran counter to a United Nations resolution adopted on December 15, 1980. Guided by principles embodied in the United Nations Charter and the Universal Declaration of Human Rights, the General Assembly expressed dismay caused "by reports of human rights violations in El Salvador and especially by the death of thousands of persons and the climate of repression and insecurity in the country, which favours terrorism by paramilitary groups and enables it to be engaged in with impunity." Those voting yes said they were "profoundly indignant at the assassination of Mr. Enrique Álvarez Córdova" and the other FDR leaders. Therefore, the UN body called upon all governments "to refrain from the supply of arms and other military assistance in the current circumstances." The vote was 70–12, with 55 abstentions, including the United States. Among the countries voting for the resolution, and thus against the United States, were Canada, West Germany, Greece, and India as well as Mexico, Panama, and Ecuador.

"The situation in El Salvador will be red hot by the time Mr. Reagan arrives," a Salvadoran guerrilla leader, Fermán Cienfuegos, boasted on December 26, in a meeting with reporters in Mexico City. The order for the "final offensive" had been given, he said. "I think Mr. Reagan will find an irreversible situation in El Salvador by the time he reaches the Presidency." And on the same day in a published interview, Colonel Majano, who was in hiding in Mexico, called for the ouster of the Salvadoran junta "by whatever means necessary."

THE music on Radio Romántica was abruptly interrupted. "The general offensive has begun," yelled an excited female, one of some twenty guerrillas who had seized the station. "The enemy is defeated. We have them surrounded. Popular justice is here."

It was January 10, 1981. In Mejicanos, one of the seedy working-class barrios that ring the capital, guerrillas commandeered five buses and roared through the streets, firing rocket-propelled grenades at the National Guard garrison. Guerrilla units attacked military barracks and government buildings throughout the country: La Unión, Zacatecoluca, San Miguel, Usulután. In the western city of Santa Ana, soldiers under the command of Captain Francisco Mena Sandoval, who had been one of the major plotters of the coup on October 15, 1979, mutinied, blowing a gaping hole in and setting fire to the barracks, which look a bit like a medieval fortress without the moat. Defense Minister García was worried that his troops would be defeated. The government declared martial law and a dusk-to-dawn curfew. The guerrillas seized another radio station and called on the populace to rise up, to join in a general strike.*

García's fear of defeat lasted no more than five hours. At a late-afternoon press conference on the eleventh, Duarte proclaimed: "The extremist guerrillas did all they could to make this a final offensive and they have failed." He was right, although his announcement might have been a day or two premature. On the day he spoke the capital was quiet. Not all shops were open, but many were. The traffic was light, but people stayed inside more out of fear than out of support of the revolution. The call for an insurrection and general strike had gone unheeded. The "final offensive" had failed. And as Duarte and García were justifiably to boast frequently thereafter, the guerrillas had been defeated "without one bullet" from the United States.

Yet, on the seventeenth, three days after it had publicly announced the resumption of military aid, the Carter administration declared its

---

*Among the casualties during the "final offensive" was Olivier Rebbot, a thirty-one-year-old French photographer for *Newsweek,* who was hit by sniper fire while he accompanied an army patrol trying to regain control of San Francisco Gotera. He died a few weeks later in a Miami hospital.

intention to supply the Salvadorans with $5 million in combat equipment, including M-16 rifles, M-79 grenade launchers, ammunition, and helicopters. And the United States was to send military advisers to help in the conduct of the counterinsurgency war. It was a complete reversal of U.S. policy toward El Salvador, which had not received "lethal" military aid since 1977. Congress did not have to approve. Carter invoked a provision of the Foreign Assistance Act, which allows the President to circumvent Congress if he determines that "an unforeseen emergency exists which requires immediate military assistance" or that "a failure to respond immediately to that emergency will result in serious harm to vital United States security interests." Unable to say that the military aid was necessary to defeat the guerrillas, the administration needed another pretext. It found one—perhaps concocted it.

On the evening of the thirteenth the Camino Real Hotel, where journalists were confined by the curfew and by their own exhaustion, was stirring with a tip from the U.S. embassy that something was developing. Something big. Something explosive. The next morning journalists scurried across town to the Presidential Palace, alerted that White would be there. He was. But the ambassador was uncharacteristically mute. After emerging from his armor-reinforced black limousine, he strode quickly through the journalist mob, divided by a wedge formed by White's bodyguards, and bounded up a few steps into the palace as soldiers slammed the tall wooden doors on reporters. But when he emerged, he had plenty to say.

"I believe reports that a group of approximately 100 men landed from Nicaragua about 4:00 P.M. yesterday." The cameras whirred. Reporters scribbled furiously. It was the first indication of outside support for the Salvadoran guerrillas. Reporters shouted questions. White responded: "There is evidence that Nicaragua has permitted its territory to be used as a transfer point for arms into El Salvador." Soviet- and Chinese-made weapons had been captured in recent days, he said. "This changes the nature of the insurgency movement here, and makes it clear that it is dependent on outside sources. . . . We cannot stand idly by and watch the guerrillas receive outside assistance." White, who had resisted military aid—his theory was that American aid would be matched by Cuban aid, which would be met by more American aid, leading to an unwanted escalation of what he saw as essentially a civil war—was now advocating more U.S. military assistance.

The journalist pack surged into the palace and up to the balconied second story for a press conference with Duarte, other members of the junta, and Defense Minister García. They said that five boats, each thirty feet long, had landed at El Cuco, a small Pacific coast village in the eastern part of the country. How did they know the boats had come from Nicaragua? several reporters shouted simultaneously. "They didn't come from Canada," García retorted. His contempt didn't faze the reporters, who pushed for some evidence that the boats had come from Nicaragua. "They were made of wood not native to El Salvador" was the answer given repeatedly during the press conference.

It was a weak case. "I had to laugh," said a prominent businessman as he jogged up the Boulevard del Hipódromo the next morning. He had seen the press conference on television. "It was better than watching a comedy," he said with a laugh. "I think they just want to get the people all excited, to get them to support the government. I've lost all faith in them." An athletically trim real estate developer in his mid-thirties said, "I'd never cross the gulf in that boat. I've scuba-dived there, done many crazy things—but not that. It's not possible."

But for the Carter administration, it was a smashing media victory. The boat landing was on the evening news. *The Washington Post* played the story on the front page. The headline screamed: 100 GUERRILLAS LAND ON BEACH IN EL SALVADOR. Inside, the story continued under a top-of-the-page banner: GUERRILLAS BELIEVED TO BE FROM NICARAGUA LAND ON SALVADORAN BEACH. With its story, *Newsweek* ran a map, an arrow leading from Nicaragua to El Salvador, depicting the route of what it called the "Nicaraguan landing."

Doubts quickly began to gnaw at reporters in El Salvador. The Gulf of Fonseca incident was too reminiscent of events in the Gulf of Tonkin, the "firing" on American destroyers off the coast of North Vietnam. That incident had led Congress to pass the Gulf of Tonkin resolution in 1964, authorizing President Lyndon Johnson to use necessary military force in Vietnam. It later turned out that Johnson had been less than candid in his description of what had happened. In El Salvador, after reporters had rushed their stories to their editors, they began to review their notes. White, outside the palace, had said about the boat landing: "I have no evidence other than what the [Salvadoran] government has told me." But Duarte at the press conference had said, "Our information comes from the American ambassador." Then Charles Krause, of CBS, went to El Cuco to investigate. He found little to match what either White or the junta had said. A naval commander told Krause that three of the five boats had landed a week earlier. As for the fighting, Krause interviewed villagers, who said that seven soldiers and two guerrillas had been killed. García had said, during the press conference, that fifty-three guerrillas had been killed.

The boat landing across the Gulf of Fonseca to El Cuco was "staged," concluded an American diplomat who was in El Salvador. Referring to the Soviet-made grenades found near the landing site, he later said, "It looks as if they were planted. I can't quite picture how people would —if they were attacked—drop grenades along the way—like Hansel and Gretel. It just seemed all too pat." Lawrence Pezzullo, who was ambassador to Nicaragua at the time of the incident, later described the boat landing as "fictional." Many months after the incident, he said, it was discovered that the fifty-five-horsepower outboard motors which powered the boats came from Panama. A former CIA agent, Ralph McGehee, who wrote about his disgust with many of the agency's tactics and methods in *Deadly Deceits: My 25 Years in the CIA,* said that the boat landing was "probably a CIA deception operation" to justify military aid.

A few days after the public statements that the boats had landed from Nicaragua, White was more subdued. He told reporters there had been "a rush to believe that wasn't totally warranted. . . . I think I overemphasized it as I examine it closely." The evidence of a boat landing was "not as compelling as the day I spoke." But while his statements about the boat landing the day he spoke in front of the Presidential Palace were on the record, his doubts were not. Moreover, he said that the military aid was justified because of other evidence that the Salvadoran guerrillas were being supplied from abroad. He declined to provide any of the evidence.

In announcing the $5 million in emergency combat equipment, helicopters, and advisers, the State Department said that "intelligence reports confirm that the guerrillas have obtained from abroad a substantial quantity of weapons, including new equipment such as grenades, recoilless rifles and mortars. The evidence also indicates that a number of countries supporting Marxist guerrillas have supplied, and are continuing to supply, these arms and ammunition."

A senior Carter administration official, who had access to all the intelligence traffic, has rebutted that statement almost totally. "The only intelligence" the United States had at the time, he said, showed that the guerrillas were receiving bullets, medical supplies, maybe some rifles, but "certainly not anything heavy." As for public statements that there had been a "massive" increase in the arms flow in the weeks before the final offensive, he noted: "How could there have been *massive* shipments? There were only two thousand to three thousand guerrillas." Reports about the increase in arms had come primarily from the Salvadorans. "We didn't have the intelligence resources [in El Salvador]. Those we did have didn't show that there was a massive arms buildup," the same former official said. As for the source of the guerrillas' weapons, "Our impression was that the guerrillas got most of their arms on the international black market, primarily in Miami." Nor, he added—contrary to public statements at the time and more forceful ones by the Reagan administration a few months later—did the United States have any intelligence information that more than "a couple of dozen, maybe four dozen" of the Salvadoran guerrillas had been trained in Cuba or Nicaragua.

Why, then, did the Carter administration in its final days reverse its four-year policy and supply combat equipment? The answer seems to be an admixture of fear and precaution, not unlike that which is present in the final days of most administrations, but which was more pronounced in the Carter White House because the election had been lost in part on charges that the nation had grown weak in the world. "We didn't want the Republicans for the next four years to say that the Carter administration had shut its eyes in the final hours," recalled one senior aide. The Pentagon was shouting apocalyptic scenarios: that unless the United States provided military aid, and fast, the guerrillas would be celebrating in the streets of San Salvador while Reagan was taking the oath of office. There is a perpetual tension between the Pentagon and State Department over the conduct of foreign policy, with the influence of the National Security Council dependent on who's in charge there. It was the Pentagon, supported by the NSC, that had more clout than State during most of the Carter administration, at least in El Salvador.

It was beginning to look more and more like Vietnam: The Republicans would be able to say they had inherited a policy of military intervention from the Democrats. Even Robert White was on board.

In a Secret cable sent four days before Reagan entered the White House, White wrote: "We are on the verge of a major policy shift on the eve of the inauguration of a new administration. Why are we faced with this important decision right now? Basically because sworn enemies of the United States are mounting a tightly orchestrated campaign of propaganda and political manipulation to cover the introduction over the last few months of hundreds of tons of sophisticated military equipment and hundreds of foreign-trained guerrilla fighters into this country."

It was a stunning cable, unlike anything White had said before, totally contradictory to what he would say in the months ahead. It read like the effort of a beleaguered man, an ambassador hoping to hold on to his job, to show his new bosses that he was one of them. White said later he was "being a good soldier," but he rejected a suggestion that he was trying to curry favor. The cable was drafted for White by one of his senior aides. "But I signed it, so I'm responsible for it," White said with obvious regret.

Still, White blocked the incoming administration from getting everything it would have liked. On the nineteenth, one day before the Reagan administration assumed full control, the senior U.S. military commander in El Salvador, Colonel Eldon Cummings, presented White with a lengthy cable requesting seventy-five military advisers. White was stunned. There had been no discussion with him or anyone else in the embassy about this dramatic increase. Why, he asked the colonel, had he drafted this cable? Cummings, a bit embarrassed, said he had been instructed to do so by the Pentagon and the U.S. Southern Command in Panama. "It was a straight power play by the Pentagon," White said later, "to have on the desk of the new administration a request for so many military advisers and to bypass the ambassador and the rest of the country team." White said he refused to approve the request, sending his own cable, which the State Department refuses to release under the FOIA.

The Pentagon, which had been itching for more military involvement in El Salvador, would have to wait. But not for long.

11

FROM A REVOLUTION
TO THE COLD WAR

TEN weeks after Reagan had become President, Archbishop Rivera y Damas, who was highly respected by U.S. embassy officials, visited Washington and provided the new policymakers with a candid assessment of the reality in El Salvador. He met with Vice President Bush, Judge William Clark, deputy assistant secretary of state at the time, and Thomas Enders, in charge of Latin American affairs at State. Clark opened the meeting "by expressing satisfaction that a man of moderation, such as Bishop Rivera, speaks for the Salvadoran church," the State Department informed all diplomatic posts in a Confidential cable. But the Reagan administration didn't listen well to the archbishop.

"In light of my conversations, I am convinced that the Administration does not understand the composition and nature of the Junta," Rivera y Damas wrote to the Vice President after his return to El Salvador. "Specifically, I think you underestimate the power and resistance of the right wing military to a true political change, including the kind of political dialogue which I am sure is the only road to peace in our country. When you and I discussed who the 'extremes' were in El Salvador, I was surprised that you defined the Junta as centrist and receiving attacks from both the right and the left which, to a certain extent, is true but what is more evident is the struggle between the Junta and the left, aggravated by the fact that the high command of the military are principally members of the far right. Therefore your views of the Junta as 'Centrist' do not concur with the reality and practice of the Junta which is greatly influenced by the right wing of the military. Failure to grasp the views of this element of the military, their power in the Junta, and their resistance to change will be a fatal mistake for U.S. policy." It was a prescient warning.

The archbishop urged the new administration not to send further military aid. "The provision of military assistance at this moment in our country's history simply strengthens the military," he wrote. He also pleaded with the administration to seek a negotiated settlement. "The United States must clearly indicate it is in favor of a political solution through negotiations or such negotiation will not occur in El Salvador. . . . [T]he U.S. role is essential in pressuring the military to accept a political solution."

The new administration ignored the archbishop on all counts.

While the administration said that it was opposed to a rightist coup —though Reagan himself during a press conference stopped short of saying the United States would cut off aid if there were one—it was only lukewarm in its support of Duarte and the Christian Democrats. The Christian Democratic party in El Salvador was far more liberal than Reagan's Republican party; expropriating farms and nationalizing banks would not be included in any Republican party platform and ran counter to the American party's emphasis on free enterprise. Rather than stress its support for Duarte and his party, the Reagan administration distanced itself from them. When Duarte visited the United States in the fall of 1981, he was not extended the reception frequently accorded leaders from even the most insignificant countries. He spent twenty minutes chatting with Reagan, thirty minutes with Bush—"and that was it," Duarte recalled. It was not an official state visit; there was no White House dinner, not even a joint press conference. These slights were strong messages to the right and military in El Salvador.

The overriding objective of the Reagan administration was to prevent a leftist government from coming to power. The cost of doing that was support for a rightist military-controlled government that was systematically murdering its own citizens—"a genocidal nun-killing" government, one anguished diplomat called it—a government that refused to prosecute the killers of the American churchwomen and the American agricultural workers. "You've really got two choices when you get into a nasty human rights situation," explained a Foreign Service officer who occupied a senior position in the embassy in El Salvador during the Reagan administration and who strongly backed its policy. "You can say, 'Oh, Jesus, these guys are real pricks, we can't have anything to do with these kind of people, we're going home'—which is basically the Patt Derian approach. Or you can say, 'All right, it's terrible, it's lousy, it's horrendous; what are we going to do about it?' " Then, recalling President Franklin D. Roosevelt's remark about the Nicaraguan dictator General Somoza—"he may be a son of a bitch, but he's our son of a bitch"—the diplomat put it in the context of the Reagan administration's policy in El Salvador: "You've just got to decide who your pricks are and go with them."

I didn't start the El Salvador thing, I inherited it," President Reagan said at one of his first news conferences. He was right—partly. What he failed to note was that when he entered the White House as the nation's fortieth President, he inherited a generally favorable situation in El Salvador. On the very day Reagan was sworn in, a spokesman for the Salvadoran junta declared that the guerrillas' "final offensive" had been "totally crushed." Defense Minister García said that his forces had killed 1,000 guerrillas, while losing only 97 men. The statements were exaggerations, but only slightly. The revolutionaries' military effort had been dealt a crippling blow. "The government is in no jeopardy at this time," Lieutenant General Ernest Graves, director of the Defense Security Assistance Agency, told the Senate Foreign Relations Committee in March 1981. It would be a full eight months before the guerrillas could take even a small town, Perquín, and they were able to hold it for only nine days. "I think the point to be drawn from this," Enders advised the House Subcommittee on Inter-American Affairs shortly after the guerrillas had been pushed out of Perquín, is that "the insurgents are not able to prevail against the Army of El Salvador nor are they indeed able to seriously push it in a military sense." Even the flow of arms to the guerrillas from Cuba and Nicaragua was reduced in the weeks following Reagan's ascension to power, according to the administration, which added that as a result, the guerrillas were running low on ammunition. A further favorable development for the new administration was that six days before it took office, the leftists expressed their willingness to negotiate a settlement, an offer that was to be frequently extended during the following months.

If El Salvador is eventually "lost" to a Marxist government, if the guerrillas do achieve a military victory or if the United States has to send American soldiers in order to prevent that, the Reagan administration will have to share much of the blame. For just as the Carter administration had not taken advantage of the propitious circumstances following the 1979 coup, the Reagan administration failed to take advantage of the favorable situation when it arrived in Washington.

For the Reagan administration, El Salvador was a place to do more than merely stop a leftist government from coming to power. It was to become a symbol of U.S. resolve, whereby the United States would show the Soviet Union it could control events and would reassert itself as a world power. The humiliating seizure of the American hostages in Iran, the Soviet Union's brazen invasion of Afghanistan, the Sandinistas' victory in Nicaragua were cited by Republicans to bolster their charge that under Carter and the Democrats the United States had grown weak in the world. El Salvador was such a tiny country it seemed a place where the United States could work its will. It would be the place where the United States would "send a message to Moscow," as White House press secretary James Brady declared, where the United States would "draw the line," as Secretary of State Haig put it.

The administration had important support for its "get tough" policy. "Haig is right, this is the place to draw the line," Senator Charles Percy of Illinois, Republican chairman of the Senate Foreign Relations Committee, told reporters in a breakfast meeting one month after Reagan had become President.

The Reagan administration presented its Salvadoran policy in terms of "vital" U.S. security interests, that if it didn't stop the leftist revolutionaries there, the security of the United States would be threatened. One of the most concise expositions of the Reagan policy in El Salvador was made during congressional testimony by Assistant Secretary of State for Latin America Enders. "There is no mistaking that the decisive battle for Central America is under way in El Salvador," he began. "If, after Nicaragua, El Salvador is captured by a violent minority, who in Central America would not live in fear? How long would it be before major U.S. strategic interests—the canal, sea lanes, oil supplies—were at risk?" he asked rhetorically.

The fear that sea-lanes could be threatened has its roots in the past. Secretary of State Kissinger made the same argument when he advocated sending U.S. forces to Angola to protect the sea-lanes in the South Atlantic, through which passed ships with oil from the Middle East. The troops weren't sent, and Angola became a pro-Soviet nation; but the sea-lanes have never been threatened.

The most appropriate response to Enders came in a *Miami Herald* editorial:

Change the place names, and the speech's familiarity comes into focus.
It was heard in the 1960s to describe Southeast Asia. The Vietnam parallel is chillingly, incontestably obvious. It is not the only recent historic parallel, however. Substitute "Iran" for Nicaragua and "Afghanistan" for El Salvador, and Mr. Enders' words echo the Soviet

Union's justification for invading Afghanistan in December 1979. To listen to Mr. Enders is to hear the voice of a fearful superpower rationalizing why it must impose its will by military means on smaller nearby nations in turmoil.

Reagan presented the threat even more ominously than Enders had. "We believe that the government of El Salvador is on the front line in a battle that is really aimed at the very heart of the Western Hemisphere, and eventually us," he declared.

Nicaragua, El Salvador, Guatemala, Mexico—that is the way the Reagan administration envisioned the dominoes falling to the Marxists, who would eventually threaten "the soft under-belly of Kansas," as White used to remark, sardonically expressing the fears of the hard-liners in the Pentagon and National Security Council who were pushing for more military aid during the Carter administration.*

It is difficult to accept that what happens in tiny El Salvador affects "vital" U.S. interests. Certainly, the United States may be said to have "important" interests there. But "vital" ones? Four years before the Reagan administration arrived in Washington, the Republican-appointed U.S. ambassador to El Salvador, Ignacio Lozano, a newspaper publisher from California, told Congress that the United States "really has no vital interest in the country." And Assistant Secretary of State for Latin America Charles Bray, who had been appointed by President Ford, had testified a few months earlier, "The United States has no strategic interests in El Salvador." As Robert Pastor, who argued for more military aid to El Salvador while a member of Carter's NSC, has written, "A 'vital interest' is presumably one for which the U.S. is willing to fight." The Reagan administration undercut its own contention that the U.S. interests were vital by repeatedly declaring that U.S. troops would not be sent there, a position endorsed overwhelmingly by the American public. The prestigious Foreign Policy Association in New York said, "The United States has no vital economic or security interests in El Salva-

*Other nations in the region worried about another domino effect. "We believe the domino theory can work in reverse," a high-ranking official from a major Latin American democracy told journalist James LeMoyne during a luncheon. While saying that his country, was a staunch U.S. ally, was worried about "Marxist, pro-Cuban states in Central America," he stressed, "We're also worried about seeing a string of extreme right-wing states." Referring to the strength of D'Aubuisson and the conservative military in El Salvador, the U.S.-backed anti-Sandinista military forces operating out of Honduras, and the grip that the military has on power in Guatemala, he said, "We think they threaten us just as much as the Marxists."

dor. . . . It is a small country 800 miles away, caught in a tide of civil war which two administrations have elevated to a battleground of the Cold War."

Not only are U.S. interests in El Salvador not vital, but it's even "too strong" to contend that they are "strategic," argued Lawrence Pezzullo, a Foreign Service officer who served in Latin America for every President from Eisenhower to Reagan. "With the advent of the ICBM and Yankee-class submarines off our coast, how the hell can you talk about strategic interests?" he asked rhetorically. "And all of that business that the traffic coming through the Caribbean is so vital to our interests—the fact of the matter is you've got Cuba in the Caribbean for the last twenty years. They could have intercepted those lanes anytime. You didn't need Nicaragua. You didn't need the airfield in Grenada. This is just hyperbole."*

Even if we assume that a leftist government in El Salvador would be pro-Soviet—an assumption that is contrary to the orientation of the strongest of the guerrilla organizations—and if we added to that an assumption of the worst-case scenario—that the Soviets would try to put missiles there—the United States could, as it did in Cuba in 1962, force the Soviets to back down.

The policy of the Reagan administration in El Salvador is best understood by looking not at U.S. military interests and concerns but at the conservative ideology of the administration. It was alarmed, for example, by the victory of Socialist François Mitterrand in France. There wasn't much the administration could do about a democratic victory in Europe. But it is not about to allow a leftist, Marxist government to come to power in the Western Hemisphere by any means: by the force of arms, through negotiations, or even at the ballot box. It was a democratically elected Marxist government in Chile that the Nixon administration—which was less politically conservative than the Reagan administration—tried to block from coming to power and eventually helped overthrow in 1973.

In El Salvador administration officials insisted that there were no major differences between their policy and that pursued by the Carter administration. "That's a lot of shit," said Wayne Smith, a diplomat who spent most of his career in Latin America, the last two years as the senior U.S. representative in Cuba. He was right. There were dif-

*At the time Ambassador Pezzullo made this statement in an interview with me, the Reagan administration was asserting that Grenada, under the influence of Cuba and the Soviet Union, was building an airfield for military purposes. Several months later the administration pointed to the airfield as one of the justifications for invading the island.

ferences—in how the situation was viewed and how it would be dealt with.

The Carter administration, or at least Robert White, saw El Salvador as a civil war, the inexorable result of generations of bitter poverty and extreme repression, with Cuba and Nicaragua taking advantage of the depressing conditions. "The revolution is homegrown, and as revolutions do, it got its arms and support wherever it could," White has said. The Reagan administration acknowledged the existence of the poverty and repression, but it saw the problem in El Salvador as "first and foremost global, second regional, with focus on Cuba, and third it is local," in Haig's analysis. El Salvador, the Reagan administration declared, was "a textbook case of indirect armed aggression by Communist powers through Cuba." Whereas the Carter administration saw the greatest threat to a democratic, centrist government in El Salvador as coming "from the right," a State Department spokesman noted a month after Reagan's inauguration, "We think it is from the leftist insurgents."

While both administrations agreed on the goal of keeping a leftist government from coming to power in El Salvador, they had markedly divergent definitions of the left and concomitantly the center. Although the Carter administration was not aggressive in trying to bring the democratic leftists into the Salvadoran government, it did meet with Ungo, Zamora, and other opposition political leaders, including Enrique Álvarez before he was murdered. The Reagan administration largely refused to talk with the opposition politicians, except on the issue of participating in elections. During the Carter administration, Ungo said, "I was in touch with every ambassador in Central America." After Reagan's inauguration "I saw no one, not even the ones I had met with before."

There were also differences over how to deal with the Salvadoran right. White sought to break the alliance between the United States and the Salvadoran political right that had governed the country with U.S. blessing for decades. "Hinton's job," said a Foreign Service officer who served both ambassadors, was to "repair the alienation" with the right that White had caused. "He accomplished that." The fundamental philosophical differences between the two administrations were portended in a debate on CBS between Jeane Kirkpatrick and Patt Derian during the transition. Kirkpatrick led: "If we are confronted with the choice between offering assistance to a moderately repressive autocratic government which is also friendly to the United States, and permitting it to be overrun by a Cuban-trained, Cuban-armed, Cuban-

sponsored insurgency, we would assist the moderate autocracy."
Derian fairly exploded: "What the hell is 'moderately repressive'—
that you only torture half of the people, that you only do summary
executions now and then? I don't even know what 'moderately repressive' is. The idea that we somehow must stand closer to dictators—
people who are cruel to their people—is absurd."

Kirkpatrick's views, which were to become the intellectual girders
of the Reagan administration's policies in El Salvador and throughout the third world, had been spelled out by her in a lengthy essay,
"Dictatorships and Double Standards." This article, which appeared
in *Commentary* in 1979, first brought Kirkpatrick, a professor at
Georgetown University, to candidate Reagan's attention and eventually led to her being named ambassador to the United Nations, with
Cabinet rank.

Kirkpatrick argued that Carter's foreign policy, with its emphasis on
human rights, had been disastrous for U.S. interests, leading to the
overthrow of Somoza in Nicaragua and the shah in Iran. They were
followed, she contended, by "even more repressive dictatorships than
had been in place before." She also set up what was to become the
much-discussed dichotomy between authoritarian and totalitarian
governments. The former merited U.S. support, she argued, because
they were pro-American and could eventually be democratized.

Senator Howard Metzenbaum, Democrat of Ohio, after listening to
Kirkpatrick outline her views at a luncheon of the Members of Congress for Peace Through Law in February 1981, said they sounded like
"the exact replay of all the Secretaries of State and all of our leadership who thought we could make deals with the juntas and dictators
and fascists throughout the world in the last 30 years. Now, maybe
that's a good policy, but it hasn't worked." In her response, Kirkpatrick
declared: "Now, if you want to say that other powers—the Soviets—can
deal with dictatorships, and suffer no loss of prestige or stature, but
that if we deal with dictators or autocrats, we lose our moral credentials, then I would simply say, that's mistaken."

About General Maximiliano Hernández Martínez, whose name and
brutally repressive methods from 1931 to 1944 have been venerated by
the Salvadoran death squads, Kirkpatrick wrote in 1981: "To many
Salvadorans the violence of this repression seems less important than
the fact of restored order and the thirteen years of civil peace that
ensued."

Kirkpatrick didn't look kindly on the work of the American churchwomen who were killed, or on the opposition FDR leaders who were

tortured and murdered, or even on U.S. congressmen who opposed the Reagan administration's policy in El Salvador. About the latter she declared that there were members of Congress "who would actually like to see the Marxist forces take power in the country."

"Let me make this last bit clear," asked the reporter who heard the remark, made by Kirkpatrick on a flight from Washington to New York. "Do you really believe there are U.S. lawmakers who would like to see a Marxist government in El Salvador?"

"Yes, of course," Kirkpatrick answered. "I don't think, I must say, that there are many, but there are some. This is, of course, in general terms."

Kirkpatrick's views about authoritarian regimes disturbed many people, including the president of the Inter-American Commission on Human Rights of the Organization of American States, Tom J. Farer. "While the eccentricity of Kirkpatrick's account may raise doubts about her competence for public service, what matters more is the effect her account is likely to have on policy makers who confuse it with reality," Farer, an American law professor, wrote in *The New York Review of Books.* The reality in El Salvador, he accurately noted, was military rule beginning in 1932. "What was the characteristic of this period was not 'evolution' toward democracy but prevention of that evolution."

As for dealing with the crisis in El Salvador, the goals of the Carter administration, at least as Robert White said frequently, were to "end the war, carry out the reforms, and get to elections." His successor, Deane Hinton, would use almost the same phrases, at least publicly, to describe the Reagan administration's policy. "Save the economy, stop the violence, have the elections, and ride into the sunset" was how Hinton put it in an interview shortly after he had arrived as ambassador.

But in a Secret cable, Hinton outlined the goals as to "win the war, avert economic collapse, and carry out democratic elections." Only on the issue of elections did the two administrations agree.

Publicly the administration insisted it backed the economic reforms. When the new administration explained its policy to the Senate Foreign Relations Committee, in March 1981, Senator Zorinsky inquired specifically if it intended "to endorse and embrace" the "government control over the export of major crops, nationalization of the banks, and the agrarian reform." Undersecretary of State Walter J. Stoessel, Jr., replied unequivocally that "yes, they are supported by the

Reagan Administration." It was not true. From the outset the administration was opposed to the nationalizations of the banks and export trade, according to several State Department officials who were involved in formulating the policy in El Salvador. The nationalizations run counter to the administration's strong views about free enterprise, for as Hinton advised Washington, in the same Secret cable mentioned above, "The economic mess here is attributable in part to agrarian, banking and marketing reforms. . . ."* But even the "agrarian reform is not something that was high on the [Reagan] administration's things when it came to power," said a senior State Department official. The administration, as late as mid-1983, declared in a public document that Phase II of the land reform "has been postponed indefinitely for lack of money, personnel, and organizational resources." It was a half-truth. Phase II hadn't been postponed. It was dead, buried in large measure because the administration was opposed to it, precisely what Ambassador-designate Hinton privately informed several congressmen and their aides in the spring of 1981, according to notes of the meeting.

But it is on the matter of the war—specifically, whether it was seeking a military victory—that there is probably the greatest gap between the public statements and classified documents. Publicly the administration insisted it was not seeking a military victory. But as Hinton declared in the Secret cable, to "win" the war was a primary objective. The Reagan policy was to "defeat the guerrillas militarily. Period. And all the rest be damned," said a Foreign Service officer who was in El Salvador for more than two years during the Reagan administration. Classified cables confirm his statement.

In his first "Annual Integrated Assessment of Security Assistance for El Salvador," a Confidential cable (only five of twenty-one pages of which were released under the Freedom of Information Act), Hinton said, "We concur with the Salvadoran assessment that substantial increases in the armed forces are a precondition for a *military solution* to the civil war [emphasis added]." Five months later, in November 1981, in another Confidential cable, Hinton reported, "While the goals and U.S. interests and objectives . . . remain essentially the same, our perception of the resources required to meet these goals has

*The administration's opposition to the reforms wasn't expressed publicly until George Shultz testified before the Senate Foreign Relations Committee during his confirmation hearings as secretary of state in July 1982. The nationalizations of the banks and export trade were "reforms we could do without," he said. Specifically as to the bank nationalization, he declared that "if we don't have that reform, I would put that down as a plus, not a minus."

changed substantially—upward." Again, only a few pages of this cable were released; presumably the other pages outline how the "military solution" would be achieved. In one of the paragraphs that weren't deleted, Hinton advised Washington that a "substantial increase in the [Salvadoran] armed forces must be accompanied by quality training" and additional military equipment from the United States "in order to *defeat* the insurgent forces [emphasis added]." Then, in his second "Annual Integrated Assessment," Hinton noted that the Salvadoran government "is fully committed to the 'victory strategy' plan proposed by El Salvador, developed in cooperation with the U.S. military strategy assistance team. . . ."

These Confidential cables contradict what administration officials were saying. Just three months before the last cable was sent, Assistant Secretary of State Enders had emphatically told the Senate Foreign Relations Committee, "Our goal [in El Salvador] is not a military victory." Hinton himself, the author of the cables, asserted to *The Washington Post*'s Christopher Dickey in January 1982, "We've never been looking for a military victory." The military strategy assistance team, which had developed the "victory strategy plan"—referred to in the final cable—had come from the U.S. Southern Command in Panama. Yet the head of that command, Lieutenant General Wallace Nutting, told the Senate Foreign Relations Committee in February 1983, "The policy being pursued does not seek a military victory."

Although a shift in United States policy toward El Salvador was expected, the speed with which Reagan changed the course caught most Americans, and the nation's allies, by surprise. Within just weeks after becoming President, he announced that he would nearly triple the number of United States military advisers in El Salvador, from twenty to fifty-five, and immediately rush $25 million of military aid, which was in addition to the $5 million Carter had just sent. And no longer would there be any attempt to maintain a distinction between "lethal" and "nonlethal" aid. Reagan's would clearly be of the former kind. The weapons to be sent were enumerated in a Confidential list prepared by the Defense Department. On that list were M-16 rifles, 81 mm and 60 mm mortars, M-60 machine guns, M-23/M-60 gun systems for the ten helicopters being supplied, M-79 grenade launchers, and ammunition for all these weapons. The military aid clearly signaled the Reagan administration's military intentions. It was being sent even though the guerrillas' "final offensive" had failed and at the same time that administration officials were saying that the guerrillas were running low on ammunition because of an apparent decision by Nicaragua and Cuba to reduce their assistance.

Archbishop Rivera y Damas pleaded with the Reagan administration not to provide any military assistance. "We do not need more arms in El Salvador from any source," he wrote in his letter to Vice President Bush. "I am opposed to any further military aid to the Junta; it will not solve our basic problem. The U.S. relationship to the military should be political: move them to dialogue." A few weeks later, after a visit to Harvard, the archbishop wrote to Massachusetts Senators Kennedy and Paul E. Tsongas and Massachusetts Representative Thomas P. O'Neill, Jr., speaker of the House. "May I be so presumptuous to ask that you use your position in the Congress of the United States to see that military aid to my country will cease and that support is given to a process of dialogue that will bring about a just and peaceful solution to the present conflict and violence."

Surprisingly, the top Salvadoran civilian and military leaders agreed that more military aid was not needed. Duarte said that what the country needed was a massive infusion of economic aid, that it had sufficient military strength to contain the guerrillas. Making the same point, in February 1981, Defense Minister García declared, "We have already demonstrated that we can defeat the guerrillas." He added, "But I insist the solution should not be military but political." And the commander of the National Guard, Colonel Vides Casanova, said, "Militarily, we have sufficient capacity to control the situation."

The Reagan administration received similar-sounding advice from America's allies in Europe and South America. The West Germans said that the solution should be political, not military, and worked to bring the Salvadoran junta and the FDR together for negotiations. The staunchly anti-Soviet Socialist government of François Mitterrand in France, while agreeing with the administration's concern about "external interference" in El Salvador, nevertheless cautioned Reagan about trying to solve the Salvadoran conflict "by purely military means." And when President Reagan visited Canada in early March 1981, he learned that it also opposed his decision to send advisers and arms to El Salvador. In Latin America the Argentines, Brazilians, and Venezuelans all expressed reservations about the increasing United States military involvement in El Salvador. The strongest opposition came from Mexico, which supposedly would be the most threatened by events in El Salvador. Warning against U.S. military action, the Mexican president, José López Portillo, said it was not "natural or reasonable" for the superpowers to "fight over our conflicts as though they were owners." As had the leaders in many other countries, he advised that "a military solution is not viable and that only a political solution will restore peace to the region."*

But the Reagan administration ignored the pleas of the archbishop, the views of the Salvadoran military, and the advice of allies. The revolution in El Salvador was no longer a civil war; it had become, by the pronouncements of the administration, part of the geopolitical cold war. It was now the United States' war. The United States would supply the helicopters and jet bombers. The United States would supply the rifles, the machine guns, the mortars, the bullets. The Salvadorans would supply the bodies—to be trained in the United States, to be trained in Honduras, to die in El Salvador.

A Secret cable sent from the U.S. embassy in August 1983—another that was denied under the Freedom of Information Act—reveals that for the two and a half years from January 1, 1981, until June 30, 1983, 2,805 Salvadoran soldiers were killed in action, and 5,298 wounded. That toll represents at least 20 percent of the Salvadoran soldiers who served during that period and a casualty rate of nearly nine per day, both of which, proportionately, are considerably higher than the losses suffered by American troops in Vietnam.

In El Salvador, the Reagan administration was propping up a rightist government that even it acknowledged lacked popular support. "Probably the overwhelming majority of people in El Salvador at the moment do not support anybody," John Bushnell informed the Senate Foreign Relations Committee in March 1981. "They do not support the left or the right or the government." (It was an assessment expressed frequently—but always off the record, of course—by the American military advisers and diplomats in El Salvador.) Senator Joseph R. Biden, Jr., Democrat of Delaware, thanked Bushnell for his "candid" assessment. But what he and other members of Congress who continually voted for increasing amounts of U.S. military assistance failed to ask was why the United States was backing a government not supported by its own people.

The position of the Reagan administration, like that of the Carter administration, was that it was supporting a moderate, centrist government, one caught between, and the best alternative to, extremes of the far left and far right. But the government supported by the Reagan administration was even less of the center, and more to the right, than

*Mexico was still strongly opposed to U.S. policy in 1984. During a news conference with foreign correspondents in February, President Miguel de la Madrid said that the U.S. government should "come to the conviction that a military intervention, far from solving the problems, would aggravate them and they would be more extensive in Central America, if not in all of the neighboring area."

the one Carter had backed. The Christian Democrats occupied key positions in the government, including Duarte and Morales Ehrlich on the junta. But the power was with the army. "The PDC [Christian Democrats] without the army would be nothing," Hinton frankly reported to Washington in the June 1981 Secret cable, the one in which he informed Washington that he talked to the press "about favorable trends," while omitting mention of "seriously adverse trends." The power of the army was one trend he did not discuss with reporters. Nor did he discuss another fact of the Salvadoran reality, which he reported in the cable: "A continuing serious problem here—despite some recent progress—is officially tolerated, if not sponsored, rightist terrorism and violence."

The situation in El Salvador was even more ominous than Hinton reported. It wasn't just the army that had control; it was the most conservative, brutal elements within that army. "The Government of El Salvador is not Duarte's but rather effectively controlled by a council of senior army officers (Gutiérrez, García, Vides Casanova, Carranza, Morán)," members of the State Department's human rights bureau wrote in an internal memorandum to Secretary of State Haig in March 1981. These senior commanders "control the security forces and they have resolved upon a policy of repression not only against the guerrillas and their active sympathizers but against those who challenge the military's pre-eminence or criticize their conduct." Duarte's utility, they wrote, "is primarily as a 'fig leaf' to cover the reality of a rightist controlled military regime—much as Ungo serves a similar purpose in fronting for the Marxist-controlled FDR."

This picture of El Salvador did not fit in with the new administration's policy, so the memorandum had to be sent through the Dissent Channel, the State Department procedure for expressing views that don't follow the prevailing winds. But the fact that this assessment accurately depicted the Salvadoran reality, and that the Reagan administration chose to ignore this reality, was underscored in the letter from Archbishop Rivera y Damas to Vice President Bush.

President Reagan had a new policy for El Salvador. What he needed was the personnel to implement it.

12

PURGE

To implement his hard-line policy in Central America, Reagan conducted one of the most thorough purges in State Department history, unlike anything since the ouster of "China hands" during the witchhunts for "Communists" by Senator Joseph McCarthy in the early 1950's. Reagan removed from the highest levels of the State Department and as ambassadors in Central America nearly everyone with knowledge about and understanding of Latin America. In their stead were substituted men who had established their conservative reputations, in many instances a bit tarnished, in Southeast Asia. "The Gang That Blew Vietnam Goes Latin" is how *The Washington Post* characterized Reagan's Central America team.

At the top of Reagan's list for Latin America was Thomas Ostrom Enders, to be assistant secretary of state for Inter-American affairs. His credentials were impeccable: born to a wealthy and conservative Connecticut banking family; prepared at Exeter; member of the prestigious secret society Scroll and Key at Yale. "Arrogant," "supercilious," "elitist" are the adjectives frequently used by aides, congressmen, and foreign diplomats to describe the six-foot-eight-inch Enders.

Enders's outlook was characterized not only by his conservatism but also by an elitism that assumed the United States knew what was best for the world. And he knew better than anyone—he thought. One American scholar, widely regarded as one of the most knowledgeable about Central America, was consulted frequently by Enders when he was assistant secretary-designate. After Enders had moved into his State Department office, the calls continued, but the scholar was stunned. Enders no longer asked questions. It was no longer a discussion. Enders presented his views, without soliciting any comment from the scholar.

However much they were put off by his haughty manner, those who had contact with Enders were unanimous on one score: He was brilliant—Junior Phi Beta Kappa; first in his class from Yale with a B.A. in history and economics in 1953; doctorate in colonial history from the University of Paris in 1955; master's in economics from Harvard two years later.

To make room for Enders, the administration unceremoniously ousted William Bowdler, who had earned the wrath of conservative Republicans because of his role in negotiating the ouster of General Somoza in 1979. During the 1970's Bowdler had been ambassador to El Salvador and Guatemala as well as served as deputy assistant secretary for Inter-American affairs. Enders was to be the first assistant secretary for Latin America in several decades without any prior experience in the region. He could speak several languages—French, German, Italian—but not Spanish. A somewhat bitter Robert White remarked to the Senate Foreign Relations Committee that while Enders was "undoubtedly a capable man," his "chief qualification appears to be that he never has served in Latin America. . . . I doubt seriously that this administration would appoint to the post of Assistant Secretary for Europe a man who never has served in Europe."

But Enders had served in Southeast Asia—Cambodia, to be exact, where he covered up government atrocities, frustrated congressional efforts to obtain information, deceived and discredited journalists, and heralded the fraudulent election victory of Cambodian General Lon Nol as "a step forward for Cambodian democracy." It was also for his performance in Cambodia, first as the number two in the embassy, later as the man in charge, that he earned the epithet "Can-Do Bombardier." Enders had selected targets for American B-52 pilots, generally using maps too old and crude to assure that there would not be villages, and civilians, where the bombs fell.

Not only had Enders assumed a role usually reserved for generals, not diplomats, but the bombings had been a violation of a law passed by Congress that severely restricted U.S. military activity in Cambodia. When the Senate Foreign Relations Committee in April 1973, sent two staff members to determine the embassy's role in the bombings, Enders stonewalled. As William Shawcross described it in his book *Sideshow,* Enders told the investigators that "special instructions" from Washington restricted the information he could provide them. Enders had drafted the "special instructions." He also denied any U.S. involvement. But on a cheap transistor radio owned by the UPI and *Newsweek* correspondent Sylvia Foa, the investigators heard embassy personnel giving bombing instructions to American pilots.

Following this incident, Foa was expelled from Cambodia at the urging of Enders, who called her dispatches "tendentious."

But Enders had pleased at least two very important people with his unquestioning execution of American policy in Cambodia. In 1974 Secretary of State Kissinger rewarded him with the position of assistant secretary of state for economic and business affairs. In 1976 he was further honored, with his appointment as ambassador to Canada. A Canadian official recalled that Enders would take long weekends for solo ventures 200 miles north of Ottawa, to the harsh, desolate stretches of the northern Canadian wilderness. "I think it was self-punishment, maybe for Cambodia—who knows?—or maybe just to show how tough he was."

The other man Enders had impressed in Cambodia was Colonel Alexander Haig, who, as Reagan's secretary of state, reached out to Enders to stop the "Communists" in Central America. When the Senate Foreign Relations Committee confirmed Enders for the economic post in 1974, it had done so reluctantly and only after having issued a highly unusual public rebuke, charging him with "grossly misleading" descriptions of the U.S. embassy's role in the Cambodian bombings. But Enders breezed through his confirmation hearing before the Foreign Relations Committee for the top-level Latin American position seven years later. Even though the committee members had been briefed by their aides about Enders's activities in Cambodia, no senator raised the matter.

A confirmation hearing serves many functions. It is an opportunity for the committee, which has primary congressional responsibility for the direction and conduct of U.S. foreign policy, to determine where that policy is headed and to extract some promises, or assurances, from the policymaker seeking confirmation. But only three of the committee's seventeen members bothered to attend the 1981 hearing, which lasted less than three hours. No one inquired about Enders's activities in Cambodia. Even Senator Dodd, a liberal who was to become one of the most persistent critics of the Reagan administration policy, praised Enders, noting that during his twenty years in the Foreign Service he had served under several administrations. "He served them all well," Dodd proclaimed. Enders was also to serve President Reagan well, faithfully carrying the administration's policy to the Hill and to the American public, until he was ousted in a showdown won by Kirkpatrick and Clark in 1983.

Enders brought in, as his chief deputy for Central America, L. Craig Johnstone to be the director of the Office of Central American Affairs. Although Johnstone as the son of a Foreign Service officer had spent much of his youth in Latin America, including El Salvador, he had never served there during his own Foreign Service career. He was another of the "can-do" types from Vietnam, where he had been directly involved with the notorious rural pacification program, CORDS (Civil Operations and Rural Development Support), which was run by the CIA and the Agency for International Development. That was merged into the Phoenix program, which targeted Vietcong cadres and sympathizers for assassination. In the spring of 1983 a CORDS-style program was brought to El Salvador, much to the displeasure of senior AID officials there. The principal architect of the Salvadoran pacification plan, according to a senior U.S. military officer in El Salvador, was Johnstone.

While Johnstone, with his Southeast Asia experience, was brought in to make Central America policy, James Cheek, who had impressive Central America credentials, was shoved out. Cheek had spent most of his Foreign Service career in Latin America, including Chile, Brazil, and Uruguay. For his work in Nicaragua, he had received one of the State Department's highest awards. And it was Cheek who had held the Salvadoran situation together during the tumultuous first months of 1980. The Reagan administration banished Cheek to the embassy in Nepal.

President-elect Reagan's foreign policy transition team had recommended that the State Department's human rights bureau should not be "in a position to paralyze or unduly delay decisions on issues where human rights concerns conflict with other vital U.S. interests." Reagan's appointment to the head of the bureau was Elliott Abrams, who was thirty-three years old when he arrived at the State Department post, after having briefly served Jeane Kirkpatrick at the United Nations. His credentials were as blue-chip as Enders's: prepped at a private high school in Greenwich Village; B.A. from Harvard; master's degree from the London School of Economics; law degree from Harvard.

While Derian had been outspoken in her criticisms of dictatorial regimes, Abrams sought to mute public condemnation of such rightist countries as the Philippines, South Africa, South Korea, and Taiwan. Abrams "betrayed" the trust as America's human rights voice, the *Boston Globe* charged in an editorial in 1983. One of the actions that reflected his view of human rights was his endorsement of R. Bruce McColm to the seven-member Inter-American Commission on Human Rights, which is part of the Organization of American States and is probably the most effective governmentally related international human rights organization. The nomination, which Reagan approved, was an affront to the organization, the other members of which were distinguished jurists from Latin American countries. They included Marco Gerardo Monroy Cabra, a member of the Supreme Court of Justice in Colombia who had been a founding member of the College of International Lawyers and was the author of nine lawbooks; Gilda Maciel Correa Meyer Russomano, a director of the Institute of International Juridical Studies and author of six books on international law; and Luis Adolfo Silas Salinas, a former Bolivian vice-president, president of the Bolivian Human Rights Assembly, and a lawyer who specialized in labor law and human rights. McColm had only "limited experience in the human rights field" and was a "polemicist who has dealt almost exclusively with the sins of the left," *The New York Times* noted in an editorial. Thirty-three years old at the time of his appointment, McColm had written one book: *Where Have They Gone?: Rock and Roll Stars.* At the conservative Freedom House, he had written that Carter's human rights policy was "counterproductive."

In December 1983 the Reagan administration went after the Inter-American Foundation, when the Reagan appointees to the agency fired Peter D. Bell as president. The foundation was established by Congress in 1969 as a quasi-independent, nonpartisan agency to encourage self-help development projects. Operating quietly and with a small staff, many of whom had been in the Peace Corps, the foundation has channeled more than $170 million to 1,700 organizations such as agricultural cooperatives and community housing groups, usually with grants of less than $100,000—to every country in the region except Cuba. The conservative Heritage Foundation accused the Inter-American Foundation of favoring "collectivism" and supporting projects that were "incompatible with the philosophy of the Reagan Administration."

George C. Lodge, a professor at the Harvard Business School who was vice-chairman of the foundation's board during the Nixon, Ford, and Carter administrations, called the firing of Bell "the latest signal that the Reagan Administration dangerously misunderstands the nature of United States interests in Latin America." And Representative Dante B. Fascell, Democrat of Florida, who was one of the foundation's originators, said that Bell's ouster violated the foundation's purpose of being insulated "from the short-term political considerations of any Administration." To replace Bell, the Reagan administration recommended that the search committee be headed by William Doherty, executive director of the AIFLD, which had recently declined to lobby for the congressional bill that would have directly linked military aid to El Salvador to a trial of the men responsible for murdering the AIFLD workers Hammer and Pearlman.

As for Abrams, during one congressional appearance he indicated that his human rights policy included the United States' forming, training, and supplying the "counterrevolutionaries" trying to overthrow the Sandinista government.

"I can't allow the hearing to close without going back to something you said, Mr. Abrams, because I hope I heard you wrong," said the chairman of the House Subcommittee on Human Rights and International Organizations, Gus Yatron, a Pennsylvania Democrat. "Did you in fact say that the pressure that the United States is bringing against Nicaragua is part of our human rights policy?"

Abrams gave an evasive answer.

Yatron pushed. "I take it you stand by the statement that the kind of pressure we are bringing against Nicaragua is part of our human rights policy?"

Abrams: "The kind of pressure that we and the whole Western world are bringing against Nicaragua."

Yatron pointed out that the "Western World is not engaged in the kind of pressure we are bringing against Nicaragua" and asked if Abrams believed that the way to advance human rights was "to engage in covert assistance."

Again, Abrams was evasive, saying that he could not discuss it in an open hearing and that "to be philosophical about the nature of covert action . . . would take a while." He did not disavow the view that the "secret" war against Nicaragua was not part of the human rights policy.

As for El Salvador, it was Abrams who had rewritten the history of the collapse of the junta after the October 1979 coup. But his views of D'Aubuisson were even more alarming. When asked by Senator Tsongas during a hearing before the Senate Foreign Relations Committee if he agreed with the view that D'Aubuisson "would fit the extreme on the right," Abrams replied, "No, I do not think so."

Tsongas: "So you would have to be to the right of d'Aubuisson to be considered extremist."

Abrams: "In my mind, you would have to be engaged in murder."

D'Aubuisson *was* engaged in murder: probably of the archbishop and of the FDR leaders and certainly of scores of others among his political opponents. When asked if D'Aubuisson was involved in the death squads, a U.S. official who had served in El Salvador for two years told *New York Times* reporter James LeMoyne, "He's at the center of it." Even conservative Republican Congressman Jack Kemp said after visiting El Salvador that D'Aubuisson "is as much a danger to the country as the insurgents."

In congressional appearances Abrams repeatedly made false statements. He testified, for example, that the Salvadoran Army had "several hundred prisoners captured off the battlefield." In fact, at the time it had few, if any.* During another appearance he assured Congress that "several hundred officers" had been dismissed or jailed for human rights abuses. Again the truth was that few, if any, had. To a House committee in 1983, he asserted that "we don't know who the death squads are." By that date the CIA and embassy in El Salvador had sent numerous cables identifying the leaders. On the issue of whether Salvadorans who had illegally entered the United States were being killed after being deported back to El Salvador—as lawyers representing the aliens said happened frequently—Abrams testified that he was aware of no such incidents. "I have asked a lot of human rights groups for information and it is a little like Sherlock Holmes' dog that didn't bark," Abrams told the members of the House subcommittees on Human Rights and Western Hemisphere Affairs on August 3 1983. "I am at the point now where I think it is quite persuasive evidence that no one produces anything," he added. But on June 28 Abrams had met with Linda Yanez, an immigration lawyer from Brownsville, Texas, who provided him with information about at least one Salvadoran who had been killed on her return. Ms. Yanez followed that meeting with a letter to Abrams on July 15 with several affidavits, including one from the brother of a man who was decapitated after being deported back to El Salvador. (In January 1984 the Immigration and Naturalization Service acknowledged, in response to a report by the American Civil Liberties Union and the Center for Immigration Rights in Los Angeles, that up to fifty Salvadorans who had been deported had been killed after their return to El Salvador.)

When Abrams appeared before the House Subcommittee on Inter-American Affairs, in July 1982, to defend the administration's certification that the Salvadoran government was making progress in respecting human rights, Representative Studds charged that the administration's report was "fundamentally a dishonest document." Abrams took offense: "I would just like to ask Mr. Studds, is it not

---

*The practice of the Salvadoran Army has been to take no prisoners, to shoot everyone, a policy that Colonel Waghelstein tried desperately to get them to change. "It's tacky to shoot prisoners," the colonel told reporters a few weeks before Abrams's statement.

possible for purposes of our debate on El Salvador to leave aside a word like 'dishonest'? I really think that we are going to get a lot further if we can say to each other that you are right on this and wrong on that, than to call us names and dishonest."

In the field, the changes of ambassadors followed the same disturbing pattern—men with Latin American experience replaced by those without. To Mexico, Reagan sent a Hollywood actor, John Gavin. Though without any diplomatic experience, Gavin did speak fluent Spanish. And he was well known to millions of Mexicans—as the promoter of Bacardi rum on television commercials.

In Nicaragua, Lawrence Pezzullo, who had devoted most of his twenty-five years in the Foreign Service to Latin America (Mexico, Guatemala, Bolivia, Colombia, Uruguay), was succeeded by Anthony C. E. Quainton, who did not speak Spanish and had never served in a Latin post. Quainton had impressed Haig with his work as director of the State Department's Office for Combating Terrorism, where he was assigned after postings as economics officer in Pakistan, political officer in India, political officer in Paris, deputy chief of mission in Katmandu, and ambassador to the Central African Empire. (In March 1984 the Reagan administration removed Quainton from Nicaragua because it felt he was being too "soft" on the Sandinistas.)

In Honduras, Ambassador Jack R. Binns (prior experience in Guatemala, Bolivia, El Salvador) was replaced with John D. Negroponte, whose performance as political officer in Saigon had earned him a position on Kissinger's National Security Council, as "my staff expert on Vietnam," Kissinger said in his memoirs. Negroponte participated in the Vietnam peace talks in Paris, where, he informed the Senate Foreign Relations Committee during his confirmation hearing as ambassador to Honduras, he felt Kissinger had been too soft. Negroponte shared the view of many in the Reagan administration that the press was largely responsible for the problems in Central America. "There is much more at stake in Central America than seems to come through in our media," Negroponte wrote in a note for the alumni magazine of the Phillips Exeter Academy, from which he was graduated in 1956. "So writing to you from one of Central America's potential dominoes, I urge fellow classmates to get more than superficially interested.... It's a helluva lot closer to home than Saigon." In Honduras Negroponte, who had only one prior Latin American post (political counselor in Quito, Ecuador, in 1973), was more than just proconsul. He was plenipotentiary, playing an active role in directing the CIA-backed guerrilla forces trying to overthrow the Sandinista government in Nicaragua.

To no one's surprise, the first Central American ambassador whose head rolled during Reagan's purge was Robert White. Less than two weeks after becoming secretary of state, Haig summoned White into his State Department office and delivered the *coup de grâce.* Under a 1946 law governing the Foreign Service, career officers of ambassadorial rank technically cannot be fired but must be either offered another ambassadorial post or an assignment of equivalent rank or else retired. White, who had served every President since Dwight D. Eisenhower, was offered only degrading demotions, and Haig personally made the decision to retire him. Senator Pell noted that the unceremonious manner in which White had been forced out of the diplomatic corps had been used only twelve or thirteen times in the history of the Foreign Service and that White was among the "distinguished victims" who included George Kennan. White responded, "I regard it as an honor to join a small group of officers who have gone out of the service because they refused to betray their principles."

J. William Fulbright, who during thirty years of Senate service was an intellectual and political force behind most of the foreign policy issues of the time, sent White a note "to express my admiration and respect for you and the way you endeavored to serve the best interests of this country." Referring to the diplomats who had been forced out by McCarthy, Fulbright, who had been one of McCarthy's earliest and most forceful opponents, added that like those men, "your wise counsel has been rejected by the government, and the people of our country will pay the price for the folly of their government."

White quickly became one of the harshest critics of the Reagan administration's policies, calling for negotiations and opposing military aid. During congressional hearings in February 1981 he charged that "the chief killer of the Salvadorans is the government security forces." Referring to the administration's request for military aid, he asked the congressmen, "Do you want to associate yourself with this kind of killing?" The administration responded with character assassination. The day after White's testimony, State Department spokesman William Dyess described White as being "somewhat emotional" about El Salvador. Later Dyess said his comments were not intended to be "pejorative," but a senior White House official, requesting anonymity with *Washington Post* reporter John Goshko, called White a "sorehead."

Replacing White was Deane R. Hinton, who by his own admission "probably wasn't" qualified for the Salvadoran post. Perhaps he was being uncharacteristically modest, but Hinton had little experience in Latin America—until El Salvador, only four of his thirty-five years in the Foreign Service were below the border—and his training and orientation were not political but economic. "Hinton is an economist who had spent some time in Latin America, but not dealing with the hard political issues, the human rights issues," said an aide who respected him. Hinton had been with AID in Guatemala (1967–1969) and Chile (1969–1971), followed by three years as the director of the White House Council on International Economic Policy. Stories that he worked for the CIA have wafted through his career, fueled by his being thrown out of Zaire, his only previous ambassadorial post, on charges that he plotted, in 1975, an aborted assassination of President Mobutu Sese Seko. Hinton has denied any connections with the CIA. As for the Zaire charges, Hinton has said: "My defense was always that if I'd been out to get him, he'd have been dead."

Born in Missoula, Montana, in 1923 to the wife of an army officer, Hinton has been married twice—once divorced and once widowed—and is the father of ten children and stepchildren. (While he was ambassador to El Salvador, he sent a birthday check to a daughter in London; she endorsed it over to a Salvadoran guerrilla solidarity group.) In El Salvador, Hinton provided some gossipy relief from the numbing effects of daily stories about atrocities with his courting of the thirty-year-old daughter of one the country's wealthy families. They were married on Valentine's Day 1983.

Given to projecting a Churchillian image—chomping thick cigars while stroking his English sheep dog, which he named Wellington—Hinton was gruff and as outspoken as White. A Foreign Service officer who served both ambassadors contrasted the two men. White, he said, was "combative toward the Salvadorans and less toward us. Hinton was more combative toward us and less toward the Salvadorans." When the senior embassy officials gathered for their regular meetings at the fortresslike embassy, Hinton would frequently "jump up and down and storm around the room," recalled another senior aide. On one occasion Hinton threw a book at his political officer. "Members of the country team used to trade jokes about who got chewed out worse by Deane Hinton," remembered the aide. "It's part of the folklore there. He was such a tough son of a bitch to work for, we figured we all had to stick together or we would get sent home separately." But Hinton won the deep respect and loyalty of his embassy staff. "We'd march to hell with him," said the same aide.

Shortly after the Reagan administration had come to power, Ambassador Kirkpatrick noted, "I think that we [Americans] have something of a reputation in Latin America for being rather overbearing and trying to order things our way, and for wanting to run the shop." She quickly sought to dispel any intentions of the new administration to act in such a manner: "No one in the Reagan Administration wants to run El Salvador." But Hinton was every bit the proconsul that White had been. "Hinton is president, and García is vice-president," remarked a Salvadoran historian in 1982, an assessment that rightists and leftists shared. During the elections in March 1982 Hinton was nearly as active as the Salvadoran politicians. After the elections he called the political leaders to his home and urged them not to raise charges of fraud, and he brokered the negotiations that kept D'Aubuisson from enjoying the fruits of his electoral triumph. But Hinton went beyond what might normally be considered the diplomatic role of even an activist Foreign Service officer. In a Secret cable sent soon after his arrival in San Salvador, Hinton urged the carrying out of "sabotage missions into Nicaragua." In the same cable (which the State Department refused to release under the Freedom of Information Act), he also recommended that mercenaries be hired to fight the war.

But Reagan needed much more than just a new team of activist ambassadors and diplomats with experience in Vietnam to implement his policy in El Salvador. He needed to convince Congress and the American people to support his policy.

13

BLAMING OUTSIDERS

THE newly elected administration issued a white paper, charging that "aggression has been loosed against an independent people who want to make their own way in peace and freedom." The "brutal campaign of terror and armed attack" was "inspired, directed, supplied and controlled" by a neighboring Communist nation. The white paper contained what the State Department described as "massive evidence" establishing "beyond question" that the Communists were carrying out the aggression against an "established government."

The date was February 27, 1965. The country seeking peace and freedom was South Vietnam. The Communist aggressor was North Vietnam. Sixteen years later, on February 23, 1981, the newly elected administration of Ronald Reagan issued a similar-sounding white paper. "Communist Interference in El Salvador" was the title. Only the names and the dates seemed to have changed much.*

"This special report presents *definitive* evidence of the clandestine military support given by the Soviet Union, Cuba, and their communist allies to Marxist-Leninist guerrillas now fighting to overthrow the established Government of El Salvador [emphasis added]." The evidence was said to be contained in some eighty captured guerrilla documents, weighing eighteen pounds. There were journals of international travels, minutes of meetings within guerrilla councils, statements of political philosophy.

*Seeking to blame Latin American turmoil on "Communists" is a long-standing American tradition. In the 1920's Secretary of State Frank Kellogg, angered by Mexico's effort to exercise more control over American oil companies there, declared that the Mexican president, in league with Nicaraguan revolutionaries and the Soviet Union, was seeking to bring about a "Mexican-fostered Bolshevik hegemony" in Central America.

The white paper concluded that these documents proved that the Salvadoran insurgency was a "textbook case of indirect armed aggression by Communist powers through Cuba." One week later the Reagan administration sent twenty additional military advisers to El Salvador and announced that it intended to provide an immediate $25 million in military assistance.

But the evidence, it turned out, wasn't quite so "definitive." And the "textbook case" of Communist aggression turned out to resemble instead a textbook case of distortion, embellishments, and exaggeration. The State Department had provided reporters with nineteen documents at the time it released the white paper. As the department almost certainly knew would happen, most reporters wrote their stories from the white paper, not having time to read the thick pile of documents, which were written in Spanish anyway. "Hardly anyone outside the communist world seemed to question the white paper," *Time* magazine reported. But although many reporters may have had suspicions about the white paper and accompanying documents, only a few pursued them. *The Nation* weighed in with a long piece by James Petras raising doubts about the white paper claims. The first analysis of the documents themselves was by John Dinges, a journalist who speaks fluent Spanish. Writing for Pacific News Service, a small independent San Francisco-based agency, Dinges reported that the documents, along with other intelligence reports available to the administration, "provide conclusions that fall far short of the administration's portrayal of El Salvador as an arena of East-West confrontation in which the U.S. faces the challenge of the Soviet Union." Dinges was also a part-time editor on the foreign desk at *The Washington Post,* where his investigative scoop prompted the editors to assign Robert G. Kaiser to probe further. Meanwhile, at *The Wall Street Journal,* Jonathan Kwitny was poring over the documents and interviewing the white paper's author, Jon Glassman, a thirty-seven-year-old Foreign Service officer who had spent several years in Moscow. When all these journalists finished their work, the white paper's claims were in shambles.

The documents, it turned out, didn't weigh eighteen pounds; that was the total weight of Glassman's suitcase, which also contained his personal belongings. Moreover, many of the documents weren't even written by the guerrilla leaders that the administration claimed had written them; there is still doubt about who did write them.

A major white paper claim was that the Salvadoran guerrillas had been promised "nearly 800 tons of the most modern weapons and equipment" by Communist nations and that "200 tons of those arms" had already been delivered, "mostly through Cuba and Nicaragua." But neither figure—800 or 200—was found anywhere in the documents. An intelligence source told me that there was no basis for the 200-ton figure, other than "wild guesses."

It wasn't enough for the administration to blame Nicaragua and Cuba for clandestine aggression. As part of its cold war rhetoric, it had to show Soviet involvement. This it did with notes that the white paper claimed had been written by the secretary-general of the Salvadoran Communist party, Shafik Handal. These notes had been first seen in Washington and had been analyzed several months before the white paper was issued. Even Glassman had seen them along with the analysis. They were dismissed as insignificant—until the Reagan administration decided to utilize them for the policy of blaming outsiders.

According to the white paper, Handal had traveled to Moscow, which had then coordinated his travels, beginning in Vietnam, then on to East Germany, Czechoslovakia, Bulgaria, Hungary, and Ethiopia. In the last country, according to the white paper, Handal was offered 150 Thompson submachine guns, 1,500 M-1 rifles, 1,000 M-14 rifles, and ammunition for all. The Soviet Union, the State Department said, had also agreed to transport weapons from Vietnam to the Salvadoran guerrillas. But Handal didn't prepare the notes; he couldn't have—they were written in Cuba at a time when he wasn't even in that country. Glassman conceded to Kwitny he did not know who had written the trip report.

Another document which the State Department said had been written by Handal didn't contain his name or any identification, and even the most casual glance showed it to be written in at least two distinctly different handwritings. Furthermore, a close reading of all the documents revealed that contrary to the white paper's assertions, Handal had not been very warmly received by Moscow. He met with a middle-ranking official in the Latin American section in the Soviet Communist party and received no firm assurances of any arms shipments.

In the white paper the administration asserted that the Salvadoran Communist party "has become increasingly committed since 1976 to a military solution." That simply was not true. As noted earlier, the Communist party which, under Handal's leadership had participated in the electoral process with Duarte and Ungo in 1972, did not join the armed revolution until 1980.

The white paper also claimed that Salvadoran guerrilla leaders met with Palestine Liberation Organization (PLO) leader Yasir Arafat, who "promises military equipment, including arms and aircraft." The document on which this assertion was based, however, contained only an elliptical reference to Arafat—"(I did not state this, on the 22nd there was a meeting with Arafat)"—and nothing about Arafat's promising any planes or other military equipment.

The administration also resorted to faulty translations—or, more accurately, mistranslations—from Spanish to English in order to make its case. In one instance, for example, the State Department's translation of a sentence from a document about guerrilla activities was: "This plan is based on there being an excellent supply source in Lagos [the code name for Nicaragua]." In fact, the author of the document had written the sentence using the Spanish conditional tense, and properly translated, it read: "This would be the plan if there is a real source of supplies in Lagos." The State Department had taken the sentence out of the conditional and put it into the absolute, and it had changed the word "real" to "excellent."

Two former CIA agents, Ralph McGehee and Philip Agee, have written that on the basis of their past experiences they believed the white paper documents were the work of the CIA. "Those happily acquired documents can only be the product of yet another C.I.A. forgery operation," wrote McGehee. He compared it to "disinformation" campaigns in Iran in 1954, in Chile during the U.S. effort to overthrow Allende in the early 1970's, and in Indonesia against Sukarno in 1965. (McGehee set out his charges and comparison in an article in *The Nation.* Because he had previously worked for the agency, he had to submit the article to the CIA for prepublication review. The agency censored words, phrases, and sentences.)

There are also serious questions about the source of the white paper documents. Administration officials, including Glassman, have offered conflicting versions of how they came into possession of the documents: whether they were supplied by the Salvadorans or whether Glassman himself found them. Investigative journalists Craig Pyes and Laurie Becklund, who spent more than a year probing the activities of the Salvadoran right, reported that some of the documents were provided to the United States by D'Aubuisson, who had them in his possession in Guatemala for a considerable period before he delivered them to the United States. According to these reporters, a Reagan adviser, retired Lieutenant General Daniel O. Graham, during a meeting in Miami in late 1980 asked D'Aubuisson to furnish evidence that would, as one Salvadoran present at the meeting put it, "influence American public opinion . . . to increase military and economic support for El Salvador."

The Reagan administration had also been guilty of selective omission when it released the white paper. Among the captured documents which it chose not to release but which were examined by *The Washington Post* were several indicating that guerrillas were chronically short of arms; these documents contradicted the State Department's contention that the guerrillas were receiving tons of arms. Other documents contradicted the Reagan administration's effort to portray the Sandinista government in Nicaragua as actively supporting the Salvadoran guerrillas. One such document recorded that the ERP had made "two serious attempts" to bring weapons from Nicaragua but that the Sandinistas had "stood in its way for reasons which in the opinion of the E.R.P. are subjective and at times wrong." The document then stated that the Sandinistas "would no longer allow the F.P.L. to bring weapons by methods it has been using."*

There were other distortions in the white paper which were related not to the documents but to the unrelenting campaign by the administration to portray the situation in terms that would justify the policy. Under the section head "The Guerrillas: Their Tactics and Propaganda," the white paper declared: "Examples of the more extreme claims of their propaganda apparatus—echoed by Cuban, Soviet, and Nicaraguan media—are: . . . That the government's security forces were responsible for most of the 10,000 killings in 1980. . . ." Those were the claims not of any "leftists" but of the church's legal aid office, of Amnesty International, of Americas Watch, and even of the U.S. embassy in its confidential cables. In the paragraphs about "The Present Government," the white paper noted innocuously that Duarte had been "denied office" by the military in the presidential elections of 1972. But as part of its efforts to enhance the image of the Salvadoran military, the State Department did not mention the blatant fraud or that the military had physically beaten Duarte before forcing him into

---

*Some of the white paper claims were contradicted by the Defense Department, although indirectly, and no one seemed to notice. Three weeks after the white paper had been released, Lieutenant General Ernest Graves, director of the Defense Security Assistance Agency, told the Senate Foreign Relations Committee that while there had been a substantial movement of Communist-bloc weapons into Nicaragua, "We haven't seen any evidence that these move on to another country, but they do go to Nicaragua." During the same hearing, however, Undersecretary of State Stoessel, who was appearing with General Graves, declared, "Soviet planes with Soviet crews have been transporting arms into Nicaragua for use in El Salvador. So that is an example of the direct involvement of the Soviet Union."

"I consider your statement to be an extraordinarily good statement," responded Senator Percy, chairman of the committee. What Percy, and the other members of the committee, failed to realize was that Stoessel's statement contradicted what General Graves had said moments earlier.

exile. And the department failed to mention that Duarte's running mate in 1972 had been Guillermo Ungo, at the time of the white paper the political leader of the leftist opposition in El Salvador. The Salvadoran military was further whitewashed when the white paper dismissed the murders of the four American churchwomen and two AIFLD workers as "unexplained."

When Kwitny confronted Glassman with the fruits of his investigative labor, Glassman, who had been promoted after his success in preparing the white paper, conceded that parts of it were "misleading" and "over-embellished." The State Department issued a rebuttal to the criticisms of the white paper, saying that they were "either based on incorrect assumptions or are inaccurate" and that the white paper's conclusions were valid. But the department did not address the key discrepancies raised by Dinges, Kwitny, and Kaiser and in issuing the written rebuttal refused to allow reporters to ask any questions.

The white paper had been a public relations success for the new administration. Its release was widely reported, while the rebuttals received considerably less media attention. Not surprisingly, the Reagan administration persisted in charging that the Nicaraguans, Cubans, Russians, and others were providing military equipment and training to the Salvadoran guerrillas. The charges were usually made when the administration was asking Congress for more aid, when it wanted to divert the public's attention from human rights atrocities, when the war wasn't going well for the U.S.-trained Salvadoran Army. In May 1981, for example, Haig told a Senate committee that there was some evidence the arms supply to the Salvadoran guerrillas was increasing. Two months earlier administration officials had said that the guerrillas were running low on ammunition, apparently, they said, as the result of a decision by Nicaragua and Cuba to reduce their assistance. In early February 1982, when the administration's policy was coming under increasing fire because of the human rights abuses in El Salvador, Assistant Secretary Enders told the Senate Foreign Relations Committee that "the clandestine infiltration of arms and munitions into El Salvador is again approaching the high levels recorded before last year's final offensive." A State Department spokesman, Alan Romberg, said the levels were approaching what they had been "just before the guerrillas' final offensive, which is to say several hundred tons per month." Not only was the department still using the discredited tonnage figures, but the administration offered no evidence to support the charges. And *The Times'* Alan Riding reported from Honduras, "Despite United States charges that Nicaragua is stepping up arms shipments to Salvadoran guerrillas, no evidence is available here to indicate that the weapons are passing through Honduras . . ."—this despite the fact that the Honduran Army, encouraged by increased military aid from the United States, had during the preceding year tightened surveillance of border areas. Moreover, Riding reported, the Hondurans had received no new intelligence information from the United States on the routes allegedly being used by the arms' smugglers.

One year after the white paper, in March 1982, the Reagan administration launched what *Time* magazine described as possibly "the most intense national security information campaign since President Kennedy went public with graphic documentation of the Cuban missile threat 20 years ago." The Defense Intelligence Agency (DIA) and the CIA put on a slide show for the press—thirty-six aerial photographs designed to demonstrate the military buildup by the Sandinista government, which the analysts contended was for the support of the Salvadoran guerrillas. Haig and CIA Director William Casey shared even more sensitive information with a group of twenty-six former security officials and advisers. "The purpose of the blitz," *Time* noted, "was to convince skeptics of the correctness of the administration's approach to the critical problems of El Salvador and its neighbors—namely, that the struggles in Central America are not simply indigenous revolts but rather are crucial battlegrounds in a broad East-West confrontation." This time, however, *Time* was more skeptical than it had been after the white paper, calling the administration's case "as yet unproved."

As part of the blitz, senior officials from all the intelligence agencies briefed the House Permanent Select Committee on Intelligence, providing the members and staff with top secret and highly sensitive information. A report by the staff of the committee's Subcommittee on Oversight and Evaluation found that the presentation "was flawed by overstatement and overinterpretation." During the briefing, for example, the intelligence officials stated that "lots of ships have been traced" from the Soviet Union, through various countries, and on to Nicaragua. But when the committee asked specifically how many ships had been traced along this route, the intelligence agencies were forced to admit very few had been. The committee also viewed a slide titled "Guerrilla Financing (Non-Arms)," which showed that in addition to weapons, the guerrillas were receiving $17 million annually. But the figure, it turned out, was an extrapolation, which the committee described as "particularly tenuous." It was based on a single piece of evidence indicating the *monthly* budget for *one* guerrilla commander.

In early March 1982 Haig declared that he had "overwhelming and irrefutable" evidence that the Salvadoran revolution was being controlled by non-Salvadorans operating outside the country. The House Intelligence Subcommittee, noting Haig's charge, said that it had received no evidence that the revolution was controlled by non-Salvadorans.

The administration wasn't deterred. Assistant Secretary of State Enders forcefully declared to the House Foreign Affairs Committee in April 1983 that "the FMLN headquarters near Managua has evolved into a sophisticated command and control center which guides operations. Cuban and Nicaraguan officers are present at this headquarters. The headquarters coordinates logistical support, including clothes, money, and ammunition." In his extraordinary address to a joint session of Congress a few days later President Reagan insisted, "The [Salvadoran] guerrilla attacks are directed from a headquarters in Managua, the capital of Nicaragua."

"Rhetorical overkill" was Lawrence Pezzullo's assessment of Reagan's claim. The U.S. ambassador to Nicaragua until August 1981 said the leadership of the Salvadoran guerrilla war "has always been in Salvador." What there was in Nicaragua, Pezzullo explained, was a communications relay station. "It's unfair to call it a command and control post."*

It wasn't that the Cubans and Nicaraguans weren't providing weapons or that their territories weren't being used. They were. (Guerrilla commanders, for example, went to Nicaragua for rest and relaxation, and some FDR leaders lived there, while others resided in Mexico.) But if the Salvadoran guerrillas had received anything close to the level of support that the administration claimed, they would readily have defeated the Salvadoran Army.

The administration's claims were "systematically overstated," said one intelligence analyst. "Intelligence does not know" how many weapons and how much training the Salvadoran guerrillas were receiving from Communist countries, he added. "I don't think there's anyone in this town [Washington, D.C.] who knows." Faced with publicly expressed doubts about charges that the weapons were coming by land through Honduras, the administration was to assert that they

*Pastor, the Latin American specialist on Carter's NSC, dismissed the claims that the Salvadorans were controlled by the Nicaraguans, suggesting that "if the guerrillas intercepted cable traffic between the State Department and our embassy in El Salvador, they might conclude that the Salvadoran government gets its instruction from a command-and-control center outside the country."

were coming by sea or air. But even the intelligence agencies couldn't agree. While the CIA would be reporting that there was an increase in the flow by air, another agency would be saying no, there is a decrease in the air traffic, but an increase in arms coming in by sea. "It was just ludicrous," said a source who had access to the intelligence reports of the CIA, DIA, and NSA (National Security Agency).

"I want to point out that the record of military intelligence in Central America has been abysmally bad," Robert White told the Senate Foreign Relations Committee. He cautioned the senators to "always worry about military intelligence because the military have oftentimes an objective: that is, the intelligence is meant to serve a particular type of solution. Therefore, I always look at military intelligence with an especially skeptical eye."

One of the most frequent military intelligence charges, especially by Colonel Waghelstein in El Salvador, was that the arms were being airlifted into El Salvadoran hills by small planes, which landed on dirt runways or dropped their weapons loads by parachute. He wouldn't provide specifics. According to a DIA officer, the landings were usually on coffee or cotton fincas, in planes belonging to the owners, who were checking on their properties. Moreover, he scoffed at the suggestion that any significant quantity of arms was being landed by parachute. Were that so, he said, at least one parachute would have become hung up in trees and been displayed publicly. None was.

There was at least one consistent element in the administration's intelligence-gathering operations: a rush to judgment, a willingness to take the smallest piece of raw intelligence and trumpet it as proof positive of outside intervention. A classic example occurred when one of the intelligence agencies intercepted conversations thought to demonstrate the link among the Cubans, Nicaraguans, and Salvadorans. When the State Department learned of the interceptions, it insisted that congressional leaders be immediately and secretly briefed. They were. But then intelligence analysts studied the intercepted conversations more closely. They concluded that there were several possible interpretations of the conversations, which were in code as well as in Spanish. But the only one that had been provided to Congress was the one that fitted the policy. "It was all a castle of sand," said an intelligence analyst.

THE United States has the most sophisticated surveillance equipment and methods in the world, including earth-orbiting satellites that can read the license plate of a moving car. From its communications center at Fort Meade, Maryland, NSA spies eavesdrop on conversations between tank commanders in the Iranian desert. In El Salvador the Reagan administration unleashed a massive intelligence-gathering operation, spending at least $50 million during just the first two years. More than 150 CIA operatives roamed through the tiny country, infiltrating peasant organizations and guerrilla groups. Even the Defense Department's highly secret Intelligence Support Activity (ISA) has agents there. And the United States trained, armed, and paid the monthly salaries of 8,000 to 10,000 "soldiers" who operated along the Honduran-Nicaraguan border; U.S. officials stated repeatedly that their mission was to interdict the flow of arms from Nicaragua to El Salvador. The CIA also financed Honduran gunboats to operate in the Gulf of Fonseca in order to halt the arms flow. A sophisticated eavesdropping post was established on a small island in the gulf.

Yet from all these massive and sophisticated resources, the evidence presented to the American public or even to Congress was paltry at best. Two or three small planes crashed in El Salvador in late 1980 and early 1981, and a semitrailer with a false roof, in which 100 automatic rifles were secreted, was seized on the Honduran-Salvadoran border. (According to the Honduran government, the truck had originated in Costa Rica, not Nicaragua as the State Department implied in the white paper, which contained a photograph of the truck.) Beyond that there wasn't much. The reason, quite simply, was that "you're just hearing bullshit; the intelligence just doesn't support the charges," as one intelligence source put it.* Another source, with access to the intelligence traffic from all the agencies, agreed. "The amount of aid has never been measured, never been quantified. . . . Let's not delude the American public; let's not delude the Congress. Let's tell the truth."

The truth hasn't been told about Cuba either. "We never had solid evidence of massive and substantial flow of arms from Cuba to Nicaragua and then to El Salvador," said Wayne Smith, the senior U.S. diplomat there from 1979 to July 1982.† Smith said that the Cubans did supply some arms, as the Cubans admitted, and did train some Salvadoran guerrillas, probably 200 at the very most. Nearly all that was

---

*I made an FOIA request to the Defense Department for all documents pertaining to the support the Salvadoran guerrillas were receiving from the outside. No documents were provided.

†The United States does not have full diplomatic relations with Cuba, so the senior U.S. representative there is called not an ambassador but the chief of the Interests Section.

prior to the "final offensive" in January 1981. And in December 1981 a senior Cuban official told Smith that the Cubans had ceased all material and training support for the Salvadoran revolution. Smith was doubtful, but the official was emphatic. So Smith cabled Washington, asking if the United States had evidence to confirm that the Cubans had ceased supplying arms. There was no response. Then Smith heard Reagan during a news conference say that the Cubans were continuing to send arms to the Salvadorans. Smith was furious. If Washington had the evidence, he wanted to know it so that he could confront the Cubans. He sent more cables. Finally, they were answered—but not with evidence that the arms flow was continuing. Lacking that proof, Washington adopted some dubious logic. The cables to Smith said there was no evidence that the arms flow had stopped; therefore, one had to "deduce" that it was continuing. "That means nothing at all; it's a nonsensical statement," Smith noted. "Our intelligence reports are like the Bible or Marxism-Leninism—you can find one that will say anything you want." Intelligence officials confirmed that the Cubans had been honest with Smith or at least that they had no evidence that any significant flow of arms continued after December 1981.

Smith had another problem with the Reagan administration. The Cubans advised him that they were willing to enter negotiations with the United States that could lead to a reduction in the turmoil in Central America. Smith informed Washington. The response was that the Cubans were interested only in bilateral issues, between Cuba and the United States, and that the United States wanted a broader agenda. When Smith cabled back that no, the Cubans were willing to discuss the broader issues, Washington's response was that it was not going to negotiate anything with Cuba because to do so would legitimize Cuba's presence in Central America. Assistant Secretary Enders, appearing before House Foreign Affairs subcommittees in December 1982, blatantly misrepresented what had transpired between Cuba and the United States. First he said that Cuba's interests in negotiations had been expressed through "private U.S. citizens" when in fact, they had been made through official channels. Then he declared that Cuba had said it was willing to discuss only the "bilateral agenda," not issues such as Central America, which to the Cubans, Enders said, "were not negotiable." (Smith, a combat marine in Korea who had served in the Foreign Service under six presidents, including in the Soviet Union and on the Soviet desk in the State Department during the Nixon years, became so disgusted with the Reagan administration's policy toward Cuba and Central America that he resigned from the diplomatic corps.)

Blaming the Salvadoran explosion on imported weapons is like blaming the Polish explosion on Radio Free Europe," *The New York Times* editorialized, putting the issue of outside involvement in the proper perspective. The *Miami Herald,* in an editorial, brought the charges of outside interference into the context of American history: "Black people challenged the long-established order of the segregationist American South during the glory years of the civil-rights movement. Champions of the immoral *status quo* oft responded by telling a favorite lie. The local 'nigrahs,' it was said, never would have made any trouble if it weren't for those rabble-rousing 'outside agitators' stirring things up." A few years later, the editorial noted, "The nation's middle-class youth turned college campuses into centers of rebellion against an unjustifiable war and a society with a dollar sign where its soul should have been. 'Outside agitators' were stirring up the kids, it was said." The editorial concluded: "El Salvador's insurgent left holds real, legitimate grievances. The solution to El Salvador's agony will be found in a ceasefire and negotiations, which the left is ready to accept. Nothing but self-deception and continued tragedy will be found by belief in ghosts from rebellions past."

"The question isn't where do they get their arms, but their right to have them," said a Mexican diplomat who served in El Salvador. "Your country is giving arms, and helicopters, and training to the government, so of course, the revolutionaries get arms wherever they can—and that is Cuba and Nicaragua. It is legitimate." Even Wayne Smith, who bluntly said, "I don't particularly like the Cuban government, I have no sympathy for the Sandinistas, and I don't want to see the FMLN win," observed: "If you look at it dispassionately, it's a rather symmetrical situation you have: The Cubans are supporting a sovereign government, Nicaragua, and they're supporting a clandestine group in El Salvador. We are supporting a sovereign government in El Salvador and clandestine groups that are operating against the Nicaraguan government."

To whatever extent the Salvadoran revolution has received material support and training from Cuba and Nicaragua, the peasants who support the revolution argue that it is justified. After all, they note, Archbishop Romero and many priests have recognized the legitimacy of their fight. But while defending their right to support from Cuba and Nicaragua, or whatever other countries, the Salvadoran leftists deny that foreign governments are the major sources of their weapons.

"It's a pity, but if you have money, you can buy weapons anywhere," Father César Jerez, the provincial superior of the Jesuits in Central America at the time, responded to my question about the source of the guerrillas' weapons. "They are in the market like bananas." Robert White said that for the Salvadoran guerrillas "the most important source of weapons has always been the international black market centered in the United States." This black market flourishes throughout the world—the United States, Europe, the Middle East, South America. This Mafia of international arms peddlers has no politics. It cares not whether the arms are going to the rightist military death squads or to the leftist guerrilla raiding parties. "Some Mafiosi are leftists, some rightists, but most are just businessmen," the guerrilla commander Jonas said with a sly smile when I was interrogating him about the source of the guerrillas' weapons. He had just slipped into Houston on an arms-buying trip, returning with machine guns, rifles, and pistols. The Mafia will sell to anyone with money. And the Salvadoran revolution had plenty of that—by conservative estimates, $60 million from kidnappings alone. It is possible to gain an understanding of the bullets and rifles that war chest could purchase by contrasting it with the $41 million in military assistance that the United States provided El Salvador in 1980 and 1981. Then remember that the guerrillas weren't putting out money for multimillion-dollar jets and helicopters.

In addition to the black market, one country has been an important source of weapons for the Salvadoran guerrillas. It wasn't Cuba, Nicaragua, Vietnam, or the Soviet Union. It was the United States.

Some Salvadoran officers sell the U.S.-supplied weapons "even before they get out of the crates," Ambassador White told a congressional committee. Usually, however, the sales were by smaller entrepreneurs. Guerrillas in Morazán told me that they could buy rifles from government soldiers and officers for from $720 to $1,200 each and bullet pouches for about 80 cents. In Guazapa, guerrillas bought bullets for $1 apiece. (It was more than material aid that the revolution received from the Salvadoran military. They had collaborators at the highest levels of the government's army. In an August 1983 Secret cable, which was not provided under the Freedom of Information Act, the embassy in El Salvador reported: "Through an insurgent intelligence collection network which penetrates the armed forces, the insurgents have acquired the Salvadoran military's call signs, broadcast frequencies and schedules, and codes which allow them to read even encoded military traffic.")

What the guerrillas couldn't buy from the army soldiers, they took from them. This was one of the primary objectives of their raids on military outposts and was a partial explanation for their benign treatment of prisoners. Surrendering or captured soldiers were turned over to the Red Cross—after being relieved of their uniforms and weapons. In October 1983 CBS's Gary Shepard interviewed Salvadoran guerrillas on a major highway twenty-five miles from the capital. "Their weapons were mostly American-made: M-16 rifles, M-60 machine guns, hand grenades, even field radios, all captured from government forces. There was no evidence of aid from the Communist bloc by way of Nicaragua." One guerrilla, whose backpack still had "U.S." markings on it, boasted, as Shepard reported, "President Reagan, by sending military aid to the Salvadoran army, is in effect supplying the rebel side as well—and he said he hopes the aid will continue."

According to a Secret cable from the embassy in El Salvador to Washington, during the first half of 1983 the guerrillas "may have obtained most of their newly acquired firearms through capture from the Salvadoran military." More than 1,800 government weapons had been captured in the period from October 1982 to May 1983, according to the cable. While the embassy contended that medicines, clothing, explosives, and money to buy food were coming from abroad, it reported: "The heaviest weapons in the insurgent arsenal are recoilless rifles, mortars, and .50 caliber machineguns, many of which also were captured from government forces." The embassy further noted that there had been "a decline in deliveries of weapons from external sources" and that the "guerrilla resupply effort" had been "gravely impaired by aggressive ESAF [El Salvador armed forces] actions within the country, U.S. supported interdiction efforts, and increasing international and internal pressure on the Sandinista Government in Nicaragua."

This cable contradicts what the top Reagan administration officials were telling the American public and Congress. The President himself, on March 10, 1983, in a speech to the National Association of Manufacturers on the subject of Central America, declared that "El Salvador's people remain under strong pressure from armed guerrillas controlled by extremists with Cuban-Soviet support." Military supplies, he said, were "coming into El Salvador from Marxist Nicaragua." Three days later Secretary of Defense Caspar W. Weinberger, appearing on CBS's *Face the Nation,* insisted that the Salvadoran guerrillas were "trained by the Cubans and by the Nicaraguans, and supplied by both, and supplied by the Soviet Union, and resupplied." At about the same time Secretary of State Shultz told the House Foreign Affairs Committee that the Salvadoran rebels were "creating hell" with Soviet-supplied weapons that flow "from the Soviet Union to Cuba, Nicaragua and these insurgents."

But at the very time that the three top civilian officials were blaming outsiders, U.S. military officials were privately telling some American reporters and visiting congressmen a different story. During his visit to Central America in April 1983 Representative Robert Torricelli, a freshman Democrat from New Jersey, was told by U.S. military officers and diplomats in El Salvador and Nicaragua that there had been no major arms shipments from Nicaragua to El Salvador for several months and that the few weapons that were reaching the guerrillas were not a significant factor in the guerrilla successes. An intelligence analyst in Washington told me the very same.

Drew Middleton, who has been analyzing armies and wars for *The New York Times* since World War II, wrote from El Salvador in March 1983: "Military aid from Nicaragua and Cuba is not a key factor in the Salvadoran guerrillas' campaign, according to an experienced intelligence officer."

14

WAGING WAR, REJECTING PEACE

IN waging the war in El Salvador, the Reagan administration made a virtual mockery out of Congress's role in the conduct of U.S. foreign policy. Policymakers scurried up to the Hill with confident assurances that were quickly forgotten, promises that were violated, deceits that weren't uncovered. When these tactics didn't suffice, the executive branch simply ignored the legislators. Reagan wasn't the first President to conduct a foreign policy in this manner, nor is he likely to be the last. Hanging over him, however, were the ghosts of Vietnam; the lessons of El Salvador should be studied carefully by future policymakers.

"All of us are very well aware of history here and what went on in Vietnam," Undersecretary of State Stoessel told the Senate Foreign Relations Committee in March 1981, the first time that the new administration was called upon to explain its policy. "We learned our lessons from it. We are doing our best to insure that a similar situation does not develop in El Salvador with what happened in Vietnam." As for the $25 million in military aid and additional advisers that Reagan was sending El Salvador, Stoessel assured the senators, "We do not foresee the necessity for increases." But the $25 million was tripled in the next fiscal year, 1982, to $82 million, and the administration reached into the triple digits ($136 million) for its fiscal 1983 request. In January 1984 the White House said it was preparing to ask for $300 million in military aid alone to carry through fiscal year 1985.

For the most part Reagan financed the war through the back door, avoiding Congress and, concomitantly, public debate. Section 506(a) of the Foreign Assistance Act authorizes the President to rush military assistance when there is an "unforeseen emergency" and the failure to respond would "result in serious harm to vital United States security interests." From the law's enactment in 1961, it was invoked six times, until Reagan became President twenty years later.* He used it twice for El Salvador. In 1981, 80 percent of Reagan's military aid for the country came from the 506(a) discretionary fund; in 1982 it was 66 percent. In addition, in January 1982 Reagan took moneys that had been approved by Congress for one country and reprogrammed them for El Salvador. By so doing, he avoided a full congressional debate.

But the Reagan administration was unable to get all it wanted for El Salvador from Congress, so it arranged for El Salvador to receive millions of dollars of economic assistance without direct congressional oversight. It used the International Monetary Fund (IMF) and the multinational banks: the International Bank for Reconstruction and Development (World Bank) and the Inter-American Development Bank. During the entire period from 1949 to 1979 El Salvador received a total of $632.8 million from these banks. In contrast, during just its first three years (1981–1983) the Reagan administration pushed through $332.4 million in loans from these banks—an average of $111 million each year, which was five times the average of $21 million a year during the thirty years ending in 1979. President-elect Reagan's State Department transition team had recommended that "foreign policy objectives and the U.S. role in the multinational banks" be regarded "not [as] an economic matter but [as] a political problem that must be seen in political terms." The recommendation was followed. The administration supported, for example, a $1.1 billion loan from the IMF to South Africa (in 1983), even though many other nations opposed it because of South Africa's racial discrimination policies. In voting for the loan, the administration argued that it was improper for the international development banks to consider political factors, that only economic conditions should be taken into account. Yet the administration opposed loans to the leftist government of Nicaragua, even though many U.S. allies supported them and that country's economy was at least as stable as the war-ravaged Salvadoran economy. Indeed, regarding El Salvador, a Confidential State Department memorandum prepared in December 1980 noted, "The IMF has found that conditions now are too chaotic" for a loan. Yet in July 1982, by which time the conditions were even more chaotic, the Reagan administration pushed through an $84.7 million IMF loan to El Salvador. From 1949 to 1980 the IMF had provided El Salvador with a total of $80.1

*Vietnam, $75 million, 1965; Cambodia, $250 million, 1974, and $75 million in 1975; Thailand, $1.1 million, 1980; Liberia, $1 million, 1980; El Salvador, $5 million, by Carter in January 1981.

million. The 1982 loan of $84.7 million was one of the most "controversial and political" loans the IMF has made, according to James Morrell of the Center for International Policy, a nonprofit organization that monitors the activities of the multinational banks.

No more Vietnams" was the theme of the congressional debate that preceded the passage of the War Powers Act in 1973, by a Congress that was resentful of the manner in which Presidents Johnson and Nixon had unilaterally carried out that war and was determined to stop further erosion of its constitutional prerogative to declare war.* Enacted over a veto by Nixon, the law requires the President to notify Congress within forty-eight hours after he has sent military personnel into combat situations. And he must withdraw those troops within sixty to ninety days unless Congress declares war or passes a joint resolution allowing them to remain.†

Reagan did not provide Congress with a war powers notification when he sent the advisers to El Salvador in early 1981. The Defense Department realized there were problems.

"It is contradictory to be stating that a War Powers report is not required when military assistance is being justified publicly as a result of a major offensive marked by intense, widespread, daily attacks draining the military resources of the requesting country," the Defense Department's general counsel's office wrote in a memorandum, dated February 12, 1981, about the applicability of the War Powers Act to El Salvador. How did the lawyers suggest avoiding compliance with the act? "Press releases concerning military assistance also need to be coordinated."

*Article I, Section VIII of the U.S. Constitution provides "The Congress shall have power . . . To declare war. . . ."
†War powers reports have been provided to Congress six times. The first one related to the evacuation of refugees from Danang and other seaports to safer areas in South Vietnam on April 4, 1975. Eight days later Ford reported again under the act during the evacuation of Cambodia. On April 30, 1975, a report was filed when American personnel were evacuated from Vietnam. When the *Mayaguez* was recaptured and its crew rescued, a report was filed on May 15, 1975. A fifth report, by President Carter on April 27, 1980, pertained to the unsuccessful attempt to rescue the Americans being held hostage in Iran. President Reagan filed war powers reports in 1983 when he sent the marines to Lebanon and when the United States invaded Grenada. But the reports only partially complied with the law. He did not report that the forces were being introduced into hostilities or imminent hostilities, which Section 4(a)(1) of the act requires.

The department had other arguments to prevent triggering the War Powers Act. Foremost among these was the contention that the mobile training teams (MTTs)—Pentagon euphemistic jargon for military advisers—"would not function in a command and control capacity, that they would not deploy to hostile areas to advise, that they would not receive hostile fire pay. . . ." These conditions were expressed to Congress in the form of assurances.

"What specific steps are being taken in El Salvador that are different from those taken in the early days of Vietnam?" asked Senator Larry Pressler of South Dakota, a Republican who had served in the army in Vietnam, during the Senate Foreign Relations Committee hearing. General Graves answered that the "most important step" was that the U.S. military personnel in El Salvador were being confined "strictly to training activities" in "the most secure areas." He stressed that the advisers would not "accompany combat operations." The assurances were repeated a few months later, when Assistant Secretary Enders appeared before the House Inter-American Affairs Subcommittee.

The Reagan administration struggled to avoid calling the American military personnel "advisers" because of the lingering connotations from Vietnam. The word "trainers" was chosen by the administration. "A lot of people said there is no distinction," Enders said. But, he insisted, "there is a distinction," and it was "important." The military men were called trainers, he explained, because "they train units in base cities or in base camps. They do not go out with any units involved on military operations. That is a very important difference, and this is why we tend to insist on the word 'trainer.' "

Nearly all these conditions and assurances were violated, some much sooner than others. But a war powers report was never filed.

The General Accounting Office (GAO), the investigating agency for Congress, issued a report in mid-1982 that received shockingly little media coverage in view of what it revealed about the improper, if not illegal, manner in which the Reagan administration was conducting the war in El Salvador. Regarding the Defense Department's representation and the repeated assurances that the advisers would be restricted to areas of El Salvador not expected to be the subject of guerrilla attacks, the GAO report noted, for example, that the advisers had been working at the Salvadoran air force base Ilopango, which might reasonably have been seen as "a potential target of the Salvadoran guerrillas and, in fact, it was." In January 1982, in one of the most devastating sabotage missions of the war, guerrilla commandos, assisted by sympathetic air force officers, penetrated security at the base, planting explosives that destroyed or crippled half of the country's helicopter fleet and several jets.

As for the promises that the advisers would not be deployed to combat areas, those, too, were broken. In June 1983 the Salvadoran armed forces launched the largest military operation of the war. Patterned after the CORDS program in Vietnam, the reinforced units swept through San Vicente and Usulután provinces in search of guerrillas. The American military advisers were present. They didn't even attempt to disguise their expanded role. Their pictures appeared in newspapers and magazines. But there were no protests from Congress. The Defense Department's general counsel's office had written in its memorandum: "If hostilities are expected to occur at a location to which U.S. forces will be assigned, a War Powers report will be required." San Vicente was unquestionably such a location. It was a guerrilla stronghold. No war powers report was filed, and Congress didn't demand one.

Probably the issue on which the administration was the most deceitful related to the dangers to which the U.S. military personnel were exposed. Under a 1963 law, armed forces personnel are entitled to an extra $65 for each month during which they are in a country designated as a hostile fire pay area, even if they are not fired upon. Only a few days in the area are needed to qualify for the extra pay, and during Vietnam officers stationed outside the country—on Okinawa, for example—routinely arranged their visits to Vietnam to overlap the end of one month and the beginning of the next, thus "earning" two months of what was called combat pay. During the final hectic days of the Carter administration the Defense Department made a preliminary decision to designate El Salvador as a hostile fire pay zone, retroactive to October 1979. The Reagan administration was troubled— not by the retroactivity provision or even by having to pay each adviser the $65 in each future month. What disturbed the administration was the realization that such a designation ran counter to its efforts to downplay the U.S. military involvement in El Salvador. The countries that had previously been designated for hostile fire pay were Vietnam, Cambodia, and Iran. But the specific reason that the administration decided not to designate El Salvador as a hazardous pay zone was that to have done so would have triggered the provisions of the War Powers Act and of the Arms Export Control Act, which prohibits military advisers from engaging in "any duties of a combatant nature."

For all practical purposes, however, the U.S. Army treated El Salvador as if it had been designated as a hostile fire pay zone. Even if a country is not so designated, a soldier is entitled to the extra $65 if he is in fact fired upon. The GAO auditors found that the U.S. military personnel in El Salvador, from early 1981 until mid-1982, were receiving hostile fire pay for 97 percent of the person-months involved.

Each adviser who received the hostile fire pay signed a statement declaring, "I was subjected to hostile fire." The declaration was verified by his commanding officer, whose statement read that the person claiming the hostile fire pay "was subjected to small arms fire or he was close enough to the trajectory, point of impact or explosion of hostile ordnance so that he was in danger of being wounded, injured or killed."

If, in fact, the American military personnel were being shot at, not only were the Defense Department's representations and the Arms Export Control Act being violated, but the State Department was regularly filing false reports to Congress. Reports about the security of the advisers had been promised by State when the House Foreign Affairs Committee expressed reservations about the increasing U.S. involvement in El Salvador and argued that the War Powers Act should be invoked. Each of State's monthly reports contained a statement to the effect that there had been no attacks on U.S. soldiers. The customary sentence was: "There were no security incidents involving US Government personnel during [the month the report covered]." But during the same months that the State Department was declaring that there were no incidents, the advisers were certifying that they had been shot at.*

Along with the War Powers Act, the Arms Export Control Act (AECA), first adopted in 1968 with subsequent amendments, is designed to allow Congress to share with the President in any decision to commit American troops. One provision of the act requires the President to notify Congress within forty-eight hours "after the outbreak of significant hostilities involving a country in which United States personnel are providing defense services." The Reagan administration did not file a report when it sent the additional advisers to El Salvador, arguing that the "outbreak" of hostilities was at the time of the "final offensive," which was during the Carter administra-

---

*If the State Department's reports were truthful, then the hostile fire pay claims were fraudulent, in which case under federal law legal actions could have been brought against the commanding officers, Colonel Eldon Cummings and Colonel John Waghelstein, who verified them. No actions were brought against either officer. After the GAO's audit the Defense Department ordered Colonel Waghelstein "to insure that absolute ethical standards are applied to any request for HFP." The hostile fire pay claims ended—except when an adviser really was shot at.

tion.* On that point the administration seemed to be legally correct, but it also argued the hostilities weren't "significant."

Senator Glenn accused the administration of "tortured logic" and introduced an amendment which became law in December 1981. It requires the President to report to Congress within forty-eight hours of the existence of *"or a change in the status of* significant hostilities or terrorist acts or a series of acts, which may endanger American lives or property [emphasis added]."

The Reagan administration ignored the new law. It filed only one report with Congress about the existence of any attacks against Americans, even though the advisers were filing monthly reports saying they had been shot at.† Nor did the administration file a report after the attack on Ilopango, which did more than merely "endanger" American property; it destroyed three U.S.-owned helicopters and damaged a fourth so badly that it had to be airlifted to the United States for repairs. Moreover, there were two teams of advisers at the base during the attack. It is difficult to imagine that the guerrilla raid didn't "endanger" their lives.

But while Reagan can be censured for ignoring and violating laws designed to give the legislative branch some voice in U.S. foreign policy, the legislators bear some responsibility for letting him walk over the supposedly equal branch. Senator Glenn did not protest the administration's refusal to file reports that his amendment required. As for the periodic reports that the administration promised and had been filing monthly with the House Foreign Affairs Committee, those simply stopped in November 1982. There was no congressional protest.‡ During a hearing of the Senate Foreign Relations Committee in early 1983 Senator Zorinsky read from an article in *U.S. News & World Report* which quoted a Special Forces sergeant as saying, "All of my men have been shot at." An army warrant officer training Salvadoran helicopter pilots, pointing to the bullet holes in his chopper, nonchalantly told reporter Carl Migdail, "The threat is always there."

Why had the incidents referred to in *U.S. News & World Report* never been reported to Congress, either in an AECA report or in one of the periodic reports? Senator Zorinsky demanded of Assistant Secretary Enders and Nestor Sanchez, deputy assistant secretary of de-

*The Carter administration did not file a report at the time of the "final offensive," a failure the Defense Department later dismissed as an "oversight."
†The one report was filed when Lieutenant Commander Schaufelberger was killed.
‡In November 1983, the administration filed another of these reports—a mere three pages, even though it purported to cover the entire previous year.

fense for Inter-American affairs, when they were appearing as witnesses. Enders and Sanchez were silent. Zorinsky went on to another subject.

"Can you imagine if that had been Fulbright or Church?" an astonished and disappointed Democratic staff member of the committee remarked later. "They'd have demanded an answer or closed the hearing until they got one."*

There were other instances of congressional silence in the face of the war's expansion. During the Senate Foreign Relations Committee hearings in March 1981, Senator Biden, at thirty-eight able to describe himself as "one of those Vietnam era guys," asked General Graves how long it would be before the United States had trained a sufficient number of Salvadoran soldiers so that they could take over their own training. "In months or at most one year" after training one battalion, General Graves assured him and the other members of the committee. In a further effort to allay fears that the U.S. was embarking on an unending involvement, the administration informally agreed with Congress that the number of advisers would be kept at 55.†

The advisers didn't come home in a year. The limit of 55 was honored but only technically; troops were trained in the United States, and more than 100 advisers were dispatched to Honduras, to train the Salvadorans there.

The first battalion trained was the Atlactl. When it quickly showed itself to be no match for the more highly motivated guerrillas, the United States brought approximately 500 Salvadoran cadets to Fort Benning, Georgia, for some of the best officer training available in the world. And a full Salvadoran battalion, the Ramón Belloso, was formed and trained at Fort Bragg, North Carolina. Upon returning to El Salvador, the Ramón Belloso boys tested their training in battle against the guerrillas in Morazán. When the shooting started, the young Ramón Belloso soldiers fled "like a covey of quail," a disappointed Colonel Waghelstein remarked at the time. When it quickly became obvious that these two battalions, along with all the other Salvadoran units, were not up to the U.S.-assigned task, the adminis-

*Senator Fulbright, chairman of the Foreign Relations Committee from 1959 to 1974, wielded his powerful position to challenge the U.S. policy in Vietnam. Fulbright was succeeded by Frank Church, a liberal Democrat from Idaho.
†While the number on its face is small, it represented a higher adviser-to-soldier ratio than during the early years of the U.S. involvement in Vietnam. In mid-1961 the ratio of American advisers to Vietnamese soldiers was one to 320; in April 1981 there was one American adviser for every 232 Salvadoran troops.

tration in 1983 trained another battalion, the Arce, and six light infantry battalions. These latter were called *cazadores* ("hunters"). They were trained to go on patrols in search of the guerrillas.

Training these later battalions was a bit of a challenge for the administration, faced with the limit of 55 advisers. Reagan first circumvented that limit by sending in 26 U.S. military personnel who were described as medics. It was true that they had received medical training; but they were Special Forces medics; that meant they had also received elite combat training. The medical training was a subspecialty. Moreover, their presence in El Salvador had the effect, and purpose, of releasing the other advisers for combat-related training. In short, the congressional limit had been exceeded by 50 percent, but there was no outcry. Still, even the 80-odd advisers were not enough. So the Reagan administration built a multimillion-dollar military camp on the northern Caribbean coast of Honduras, at Puerto Castilla. Some 125 Green Berets from Fort Bragg, most of them Vietnam veterans, were dispatched to train the 1,040 Salvadorans there. "If it were not for the Spanish that floats from the tents, this could be Vietnam," Loren Jenkins, the Pulitzer Prize-winning correspondent for *The Washington Post,* wrote from Puerto Castilla in September 1983. The effect was more money and advisers for El Salvador. Congress acquiesced.

At the beginning it all had seemed so easy. Surely this would be a place where the United States could win a guerrilla war, where Haig and others could expiate the haunting memories of Vietnam. A few score advisers and less than $100 million would be sufficient. El Salvador wasn't another Vietnam, at least not militarily. El Salvador is one-eighth the size of South Vietnam—8,124 square miles compared to 67,108 square miles. In tiny El Salvador there are forested mountains, but not tropical jungles as in Vietnam, so thick that American soldiers had to cut their way through them inch by inch with machetes, while the Vietcong waited within the distance of a soldier's breath. There was no North Vietnam on El Salvador's border, no country that would supply troops. Nor were there supply lines of the magnitude of those in Vietnam. There was no Cambodia or Laos to serve as a sanctuary. Guatemala was ruled by right-wing dictators; Honduras was an ally controlled by the United States. Nicaragua and El Salvador do not share a land border.

"El Salvador is a place where we can win," William Safire, the Nixon speech writer turned conservative columnist for *The New York Times,* wrote soon after the Reagan administration had come to Washington. "Logistics, for a change, works against the Communists and for us."

The optimism was misplaced. In June 1981 Ambassador Hinton advised Washington that the Salvadoran regular army would have to be almost doubled, from 12,000 to nearly 23,000 troops, in order to achieve the military victory. The navy would also have to double, from 350 to 700, and the air force would have to increase from 450 to approximately 600. A mere five months later Hinton cabled Washington: "Our perception of the resources required to meet these goals has changed substantially—upward." The armed forces, excluding the security forces, would have to be increased from its level at that time of 14,000 to 41,000 "in order to defeat the insurgent forces." The deadline was 1985. By mid-1983 those numbers had nearly been reached and in the case of the air force had been exceeded. There were 1,287 in the air force, nearly double the number originally thought necessary. As of June 1983, the total strength of the Salvadoran armed forces, including the security forces, was 37,397 officers and troops. This figure, contained in a Secret cable, which was not released under the FOIA, contradicts what U.S. officials were telling reporters at the time. They were asserting that the size of the armed forces was about 32,000. The lower figure was being used because the officials did not want to acknowledge that the Salvadoran Army was nearly twice as large as the Nicaraguan Army—22,000 regulars at the time—which the Reagan administration was charging with being engaged in a threatening military buildup.

But something happened on the way to the victory in El Salvador. The fifty-five advisers weren't enough. The two score UH-1H helicopters, the nearly dozen A-37B fighter bombers, the navy patrol boats weren't enough. The CIA wasn't enough. One U.S.-trained battalion wasn't enough. Victory didn't come as swiftly and easily as the Americans had thought for a number of reasons. On one side of the equation, U.S. policymakers underestimated, or refused to accept, the level of popular support for the revolution. On the other side, they were blind to the weaknesses—the incompetence—of the Salvadoran armed forces.

"This is evidence of an Army trained only to fight civilians," Safire caustically observed about the Argentine Army after its defeat by the British in the Falklands in 1982. The same was true about the Salvadoran Army. It was brutally competent at the repression of unarmed civilians, but it couldn't fight a war, even with all the hardware and training that the Americans gave them.

The Reagan administration, intentionally or otherwise, remained ignorant about the institutional impuissance of the Salvadoran armed forces until late 1981, and when it did discover the dire reality, it kept the American public from knowing. The bad news was delivered by Brigadier General Frederick F. Woerner, Jr., who is highly respected for his understanding of Latin American armies. After he and his seven-member military team had spent eight weeks in El Salvador, they concluded that only a dramatic restructuring of the Salvadoran military, including the removal of many senior officers, a crackdown on corruption and violence, and the adoption of more aggressive counterinsurgency tactics, could turn it into an effective fighting force.

"If anybody at this table read that Woerner report with a God-given brain, I can't understand how that person could think you can attain a military victory," exploded Senator Zorinsky during a hearing of the Senate Foreign Relations Committee in February 1983. Yet neither Zorinsky nor any other member of Congress demanded release of the report before he would vote for further military aid to El Salvador.

The Defense Department did not even want to show the Woerner report to members of Congress. When some congressmen suggested that they would not vote for additional military aid unless they saw the report, they were allowed to read it, but only after signing an oath that they would not divulge its contents. Even the General Accounting Office, which was asked by Senator Zorinsky to prepare an assessment of the military needs of the Salvadoran Army, was initially denied access to the Woerner report. Eventually the GAO auditors were allowed to read, but not copy, it. Then the Defense Department insisted that the GAO's own forty- to fifty-page report be classified.

Both the Woerner report—350 to 400 pages—and the GAO's report are highly classified and tightly guarded, unnecessarily so, according to sources who have read them. The contents of the reports, they said, would not jeopardize United States security interests, but they would surely reflect badly on the Salvadoran military. The Woerner report underscores the fact that the Salvadoran military "lacks the doctrine, structure, ideology, and mentality" to fight a counterinsurgency war, said a diplomat who read it. "The issue is the same as it was in Vietnam," said a Pentagon analyst. "How do you get rid of these incompetent bastards?"

The primary reasons the Salvadoran military has not defeated the guerrillas are not the weapons and assistance from Cuba and Nicaragua but the structure, incompetence, and especially the near cowardice of the Salvadoran officer corps. The Americans provided the Salvadorans with intelligence information about guerrilla locations and activities. The Salvadorans did nothing. Common sense and intelligence information, for example, said that the Puente de Oro, the span bridge linking the eastern third and western two-thirds of the country, was a prime guerrilla target. It was destroyed by a sapper operation on October 15, 1981—to commemorate the coup. When another major bridge was blown, the lieutenant on duty was asleep. No disciplinary action was taken against him. When the "crack" Ramón Belloso Battalion, the one trained at Fort Bragg, went into combat against the guerrillas in Morazán, the commanding officer drew its area of operation (AO) on the transparent plastic overlying his topographical map. The AO was a piece of military gerrymandering; it excluded the areas where the guerrillas were known to be located. "This is the best battalion!" exclaimed a diplomat who related the incident.

"It's an army that's pushed, not led," said an American diplomat with no attempt to disguise his disgust. "It's 'You take that hill—and when it's over, come back and tell me about it.'" In any good army the officers, especially the young lieutenants, do the dying, leading their troops in combat. But according to a Secret cable, the number of officers killed or wounded in action during two and a half years of the war in El Salvador (January 1981 to July 1983) was, from the perspective of an army at war, astonishingly low: 39 KIAs and 133 WIAs.

"You know the Atlactl [Battalion]. You wanna know how many officers they've lost in combat since day one?" exclaimed the same diplomat in mid-1983. "One! That's right, one, a captain." When a lieutenant from the Ramón Belloso Battalion was killed in battle, along with nearly 70 young soldiers, there were black-bordered memoriams in the newspapers and an elaborate funeral ceremony with a military honor guard. American diplomats and advisers were appalled. "What is this shit?" one senior diplomat in the embassy grumbled to Colonel Waghelstein. "Jesus, you think they could have raped the Virgin Mary by killing this guy."

Too many Salvadoran commanders "spend their time at the beach or hitch rides into San Salvador on weekends to play tennis with their girl friends," complained a senior U.S. military officer in El Salvador in mid-1983. The guerrillas were motivated, he said, but the government's army had "no inspired leadership, no real ideology, no leaders."

The dying was done by the troops, and they were for the most part poor peasants, often as young as fourteen and fifteen years old, impressed into service during raids of rural villages or rounded up as they came out of movie theaters. "The solution is to draft the sons of the rich," suggested a senior embassy officer. "Then the wealthy of this country won't tolerate the corruption, the brutality."

The highest-ranking Salvadoran officer to become a combat casualty was Colonel Francisco Adolfo Castillo, deputy minister of defense, who was taken prisoner after his helicopter had been shot down a few kilometers west of Perquín in June 1982. A few weeks after the incident, Assistant Secretary Enders testified to the Senate Foreign Relations Committee, "The deputy minister of defense was shot down in a helicopter and taken prisoner coming back from a distribution of provisional titles." Provisional titles are what peasants receive under the land-to-the-tiller law, and Enders was seeking to demonstrate that the Salvadoran armed forces supported the land reform program. But Enders's statement was a half-truth. It was true that Castillo had been distributing provisional titles in the eastern part of the country. But that had been early in the morning. When his helicopter was shot down, Castillo was "coming back" from a meeting with Honduran military commanders just across the border from El Salvador in Honduras. Indeed, when he had told them of his intention to fly over the guerrilla zone, they had advised against it.

The Reagan administration, unable to achieve a victory in El Salvador with the Salvadoran Army, expanded the war—covertly. From American bases in Panama, C-130's loaded with electronic surveillance gear flew over Salvadoran guerrilla strongholds. The CIA set up operations in Honduras for patrols into Salvadoran territory "to destroy Salvadoran guerrilla bases," according to a top secret paper prepared by an interagency task force for a meeting of the National Security Council on July 8, 1983.

Overtly the Reagan administration transformed Honduras from a banana republic where the United Fruit Company picked the country's presidents in the early twentieth century into a virtual U.S. military base ruled by Ambassador Negroponte and the Honduran minister of defense, General Gustavo Álvarez Martínez. U.S. military aid to Honduras in fiscal year 1982 alone was $31.3 million, compared with a total of $32.5 million for the entire period between 1946 through 1981. The Reagan administration delivered helicopters, counterinsurgency planes, mortars, howitzers, communications equipment, and patrol boats—built airfields and dispatched military advisers.

The military aid wasn't needed by the Hondurans. The country's air force was already the most formidable and professional in Central America. Moreover, Honduras, the most backward of the Central American republics—the road between the capital, Tegucigalpa, and the major industrial city, San Pedro Sula, wasn't even paved until 1971 —has been spared, unlike its neighbors on all sides, any revolutionary or guerrilla activity. The country's peace stems largely, it seems, from an absence of wide disparities between rich and poor. There has been no single dictator like Somoza or a ruling oligarchy as in El Salvador.

The military has been corrupt—in 1975, as part of what became known locally as Bananagate, United Brands paid a $1.25 million bribe to high military officials for a reduction in the banana export tax —but by Latin American standards relatively benign. Prodded by Carter's human rights policy, the Honduran armed forces conducted free and honest elections, and in 1981 a civilian, Roberto Suazo Córdova, was sworn in as president.

Bringing Honduras into the war against El Salvador was not an easy task. In 1969 the two countries had fought a brief but bloody war, commonly and comically referred to as the Soccer War because it broke out after a soccer match between the two nations. But the primary cause of the war had been a decision by the Honduran government to expel Salvadoran peasants who had left their tiny, over-populated country in search of land in vast, sparsely populated Honduras. The war was over within a week, the truce arranged by the OAS with Saivadoran troops poised on the outskirts of Tegucigalpa. There are still deep feelings of bitterness and distrust between citizens and especially soldiers of the two nations.

By the middle of 1982 the Honduran Army, under the onslaught of intense pressure and millions of dollars from the United States, was actively involved in the Salvadoran civil war, acting as blocking forces along the border, even entering territory claimed by El Salvador.

Militarizing Honduras, done as part of the U.S. war against the Sandinista government in Nicaragua as well as the civil war in El Salvador, was a brilliantly successful ploy by the Reagan administration. There were only a few voices of opposition in Congress and no public demonstrations. But the move may over time generate the saddest legacy of the Reagan administration's policy in Central America: the smothering of a fledgling democracy and the engendering of deep resentment against the United States. As the Reagan administration poured in more military aid, General Álvarez Martínez, the country's strong man, grew even stronger, bolder, and more repressive. He ignored the country's Congress and the figurehead President Suazo Córdova, a country dentist, when he worked out the deal with the Reagan administration to set up the training camp for the Salvadorans. Torture, clandestine jails, and disappearances were beginning, in 1983, to give Honduras the ugly face of El Salvador. The seeds of a revolution were being planted. They may well be fertilized by anti-Yankeeism, always a convenient rallying cry for revolutionaries. In contrast with El Salvador, where the American military personnel have maintained a low profile, in Honduras they swagger into Tegucigalpa bars, pistols on their hips, patches on their combat fatigues identifying them as "jungle experts." One can imagine a few years hence university students demonstrating in front of American military bases in Honduras, shouting, "Yankee, go home."

But bringing Honduras into the Salvadoran civil war was not the only tactic employed by the Reagan administration to compensate for the impotence of the Salvadoran Army. Within a month after he had arrived in El Salvador, Ambassador Hinton, in addition to recommending sabotage actions inside Nicaragua, suggested, in a Secret cable, "contracting non-Salvadorans" to fly and maintain the country's helicopters. In other words, hire mercenaries—precisely what was done.

Several diplomats who served in El Salvador said that mercenaries were used to fight the war, but they said that information about their numbers and activities was so closely guarded that only two or three people in the embassy knew. Some worked for the CIA; others for ISA. For two weeks of work in El Salvador in late 1982, one American aviator with experience in Vietnam said he was paid $12,000, the money being deposited directly in his Swiss bank account. He said that the planes were owned by Air America, the company used by the CIA in Vietnam. The planes flew Salvadoran troops into combat, an action from which the American advisers were prohibited. Another pilot clandestinely ferried men and matériel in unmarked planes from Homestead Air Force Base in Florida to Ilopango Air Base in San Salvador. He had been an air force pilot in Vietnam and was now paid in cash for his work. And Americans, working either for the CIA, for ISA, or directly for the military, operated on the ground with the Salvadoran troops. Indeed, among those who received hostile fire pay from the U.S. Army were individuals with Spanish surnames whose names did not appear on any official U.S. Army records.

IT didn't have to be this way, with the Reagan administration pouring nearly $1 billion in aid into El Salvador, the militarization of Honduras, the hiring of mercenaries, the support of a repressive right-wing military-controlled government. There was a way out of the quagmire: negotiations.

Shortly after the Reagan administration had arrived in Washington, it had several possibilities to negotiate a settlement. The Organization of American States offered its services. When Senator Tsongas questioned Assistant Secretary Bushnell about this during Senate Foreign Relations Committee hearings in March 1981, Bushnell tried to avoid giving a direct answer. But Tsongas persevered, and Bushnell conceded that the Reagan administration had not encouraged the Salvadoran government to accept the mediation offer. In the spring of 1981 the Nicaraguans, Hondurans, and Costa Ricans met to discuss ways of reducing tensions in the region. The Cubans were also interested. Smith in Cuba and Pezzullo in Nicaragua urged the State Department to pursue the opening. The department told the diplomats the administration wasn't interested.

Most significantly, the administration was offered another, much more promising opportunity, one that had not been available to, though it was sought by, the Carter administration. In October 1980 Ambassador White had pressured the Salvadoran military commanders into agreeing to allow the Salvadoran bishops to act as mediators. The FDR-FMLN rejected the offer.

In 1981 Archbishop Rivera y Damas was to play the mediator's role. First he received an amber light from Duarte. Then the archbishop traveled to Panama, where he met with representatives of the guerrilla groups and the FDR. They also agreed to negotiations. Having accomplished that, Rivera y Damas flew to Europe, where he sought and obtained the backing of the International Social Democrats and the International Christian Democrats. The pope also blessed his archbishop's efforts to achieve peace. Now only the key player remained to be brought on board. So in April 1981 Rivera y Damas went to Washington, where he met with Vice President Bush and William Clark, at the time number two in the State Department and one of Reagan's most trusted advisers. They delivered the crushing message: The United States was not interested. A disappointed archbishop wrote to Bush after the meeting: "The United States must clearly indicate it is in favor of a political solution through negotiations or such negotiation will not occur in El Salvador. In addition to declaring its support for dialogue/mediation/negotiation, the U.S. role is essential in pressuring the military to accept a political solution."

The Reagan administration repeatedly sought to blame the leftists for the lack of negotiations. When, for example, Enders appeared before the House Subcommittee on Inter-American Affairs in September 1981, he testified that the FDR "has made no proposal for negotiation. It has said that it is for negotiations, but it has said at the same time that for negotiations to occur—unspecified negotiations—two conditions will have to be met." Enders told the subcommittee members, "The army will have to be restructured and the government will have to be substituted by an unspecified new order."

It was a false representation. Three months earlier, in June 1981, the FDR-FLMN had expressed its willingness to negotiate without preconditions. Moreover, even if the leftist opposition had imposed these conditions, one has to wonder why the Reagan administration was opposed to them. It, too, was in favor of a restructuring of the armed forces, as outlined in a Confidential cable from the State Department to the embassy several months later. There was also an internal inconsistency in Enders's statement that presented a Catch-22 dilemma for the FDR-FMLN: When the Salvadorans offered proposals in the form of an agenda—such as reopening the National University, release of political prisoners, lifting of the state of siege—they were told these were preconditions. When they offered to negotiate without preconditions, they were told there could be no negotiations without proposals.

A testy exchange, during the same September 1981 hearings, between Enders and Representative Studds is illustrative of how the administration sought to avoid responsibility for the absence of negotiations.

STUDDS: Let me try one more run around this, then we will give up. Would the United States have any objections of any kind to totally unconditional face-to-face discussion between the Duarte government and the Frente [FDR] designed to find a solution to the violence?

ENDERS: Look, Mr. Studds—

STUDDS: It is a fairly simple question.

ENDERS: One can imagine hundreds of negotiating scenarios.

STUDDS: I did not ask you for any of them.

ENDERS: The point is that a series of proposals have been made which remain without any response. There is no point in trying to negotiate with yourself in order to see whether you can imagine something which might appeal to oneself. You talk about reality. The reality down there is that the violent left does not wish to pick up opportunities for discussions and talks open to it. There is no point in making hundreds of hypothetical questions.

STUDDS: I did not ask any, much less hundreds. I asked a simple, straightforward question. The record will reflect that you are unwilling to answer it. But the question is, would the United States have any objection of totally unconditional face-to-face discussions between the Government and the Frente? If so, on what conceivable basis?

ENDERS: If the proposal were made by the authorities of El Salvador, that would be on their responsibility. We are not going to make additional proposals for this—

STUDDS: I did not ask for any proposals. I said would you object to their talking unconditionally.

ENDERS: They have plenty of opportunity to talk now. Indeed, if I am not mistaken—

STUDDS: Let the record reflect your unwillingness to answer the question, if you are not going to. It did not seem to me to be a trap, particularly. I cannot imagine the United States' unwillingness to answer such a question. I am compelled to attempt to imagine it by your unwillingness to answer it.

Enders had been less than truthful with the committee. It was not true that "a series of proposals" had been made. And it wasn't the "violent left" that was opposed to negotiations. It was the high command of the violent Salvadoran Army and the Reagan administration that were flatly opposed to the negotiations.

According to one Confidential cable from Secretary of State Haig to all U.S. diplomatic posts on June 2, 1981, "Canada's Ed Broadbent, a vice president of the Socialist International, met with President Duarte May 27 in an effort to promote a negotiated settlement." The cable continues: "Q: Is the US supporting the new Socialist International mediation effort of Canada's Ed Broadbent? A: No." Moreover, the cable notes that Haig would not meet with Broadbent when the latter was in Washington.

Enders would not even provide the committee with a straight answer about the attitude of the Salvadoran church. Representative Gus Yatron asked him, "Does the church in El Salvador favor a negotiated settlement among the warring factions in order to bring about a political solution?"

The answer was a simple and unequivocal yes. Enders said, "The church definitely favors a political solution and would favor all means of reaching that political solution, and it, of course, has not defined detailed negotiating proposals of its own." It would have, of course, been improper for the church to have offered any proposals; it was not a party to the negotiations but was seeking only to act as mediator, to get the parties talking.

The calls for a negotiated settlement continued. In August 1981 France and Mexico recognized the FDR-FMLN as a "representative political force." The Reagan administration, stunned and angry, "diplomated like crazy," as one senior State Department official put it, to get a number of Latin American countries to label the French-Mexican resolution "interference"—a bit paradoxical in view of the high level of U.S. involvement. The administration's approach toward Mexico, which also adopted a conciliatory attitude toward the Sandinistas, was not to try to work with this most important neighbor, but to "keep them [the Mexicans] isolated," according to a highly confidential memorandum prepared for the National Security Council. The extent of what the administration did to counter the French-Mexican recognition is still being withheld. Pursuant to an FOIA request, the State Department said it had located twenty-three documents. It refused to release any of them.

Other foreign nations, even Nicaragua, which the Reagan administration was blaming for the problems in El Salvador, also pushed for negotiations. In October 1981 one of the Sandinistas' most important leaders, Daniel Ortega, in a UN speech called for negotiations leading to internationally supervised elections in which the guerrillas would participate. The UN followed with a try for peace. Over the strong objections of the U.S. ambassador to the UN, Jeane Kirkpatrick, the General Assembly by a vote of 68 to 22, with 53 abstentions, passed a resolution, saying that it "deeply deplores" the continuing human rights abuses, and calling for a "negotiated political solution." Two weeks later, on December 27, 1981, the FDR-FMLN made another offer for peace. In one of their first displays of unity, all five guerrilla commanders, including Cayetano Carpio and Joaquín Villalobos, signed a letter to President Reagan. In it, they reiterated "our disposition to undertake them [negotiations] at any time, without pre-conditions placed on any of the parties in the conflict." The offer was frequently repeated. (It is somewhat surprising that the guerrillas were willing to negotiate since "the far right here doesn't have a good record for playing fair," as a senior U.S. military officer in El Salvador told a State Department official.)

Administration officials said that they were opposed to "power sharing" and that the guerrillas would not be allowed to "shoot their way into power." If the Reagan administration were really troubled by governments that come to power by force, it would have had to sever diplomatic relations with nearly half the Latin American nations and scores of others throughout the world. Moreover, the administration was arming, training, and paying the salaries of guerrillas trying to shoot their way into power sharing in Nicaragua. President Reagan called them freedom fighters. The argument was not only hypocritical but an overly simplistic response to a complex issue. It was possible to have negotiations without power sharing. One negotiated scenario might have been a cease-fire, with an international peacekeeping force to enforce it and to supervise elections in which all parties could participate.

Publicly the Reagan administration consistently professed to be in favor of "negotiations" and a "political solution." This was the primary assignment for Richard Stone, whom Reagan appointed special envoy to Central America in April 1983. But his assignment—what the words meant—was something considerably less than what is commonly thought to be implied in the words. The issue Stone was authorized to negotiate was the FDR-FMLN's participation in elections.

The administration first outlined its pursuit of a political solution in a speech by Thomas Enders to the World Affairs Council, a private foreign policy discussion group in Washington, D.C., in July 1981. His remarks were widely hailed, in front-page stories and editorials, as demonstrating that the administration had adopted a more flexible, less militaristic approach to the Salvadoran turmoil. Enders had selected the phrase carefully. A "political solution" was what the Salvadoran church was calling for. But what Enders meant by the words "political solution" wasn't the same thing that the church, and others, meant.

15

ELECTIONS SÍ, DEMOCRACY NO

THE fact that the elections were held was a justifiable cause for celebration in Washington. The turnout on election day was the ticker-tape parade for an administration that had few other successes in the conduct of its foreign policy—in El Salvador or elsewhere. But the hopes were dashed by the Reagan administration's own antidemocratic behavior and by the torrents of blood unleashed by a military that was not about to relinquish its sovereignty to a civilian government.

The U.S. belief that elections were the "political solution" to the Salvadoran bloodshed was met with widespread skepticism. "The best case for a bad policy," Representative Stephen J. Solarz, a liberal Democrat from New York, who had just returned from a ten-day fact-finding trip to the region, commented in reaction to Enders's announcement of the administration's new approach to the World Affairs Council. "It is totally unrealistic to expect the guerrillas to renounce violence without direct negotiations with the junta that insure that the subsequent electoral process will be safe and fair." Colonel Majano, who had been forced into exile, called the plans for elections "madness." The guerrillas, he said, could not be expected to take part "if there is not dialogue first." In El Salvador a group of business leaders expressed opposition to the elections in a dinner with Ambassador Hinton. The businessmen said that the Christian Democrats "would rig" the elections and that "the electorate, although overly politicized, is not ready to deal with political issues in a sensible and sophisticated manner," Hinton reported to Washington in a Confidential cable.

The army was also opposed to the elections, as Ambassador Hinton reported in a Secret cable shortly after his arrival in El Salvador. The cable, which was not released under the FOIA, was the one in which Hinton declared that there were "seriously adverse trends" which he did not discuss with the press. One of the things that he did not mention to reporters but did report in the Secret cable was: "There is now circulating among officers a document explaining that a Constituent Assembly which resulted from elections would perpetuate the hated PDC [Christian Democratic party] in power, and worse, give civilians authority to undermine the 'military institution.' Col. Gutierrez and Vides Casanova, among others, have told the DCM [deputy chief of mission] and myself of their concerns that elections will result in a one-party state, the retention of Duarte, and the strengthening of their bête noir, Jose Antonio Morales Ehrlich."* (Asked what had convinced the senior Salvadoran Army officers to permit the elections, a senior U.S. diplomat who was in El Salvador at the time said, "I assume they [the CIA] bought them.")

El Salvador's National Federation of Lawyers, which represents all of the country's bar associations, declined an invitation to work with the Central Elections Council in drafting the 1982 electoral law. The lawyers said that there could not be meaningful elections while there was a state of siege, which suspends such constitutional rights as freedom of speech and press and prohibits mass demonstrations and rallies. The archconservative *News-Gazette,* the country's English-language weekly, endorsed the national bar association's position. "Elections are held in times of war, but not in the midst of battles, nor on the front lines, and all El Salvador is the front line in this war," the paper maintained in an editorial. "Nor do we believe that free elections can be held while the country is in a state of siege and restrictions on individual liberty and freedom of expression exist."† In his

*At the time the cable was sent, June 24, 1981, Vides Casanova was commander of the National Guard. That he was minister of defense at the time of the 1984 elections underscored the likelihood that even if Duarte and the Christian Socialists were victorious, the military would not allow them to exercise any meaningful power. In addition to Duarte and D'Aubuisson, the other presidential candidate for the 1984 elections was Francisco José Guerrero of the National Conciliation party (PCN). A Guerrero victory would return El Salvador to the status quo ante. A conservative landowner, Guerrero had represented large landowners who successfully thwarted the land reform efforts in the mid-1970's, and his PCN was the army's party, which had ruled El Salvador for more than a quarter of a century until the coup in 1979.

†The state of siege was lifted a few days prior to voting day, but this was done without any public announcement, so the effect of the new freedom was at most minimal.

Sunday homily following Enders's speech, Archbishop Rivera y Damas reiterated his call for negotiations and said that meaningful elections were not possible in the climate of violence and lack of confidence in the government. Monsignor Ricardo Urioste, the vicar-general, said in an interview, "The United States is playing only one key on the piano."

The Reagan administration played that key masterfully. Even the Salvadoran bishops' council eventually endorsed the elections. Although the administration made much of the bishops' support for the elections, "it was not very surprising," said a senior U.S. diplomat who was in El Salvador at the time, noting that the conference is "very, very rightist." Even at that the endorsement was tepid, though the U.S. embassy in El Salvador sought to enhance it. In the packet of election materials the embassy provided journalists, it quoted the following from the bishops' statement: "We see in the elections . . . a possible beginning of a solution to the current crisis. . . . It would be ideal for all citizens to participate in the elections." The bishops had, however, been more restrained, saying: "We see in the elections *a faint glimmer of hope,* a possible beginning of a solution to the current crisis [emphasis added]."

The Reagan administration made every effort to bring off the elections, though just how much and what it did it won't say. The Agency for International Development (AID) spent at least a quarter of a million dollars from its human rights fund and from money that had been earmarked for the Salvadoran Ministry of Planning. The American Institute for Free Labor Development (AIFLD) funneled in more money, though it won't say how much, and there are conflicting reports about what it was used for. The Defense Department sent one of its superspook teams from ISA, which was established during the planning of the 1980 raid to free the Americans being held hostage in Iran because the department was dissatisfied with the work of the CIA. For nearly a year ISA operated without a "presidential finding," which is required for covert operations. Nor did the Defense Department notify the Senate and House intelligence oversight committees, as required by law. In addition to conducting paramilitary operations, ISA provides military equipment to foreign forces and deploys servicemen using false identities to collect intelligence inside a foreign country. In El Salvador, where it began its spying and covert operations shortly before the elections, only a handful of officials within the U.S. embassy were even aware of the unit's presence. One diplomat said that some of ISA's agents were members of the armed forces, that others were civilians, and that they included women as well as men. He declined to provide any details about what they did, except to say "they were very useful."

Similarly, the extent of the CIA's participation is a closely guarded secret. The CIA's involvement first surfaced in *The Wall Street Journal,* which quoted the director, William Casey, as saying that "we helped in the El Salvador election." In an effort to mitigate the adverse impact of the appearance of untoward U.S. involvement, Casey, in a dramatic departure from the agency's policy of not making any comment about its activities, said that the CIA's role had been limited to providing intelligence information about guerrilla plans to disrupt the elections and to supplying invisible ink to mark voters' fingers along with small hand-held battery-powered devices to detect the ink —designed to prevent people from voting more than once. He declined to say what else the CIA had done, and the agency has thwarted efforts to find out. Using the Freedom of Information Act, Jay Peterzell, of the Center for National Security Studies, requested documents relating to the CIA's role in the Salvadoran elections. The agency said that it had five documents. It refused to release four of these; the fifth had substantial deletions, and what was released was only what Casey had said publicly.

Relying on his own sources within the U.S. intelligence community, Philip Taubman of *The New York Times* reported that the Reagan administration had considered sending funds covertly to Duarte and the Christian Democrats. Casey refused to comment on this. But according to a State Department official, the United States did channel money to the Christian Democrats through AIFLD. He said that at least $50,000 in cash was carried into the country by AIFLD representatives. The money was given to the UCS, the Salvadoran peasant union, for use on behalf of the Christian Democrats. Other diplomats who were posted in El Salvador at the time of the elections said AIFLD gave several hundred thousand dollars to the UCS for use in the election, but they thought it was for the purpose of a get-out-the-vote drive among the peasants. AIFLD says it gave no more than $10,000 for that purpose; the UCS says it spent no money on the election, for any purpose.

Much of the AID money was for posters, plastered everywhere, as well as for radio jingles and television commercials that saturated the airwaves. As part of the effort to reach illiterate peasants, the voting campaign included thousands of copies of a brightly colored comic book, some dropped by helicopters into rural areas controlled by the guerrillas. In the comic, the guerrillas were portrayed as snarling terrorists with red berets who in one frame were shown torturing a cow. Enemies of the government's land reform, the extreme right, were shown with Rolls-Royces and uniformed thugs as body-guards. The theme, expressed in the comic book as well as all the other posters and jingles, was "Your vote will help end the violence, because it will strengthen the democratic Government while the loyal army eliminates the Communist threat." Nowhere in the comic book or in any of the propaganda effort was there any mention of the U.S. involvement and financing; the omission was consistent with the U.S. effort to avoid the impression that the elections were an American idea.

However much the Reagan administration spent, and for whatever purposes, it was a well-placed investment.

Election day was chaotic. In Ahuachapán, the capital of the country's westernmost province, soldiers struggled patiently to maintain order as hundreds shoved to get to the voting tables. Lines a block long descended a street between towering coconut palms plastered with political party posters, to the cyclone fence surrounding a school. Inside, the voters slid down low embankments, trampling and uprooting shrubs and small trees as they pushed their way to voting tables. At another school, near the central plaza, rifle barrels protruded above the crowd as soldiers found themselves trapped by the shoving throng. In nearby Juayúa, a bucolic coffee plantation village which had been sacked by peasants during the 1932 uprising, peasants waited in several long lines, extending from the twenty voting tables on the cement yard inside the run-down cinder-block elementary school. Hundreds more crowded in the dirt street littered with garbage. Many of the voters had walked from hillside hamlets three or four miles distant. Supporting himself with a gnarled stick crudely fashioned into a cane, a weathered man in tattered clothes waited with peasants whose bare feet were caked with thin layers of dirt. Women nursed their babies under parasols to protect them from the blistering sun. *New York Times* reporter Richard Meislin journeyed to Zacatecoluca on election day. "The dusty roads outside this country's major eastern cities were awash with hundreds of people, walking and walking—sometimes for miles—to cast their ballots," he reported. "There were people young and old—men with canes, women carrying babies and women expecting them. Their attire of vivid yellows and greens and reds and magentas gave the impression of a traveling rainbow as they surged on foot along the scorching highway toward voting places." The Salvadoran government reported that 1,551,687 people had trudged to the polls. An elated Secretary of State Haig called it a display of "awesome courage and civic responsibility" and "a military defeat for the guerrillas quite as much as a political repudiation." His sweeping pronouncement was sounded by the U.S. delegation that had been sent to observe the voting. The delegation, headed by Senator Nancy Landon Kassebaum, Republican of Kansas, declared that "the election clearly is a repudiation of the guerrillas' claim that they represent the will of the Salvadoran people."*

The journalistic reports about the elections echoed the administration's euphoria. On a CBS special Dan Rather exulted, "It's a triumph! A million people at the polls." ABC anchorman Frank Reynolds heralded "this exercise in democracy" as "gratifying, even inspiring." And at NBC Tom Brokaw described it as "one of the most remarkable election days anywhere."

The media turnout for the elections had been as awesome as that of the peasants. Nearly 700 correspondents, photographers, television technicians from all over the world—Japan, Denmark, Germany, Argentina—overran the tiny country. The journalists descended on El Salvador, filling hotels beyond the levels known even in the most peaceful days, in spite of a couple of ominous events. Eleven days before the election four members of a Dutch television crew had been killed. The producer was Jacobus Andries Koster, forty-six years old, who lived in Mexico. The others, all based in Holland, were the cameraman, Johannes Willemsen, forty-two; sound man, Hans ter Laan, twenty-five; and director, Jan Kuiper, two days shy of his fortieth birthday. The government said they were caught in a fire fight between soldiers and the guerrillas. But U.S. military advisers based at the headquarters of the Fourth Brigade at El Paraíso, two miles from the dry hills where the journalists died, reported to the embassy that the soldiers had set an ambush for the four, who they knew, on the basis of surveillance and intelligence, would be meeting with guerrillas at the spot they were cut down. The Dutch crew had previously made a film about life in the guer-

*Other members of the delegation were Representatives John Murtha (Democrat, Pennsylvania) and Robert Livingston (Republican, Louisiana); Father Theodore Hesburgh, president of Notre Dame University; Dr. Clark Kerr, president emeritus of the University of California; Deputy Assistant Secretary of State for Inter-American Affairs Everett E. Briggs; and election specialists Richard Scammon and Howard Penniman, who had observed elections in South Vietnam in the 1960's. According to AID documents obtained under the Freedom of Information Act, the expenses for the American delegation, as well as for observers from other countries, were paid for with $200,000 from AID and with $150,000 from four American business foundations—Scaife, Olin, Smith Richardson, and Grace. The Salvadoran government contributed $120,000.

rilla zones that had angered the Salvadoran military.

On the day the Dutchmen were killed, a list of persons accused of being "principals of Soviet, Cuban and Sandinista Communism" began circulating in the capital. Signed by one of the country's death squads, it called for death to "pseudo-journalists in the service of international subversion." A few of the journalists on the death list left the country, but most of us remained. It seems likely that the death list was meant to intimidate reporters, and one can only wonder about the degree, if any, to which it and the deaths of the Dutch journalists affected reporting.*

But the election day turnout by peasants silenced the administration's critics in Congress and on editorial boards, as well as the FDR-FMLN backers in Europe. "It was a public relations triumph," said a senior State Department press officer. "It got the reporters and the Europeans off all this other shit about human rights." The administration's loudly trumpeted conclusion—that the elections had been a defeat for the guerrillas—was accepted and repeated by journalists. But it was a superficial analysis and does not stand up to a closer examination of the more complex reasons that explain the turnout and results.

It has to approach the height of journalistic arrogance to pronounce upon elections on the basis of having been present on voting day and perhaps a few days before and after. But that is precisely what was done by the journalists as well as by the international observers; the U.S. delegation was in the country for four days.

The barometer of media interest in El Salvador is the style in which meals are served at the Camino Real, the journalists' favored hotel. When the story is running hot, there is a buffet; during slack times there is table service. The days before the election the breakfast buffet of fresh fruits, sausage, and all kinds of eggs was barely removed before the vegetables, slabs of beef, and rich pastries were set out for lunch. The roof of the high-rise hotel was a tangle of cables and cameras as television networks competed for space to conduct interviews with Hinton, Duarte, D'Aubuisson, using the lush volcanoes as backdrop. Then it was over. Within days the buffet was dismantled at the Camino Real; other hotels were again vacant. The television crews, having packed their gear, departed along with newspaper reporters

---

*The media protested only mildly the killing of the Dutch journalists, prompting I. F. Stone to write from Washington, D.C.: "After a lifetime of journalism, I still do not understand the media. I cannot fathom the pool of silence into which the killing of the four Dutch journalists in El Salvador has been dropped. Why is there so little capacity for caring?"

for home or for the war in the Falklands, which broke out six days after the Salvadoran elections.

There is more, however, to an election or to the "democratic process," as the Reagan administration described what it was trying to encourage in El Salvador, than the one day of voting. "Elections do not necessarily mean democracy, but that is something you Americans do not understand," a prominent Salvadoran businessman remarked during a conversation when the elections had been announced. Some weeks after March 28 I asked if he still held the same view. "Absolutely!"

His observation applies as well to the Salvadoran elections scheduled for March 1984. Indeed, the elections of 1984 will be in many ways a replica of those two years earlier. Just as the military remained the dominant political institution in the country after the 1982 elections, so will the military officers, not the civilians—whoever is elected—continue to run the country after the elections in 1984. And just as leftist politicians could not have safely participated in the elections in 1982, so it is not safe for them to participate two years later.

To call the Salvadoran elections—in 1982 or 1984—democratic would be akin to describing a U.S. election democratic if the liberal wing of the Democratic party were not allowed to participate. No parties representing political views to the left of the Christian Democrats were—or would be—represented in the Salvadoran elections. But even if the elections could be judged as democratic as possible within the context of a civil war, the absence of the FDR or any other leftist parties challenged—arguably rebutted—the conclusion that the vote was a defeat for the revolution.

The Reagan administration and Duarte had said that the left could participate; the only condition was that they renounce violence and lay down their arms. (A similar condition, however, was not imposed on the rightist political party, the Nationalist Republican Alliance [ARENA], the death squads of which continued to murder.) But in fact, the FDR could not have participated. Colonel Gutiérrez, as a member of the junta, had stated categorically that it could not participate in the elections because it was not a political party but "the democratic façade for the guerrillas," the State Department advised all diplomatic posts in one of its Confidential "Summary of Developments in El Salvador." Similarly, during a dinner at the embassy residence guests from the private sector "representing a diversity of views" were unanimous in their insistence that the FDR "could not participate in the elections," according to a Confidential cable, which was released under the FOIA, with the names of the private-sector individuals deleted.

No one could seriously argue that even if they had been allowed to participate, it would have been safe for Ungo, Zamora, or any candidate representing the left or the guerrillas to enter the country for the election. They would have been murdered as surely as had been Enrique Álvarez and the other FDR leaders in November 1980. In a Secret cable the CIA reported on information that had come from a former officer of the civil defense organization and "anti-guerrilla National Guard unit" in Cinquera. The officer had said he did not believe that Duarte "could guarantee the safety of any rebel who wanted to participate in the March elections. He considered that too much blood had been shed over recent years for any guarantee to have validity and Duarte's writ did not run through the Army and National Guard." He was right. Underscoring the risks that any leftist candidate would have faced was the fact that the armed forces themselves, not some clandestine death squad, had issued a communiqué, prominently reported in the newspapers, describing the FDR and even the MNR as terrorist groups. (The MNR was a legal political party, founded in the 1960's, representing social democratic views.) The list, disseminated in March 1981, also contained the names of 138 "traitors," including Ungo, Zamora, and nearly all the other leaders of the FDR and MNR. "The armed forces, complying with its constitutional mission to defend the Salvadoran people, incessantly pursues all traitors to the country, in order that they pay for the great damage done to our country," the communiqué concluded. In short, it was an invitation for anyone to shoot any of the leftist political leaders; doing so would be a patriotic act.

The U.S. embassy in El Salvador was aware that any leftist politician who appeared in the country would be risking his life. Hinton suggested that they campaign with videotapes. He, as well as others in the embassy, also argued—as they have again argued for the 1984 elections—that no politician was completely free of risk during the campaign. While they were right, there was a quantum difference in the degree of risks to which the candidates exposed themselves. It was the difference between walking through a crime-ridden district of a major U.S. city in broad daylight surrounded by police and strolling alone there in the dark of night. Moreover, no leaders of the Christian Democrats, ARENA, or the other political parties had been on the military's list of "traitors." Finally, whatever protections might be possible for the leftist candidates—embassy officials argued that they be allowed to have their own bodyguards—ignored the fate that would befall anyone who attended their rallies; thousands of Salvadorans have been murdered on nothing more than the suspicion that they were merely sympathetic to the leftists.

In pronouncing the 1982 elections a defeat for the guerrillas, U.S. officials stressed several related aspects of guerrilla activities: that there had been threats to disrupt the elections; that there had been attempts to intimidate voters; that there had been shooting on election day. ("If they really want to disrupt elections, why didn't they shoot candidates? I wonder," said a U.S. diplomat who was in El Salvador.) President Reagan summed it up in a speech to the British Parliament a few weeks after the election. The Salvadoran guerrillas, he said, "threatened death to anyone who voted and destroyed hundreds of buses and trucks to keep people from getting to the polling places. But on election day, the people of El Salvador, an unprecedented 1.4 million of them, braved ambush and gunfire, trudging miles to vote for freedom. They stood for hours in the hot sun waiting for their turn to vote. Members of our Congress who went there as observers told me of a woman wounded by rifle fire who refused to leave the line to have her wound treated until after she had voted.

"A grandmother, who had been told by the guerrillas she would be killed when she returned from the polls, told the guerrillas, 'You can kill me, kill my family, kill my neighbors, but you can't kill us all.' " It was a little story the President liked so much that he repeated it often, including during his address to the joint session of Congress in April 1983.

There were indeed guerrilla attacks on election day—in Apopa, San Antonio Abad, Zacatecoluca, Usulután. But in total there was one major battle and fewer than a dozen fire fights. "Despite the 'ballots over bullets' news frame, over 85 percent of the 260–300 (reports vary) polling places were opened and peaceful, and two to three percent experienced fighting," wrote a professor of political science at the University of Massachusetts, Boston, Jack Spence, who analyzed all the election coverage in the major newspapers, in the magazines, and on the networks.

As for guerrilla efforts to disrupt the elections, this, too, was a mixed and complex picture, which has been presented simply. Two days before the elections, for example, an ABC correspondent held a box of captured explosives which he said the guerrillas had planned to use to disrupt the elections. But it was impossible to know whether the explosives were intended for such a specific purpose or were simply part of the guerrillas' overall military effort. Similarly, the destruction of buses, which was said by journalists and the administration to be part of the guerrillas' effort to keep people from reaching polling stations, was, in fact, a tactic that long predated the elections and continued afterward. Moreover, not all guerrilla units tried to disrupt the elections. While Roberto Roca, leader of the tiny and militarily almost insignificant guerrilla group the Revolutionary Party of Central American Workers, declared that "we will defeat the elections, not by attacking voters or polling booths, but by making the war felt at all levels everywhere," the most powerful and influential guerrilla leader at the time, Salvador Cayetano Carpio, argued that they were insignificant in the long struggle. On election day it was quiet in Chalatenango, the stronghold of Carpio's FPL forces.

Guerrilla attempts to intimidate Salvadoran peasants not to vote appear to have been isolated—and magnified by the press—rather than an overall strategy. Many of the charges of intimidation were based on a report in *Time* magazine about a graffiti slogan: "Vote in the morning, die in the afternoon." But there was only one such slogan spotted by the hundreds of reporters in El Salvador, and it apparently was the work of an individual rebel or rebel unit. Moreover, five days before the elections the guerrillas' clandestine Radio Venceremos advised rebel supporters "not to worry" about whether or not they voted. "There should be no concern about whether or not one votes, because the elections have no significance for the Salvadoran people." In an effort to encourage voting, the Salvadoran newspapers, which rarely made any mention of the leftist political leaders except to condemn them in strident language, prominently reported, just prior to the elections, a declaration by Ungo that there would be no attempts to interfere with the voting. (On the advice of Ungo, Zamora, and other FDR leaders, the FMLN guerrilla commanders announced in February 1984 they would not interfere with the March 1984 elections.)

While many Salvadorans voted in 1982 in spite of fears of guerrilla retaliation, another fear contributed to the massive turnout. That was the fear of reprisals by the Salvadoran armed forces against those who did not vote. Twelve days before the voting I wandered through the capital barrio Mejicanos, talking with women squatting next to little piles of bright red tomatoes, cabbages, and watermelons, displayed under torn pieces of plastic in the congested open-air market, and with merchants in the rows of ramshackle structures that open onto the narrow streets plied by clanking, soot-belching buses. A muscular twenty-four year-old man working in his T-shirt in a tiny windowless shop explained the dilemma. "We think about this much, to vote or not to vote," he said in a barely audible voice, reflecting the widespread fear of talking about politics. Passing the collar of what would be a sport shirt under the needle of his foot-trundle sewing machine, he continued: "The government says if we don't vote, we're terrorists. The guerrillas say if we do, we're against them." Many of the residents of Mejicanos were guerrilla supporters, he said. His wife, a few feet behind him, leaning on a cloth-covered cutting table, nodded in agreement. But they had decided to vote, because, he said, the army would "maltreat" those who didn't.

Minister of Defense García and other senior government officials publicly declared on numerous occasions that not to vote was treason. Lynda Schuster, of *The Wall Street Journal,* reported that soldiers had surrounded the village of San Benito, threatening to kill everyone who didn't vote. In January 100 people had been massacred there. "I'll vote because they're forcing me to vote, but I don't have the slightest idea what it means," María Amanda Parada told Schuster. Sobbing, she added, "I just want to find my daughters; I miss them so much." Mrs. Parada said that her three married daughters had been kidnapped by soldiers after they had shot and killed her sons-in-law and burned her house.

The Reagan administration ignored these threats by the army, along with the effective means the Salvadoran government had of enforcing them. Salvadoran citizens, like those in most Latin American countries, are required to carry identification cards, called *cédulas.* On election day each *cédula* was stamped after the person had voted. Thousands of Salvadoran peasants walked many miles, endured long lines, stood in the blistering sun solely because they wanted their *cédulas* stamped, not because they had faith in the democratic process or were opposed to the guerrillas.

The stamp was supposed to be invisible, so that the guerrillas would not know if the person had voted. But many journalists reported seeing *cédulas* on which the stamp was visible. Moreover, "campesinos in El Salvador have always believed that the government has ways of knowing how you voted," said Leonel Gómez, the former head of the Salvadoran land reform agency. "They always believe the government is watching."

The voting procedures were devised in such a way to reinforce this belief. All the ballots were numbered. "Numbered ballots have been the traditional means of making sure that Juan Pueblo votes as the authorities want him to," said Robert White, who described the Salvadoran election as a "distortion" of the democratic process. "No power on earth can convince a poor, unlettered campesino with a numbered ballot in his hand that the military commandant of his district will not know for whom his vote was cast." Even the president of the Central Elections Council, Dr. Jorge Bustamante, a University of Chicago-educated gynecologist who was widely heralded for his exemplary performance in conducting the elections, was so disturbed by the numbered balloting procedure that he cast a blank ballot. And the U.S.-backed peasant organization, UCS, convinced that the government would know how people voted, instructed peasants not to cast blank ballots, which would have been considered votes for the left, because to have done so would have endangered the voters' lives.

Whatever combination of factors accounted for the voter turnout, to interpret it as a demonstration against the leftists fails to take into account the nature in which the election was presented. Much of the get-out-the-vote sloganeering was the creative work of the CIA. One poster depicted the country of El Salvador sundered down the middle, with blood dripping from the center. Pulling on one side were the oligarchs, portrayed by an individual with money spilling out of his pocket; on the other side was a guerrilla, wearing a red bandanna and carrying a rifle. A television appeal showed a grieving woman lighting candles at the four corners of a body covered by a sheet. The narrator asked viewers if they wanted the violence to continue. "El Salvador deserves your vote," said the bereaved woman. This was the theme: that voting would bring an end to the violence. But the violence came from the right and the left. There was no mention of who had killed the grieving woman's friend or relative.

"We are voting for peace and an end to the violence," the American observer delegation reported hearing "over and over again" from voters. That is precisely what the Salvadorans were longing for: respite from the violence. But as every Salvadoran peasant knows, the government's army and security forces have long been responsible for most of the violence against the people. So going to the polls, even when not done out of fear, can just as easily be interpreted as a vote against the violent right and the violent government as against the violent left.

The lines on election day were long, to be sure, just as journalists noted. But what did that indicate? A massive turnout, as commonly interpreted? Or that the limited number of polling places allowed for the impression of a massive turnout? In the capital, for example, there were only thirteen polling places. If the turnout had been only half what the government reported (187,916), reporters would have been awed by scenes of 7,200 people crowding each place.

According to the Salvadoran elections council, 1,551,687 persons went to the polls. But researchers at the University of Central America, the Catholic university, in San Salvador have charged that there was "massive fraud in the number of votes." According to university studies, the number of voters was probably between 600,000 and 800,000, and no more than 1,281,600.

In reaching its conclusions about the number of people who voted, the researchers considered three factors: the time it took to vote; the number of polling places; and the number of hours the polls were open. Regarding the first, they concluded that it took an average of two minutes for each voter to complete the multiple-step balloting process. This included a check of fingers to make sure that the person had not already voted; receiving the ballot; walking a few feet to the voting box; marking the ballot; folding it; stuffing it into the box; returning to the voting table to sign the register, have the *cédula* stamped, and get the fingers marked with indelible ink to prevent voting again. Between two and three minutes was what it was taking each voter to complete the steps in Juayúa and the provincial capital of Ahuacha-pán where I observed the voting, and several election officials said three minutes was the average voting time.*

The university researchers also calculated the hours of continuous voting that would have been necessary in order for the number of officially reported votes actually to have been cast, again if one assumed it took two minutes for each voter. In six of the country's fourteen provinces, it would have required uninterrupted voting for more than twelve hours. (The official voting hours were from 7:00 A.M. to 7:00 P.M. in places where there was electricity and until 4:00 P.M. in villages without. Few polling places opened on time—some not until early afternoon—and many closed early. The U.S. observer delegation reported that polls closed at 6:00 P.M.) In Sonsonate, for example, the government claimed that 133,313 persons voted. If each voter took two minutes, which was about the average time on the basis of my observations there, there would have had to have been continuous voting for 15.6 hours; in La Libertad, it would have required 14.9 hours, and in Ahuachapán, 13.4 hours. In only five of the provinces could the officially reported number of voters have completed the process in fewer than eleven hours and in only one in less than ten hours.†

*The day after the voting, the country's most conservative newspaper, *El Diario de Hoy,* reported that it took "up to 10 minutes" to vote. When the charges of vote inflation surfaced, Howard Penniman, of the conservative American Enterprise Institute, who had been part of the American observer delegation and had worked closely with the Salvadoran elections council, said that he had clocked the average voting time of each person at under one minute. But John Carbaugh, a staunch conservative who was an aide to Senator Jesse Helms when he went to El Salvador for the elections, determined that the average time was three minutes.

†There were other irregularities in the voting. For example, according to a computer printout from the Central Elections Council dated April 13, there was no voting in nine villages in Chalatenango. But the printout dated April 14

Other suspicions about the vote total are raised by predictions of Salvadoran and U.S. officials *prior* to the election. In a preelection day interview at his modest election office headquarters, Dr. Bustamante calculated that there were only about 1 million eligible voters in the country. In painstakingly explaining how he arrived at this number, he referred to the total population, the Salvadorans who were too young to vote, the refugees who had fled the country, and the reasons why many peasants lacked the identification cards needed to vote. Ten days before the voting Richard Scammon, an elections expert who was an adviser to the Central Elections Council and a member of the U.S. observer team, appeared at a briefing for reporters given by the State Department. He told them that the maximum expected turnout was 640,000. During a meeting of embassy officials in San Salvador one political officer predicted that 1 million people would vote. "We wanted to put him in a rubber room," said another diplomat who was present.

When the charges that the totals had been inflated surfaced, one elected deputy, from the Democratic Action (AD), a small, moderate party of lawyers and businessmen, said in an interview, "One and a half million? It's impossible." He thought that the actual number of voters was probably between 900,000 and 1 million. He explained that no political leader wanted to discuss the likelihood of fraud because it was to everyone's benefit for the number to appear high. "In the end we all understood that the country is going through difficult times and this was not the moment to inject another problem." A year later AD politicians were more openly saying that the vote total had been inflated and that Robert Driscoll, the U.S. embassy political officer at the time, was the person responsible. Driscoll laughed at the charges. "It's more of the Latin demonology, that nothing ever happens on its own merits," he said.

D'Aubuisson also said that there was "massive fraud" during the elections but that ARENA had been involved, so he could not say anything publicly. He told this to a gathering of his party faithful a couple of months after the election, and two reporters waiting to interview him were in the audience. A high-ranking ARENA leader explained that when the results came in by telex from the outlying voting districts to ANTEL, the state communications company controlled by the military, they were inflated before being sent to the elections council's counting headquarters. (In view of the capability of

shows voting in those nine villages. There are similar discrepancies between the April 13 and 14 computer printouts in two other provinces.

computers and the inclination of the CIA, it is certainly possible that the intelligence agency arranged just such an operation.)

"Bullshit!" said Ambassador Hinton in response to the university's conclusion that the vote total was vastly inflated. "It would take a professor in an ivory tower who didn't go out to vote because the guerrillas told him not to to come up with a theory like that."

But Hinton rejected a suggestion by the professors that an investigation be conducted. The ambassador's relationship with the Catholic university had been cool and distant; while many on his staff respected the work of the professors, Hinton thought the university was too antigovernment and too leftist. It was not until he had been ambassador for two years that members of his staff persuaded him at least to meet with university officials. A few months after the elections, the university's rector, Ignacio Ellacuría, and three other Jesuit professors were invited to the embassy residence for lunch. When the discussion turned to the recent elections, Hinton made it clear that he was "extremely angry" with the university's charges that the vote total had been massively inflated. Father Ellacuría responded by proposing that an independent commission, including one or two people appointed by the U.S. Congress, be established to investigate the charges. Hinton was not enthusiastic and said that if there were to be any investigation, it should be by the people who had conducted the elections. The priests viewed this as allowing those who were possibly involved in the fraud to investigate themselves. The possibility of an investigation went no further.

Hinton also played a role in suppressing other charges of fraud. On the day after the elections he invited the leaders from each of the participating parties to the embassy for lunch. The campaign had been bitter, and the luncheon was a "low-key social affair," said an American diplomat who was present, "to allow the warring parties to begin talking civilly." Hinton suggested to the politicians that they not start hurling charges of fraud. "It was more a plea than an order," said the diplomat, made "in the spirit of not destroying the incipient democracy with fraud charges." While the diplomat may have thought it was only a plea or suggestion, it is likely that the Salvadoran politicians present interpreted more seriously the remarks of the powerful American ambassador.

Elliott Abrams, of State's human rights bureau, declared to the House Foreign Affairs Committee four months after the elections, "[T]here was absolutely no indication of fraud." It was an overstatement. While in comparison to previous Salvadoran elections, those in 1982 were honest, there was some fraud.

In the province of Cabañas, where he was commander, Lieutenant Colonel Ochoa "stuffed the ballot boxes" for D'Aubuisson's ARENA, according to a senior American diplomat who was deeply involved in the Salvadoran elections. Ochoa was the military commander most admired at the time by the military advisers. "As a military commander he was very good," said the diplomat who provided the information about stuffing the ballot boxes. "But he got frustrated and sold his soul to ARENA." Ochoa and D'Aubuisson are members of the same *tanda*.

Other charges of fraud have surfaced. Raúl Molina, secretary-general of the National Conciliation party (PCN)—the official military party that was founded in 1961 and stole the elections from Duarte and Ungo in 1972—has charged that ARENA and the Christian Democrats committed fraud. He told Robert Leiken, director of the Soviet-Latin American Project at the Georgetown University Center for Strategic and International Studies, that PCN ballots had been annulled and that official PCN poll watchers had been prevented from entering some polling places. He also claimed that some ballots had been burned. D'Aubuisson said that the fraud cost ARENA three deputies in San Salvador, one in Usulután, and one in La Libertad.

Publicly Dr. Bustamante denied that there was an inflation of the vote total or any fraud. Privately, however, he told U.S. embassy officials that some of the ballot boxes were "picked up by unauthorized people" and that "in the haste" ballots marked for one party were tossed into boxes for another party.

In some measure, maybe all the fraud charges are moot. The elections did not bring an end to the violence or the beginning of a moderate, civilian government that could control the military. But it wasn't the political left, the Marxists, that subverted the incipient Salvadoran democracy. That was done by the United States and the Salvadoran armed forces, first working together, then by the latter operating alone to control the country, as it has always done.

In the voting on March 28, the Christian Democrats emerged with 35 percent of the ballots cast, and twenty-four of the sixty deputies in the Constituent Assembly. Finishing second, with 26 percent and nineteen deputies, was the ultraconservative Nationalist Republican Alliance (ARENA) led by D'Aubuisson, followed by the PCN, with 17 percent and fourteen deputies.*

*Two of the elected deputies were from the Democratic Action (AD), which had been formed in late 1981 for the express purpose of participating in the elections and was supported primarily by moderate to conservative lawyers, mid-

That the Christian Democrats did not fare better and that ARENA did as well as it did were a surprise and something of an embarrassment to the U.S. embassy, which did not begin to sense ARENA's strength until a few weeks before the elections. The relative failure of the Christian Democrats was attributable to a number of factors. While the party enjoyed some advantages of incumbency, these were more than offset by the disadvantages: The economy was in shambles, unemployment was rampant, prices were rising, and the war was making everyone's life miserable. The Christian Democrats were blamed for all these maladies. Moreover, the other five political parties all campaigned against the Christian Democrats and only against the Christian Democrats—that is, not against each other. Hinton tried to convince the candidates in the other parties that in a truly democratic process they should criticize each other as well. He did not succeed.

None of the parties has said publicly how much it spent on the campaign, but an embassy political officer estimates that the Christian Democrats and ARENA each expended about $1 million. Most of the Christian Democrats' money came from Venezuela, where the Christian Democrats' party was in power, as well as, almost certainly, from funds channeled to it by the CIA and AIFLD. ARENA was financially backed by wealthy Salvadorans, most of whom were living in Miami. The party had the slickest and most professional campaign, managed by the New York-based international advertising agency McCann Erickson.

Much of ARENA's structure and ideology was provided by Mario Sandoval Alarcón, leader of Guatemala's ultraright National Liberation Movement (MLN), which calls itself "the party of organized violence." Sandoval's inspiration in turn comes from the Taiwan-based World Anti-Communist League (WACL). The league's Latin American branch, of which Sandoval has long been a leader, is dominated by anti-Semitic, neofascist groups. Sandoval was approached by D'Aubuisson in 1979 and helped raise millions of dollars for the Salvadoran rightists as well as assisted them in smuggling arms into El Salvador, according to Laurie Becklund and Craig Pyes, the investigative reporters who spent nearly a year and a half tracing the rise, structure, and activities of the right in El Salvador.

---

dle-level business managers, owners of medium-size farms, and other professionals. The tiny Popular Salvadoran party elected one deputy, and the Popular Orientation party, headed by the founder of ORDEN, General José Alberto "Chele" Medrano, was shut out at the polls.

"Arena is a fascist party modeled after the NAZIs and certain revolutionary communist groups," former Ambassador White told the House Subcommittee on Western Hemisphere Affairs in February 1984. Though D'Aubuisson usually disguised his admiration for Adolf Hitler, he once told three European reporters, "You Germans were very intelligent. You realized that the Jews were responsible for the spread of communism, and you began to kill them." ARENA is more than just a political party, formed and supported by the same members of the oligarchy and conservative military elements who have ruled the country for generations. It is a paramilitary organization as well.

The Reagan administration, so intent on convincing the world that outsiders were behind the guerrilla effort, ignored the foreign influence on ARENA. Sandoval was ARENA's Castro. One of Sandoval's nephews, Carlos Midence, who proudly wore a Nazi swastika medallion—he told Pyes and Becklund that it was given to him by the private secretary of Hitler's propaganda minister in Argentina—advised the Salvadorans on underground techniques. Veterans of the French Secret Army Organization (OAS), who had fought against the nationalists in Algeria, worked with D'Aubuisson to develop a plan of terror, kidnappings, and assassinations. Advisers from Argentina, who had conducted the brutal campaign against the leftists in that country in the 1970's, taught them to set up safe houses, where torture was often carried out with cooperation from the government's military forces.

"Terrorism cannot be fought with conventional methods," one of D'Aubuisson's earliest financial backers, Guillermo Sol, told Pyes and Becklund. The only answer, Sol said, was to "destroy it." To do that "you need excellent intelligence. D'Aubuisson is excellent on that. He's U.S.-trained."

A graduate of the Salvadoran military academy, D'Aubuisson was also trained at the U.S. Army's school in Panama and the International Police Academy in the suburbs of Washington, D.C. In Taiwan he studied "Communist infiltration." His military career ended with the coup in October 1979. At the time he was a National Guard major; he is widely referred to by Salvadorans as Major Bob. According to most accounts, he was forced out of the armed forces. D'Aubuisson said he voluntarily retired. In any case, he remained an active leader of radical right-wing causes, couching them in strident anti-Communist rhetoric. In the spring of 1980 he accused the Carter administration of trying to bring communism to El Salvador; during one public appearance he drew his finger across his throat, saying that James Cheek, in charge of the embassy in El Salvador at the time, would "get what he deserves" for "leading El Salvador to Communism." Soon thereafter came his arrest on charges for plotting to overthrow the Salvadoran government. It was during this arrest that he was caught with the documents that Robert White said provide "compelling if not 100-percent conclusive evidence" that D'Aubuisson was responsible for the assassination of Archbishop Romero and led to White's calling him a "pathological killer." Also among the documents were the organizational diagram that resulted in ARENA and plans for attacks on the U.S. embassy. When the embassy was machine-gunned in March 1981, the U.S. chargé d'affaires, Frederic Chapin, said, "[T]his incident has all the hallmarks of a D'Aubuisson operation."

After D'Aubuisson's success in the March elections, two U.S. intelligence agencies altered their biographical profiles of him, eliminating much of the negative data. Before the elections one agency's profile had mentioned the charges that D'Aubuisson had been involved in the assassination of the archbishop. Two months later the same profile made no mention of the charges or the assassination. Similarly, another intelligence agency's profile, prepared in June 1980, reported that D'Aubuisson had been charged with leading death squads that in recent months had assassinated hundreds, including Archbishop Romero. These charges were omitted when the agency issued a revised profile in May 1982.

The State Department is covering up information relating to D'Aubuisson's involvement in the killings of the AIFLD workers, Hammer and Pearlman, by classifying and refusing to release documents, which it acknowledges exist. During a lawsuit in Los Angeles, brought by the ACLU Foundation of Southern California in behalf of Salvadorans who were seeking to avoid deportation, Peter F. Romero, a State Department officer, was asked, "Have you seen any information that would link D'Aubuisson with the frustration of the investigation into" the deaths of Hammer and Pearlman? Romero declined to answer, saying, "I think we are getting into an area that's classified."

D'Aubuisson's rehabilitation by the Reagan administration and political comeback began when Hinton arrived as ambassador. One of Hinton's missions was to repair the U.S. relations with the Salvadoran rightists, which had been severed, intentionally, by Ambassador White, who had instructed his staff not to meet with D'Aubuisson. Hinton developed an "almost father-son relationship with D'Aubuisson," said one of Hinton's aides. "He thought he could channel him, push him along the democratic path, and theoretically curb his more violent tendencies. In the process he created a monster."

During the campaign the ultraright-wing ARENA officials talked about using napalm against the guerrillas and releasing the army from all human rights restraints. The party also pledged to reverse the land reforms and the nationalizations of the banks and export trade. But in a country where probably half the voters had only a sixth-grade education, if that, it is not derogatory to suggest that the people voted less on the issues than on the men.

D'Aubuisson, born in 1944, was by far the most charismatic candidate, much in the tradition of the Latin American caudillo, or strong man. Women found him charming and handsome. Hinton once joked with reporters that he "ran a risk" when at the request of his then thirty-year-old Salvadoran girl friend, later to be his wife, he introduced her to D'Aubuisson. Taut and very muscular, with thick, curly hair, D'Aubuisson, noted Warren Hoge of *The New York Times,* bears a striking resemblance to singer Eddie Fisher. He wears high-heeled boots to elevate his five-foot-six-inch height, chain-smokes, usually Marlboros, drinks heavily, and is a caricature of kinetic energy. While he is seated during press conferences or interviews, his legs are perpetually jiggling.

Escorted by armor-reinforced vans loaded with heavily armed bodyguards, D'Aubuisson took his campaign into remote, dusty villages where the Christian Democrats were afraid to tread. But D'Aubuisson had the protection both of former ORDEN members, whom he had incorporated into his own political organization, and of military commanders. With his pistol bulging under his loose-fitting shirt, he would lead handclapping rallies in the party's catchy campaign song: "Tremble, Tremble, Communists." The Christian Democrats' party color is green, and D'Aubuisson would often hold up a watermelon and slice it through with a machete, telling the crowd this was what Duarte and his party were: green on the outside but red (Communists) on the inside.

In addition to its primary task of drafting a constitution, the sixty-member Constituent Assembly had the power to name a provisional president to replace Duarte and the junta. D'Aubuisson had the necessary support—nineteen members of his own party and fourteen deputies from the conservative PCN. But then the Reagan administration stepped in. It knew that it would be difficult, if not impossible, to convince Congress and the American people to send millions of dollars of military and economic aid if D'Aubuisson were running the country.

"I worked harder after the election than before," Hinton remarked privately at the time, referring to his efforts to stop D'Aubuisson. Embassy political officers worked sixteen- to eighteen-hour days, in tough, smoke-filled negotiating sessions with leaders of ARENA and the PCN. Reagan dispatched a high-level congressional delegation, led by the House majority leader, James C. "Jim" Wright, Jr., Democrat of Texas, to reinforce the message that a D'Aubuisson government would not be palatable. It's questionable how much impact the message had since Wright publicly praised D'Aubuisson as being "very bright, very intense, very sincere." Wright added, "I don't accept the most severe characterizations about him at all. I don't think he's that bad at all. I believe he's dedicated to the democratic process."

The rightists held together. They had been democratically elected, and D'Aubuisson was their man. Reagan turned to his special envoy Vernon Walters, a retired army general who had been a deputy director of the CIA under Nixon. Walters had spent much of his cloak-and-dagger career in Latin America; colonels and generals liked his tough anti-Communist style. After hearing Walters, Salvadoran Defense Minister García and the military high command believed that U.S. military support might just be jeopardized if D'Aubuisson were named president.

For fifty years the Salvadoran armed forces had chosen the country's president. It would be no different now. The military high command summoned Duarte and D'Aubuisson and bluntly informed each, in separate sessions, that he was not going to be president. Then the senior officers gave the newly elected Constituent Assembly three names to choose from, but they made it clear that the man they expected to be named president was Álvaro Alfredo Magaña. In El Salvador, Magaña, who has a law degree from the University of El Salvador and a master's degree in economics from the University of Chicago, was jokingly referred to as Dr. Yes, in contrast with another businessman who was called Dr. No. The latter had been asked several times to be president and had always said no. Magaña had said yes, he would like to be president, but he had never been asked. Now the military was asking him, repaying an institutional debt. For seventeen years Magaña had been president of the nation's mortgage bank. In that capacity he had regularly lent officers money to buy houses and farms, loans which were not justified by the officers' salaries and credit ratings. Some officers turned to corruption—selling drivers' licenses, extorting protection money from businessmen and small farmers—to repay the loans; many others simply defaulted. Magaña himself didn't profit "inordinately" from making the improper loans, said one U.S. diplomat. Another described the practice as "structural corruption," using the national budget "to keep the army from going on a rampage." Magaña was one of the people whom the young coup plotters had wanted to put on trial in October 1979, before they were thwarted by the military conservatives.

As president, Magaña, who admitted to reporters that he had a serious drinking problem (judged by its high incidence an occupational hazard of political office in El Salvador), was powerless, serving as a figurehead, as had Duarte and the Christian Democrats. Reporters and congressional delegations found they could spend hours with the president in his spacious office and not be interrupted by phone calls on any of his several telephones. "Why is President Magaña like a public telephone?" began a joke told by Salvadorans and U.S. diplomats. "Because he's on the street and he doesn't receive calls." Magaña had no delusions about his power or, more accurately, lack thereof. "I have no power, no authority," he told a congressional delegation a year after he had become president. "The extreme right here is incredible the way they are." Magaña's impotence was driven home to him when he paid a visit to the commanders at the Treasury Police in an effort to curtail their death squad activities. The commanders all but laughed in his face.

Contrary to Reagan administration claims about democracy in El Salvador, the reality was that political power after the elections belonged to the military, as it always has. This was underscored in early 1983, when Lieutenant Colonel Ochoa staged a rebellion, refusing to obey any further orders issued by the minister of defense, General García.

Reagan administration officials maintained that Magaña ended the rebellion and obtained García's resignation, which Ochoa, along with several other field commanders, was demanding. In January 1983 the administration reported to Congress that "the successful resolution of this internal problem by President Magaña in his capacity as Commander-in-Chief of the Armed Forces is an affirmation of adherence by the military to civilian governmental authority." Six months later, in another report to Congress, the administration declared again that Magaña had played a key role in the resolution of the conflict, which "served to strengthen civilian control of the military institution."

The administration's statements can charitably be described as a view of the world as Reagan wished it were but not as it really was— or even as it was reported by the U.S. embassy. García was forced out only after air force jets had buzzed his residence and the commander of the air force had warned Magaña that unless García were replaced, the air force would go on strike. In a Secret cable, which was not released under the FOIA, the embassy reported: "In the end, at the stubborn insistence of the Air Force and its commander Col. Juan Rafael Bustillo, García was finally forced out of office and replaced by Gen. Carlos Eugenio Vides Casanova." Vides's appointment was by the military, not by Magaña, and the subsequent reassignments of commanders that he made was a "shift to the right," the embassy informed Washington.

The shift to the right began when D'Aubuisson, even though he was denied the presidency of the country, was named president of the National Assembly. In charge of security for the Assembly he named a dentist from San Miguel, Héctor Antonio Regalado, who was notorious in El Salvador for leading his own death squads.* "Archbishop Rivera y Damas shudders at the mere mention of his name," said one American diplomat.

The Salvadoran political right was furious with the Reagan administration's interference. It had participated in the elections that the United States had insisted upon. Now the United States had refused to accept the results. D'Aubuisson and the rightists "took their revenge," as one U.S. diplomat in El Salvador at the time put it, on the land reform. Named minister of agriculture was Miguel Muyshondt, an archconservative opposed to the land reform who had been captured along with D'Aubuisson and the other coup plotters in the spring of 1980. One of the Assembly's first legislative acts, in May, was to suspend certain provisions of Decree 207, the land-to-the-tiller law, which allowed peasants to buy the small parcels of land they were working as tenant farmers. The Assembly sought to protect the rights of tenant farmers who had already applied for title or had acquired the right to do so. Those guarantees were "fine on paper," said a Christian Democratic party deputy who had voted against the suspension, but "in practice" the legislation was a "victory for landowners." Buoyed by the legislation, landowners began massive evictions of tenant peasants, who were largely illiterate and had no access to lawyers who could explain their rights. The land reform, especially this phase, which was the linchpin of the U.S. policy under Carter, was being dismantled; in Washington Senator Percy, chairman of the Foreign Relations Committee, reacted with a strong warning that "not one cent of funds shall go to the Government of El Salvador" if the land reform program was halted.

*In late December 1983 Regalado left his post. The Reagan administration declared that he was forced out as part of the measures that the Salvadorans were taking to eliminate the death squads. But according to several Salvadoran political leaders, Regalado voluntarily resigned after his mentor, D'Aubuisson, had left the Assembly to campaign for the 1984 election.

I was in Guatemala when the chaos erupted, and the foreign desk of *The New York Times* asked me to return to El Salvador immediately. I did. The lead of the front-page story I wrote was: "In less than one month as a legislative body, El Salvador's Constituent Assembly has blocked most of the country's land redistribution effort from being carried out." In addition to the suspension of 207, I reported that Phases I and II of the land reform "have been affected by the assembly's actions." The latter was based on what I was told by Assembly deputies, as well as by a lawyer, highly respected by the U.S. embassy, who explained the legal ramifications of the Assembly's acts. I also reported that in his Sunday homily Archbishop Rivera y Damas had indicated that the deputies had wanted to repeal the land-to-the-tiller law and that the suspension was a "political maneuver," designed "to leave open the possibility of American aid, which is conditioned on the reforms not being halted." Finally, I noted that according to the major Salvadoran peasant organization, 9,600 peasant families had been evicted from their plots since the elections.

U.S. embassy officials in El Salvador reacted with a vengeance to the story. Gale Rozell, the AID officer in El Salvador responsible for the land program, circled what he said were twenty-two "factual errors and misleading statements" in the story. Several of the objections related to the headline and subheads. Six of the "errors" were because of my use of the phrase "land to the tiller," which Rozell objected to, because it had been used by Lenin around 1917. But "land to the tiller" is what the program was called by most American diplomats, as well as by Roy Prosterman, the program's principal architect. Rozell also said that it was "factually incorrect" to have reported that the land-to-the-tiller law was "suspended." In Washington, shortly after my article had appeared, Ambassador Hinton, always blunt and outspoken, exploded. During a breakfast with reporters he charged that I was "an advocate journalist" and that the story about land reform was "not based on an accurate reading of the situation."

But President Magaña, who had proposed the legislation affecting Decree 207, told me in an interview that 207 had been "suspended." Moreover, classified State Department documents written at the time use the words "suspension" and "suspended" when describing the legislative action.

Hinton was right, however, that my story was not based on an accurate reading of the situation. The situation was worse than I had portrayed it. One State Department memorandum written at the time of my story noted, for example, that the director of AIFLD, William Doherty, was telling congressmen that the State Department was giving the "false impression" that "the benefits of Decree 207 have not been eliminated, but only suspended." Another said: "AID reports evictions, pessimism and insecurity about future of land reform in all Departments." The same document noted that the new head of the Salvadoran land agency (ISTA) was a veterinarian with "no qualifications for the job." As for claims by Magaña and other newly elected leaders that "we are not going back on the reforms," the State Department document described them as "verbiage" which "contradicts what is actually happening." The document adds that both Magaña and D'Aubuisson were refusing to meet with peasant leaders.

Nevertheless, the embassy's deputy chief of mission, Kenneth Bleakley, transmitted to Washington the "factual errors and misleading statements" which Rozell said my article contained.

It was not the first time I had run afoul of the embassy. Some of the officers had long believed that I wrote too many stories about the human rights abuses and was too sympathetic to the guerrillas. The four stories that were based on my experiences with the guerrillas in Morazán, including one about the massacre in Mozote, exacerbated the friction. Following that series, *The Wall Street Journal,* in an unusually long editorial, harshly criticized me and *The New York Times.* I had been "overly credulous" in accepting the guerrillas' accounts of the massacre, the editorial said. A few weeks later, on the *MacNeil-Lehrer Report,* George Melloan, author of *The Wall Street Journal* editorial, said, "I think some reporters tend to identify with guerrilla and revolutionary movements to some degree. . . . This comes partly out of the tradition of American journalism to support the underdog and sometimes it goes somewhat beyond that into the genuine political orientation that is Marxist in nature, but that's in very few cases, I think." Also appearing on the program was Sydney Schanberg, who had been criticized in the same *Wall Street Journal* editorial for his reporting from Cambodia at the time of the Khmer Rouge conquest and subsequent butchery.* Schanberg challenged Melloan to name the newsmen with this "political orientation." Melloan responded, "Well, Ray Bonner, of course. Obviously Ray Bonner has a political orientation."

Ambassador Hinton complained about my reporting to other journalists and visiting congressmen, as did other State Department offi-

*The *Journal* also used the editorial to raise anew its criticisms about David Halberstam's early coverage in Vietnam. Both Halberstam and Schanberg won Pulitzer Prizes for their coverage.

cials in letters to *The New York Times* and conversations with editors.*

Another senior official who made no attempt to disguise his contempt for my reporting was Colonel Waghelstein. For several months he barred me from briefings, and he continued to criticize me stridently to other reporters long after both he and I had left El Salvador.†
Waghelstein's animosity grew out of an article published on January 11, 1982, in which I related the allegations of a Salvadoran army deserter, Carlos Antonio Gómez Montaña, that "United States military advisers were present at two 'training sessions' early last year when two suspected guerrillas were tortured by Salvadoran army instructors." I had spent several hours interviewing Gómez on two occasions, and a veteran *Times* reporter interviewed him separately for several hours. The Salvadoran military denied that Gómez had ever been in the service, but his military serial number and rifle number, which he provided to *The Times,* checked with military records. Even though an embassy officer told me many months later that there was "some truth" to the story and that there were indeed occasions when U.S. advisers were present while suspected guerrilla sympathizers were tortured, I now believe that I should not have written Gómez's account without seeking a second source to verify what he related. Though

*Hinton did more than just complain. Over the mild objections of some embassy officers, he cooperated with an archconservative organization, Accuracy in Media (AIM), which published a series of articles denouncing me. I learned that Hinton was up to something, though at the time I didn't know what, in an inadvertent and somewhat amusing fashion. One day I asked the embassy spokesman, Don Hamilton, to provide me with some documents relating to U.S. military and financial aid. But the brown envelope with my name on it, which Hamilton had taken from his desk and handed to a journalistic colleague to deliver to me at the hotel, did not have those documents. When I opened the sealed envelope, I found copies of all the articles I had written while in El Salvador. As for AIM's attacks, *The Times'* foreign editor, Craig Whitney, responded: "Accuracy in Media ought to change its name. Its attack against Bonner is clearly filled with so much rumor, innuendo, and mistakes that they clearly don't know accuracy from a hole in the ground, and maybe a good lawyer ought to take them to court and teach them what libel is." The head of AIM, Reed Irvine, wrote to *The Times'* most senior officers asking that they question me about my background. Sydney Gruson, vice-chairman of The New York Times Company, wrote back to Irvine: "If he [Bonner] wrote his dispatches with a fraction of the bias and innuendo contained in your letter, he would have been fired long ago."
†I was not the only reporter to run afoul of Colonel Waghelstein. When John Dinges was introduced to the colonel at a Fourth of July reception at Ambassador Hinton's residence in San Salvador, Waghelstein responded, "Fuck you." Later during the reception, the colonel remarked to another reporter, "I'd like to get Dinges and Bonner up in a plane."

Gómez probably witnessed brutal torture—what he described was not uncommon—I suspect now that he embellished what had happened, and I do not believe that the American advisers had been present as he described.

THE Assembly's actions against the land reform created serious problems for the Reagan administration. In order to continue military aid to El Salvador, the administration had to certify every six months that the Salvadoran government was making "continued progress" in implementing the land redistribution program. After the suspension of the land-to-the-tiller law, the Salvadoran government launched a highly visible campaign designed to demonstrate that it was still committed to the land reform. Army units reinstated some evicted peasants, and in ceremonies around the country attended by high-ranking civilian and military officials, titles were delivered to peasants. During one elaborate affair in the ornate second-floor chamber of the Presidential Palace, President Magaña, flanked by a military honor guard of white-gloved soldiers holding rifles mounted with silver-plated bayonets, candidly acknowledged that the delivery of the titles was designed primarily for foreign consumption, to demonstrate "to the entire world" that El Salvador's land program was "going forward." The ceremony was held on the very day that President Reagan sent his certification to Congress. "Pure theater," said a senior Salvadoran official who was present. He was right. "After certification" there was "a lack of interest in completing the [land reform] program," Deputy Agricultural Minister Jorge A. Peña Solano told *New York Times* reporter Bernard Weinraub three months later. "Before certification we wanted to give an impression to the American people and Government how fast we were giving titles. Now certification is over." A few months earlier Peña Solano had told me, "If I were in their [the Reagan administration's] socks, I would stop aid, if what I believe is they [the Salvadorans] should go on with the reforms."

The Salvadoran land reform program never fully recovered from the assaults in the spring of 1982, failing even to meet the minimal goals set by the Reagan administration. The number of potential beneficiaries under the land-to-the-tiller program, according to the Salvadoran government, was between 125,000 and 150,000. In June 1982 the State Department in a Confidential cable to the embassy in El Salvador established certain goals that would be necessary in order to justify certification. Among them was the issuance of 12,000 definitive titles to land-to-the-tiller beneficiaries by the end of 1982. When the administration issued its certification in January 1983, the number of definitive titles issued was only 408. At the end of June 1983 the number had risen to 2,453. Yet the Reagan administration again certified that progress was being made on the land reform. And Senator Percy, along with other members of Congress who loudly protested the actions against the land reform, routinely voted for more aid.

More titles had not been issued primarily because of guerrilla attacks, Enders told the Senate Foreign Relations Committee in August 1982. Senator Dodd questioned this, saying that he had been told by the peasants "that in fact the left really did not bother the land reform that much because it was too sacrosanct an issue to really disrupt it and thereby run the risk of incurring even further opposition in the countryside." Roy Prosterman, who was also appearing before the committee, said that "there is actually very little substance, very little support, for Secretary Enders' suggestion." He explained that the guerrillas were not willing "to interfere physically with the actual land reform process, because they know if they do that they will gain the enmity of vast numbers of campesinos who are beneficiaries of that process."

Nevertheless, a few months later, at the time of the January 1983 certification, the administration again insisted that "guerrilla attacks" on agrarian reform promoters and workers in the Salvadoran National Financial Institute for Agricultural Lands (FINATA) were interfering with the titling process. But the independent consulting firm hired by AID to evaluate the land reform reported: "FINATA staff told us that the guerrillas have seldom attacked them, and at times when FINATA promoters have been stopped by guerrilla roadblocks, they have been released with good wishes."

The administration also distorted the problem of evictions. In its July 1983 certification it reported that 3,656 evicted peasants had been reinstated. That may well have been accurate. But the administration failed to advise Congress on the number of peasants who had been evicted and not reinstated—nearly 10,000, according to the Salvadoran peasant organization—and also failed to report that many peasants reinstated one day were evicted the next.*

---

*Although Salvadoran peasants continued to suffer from the dismantling of the land reform program begun by the Assembly in 1982, progress was made on behalf of the former owners, reflecting the priorities of the Reagan administration and the Salvadoran government. Prior to the elections in March 1982, no landlord of parcels claimed by peasants under the land-to-the-tiller law had received any compensation. By July 1983, $6,022,412 had been paid to 271 former owners.

The Salvadoran Assembly delivered its final blow to the land redistribution effort in December 1983, passing a constitutional provision that cut in half the amount of land available for distribution. As originally drafted, El Salvador's land program placed a limit of 360 acres on the size of farms that could be privately owned. The constitutional provision, adopted by a coalition of ARENA and other rightist parties, permits individual ownership of up to 600 acres. "I congratulate it [the rightist coalition] for succeeding in definitely ending agrarian reform," said Julio Rey Prendes, a leader of the Christian Democrats, whose deputies voted against the provision.

But peasants who lost only a future right to become landowners or were merely evicted from their lands were in some respects fortunate, as the army continued gruesome attacks on cooperatives. A unit of some 150 soldiers, for example, raided La Florida, a cooperative sixty-five miles west of the capital that was financially supported by the Episcopal Church in the United States and the Anglican Church of Canada. The soldiers seized seven members of the cooperative, hauled them away, tortured and killed them. One man had his nipples cut out. The testicles were slashed off another; the ears off a third. Brains spilled out of one man's head. All had their heads partially or completely severed. None had any bullet wounds. "This is the most horrendous thing I have ever seen in my entire ministry," said the Reverend Luis Serrano, the priest for the 220-member congregation at the cooperative, as he wept. The assassinations left behind widows and 24 orphans. No one was prosecuted.

The elections were "the best available means" to "help break the cycle of violence that has plagued the country in recent years," the Reagan administration declared. They would "strengthen moderation and the political center." In fact, the elections accomplished none of these goals; instead, the government moved to the right, and the cycle of violence escalated.

ON weekends the forested acres of Balboa Park, in the mountainous hills at the top of a twisting road just south of the capital are filled with frolicking families: boys kicking soccer balls with their fathers; girls helping their mothers spread picnic lunches; merchants selling ice cream and sodas from pushcarts. Small wooden signs placed by the national tourist agency direct visitors to Puerto Diablo ("Devil's Door"), a cliff that offers sweeping vistas of tranquil hills. In recent years Devil's Door has brought families in search of relatives who have disappeared.

On a Sunday a few weeks after the election, a trek along trails barely visible in the thicket of vines and trees was rendered more treacherous by heavy fog and mist, which broke into rain at times. In a craggy crevice, desperate families found the bodies of four strapping men who appeared to be laborers in their twenties. They had been tossed, along with rotting cartons, shattered glass, and other garbage, from a cliff 100 feet above. One man in green work pants, shirtless and shoeless, had come to rest facing up the draw. Just below him, two bodies were entwined. The fourth, his trousers twisted around his ankles, had the skin peeled off his chest, revealing his rib cage. His head was not to be found. The military death squads were back in action, after a few weeks of relative quiet preceding the elections.

During one forty-eight-hour period, in early May, there were discovered nine decapitated bodies, six of them young people whose heads were not found. The arms and legs had also been severed from one. Also in May, four Christian Democratic mayors and seven of the party's election day poll watchers were murdered, underscoring what would have happened to any leftist politicians had they participated in the elections—or should they try to enter the country for the elections in 1984. Two hours after being appointed, the mayor of Chinameca, Evangelina García de López, and her eighteen-year-old daughter were killed in the kitchen of their home by members of the rural civil defense force.

Regular army commanders, beholden to no civilian government, continued their campaign against peasants who they thought were sympathetic to the guerrillas.

"I was making coffee when they arrived," explained pert ten-year-old Mercedes Umana, a green parakeet perched peacefully on the top of her long brown hair. "The armed men said, 'Go all of you, get in line to be killed.' I screamed, 'We didn't do anything.' " In the commotion Mercedes fled into the hills. Eleven-year-old Fidel's life was spared, for some unknown reason, as he stood by, watching his aunt and grandfather shot. Twelve-year-old María Dolores Turcios was splashed with her father's blood.

The soldiers had arrived at Barrios, a cluster of daub-and-wattle huts on the banks of the shallow Río Seca in Morazán Province, during the first light hours on the third Sunday after the elections. They killed forty-eight people. Twenty-five were children younger than twelve years old; twelve of them had not yet celebrated their fifth birthdays. Two women were pregnant. One man was nearly ninety.

"A crude cross carved on a tree trunk marks one of the graves where peasants said today they had buried at least 48 people killed by the armed forces," wrote *The Washington Post*'s Joanne Omang, who went to Barrios the day after Juan Vasquez of the *Los Angeles Times* and I had gone. "Nearby is another tree, its gnarled roots matted in blood and human hair. Dogs have dug up at least one body." The tree roots were "sticky with blood where bullets have torn away the bark. A few shell casings, not many, share the dirt, with a campesino's straw hat, a woman's plastic sandal, a few bits of clothing."

Washington's response to the massacre? Relief that it wasn't widely reported in the press. At the time of the second certification Craig Johnstone, assistant secretary of state for Central America, wrote in a Confidential memorandum to his boss, Thomas Enders, "[W]e cannot argue that violence is down since the first certification." But he added, "Fortunately, we have had no major massacres to report since the last certification. (There were press accounts of an alleged massacre at Barrios, Morazán, but no bodies could be found and the story quickly died.)"

In other words, the Reagan administration could ignore another mass killing of peasants and continue to send military aid to the government that permitted it. It was a policy of speak softly—and carry no stick.

16

QUIET DIPLOMACY

INTERNATIONAL terrorism will take the place of human rights in our concern," Secretary of State Haig said one week after Reagan had been inaugurated.

What that meant for El Salvador was explained a month later, when the new administration presented its policy to the Senate Foreign Relations Committee. "Has the administration decided to offer unconditional military and economic aid to El Salvador, or will we hold the El Salvadoran Government to a commitment to efforts trying to stop rightwing terrorism and to achieve land reform?" inquired Senator Alan Cranston, Democrat of California. Undersecretary of State Stoessel answered, "Senator, we have not made specific conditions with regard to the assistance we are providing to the Government of El Salvador."

In El Salvador Reagan's man, Deane Hinton, explained quickly after arriving as ambassador that he would pursue human rights cases "quietly, not planning any press conference to denounce anything or anybody."

What constituted "quiet diplomacy" to the Reagan administration was a blank check for the Salvadoran military. And it wasted no time filling it in, swinging into action throughout the country against anyone perceived to be sympathetic to the revolution or critical of the government or the armed forces. In Tonacatepeque, San Salvador, on February 25, 1981, three schoolteachers, their wives, and town officials were killed by gunmen who forced the victims' children to watch.

In the small town of Chalchuapa, located in the southern part of Santa Ana Department, in the month of March alone thirty-four people were murdered, some "in ways that revolt even atrocity-numbed Salvadorans," the embassy reported in a Confidential cable. "Teachers, for instance, are a favorite target in Chalchuapa, and the entire family of one was slaughtered, including his two teenage daughters, who were found raped and with their breasts cut out." The embassy cable noted that the town had recently been attacked by guerrillas but that "what Chalchuapans fear now is not a new attack, but a knock on the door in the middle of the night." Villagers said the killers were members of the death squads and the security forces. "The motives for the murders," the embassy reported, "could be characterized as a combination of repudiation of GOES [government of El Salvador] policies and of an inability to distinguish a reformer from a guerrilla." The embassy described Chalchuapa as "an extreme case. But it is far from unique." Nor was it the end for Chalchuapans. On a Thursday in August the headless bodies of twenty-seven nearly nude people were found on the streets.

The Salvadoran armed forces routinely denied any wrongdoing. During the early-morning hours of April 7, 1981, for example, the Treasury Police conducted a house-to-house raid in the capital's working-class barrio of Soyapango. At least twenty-three civilians were killed. The Treasury Police held a press conference to declare that the civilians had been killed during a shoot-out with guerrillas. The U.S. embassy concluded that the official report was "not credible." One woman told the embassy that three pickup trucks of heavily armed men had arrived at her house while her family was sleeping. They banged on the door, then fired through it. A man wearing a hood pointed to the woman's brother. He was taken away and shot. Residents too frightened to come out of their houses heard cries of "Don't take me!" Many of the victims were clothed only in their underwear. The soldiers cut the testicles off one man and placed them on top of his bullet-ridden body. They shot a forty-eight-year-old man and his two sons, seventeen and nineteen, a sixteen-year-old girl, and her eighteen- and twenty-four-year-old brothers. Eight of the victims, whose bodies were found in distant gullies, were teenagers, one thirteen years old.

In the tiny, squalid, dusty rural village of Los Hernández, just off the main highway leading north from the capital, the armed men arrived at about 6:00 P.M. on July 7. They hauled away virtually all the village males, ranging in ages from fourteen to sixty-five. Twenty-eight bodies were found thirty kilometers away, beneath the silver-painted cables of a one-lane bridge by the still waters of the Metayate River. Two women, ages fifteen and twenty, had been raped, then mutilated and murdered. All of the victims' throats had been cut. Most had been hacked by machetes. The Salvadoran armed forces put out a statement saying the victims were members of the civil defense forces killed by "terrorists." But one source, whom the embassy described as "absolutely credible," said it was the work of the Treasury Police and death squads, acting because they suspected the men supported the guerrillas, according to a Confidential cable.

A few weeks later, on July 30, the soldiers struck in Armenia, in what *The Washington Post*'s Christopher Dickey described as "one of the most capricious massacres to date." At least forty residents of Armenia, including all the members of a soccer team, were killed. The massacre followed an incident at a military checkpoint, where the soccer team playing for the Las Lajas plantation was stopped on its return from a game in Sonsonate. Emboldened by a bit of alcohol, a member of the team, recently discharged from the army, had some unkind words for his former comrades, and a brief fistfight followed. Four days later soldiers returned and began breaking down house doors and dragging away village men. Twenty-three bodies were found the next morning in the Talnique River; fifteen were dumped in the Sucio River and the rest in nearby villages. Duarte flatly denied that there had been any killings at Armenia.

WHEN it comes to human rights in a situation like that [El Salvador]," said a diplomat who served Carter and Reagan in El Salvador, "either you're a hundred percent for it or you're completely ineffective. . . . Unless you keep the pressure on, unless you keep their feet to the fire, the chances of succeeding are practically nil."

During the first six months of the Reagan administration (February through July 1981), 7,152 Salvadorans were killed, according to the archdiocese's legal aid office—compared with that group's figure of 8,062 for all of 1980. More than half the victims were peasants, and a substantial number of killings occurred during the curfew hours, when the soldiers conducted their house-to-house searches, hauling their victims to isolated spots to be tortured and murdered, free of whatever minimal restraints might have influenced them when there was no curfew. The Christian Democrats in the government wanted the curfew lifted, but the armed forces' high command refused to accede to the request.

If there is ever peace in El Salvador, El Playón should be a national park, similar to the one on the island of Hawaii where visitors stroll on wooden walks through the peaceful lava fields. Backdropped by the verdant slopes of the 6,400-foot-high, almost perfectly conical San Salvador Volcano, El Playón is a vast expanse of undulating, porous coal-black lava rock. In mid-1981 it was a macabre scene from a surrealistic canvas. Sun-bleached femurs, tibias, jaws, and skulls, each usually with a single bullet hole in the back, littered the jagged black moonscape surface. A knot of stringy dark hair spun a cobweb on the rocks. A foot or so away, decayed women's undergarments clung to pelvic bones protruding from beneath the rocks—as if someone had tried to give a woman a decent burial. The human skeletons collected in depressions, along with rotting garbage, plastic soda bottles, rusting tin cans, soggy cartons. El Playón was a dump for garbage as well as for humans.

One day a twenty-two-year-old peasant was scavenging through the garbage with the tip of his machete. I offered him a cigarette and asked him where he was from, what he did for a living, if he was married, had children—the customary small talk. Did he know who had killed these people and dumped the bodies? A long silence. Finally, looking blankly at the garbage, his voice barely audible, he said, "I suppose the army." Not more than 200 yards away, black vultures, some too bloated to fly, and scrawny dogs, tore at the genitals of the latest victims, three men who appeared to be in their twenties. They had been dumped in the weeds off the side of the paved road, at the edge of a real cemetery, its pink and pastel green tombstones now overgrown with weeds. One of the dead, shoeless but wearing socks, had a heavy rope tied around his wrists; the wrists of another were tied and laid across his stomach.

Alma Guillermoprieto, correspondent for *The Washington Post,* was one of the first to discover and write about El Playón. Duarte's response was to deny that there were any bodies there. The stories had been "fabricated," he insisted. But when Carol Doerflein, an embassy spokesperson, heard about about El Playón from Guillermoprieto, she drove out to the lava field to decide for herself. A small, frisky woman widely respected by the press corps for her honesty, Doerflein had been in El Salvador long enough not to be shocked every time she saw a body. But the scene at El Playón horrified her. It was more gruesome than reporters had described it, she said. The embassy took photographs. Duarte and the military high command promised an investigation. Several months later, when reporters discovered new pockets of skeletons at El Playón, the embassy acknowledged that there had been no investigation.

There couldn't be an investigation, for it would have led to the government forces. El Playón was on a paved road less than three miles from the headquarters of three major military units, including that of the U.S.-trained Atlacatl Battalion. Americas Watch, the nonprofit human rights monitoring organization, noted in one of its reports about El Salvador that the road that bisected the lava field "was heavily patrolled by army troops and security forces."

"[Y]our statement is not true" that "El Playón, infamous body dump, could not be approached without the knowledge of military personnel," Elliott Abrams wrote to Aryeh Neier, director of Americas Watch Committee. In support of that contention, Abrams continued, "Our Embassy officers who went to that hellish place did so unobserved." But, how could the embassy officers have known that they were *not* observed? If they were, what soldier would interfere with a big, modern, bulletproof vehicle, which, if it didn't obviously belong to the embassy, certainly wasn't the kind driven by guerrillas. In fact, embassy officers in El Salvador told reporters that the army cavalry unit located nearby was responsible for most of the bodies dumped at El Playón.

The Reagan administration repeatedly insisted that the Salvadoran government and armed forces were not responsible for the violence. That which wasn't the work of the guerrillas, administration officials insisted, was the responsibility of the death squads and the "extreme right." As President Reagan himself declared in a speech to the International Longshoremen's Association in July 1983, "Much of the violence there [in El Salvador]—whether from the extreme right or left— is beyond the control of the government." A month later Abrams insisted to the House Subcommittee on Western Hemisphere Affairs* that it was "unfair" to blame the military for the violence because "we really don't know who the death squads are."

But most of the violence wasn't beyond the control of the government; it was carried out by the government. "The 'extreme right' is just a convenient term for sort of this government unto itself," said a diplomat who served in El Salvador during the Carter and Reagan administrations. "Of course, the military is the violent arm of the extreme right. . . . It is part and parcel of the so-called extreme right."

Surely Abrams knew who the death squads were; nearly everyone else did. During the same hearing Representative Studds quoted Magaña as having recently told a congressional delegation, "all of the death squads are related to the army or paramilitary." If Abrams didn't know, it was because he was ignoring reports from the embassy

---

*The name of the House Subcommittee on Inter-American Affairs was changed to Western Hemisphere Affairs in January 1983. This committee, under the leadership of Michael D. Barnes, Democrat of Maryland, held most of the hearings about the U.S. policy and activities in El Salvador.

in El Salvador. For example, one Secret CIA cable, which was not provided under an FOIA request, reported that a former officer of a rural National Guard unit had explained that while there were "right-wing groups" that were responsible for some killings, "they were more prone to long-distance violence, i.e., murder by rifleshot rather than the kind of brutal killings attributed by the press to 'death squadrons.'" And in the summer of 1983, at the time that Reagan and Abrams were making their exculpatory declarations, the administration wanted the secretaries of state and defense "to prepare immediately a plan of action" that would result in the "elimination of military participation in death squads," according to a highly secret working paper prepared for a meeting of the National Security Council.

Like the policymakers, most journalists long treated the death squads as if they were *sui generis* units without any links to the government, which lurked in the night, chopping people's heads off, tying thumbs, peeling back skin. Largely overlooked by the media was what a Salvadoran Army captain told a congressional committee in April 1981.

"It is a grievous error to believe that the forces of the extreme right, or the so-called 'Death Squads,' operate independent of the security forces," Captain Ricardo Alejandro Fiallos began. "The simple truth of the matter is that 'Los Escuadrones de la Muerte' are made up of members of the security forces and acts of terrorism credited to these squads such as political assassinations, kidnappings, and indiscriminate murder are, in fact, planned by high-ranking military officers and carried out by members of the security forces. I do not make this statement lightly, but with full knowledge of the role which the military high command and the directors of the security forces have played in the murders of countless numbers of innocent people in my country."

Captain Fiallos, a sixteen-year army veteran, had graduated first in his class from military school, had been promoted to first lieutenant with honors, then with a president's scholarship had studied medicine. While working as a doctor in the military hospital, he treated numerous people who had been injured while "eliminating" people. "For example, on one occasion," Fiallos testified, "a member of the Treasury Police, in civilian dress, was brought to the hospital with a fractured tibia. I asked him how he had been injured and he told me that he and another member of his unit had received orders to 'eliminate' a woman school teacher in the town of Aguas Calientes who he had been told was a subversive. In the act of pursuing the school teacher in her car, the motorcycle driven by this man and his associate struck the rear of the automobile and overturned, causing the injury. However, the other man was not hurt in the accident and murdered the school teacher before she could get out of her car. Afterwards, he brought his companion to the hospital for treatment."

Another captain, recruiting for the death squads, told René Hurtado, "You will be paid well, and you will be able to carry good weapons." Hurtado was a soldier who had received parachute training, and he recalled the army captain saying, "You were a good parachutist. We need people like you." Hurtado was promised 1,000 colones a month ($400), nearly eight times his regular army salary of approximately 130 colones ($52) a month. (This amount, 1,000 colones a month, was what Duarte once told me that the militant members of the Nationalist Democratic Front, which was founded by D'Aubuisson as the forerunner to ARENA, were paid. They were also provided with substantial life insurance policies.)

"They told me that the only requirement was to be able to kill without any compassion or pity," Hurtado said during an interview at the St. Luke's Lutheran Church in suburban Minneapolis, where he had been given sanctuary after deserting from the army and illegally entering the United States. Hurtado deserted after he had been caught reading the Bible and accused by officers of being a "subversive."* He had entered the army when he was fifteen years old. After a couple of years he passed a test and was transferred to the Treasury Police, where he observed common torture practices. One was to put a hood over the prisoner's face, then throw lime inside "so when the person tries to breathe, they inhale lime," Hurtado explained. Electric shock was also common, he said, with wires tied to the penis, or breasts, fingers, and ears. "Well, after two or three shocks, the person would faint. So, to bring him around, they would throw water on him." The torture chambers, he said, were equipped with stereophonic speakers. "When they torture somebody, they turn up the volume all the way and play music, so nobody can hear the screams." The victim is told, "If you don't confess, we'll kill you. Little by little, we'll kill you. You are going to suffer, so it's better you confess, and then we'll let you go." If the prisoner continued to resist, "then they begin to cut pieces of flesh off the fingers, this part here on the fingers," he said, pointing to the last knuckle. "They cut off more, piece after piece, until the whole

*Hurtado was not his real name, which he told me but asked me not to print because he still had family in El Salvador. His accounts of the torture practices conformed to what U.S. embassy officials also described in cables and interviews.

hand is cut off. And of course, while this happens, the person is already losing a lot of blood, and so they faint. Then they cut off this here," he said, pointing to his crotch. "They cut it like this," his hand making a slicing motion. "And they go throw it in the garbage." Before discarding the mutilated body by the side of a road or in a garbage dump, at El Playón, at Puerto Diablo, "they hang a sign on him that says 'death squad.' But it's really in the torture chambers that they are killed—by the National Guard, the National Police, the Treasury Police."

One death squad member, when asked about the types of tortures used, replied, "Uh, well, the same thing you did in Vietnam. We learned from you. We learned from you the means, like blowtorches in the armpits, shots in the balls." But for "the toughest ones"—that is, those who resist these other tortures—"we have to pop their eyes out with a spoon. You have to film it to believe it, but boy, they sure sing." The death squad member was interviewed by a reporter preparing a *Frontline* program for WGBH, the public television station in Boston. He used a pseudonym, Ricardo, and appeared in silhouette to protect himself. Ricardo said that he had joined the death squads in Usulután after the guerrillas had killed his uncle. "I decided to take revenge." He explained that there were three paramilitary groups of between thirty and forty members each and that they operated in small groups —"what you might call a hit team"—of three to five. "Ninety percent of our members are graduated from the United States, and we are members of high-middle-class families," he said.

Some insight into how these death squads operate is contained in a Confidential embassy cable. The cable was released under the Freedom of Information Act. The cable was based on an incident on January 27, 1981, in Amatepeque, a poor suburb of the western province of Santa Ana, and was related to the embassy by Maryknoll missionaries. The account as it appeared in the cable, with the State Department deletions noted read:

Last Tuesday some time around eleven o'clock—well after curfew—seven heavily armed men dressed in civilian clothes raided two houses near the the little convent where the Maryknollers live. The men are believed by all the neighbors to have been [several words deleted] members of one of the death squads operating in the town. [Line and a half deleted.] In both houses the families had gone to bed, in one place after having watched the last television serial of the evening. An 18-year old son was was taken from one house, and a 16-year old son from another. There were several young adults in one of the families, leading to the conclusion that the two people taken had been fingered with precision [line deleted]. The two young men were taken a short distance down the street and killed—close enough that the families of both heard the shots, although because of the curfew they could not go out until five o'clock the next morning to recover the bodies. Both young men had been working for some time in Mexico, and returned to El Salvador for the Christmas holidays against the advice of their families. They returned "well fed and happy because of the good jobs they had found," and both planned to leave again for Mexico on February 3. . . . No one will know for sure why the young men were hunted and gunned down. Perhaps this was the result of a grudge or a rumor. Perhaps they were members of a terrorist organization—their happy circumstances in Mexico seem unusual; and insistence on returning to El Salvador and remaining through the "offensive" raises suspicion. All that is certain is the legacy of rage and sadness that keeps building in this country.

In sum, the death squads are financed by right-wing Salvadoran businessmen, commanded by military officers, and made up of soldiers, ex-soldiers, and civilians. They have adopted colorful names, such as the White Warriors Union, whose calling card is a white handprint, the Secret Anti-Communist Army, and the Maximiliano Hernández Martínez Anti-Communist Brigade, which proudly takes its name from the infamous dictator. They defend their work in "patriotic"—that is, anti-Communist—and law-and-order rhetoric.

Six months after Reagan became President, the Maximiliano Hernández Martínez Brigade publicly announced its intention "to cleanse San Salvador of thieves, muggers, miscreants, and swindlers." It noted that it had already been at work in Santa Ana. During one operation there the brigade had murdered ten circus workers, including two clowns. It said that the ten were drug traffickers and had been executed after a summary trial. During five days in August eighty-three decapitated bodies were found in Santa Ana Province. The heads had been so cleanly severed that there were reports that they were being murdered in a meat factory.

The matter of rightist violence, death squads, and the military involvement in them has been of little concern to U.S. policymakers, as the House committee that oversees the activities of all the U.S. intelligence agencies discovered during an investigation.

The Subcommittee on Oversight and Evaluation of the House Permanent Select Committee on Intelligence was so disturbed by what it found during its investigation of the intelligence agencies' activities in El Salvador that the subcommittee chairman, Charles Rose, Democrat of North Carolina, decided to make some of the findings public. "Sometimes a public report is needed. This is one such time," Rose said. It was only the second time that the subcommittee, which operates in cloistered secrecy, had issued a public report. (The other time was an evaluation of U.S. intelligence gathering in Iran prior to the fall of the shah in 1979.) Further underscoring the significance of the report, which received little media coverage, was the intense campaign by the intelligence agencies to keep it from being released. The report, which the subcommittee completed in May, was not released until September 1982, and the intelligence agencies succeeded in watering down some parts of the report as well as in deleting nearly all specific references to them—that is, whether an individual reference was to the Central Intelligence Agency (CIA), the Defense Intelligence Agency (DIA), the National Security Agency (NSA), or the State Department's Bureau of Intelligence and Research (INR).

"[I]ntelligence has provided little firm information about the subject of violence by the right and the security forces," the subcommittee reported. An intelligence study in mid-1980 noted that "there is scant intelligence on right-wing terrorist organization membership and the groups' relationship to each other, to the wealthy elite, or to the military." That was still the situation in 1982, according to the report. Although the embassy reported on right-wing terrorism, the subcommittee concluded that the intelligence agencies "have simply not considered the subject of Salvadoran rightist violence as a target for collection." This was in part attributable to the agencies' "limited collection resources," which the subcommittee noted in the case of the CIA "have been devoted almost exclusively to the insurgency."

The lack of U.S. government interest in, or concern about, rightist and armed forces violence in El Salvador is illustrated by the treatment given to the thick pile of documents seized from D'Aubuisson when he was caught plotting the coup in the spring of 1980. The incriminating documents included logs of meetings, lists of expenditures for submachine guns, 9 mm pistols, silencers, sniperscopes, and ammunition, along with the names, addresses, and phone numbers of right-wing Salvadoran businessmen and military officers. "In these documents there are over a hundred names of people who are participating, both within the Salvadoran military as active conspirators against the Government, and also the names of people living in the United States and Guatemala City who are actively funding the death squads," Robert White informed the Senate Foreign Relations Committee in April 1981.

Yet "during the two years since their capture, these documents had been virtually ignored not only by policymakers, who felt they had no immediate use for them, but more importantly [sic] by the intelligence community," the House subcommittee found during its probe. "They did not receive the kind of routine intelligence evaluation given to a large number of the Salvadoran guerrilla documents captured later that year," said the report, referring to the cache of documents that were the basis of the white paper issued by the Reagan administration in February 1981.

The subcommittee's report on how the documents were treated— "their whereabouts is unknown"—reads like the script for a slapstick routine in a banana republic:

> The CIA analyst who covered El Salvador at that time vaguely recalls seeing a couple of pages containing many names and receipts for weapons, but did not examine them closely, although he thought that personnel in CIA's collection organization, the Directorate for Operations (DDO), might have analyzed them. However, CIA's DDO could find no record of the documents or of any analysis. DIA analysts in Washington never received or analyzed the documents.
>
> Policymakers at the State Department learned of the documents through Ambassador White's June 1980 cable, but chose not to make any immediate use of the documents. Former Deputy Assistant Secretary James Cheek, however, believed they were significant and assumed that CIA would receive and examine them.
>
> State Department officers at the Inter-American Affairs Bureau and the Bureau of Intelligence and Research (INR) responded to staff queries by saying that they had heard "rumors" of such documents and had been looking high and low for them. INR noted that they and State Department attorneys would have liked to see such documents in connection with the Department's earlier efforts to exclude d'Aubuisson from the United States, and asked the staff [of the House subcommittee] to notify them if it should locate the documents. The staff was soon able to do so, having learned that the Senate Foreign Relations Committee published the documents, along with former Ambassador White's testimony, in April 1981. After staff inquiries, INR also found the original State Department cable, which had transmitted a translation of the original document.

Members of Congress also discovered that the Reagan State Department preferred to look the other way when it came to violent activity by Salvadoran rightists. In early 1981 Senator Tsongas as a member of the Foreign Relations Committee requested from the department a report "on the money coming from Miami, allegedly, to the right-wing terrorists." When the Massachusetts Democrat asked, during a committee hearing, why there had been no response to his request, Acting Assistant Secretary of State for Inter-American Affairs Bushnell replied that it was not for the State Department to report on such activity. An FBI official who was seated at the long table with Bushnell interjected that it was the FBI's jurisdiction but that the agency had never received a request from State to conduct such an inquiry.

"You target your intelligence sources to win your war, and you try to find out things which more or less support your point of view, the policy," said a senior embassy officer explaining the intelligence-gathering process. "What would it matter if D'Aubuisson had pulled the trigger on [Archbishop] Romero? Would our position about the war in El Salvador change? Our position about D'Aubuisson would. We'd hold our nose. But our policy wouldn't change."

The United States had to ignore the death squads since they were part of the military that the Reagan administration was backing. The death squads were operated by military officers in the National Police, the Treasury Police, the National Guard. Civilians provided the military units with names of persons suspected of being leftists or of being sympathetic to the revolution, and the military forces eliminated them. National Police commander Colonel Reynaldo López Nuila, who was generally heralded by American diplomats for being one of the less brutal military commanders, told investigative reporters Craig Pyes and Laurie Becklund that he couldn't understand why the United States disapproved of the activities. "War is by definition inhumane," he said. "When someone has an important bit of information, they don't want to consign him to a judge. They want to eliminate him."

It wasn't just the guerrillas who had foreign advisers; it was also the Salvadoran military. American advisers worked with combat units; Argentines instructed the security forces in torture methods. "There would be two or three persons from the National Guard" in each house where the Argentines taught torture techniques, D'Aubuisson explained to Pyes and Becklund. They instructed the Salvadorans how to do things "without being medieval about it," said another Salvadoran who knew the advisers personally. They taught the use of a hood filled with powdered ant poison and tied over the suspect's head. And there was the technique called the *aviador*—tying the prisoner's hands behind his back and then hoisting him off the floor by the hands with a rope through a pulley. The Argentines emphasized the need for psychological torture as well. This was accomplished with isolation, strapping the suspect to a chair, then leaving him alone, naked and blindfolded, for several hours with the air conditioner turned up. If that didn't induce him to talk, electric shocks would be applied. (The head of the National Guard while all this was going on was Colonel

Vides Casanova, later promoted to general and in 1983 becoming the minister of defense.)

To the extent that it acknowledged there was indiscriminate violence, the Reagan administration argued that it was primarily the responsibility of the security forces—Treasury Police, National Police, and National Guard—as opposed to the regular army units. But the latter, including those trained by the U.S. advisers, also carried out massacres.

T HE helicopter wheeled so low over the river that it was possible to see the face of the door gunner who was taking aim on the peasants trying to flee to safety, clinging to a rope line which had been strung across the Río Lempa by the only five peasant men who knew how to swim. On the ground Salvadoran soldiers on a ridge above the river fired their automatic rifles at the refugees. "I saw a little boy with an arc of bullets across his back fall into the water," recalled Yvonne Dilling, a twenty-six-year-old from Fort Wayne, Indiana, who taught reading and writing to Salvadoran refugees at camps in Honduras. Heads slipped under the water, never to reappear. Children clung to the beard of Father Earl Gallagher, the Brooklyn-born Capuchin priest who also worked with the refugees. Dilling ferried tiny infants to safety by tying them to her bra strap, then swimming across the raging river, thirty-five feet wide and twenty-five to fifty feet deep. But once on the Honduran side, helicopter machine-gun fire "cut up a line in the earth as close as I'm sitting to you right now," Dilling recalled to *New York Times* reporter Warren Hoge a few weeks after the incident in the spring of 1981. It had been the regular army, along with the air force that had cut down the fleeing peasants at the Río Lempa.

It was also the regular army that stormed into the village of Cerros de San Pedro after a day of mortar shelling. A survivor told the archdiocese's legal aid office that the soldiers seized fifteen people, including a sixty-five-year-old woman, her sister, and the latter's children, ages three, five, and seven. All those taken away were shot, after the soldiers had "smashed in their heads with rocks," the survivor said. The bodies were found in a cornfield.

The Río Lempa and San Pedro weren't isolated instances. They were illustrative of the manner in which the Salvadoran Army fought the counterinsurgency war. And contrary to the claims from U.S. officials that the American training produced commanders who respected human rights, the U.S.-trained battalions, as well as the commanders most highly regarded by the advisers, also carried out massacres.

After the elite Atlacatl Battalion, which was the first trained by the advisers, swept through the Guazapa Volcano in the spring of 1983, "the signs of slaughter were everywhere," free-lance journalist Don North reported for *Newsweek*. North, who spent forty-two days with the guerrillas in their Guazapa stronghold, wrote about the "charred and scattered bits of clothing, shoes and schoolbooks." A villager from Tenango showed him shallow graves in which he said the soldiers had buried dozens of men, women, and children after executing them with guns and machetes. "When I saw the bodies of the victims," North wrote, "vultures had already picked their skeletons clean and village dogs had begun to carry away the bones." On the adobe walls were "graffiti marks left by the soldiers congratulating the Atlacatl Brigade on its second anniversary."

In the province of Cabañas, along the border with Honduras, soldiers killed scores of civilians, mostly old people, women, and children who could not flee. Again, the American-trained Atlacatl Battalion was involved, along with the troops under the command of Lieutenant Colonel Ochoa. "You should go up and speak to Ochoa," Colonel Waghelstein, the senior adviser during 1982 and 1983, was continually urging reporters. Ochoa fought the counterinsurgency war in Cabañas the way Waghelstein, one of the U.S. Army's premier counterinsurgency experts—he was an adviser to the Bolivian Army when Che Guevara was captured and killed in 1967—wanted it fought. "He has the best organized patrols in the country, loyal to a man and tougher than lizard lips," Waghelstein, a huge man who delighted reporters with his salty language, cowboy boots on the table, and big cigars, was fond of saying about Ochoa. Numerous reporters filed glowing paeans about Ochoa.

But another side of Ochoa's methods was revealed by Philippe Bourgois. Bourgois wasn't a journalist but a Harvard graduate doing doctoral work in anthropology at Stanford. He had entered Cabañas in November 1981 as part of his research on Salvadoran peasants. He had intended to remain for two days, but after a day of interviewing peasants about their daily lives and history of the villages, he got caught in a government sweep and was trapped for two weeks. Bourgois recounted his harrowing experiences—at one point, when he thought he was about to be captured, he took out his knife, ready to kill himself rather than be tortured—in an article for *The Washington Post* and later in testimony to the House Subcommittee on Inter-American Affairs.

On the first day of the operation Bourgois crouched in a muddy cavity with a woman and two-year-old boy as a helicopter gunship sprayed the huts with machine-gun fire. "A man, unable to fit into the cave with us, could be heard saying his prayers outside." When the soldiers "apparently heard the wails of the babies that the mothers were carrying . . . they actually changed the direction of their fire, and started shooting directly at us. If you can imagine, in the darkness of the night, the government troops were firing into the sound of screaming babies." Bourgois found a little boy who had been hit by a grenade "staring up at me, writhing, with his hands on his hips, a gargling noise coming out of his throat. . . . Then I looked more closely and saw there was nothing below his hips. His legs were blown away." And while mortar shrapnel was removed from the legs of an eight-year-old boy, a rag was stuffed in his mouth "so that his screams would not reveal our location to the Government troops on the hills above," Bourgois testified. "He died the next day, but we could not even leave our hiding place to give him a proper burial because the Government helicopters and planes patrolling overhead in search of us might have located us." There was a two-month-old girl whose mother was killed "on the night we ran through the line of fire." Because the breast milk of lactating mothers had dried up, there was no one to breast-feed her. "There was nothing we could do except watch her shrivel up and dehydrate in front of us," Bourgois recounted.

U.S. intelligence officials described Bourgois's account as the type of guerrilla "propaganda" reaching the American public. In a briefing to the staff of the House Intelligence Subcommittee, the intelligence officials described those who were killed while fleeing as "guerrillas," not "peasant farmers," as Bourgois had reported. They contended that he had been "with an FMLN (guerrilla) fighting unit," not noncombatants, as he had claimed.

The staff concluded, on the basis of follow-up interviews with intelligence officials, that "it was misleading to present [Bourgois's report] as an example of guerrilla propaganda and that *no intelligence existed to contradict Bourgois' claim that he was with noncombatants* [emphasis in the subcommittee's report]."*

---

*Bourgois had also reported that the guerrilla fighters were poorly armed, with unsophisticated World War II vintage rifles. In their presentation to the congressional subcommittee, the intelligence officials, as part of the administration's campaign to blame the revolution on outsiders, had said the guerrillas had automatic rifles, machine guns, and mortars. In interviews with the staff, however, the officials acknowledged that Bourgois probably reported accurately what he saw, but contended that he probably had not seen the best-armed guerrillas.

A few days before the incident in Cabañas there was another army massacre, which the State Department is still covering up. On November 10, 1981, Ambassador Hinton sent a two-page Confidential cable summarizing his conversations with "a prominent Salvadoran private citizen and a high Salvadoran official," according to a U.S. government document. The cable is described as a report "of a particularly violent military operation," along with Hinton's "comments about the impact of the incident and a request for any additional information from the State Department." The department refuses to release any part of the cable under the Freedom of Information Act. But a U.S. government official who read the cable said that it contained a report that at least 200 noncombatant civilians, primarily women and children, were killed during an army operation. The cable explained that the army had attacked the guerrilla stronghold on two or three previous occasions without success but this time, as the official put it, "had literally cleaned up the area."

It is not the only State Department cover-up of an army massacre.

A pleasant breeze lightly rustled the leaves, about the only sounds in the pastoral mountain village of Mozote. There was no chatter at the rectangular cement cistern where peasant women, protected by a tin roof, once gathered to scrub clothes. The fragrance of tropical flowers was overwhelmed by the stench of decaying bodies. In one adobe hut after the other, charred skulls, legbones, pelvises, femurs, rib cages, and spinal columns protruded from the rubble of sewing-machine parts, simple family belongings, smashed red roofing tiles, and the charred beams that had held them. The small whitewashed church on the long end of the weedy central plaza had been ransacked. In the rubble of the adjacent sacristry were more bones.

On the dirt trail leading out of Mozote to other clusters of huts there was more of the same. In front of one hovel lay a blue knit infant's bonnet near a plastic baby bottle. Inside, among the ruins, skeletons of two bodies were discernible, along with the jumble of bones from an undetermined number of others, possibly members of the same family or maybe friends. Down the mountain trail a short distance, twelve recently cut twelve-foot planks, maybe ten inches by three-eighths of an inch, were propped against the trees. On the patio of the adobe hut, the saws, machetes, and crude homemade hammers were stained with drops of blood. Inside, five skulls were strewn among the smashed tiles. The men had been carpenters. A couple of hundred yards away, on the other side of some beehives, the lone, partially burned body of a man who appeared to be about forty years old was sprawled on the dirt floor, his head a few feet from the family's altar on which rested three crudely framed religious pictures torn from a magazine—one of Mary and the Christ Child, another of Christ on the cross. Brown beans from a ruptured white bag had spilled under his torso.

At the edge of a cornfield, under the swooping green leaves of the banana trees, was a pile of fourteen bodies—infants and men and women in their teens and early twenties. Horrified disbelief was reflected in their wide eyes and gaping mouths. In the heap was a child perhaps five years old. There was a months-old infant wrapped securely around the buttocks in a cotton bath towel, as if he or she were being carried, perhaps by the facedown woman in plastic sandals. The earth was littered with spent M-16 automatic-rifle cartridges. The victims were members of an evangelical group and had gathered in a house for protection. The house was a shambles.

The carnage was wreaked during a ten-day military operation through the northern part of Morazán Province just before Christmas 1981. Again, it was the U.S.-trained Atlacatl Battalion, reinforced by helicopter gunships and heavy artillery. The guerrillas had warned the peasants in the zone about the impending invasion. But most had remained in their villages. Only the hard-core revolutionaries had fled. Those who hadn't were like so many Salvadoran peasants—offering food and shelter to the guerrilla forces when they were present, to the government soldiers when they were posted in the village.

The first column of soldiers arrived on foot in Mozote at about 6:00 A.M. More soldiers were landed by helicopter. The villagers were ordered out of their houses, into the tiny square in front of the church, men in one group, women in another. The men were blindfolded, taken away in small groups of four and five, and shot. Women were raped. Of the 482 Mozote victims, 280 were children under fourteen years old.

"Mama, they're killing me. They've killed my sister. They're going to kill me," screamed the nine-year-old son of Rufina Amaya, who managed to escape during the confusion.* In addition to her son, somewhere among the ruins in Mozote were the skeletons of her blind husband and three daughters, ages three years, five years, and eight

---

*Mrs. Amaya provided her account to me and Alma Guillermoprieto in interviews on different days, while we were, independently, with the guerrillas and their peasant supporters in Morazán in January 1982.

months. While the villagers were being herded together, Mrs. Amaya had slipped away. From her hiding place in the trees, she heard the soldiers' conversation: "Lieutenant, somebody here says he won't kill children," said one soldier. "Who's the son of a bitch who said that?" the lieutenant answered. "I am going to kill him." Mrs. Amaya recalled, "The soldiers had no fury. They just observed the lieutenant's orders. They were cold. It wasn't a battle."

When the soldiers and helicopters began arriving in La Joya, a smaller village south of Mozote, the older boys and men fled. "We didn't think they would kill children, women, and old people," explained César Martínez, a weathered man with two years of formal schooling who looks a couple of decades older than his forty-six years. Thus many of the villagers remained. But the soldiers killed Martínez's mother and sister and his sister's two children, ages five and eight. Sitting next to Martínez on a rope bed as we talked during the first morning light a few weeks later was fifteen-year-old Julio, who had hidden in a gully when the shooting started in La Joya. The soldiers killed his mother, father, nine-year-old brother, and two sisters, ages seven and five. Julio returned to La Joya to bury his family and two of his friends, ages seven and ten. Another villager from La Joya, Gumersindo Lucas, held his half-naked chubby-cheeked four-month old daughter, wearing a red T-shirt and tiny red bracelet, while a three-year old girl in a yellow dress, her face filthy, tugged at his trousers, crying "Papa, Papa," as he explained that before he fled from the advancing troops with his wife, children, and other relatives, he had taken his sixty-two-year-old mother, too sick to walk, to a neighbor's house and hidden her under some blankets. He returned to find that she had been shot in bed; then the soldiers had burned the rough logs that supported the roof, burying her under the heavy red tiles. Among the victims in La Joya were a seventy-year-old woman, a mother, and her three-day-old baby. On the adobe walls, the soldiers had scrawled, "The Atlacatl Battalion will return to kill the rest."

In the tiny hamlet of La Capilla, soldiers raped Chona Díaz and her twelve-year-old daughter, then killed them both, along with four other children in the family. They murdered Juan Savaria and his eight children. Another victim in La Capilla was seventy years old.

In Cerro Pando, the toll of 149 included twenty-four-year-old Rosalda Argueta, who was pregnant, one-month-old Jeremia Argueta, and ten men and women in their seventies and eighties. In Guacamaya the soldiers went house to house, killing tiny infants and old people. They hauled ten villagers to the church, where they executed them.

At the time I was with the rebels in Morazán, a few weeks after the massacre, they had prepared handwritten lists with the names, ages, and villages of 733 victims. More victims were discovered later, in isolated huts throughout the mountains.

Stories about the massacre appeared in *The Washington Post* and *The New York Times* on January 27, 1982.* The next day President Reagan certified that the Salvadoran government "is making a concerted and significant effort to comply with internationally recognized human rights" and that the government "is achieving substantial control over all elements of its own armed forces, so as to bring an end to the indiscriminate torture and murder of Salvadoran citizens." Five days later Thomas Enders went before Congress to defend the President's conclusions. "There is no evidence to confirm that Government forces systematically massacred civilians in the operations zone, or that the number of civilians even remotely approached the 733 or 926 victims cited in the press," he told the congressmen. Then, for good measure, he added that "there were probably not more than 300" people living in Mozote at the time of the massacre.

"Does it ring familiar?" Sydney Schanberg asked in his *New York Times* column a few days after Enders's exculpatory testimony about the Salvadoran massacre. Schanberg had been the *Times* correspondent in Cambodia in 1973, when Enders, as the number two man in the embassy, had selected targets for the American B-52 bomber pilots. On August 6, 1973, a B-52 accidentally dropped its twenty-ton load on a village. "Mr. Enders tried to cover up the incident—first by sending an aide to tell the press corps that the death toll was probably only 25 but certainly no more than 65, and then by issuing orders to block reporters from getting to the town, 38 miles down the Mekong River from Phnom Penh," Schanberg recalled in his column. But Schanberg had circumvented the obstacles to reach the Cambodian village. The toll had not been 25 or 65 but nearly 200 dead and more than 300 wounded.

The Wall Street Journal, on the other hand, accepted Enders's statements about the Mozote massacre. In an editorial the *Journal* charged that I had been "overly credulous" in accepting the peasants' accounts. Then the editorial referred to a "News Analysis" written by *The Times'* Barbara Crossette, now the paper's deputy foreign editor. Crossette noted that the administration was challenging press reports

---

*I had filed my story after leaving the rebel zone. The *Post* reporter, Alma Guillermoprieto, who had clandestinely entered with the guerrillas as I was leaving, did not want to be "scooped." She wrote her account in longhand while still in Morazán, then had it smuggled out of El Salvador and transmitted to the *Post.*

about the massacre "without presenting detailed evidence to support its position." With this "News Analysis" and Schanberg's column, the *Journal* charged, *The Times* "has closed ranks behind a reporter out on a limb, waging a little campaign to bolster his position by impugning his critics."

But it was Enders, not *The Times,* who was out on a limb.*

"I wouldn't say Enders lied, but he spoke through the glasses of the policy, and what he said wasn't exactly supported by the report," said a U.S. diplomat who was in El Salvador at the time of the massacre and was intimately involved with the embassy's investigation.

After the massacre accounts had appeared in the *Post* and *The Times,* Ambassador Hinton sent two embassy officials, Todd Greentree and John McKay, to investigate. Greentree, a political officer, was one of the youngest—twenty-eight years old at the time—and brightest members of the embassy staff. With a pistol tucked into his boots, he, more than any other embassy official, ventured outside the capital for an understanding of what was happening in the countryside, where the war was being fought. McKay was a Marine Corps major. (He and I had been in the same officer corps class at Quantico, Virginia, in 1968, and had served together in Vietnam, where McKay had been wounded.) Their mission in going to Mozote was "aimed at proving it didn't happen," said a diplomat who was there at the time. But Greentree and McKay concluded "there had been a massacre." The embassy knew this wasn't what Washington wanted to hear, so it filed a report that was "intentionally devoid of judgment," said a diplomat who helped prepare the report forwarded to Washington.

Enders's statements were based on the embassy's investigation, which was reported in an eight-page cable. He refused, however, to make the cable publicly available, on the ground that it was classified. But there is nothing in the cable that would jeopardize U.S. security interests. There is much in it, however, that raises doubts about the administration's account of the massacre—by Enders in his testimony and later by other State Department officers. And even though the cable has now been released under the Freedom of Information Act, several crucial words and paragraphs, which further undermine the administration's position, are still being withheld.

*It is widely believed that the *Journal*'s editorial had a significant impact on the reporting from El Salvador, in favor of the administration. The editorial "turned the press around," General Nutting told a reporter some months later. The foreign editor of one major newspaper sent copies of the editorial to his correspondents in Central America. "Let's not let this happen to us" was the message, according to one of the paper's reporters.

What the cable does reveal, and what Enders did not tell the committee, is that the investigators never reached any of the villages where the massacres occurred. The closest they had come was Jocoaitique, several miles from Mozote. Moreover, Greentree and McKay interviewed no one who had been present when the people were killed. "Civilian authorities, church officials, relief workers, and Socorro Jurídico representatives were unable to provide first-hand information on El Mozote," the embassy reported in the cable. The embassy's report suggested that the peasants were killed in a fire fight, not massacred. But this conclusion was based on an interview with a peasant who had not been present. The peasant "intimated that he knew of violent fighting in Mozote and other nearby cantones," the embassy's cable read. The word "intimated" was deleted from the cable released to me under the FOIA. Thus the impression was left that the man, in fact, "knew of" fighting. Also deleted was the following: "He was unwilling to discuss comportment of Government forces saying 'This is something one should talk about in another time, in another country.' "

In sum, Greentree and McKay had gathered circumstantial evidence to support what the villagers had told *The New York Times* and *The Washington Post*.

Enders's effort to rebut the massacre reports by contending that there were no more than 300 people living in Mozote in December was, first of all, a distortion since the accounts in the *Post* and *The Times* had clearly indicated that the massacre had taken place in Mozote *and several nearby villages*. It was also not true. A representative of the International Red Cross told me a few months after the story about the massacre that there had been at least 1,000 people in Mozote at the time. Red Cross workers had firsthand knowledge about life in northern Morazán, which the State Department knows but is still not interested in disclosing. In the cable released under the FOIA, the following was deleted: "The International Red Cross is the only relief agency permitted to move freely in Morazán Department, making weekly trips with relief supplies to the towns on the north-south road and in other areas." Along that north-south road are La Capilla, La Joya, and the other villages where the peasants said the massacre occurred.

The State Department eventually strayed even farther from the facts than Enders had on the subject of the massacre at Mozote. In a letter to Representative Richard L. Ottinger, New York Democrat, the State Department declared that the embassy investigators had "interviewed a wide variety of sources, including refugees from El Mozote, who said they witnessed the events of December 11." But Greentree and McKay talked with no eyewitnesses, and the embassy cable specifically states that civilian authorities, church officials, relief workers, and International Red Cross delegates "were unable to provide first-hand information."

The department also sought to lay the responsibility for the deaths of the civilians on the guerrillas, saying that "it is clear that the guerrilla forces defending El Mozote did nothing to remove civilians from the path of the battle they knew was coming and had prepared for." The same assertion was made in the opening "Summary" paragraph of the embassy's cable. But it is contradicted in the body of the cable. Greentree and McKay talked with one old couple. "According to them, guerrillas had told them to leave in early December because they were so old, but they did not want to because they had spent their whole lives there and had never been outside the community."

In its letter to Ottinger the department argued that the lists of "victims" (the department used the quotation marks to imply doubts about whether anyone had been unjustifiably killed) had probably been "extracted from civil registries stolen from the nearby town of Jocoaitique when guerrillas occupied it." The embassy had made the same contention in its report. But the guerrilla attack on Jocoaitique was on January 12, as the embassy cable noted. It was several days before that attack that I was shown the list with the 733 names, ages, and villages. The State Department was responding to a letter from Ottinger, signed by fifty-four other members of Congress, calling on the President to withdraw his certification of January 28, 1982.

The certification requirement was another attempt by Congress to have a greater say in the U.S. foreign policy, at least with regard to El Salvador. Military assistance and human rights were already linked by the 1974 amendment to the Foreign Assistance Act. That law had deterred neither Carter nor Reagan.

Specifically, the certification law, which was enacted in 1981, conditioned further military assistance to El Salvador, and the continuation of the U.S. military advisers there, on the President's certifying every six months that the Salvadoran government "(1) is making a concerted and significant effort to comply with internationally recognized human rights; (2) is achieving substantial control over all elements of its own armed forces, so as to bring to an end the indiscriminate torture and murder of Salvadoran citizens by these forces; (3) is making continued progress in implementing essential economic and political reforms, including the land reform program . . ."*

*For the first six-month period, the administration had to certify that the Salvadoran government was committed to holding free elections. In addition, the

"This vote represents a decisive repudiation of the blank-check military policy of the Reagan administration in El Salvador and constitutes a significant victory for those who believe we should not provide unconditional military aid to the government of El Salvador," Representative Solarz, who had sponsored the certification legislation along with fellow New York Democrat Jonathan B. Bingham, said at the time of the House committee approval.

The State Department and the Reagan White House lobbied against the law, and Ambassador Hinton, in a public address to Salvadoran businessmen at the Sheraton Hotel, called the law "stupid." To the Salvadoran military, the message was clear: It could ignore the law, as for the most part did the administration. About all that the certification requirement did was to ensure that the atrocities in El Salvador would be publicly exposed every six months. Each certification also "made us look like hypocrites," said a senior diplomat who had served in El Salvador. "The President has made the decision that he wants to back the government of El Salvador," he continued. "In order to do this, he has to put a good face on what's happening down there, to put it in the best possible light—to make a silk purse out of a sow's ear, I suppose. He has to stretch the facts to the breaking point," he said. "I'm sure he doesn't think of it as a lie. But there may be some of that. But rather than a lie, it may be not telling the whole truth."

In the year preceding Reagan's first certification (January 28, 1982) that the Salvadoran government was making a serious effort to respect human rights, 13,353 Salvadorans had been murdered by the Salvadoran Army, security forces, and paramilitary groups, according to the archdiocese's legal aid office. There had been the massacres at the Río Lempa, Cabañas, Mozote, the small-unit sweeps through Soyapango and Armenia, the decapitations in Santa Ana. And three days after the President had issued his certification, a patrol of soldiers from the First Infantry Brigade attacked San Antonio Abad, a warren of mud huts and tin shacks where pigs and children wander in the rutted, garbage-littered dirt streets abutting a wealthy residential neighborhood, where the streets are paved and lined with trees. The army said there had been a shoot-out with "subversives." But the slum residents and a nun said that the soldiers, accompanied by several men with hoods, arrived during the still-dark morning hours and went house to

President had to certify that the Salvadoran government was making good-faith efforts to investigate the murders of the four American churchwomen, the two AIFLD workers, and the American journalist John Sullivan.

house, dragging out people dressed in their underwear or without shoes and socks. Many were shot in the back of the head or the heart. Among at least twenty victims were a fifty-seven-year old couple and their twenty-two-year-old son. The soldiers raped three sisters, ages sixteen, fourteen, and thirteen, and shot their twenty-year-old brother.

Two days after the incident at San Antonio Abad, Enders appeared before the House Subcommittee on Inter-American Affairs to defend the President's certification, and Representative Studds said: "The President has just certified that up is down and in is out and black is white. I anticipate his telling us that war is peace at any moment."

Such colorful rhetoric was probably not surprising from a persistent liberal critic of Reagan's Central America policy, but the sense of his disbelief was heard in El Salvador as well. "It's absolutely cynical," César Jerez, the then-ranking Jesuit in Central America, said of the certification. "It's incredible, so totally contradictory to the reality here," Vicar-General Urioste said in a separate interview. "Would Mr. Reagan certify that they respect human rights in Poland?" he asked rhetorically. Two months earlier the Polish government had imposed martial law as part of its effort to crush the workers' union, Solidarity, and all dissent; seven workers had been killed. By contrast, Urioste noted, "Here hundreds, thousands, of workers have been killed," and the state of siege, which, like martial law, suspends all basic freedoms and liberties, had been in effect for two years.

The religious leaders' sentiments about the certification were echoed by a wide range of Salvadorans interviewed at the time. "It's a lie. In no moment has it [the human rights situation] improved," said a twenty-seven-year-old bank teller whose brother had recently "disappeared" after being seized on the street. A U.S.-educated business leader said without hesitation that the human rights situation "has not improved; it has worsened." And a twenty-two-year-old who worked with one of the human rights organizations invited Reagan to "come down here, to walk the streets of El Salvador at six A.M. every day, then tell us if there is progress in human rights here."

The Reagan administration had certified, in January 1982, that the Salvadoran government was making progress on human rights and in implementing the land reform. Another picture was presented by an internal State Department memorandum dated March 9, 1982. The memorandum, which was released under the FOIA in late February 1984, was based on a conversation with Jorge Camacho, the leader of a peasant organization.

"Soldiers sometimes get together in larger groups and kill whole groups of campesinos on a weekend away from their barracks," the memorandum stated. Camacho told the American AID officials in El Salvador that his organization had "proof that in one town, only six of 23 in one campesino family survived one of the 'death squads.' "

The memorandum reported another incident. "Recently, an Army Captain's father was killed. He was a landowner, who killed some of his workers. The guerrillas killed him and turned the farm into a guerrilla base. The captain has killed 20 guerrillas, but he will create 50 new ones with his attitude. (The captain is U.S. trained.) The U.S. must prepare the Salvadoran trainees in the U.S. for social change as well as give them military skills."

The Americas Watch Committee, the nonprofit human rights monitoring organization in New York, and the American Civil Liberties Union (ACLU) called the January 1982 certification "a fraud," and jointly issued a 280-page report with statistics and gruesome details designed to support their conclusion. The human rights bureau of the State Department, in an internal memorandum, described the report as "an extremely well-prepared, effective documentation of human rights violations in El Salvador by government forces." But, the bureau added, it was "obviously slanted and totally one-sided in its presentation." Then the bureau proceeded to impugn the political orientation of the individuals who had helped prepare the report. The organizer and director of the Americas Watch-ACLU project was Roberto Álvarez, a lawyer from the Dominican Republic who had once worked for the OAS's Human Rights Commission. State's human rights bureau sought to denigrate him with the charge that he "shows an apparent partisanship for the left wing" of a Dominican political party that is affiliated with the Socialist International. Another lawyer who worked on the study was Michael Posner, executive director of the Lawyers Committee for International Human Rights. Posner and the committee represent the families of the murdered American churchwomen in their efforts to obtain information about the killings from the U.S. government. The State Department referred to the Lawyers Committee as "an organization with obvious liberal leanings." Two other persons who worked on the report were Heather Foote and Leyda Barbieri, staff members of the church-supported Washington Office on Latin America. The State Department said that WOLA had "long opposed American policy in Central America" and declared that "Ms. Foote in particular is a partisan of the FDR." But it had been WOLA that had brought Duarte to the United States in 1977 and that had testified to Congress about the fraud against the Christian Democrats during the elections that year, both of which were of little interest to the State Department.

The import of all this was unmistakably clear: Critics of the U.S. policy could not be expected to report truthfully and were by definition leftists. But the Americas Watch report was a largely accurate and honest appraisal of the human rights situation in El Salvador.

During 1981 the embassy reported that 5,407 people died as the result of political violence. The archdiocese's legal aid office said it was almost three times that many—13,353—and the Center for Documentation and Information at the Catholic university put the toll at 13,229.

The embassy in El Salvador knew that its murder statistics were "not realistic," that they represented only "a tiny portion" of the people killed, as a diplomat who helped prepare the statistics said at the time. The sources for the embassy figures were the Salvadoran dailies. But they reported principally on deaths in the capital and large cities, while it was in the rural countryside that peasants were being slaughtered. Moreover, both of the major newspapers are ideologically conservative and more inclined to cover up than to expose human rights abuses. The other organizations had more accurate and higher numbers because they had offices and staffs where relatives and friends could report assassinations and mass killing. These people would never take their case to the U.S. embassy or to any of the Salvadoran police or military units since the latter were the perpetrators of most of the violence.

Enders sought to defend the embassy's reporting by attacking the other groups. As for the archdiocese's legal aid office, Socorro Jurídico, Enders asserted that Archbishop Rivera y Damas had "deprived the Legal Aid Office of any right to speak on behalf of the Archbishopric," a contention repeated so often that it acquired a truth of its own. But the statement is only partially true and highly misleading.

Because of its reporting on human rights, Socorro Jurídico became well known internationally. And because of its close links to the church, Rivera y Damas was concerned that its role be made clear. He withdrew from the legal aid office its function to speak for the archbishopric *"in issues of displaced persons with which it usually deals* [emphasis added]," as the State Department reported in a Confidential cable to all diplomatic posts. He also criticized it for not compiling statistics about leftist violence. But the archbishop did not, contrary to what Enders sought to imply, cast any doubts on the human rights work of Socorro Jurídico—except for its failure to monitor human rights abuses by the left. Indeed he continued to cite the statistics in his Sunday homilies.

When Socorro Jurídico was established in 1975 by a small group of

Catholic lawyers and law students, it functioned as do legal aid organizations in the United States: providing legal representation for the poor. In 1977 Archbishop Romero began sending the volunteer lawyers human rights cases, and later he gave the agency official status within the archdiocese and quarters on the church's premises. The office was financed by donations from Catholic and Protestant churches worldwide. As the human rights abuses escalated, so did the armed assaults on the Socorro Jurídico office. And on the armed forces list of "traitors" published in March 1981 were several Socorro Jurídico workers. (As part of a general reorganization in 1982 Socorro Jurídico became Tutela Legal del Arzobispado.)

As for the University of Central America and the Center for Documentation and Information there, Enders charged the university with "bias" and "prejudice" and called the center a "leftwing organization." Though the university is nondenominational, most of the administrators and professors are Roman Catholics, predominantly Jesuits. Its small campus, on the eastern edge of the capital, is nestled among pines and leafy oaks, and the air is fragrant with the scents of tropical florae. From its hilltop acres one can look across the capital, along a straight line of about three miles, to the tops of the high-rise buildings of the National University, which looks like a tenement project. It has been closed since 1980. Like most Latin American universities, the National University of El Salvador was the focus of leftist activities. In the 1950's most of the country's few Communists taught or studied there. Most of the current guerrilla leaders read Marx and Mao at the National University in the late 1960's or early 70's. And before all the revolutionaries went underground or into the hills, reporters would head to the National University to seek them out.

Disturbed by the goings-on at the National University, fifty members of the country's oligarchy donated about $1 million in the mid-1960's for the establishment of a university where they hoped the young would not be exposed to all these radical ideas. The result was UCA, which over the years has been as calm as the National University was stormy. It has the feeling of a small midwestern college. The university's modern structures—a pleasant mix of low-rise concrete and one- and two-story red brick—are graffiti-free. Male students, whose hair is usually trimmed, wear slacks and sport shirts; the women, skirts and heels.

Nonetheless, the university has been the intellectual center of opposition to the country's military governments. The university's magazine *Estudios Centroamericanos,* known by its Spanish acronym *ECA,* is the only scholarly, general-interest journal published in El Salvador. In it have appeared lengthy academic analyses of the electoral frauds of 1972 and 1977, treatises on the Salvadoran military, the left, and the economy. A book about the historical development of the Salvadoran economy, *Fundamentos Economicos de la Burguesia Salvadoreña,* which was edited and published by the university in 1977, is the seminal and still most comprehensive work on the subject. The human rights statistics are maintained by the university's Center for Documentation and Information, which somehow manages to put out *Proceso,* a weekly summary of events and analysis of everything from human rights to the economy to the status of the war. On the third floor of the cement structure that houses the university library, student volunteers cut, paste, and analyze in sparsely furnished offices. Gray metal shelves are crammed with back issues of the country's newspapers, the most complete collection in El Salvador.

A U.S. embassy political officer regularly visited the *Proceso* offices, realizing that their studies were academically sound. Indeed, the embassy described UCA in 1982 as the country's "most academically credible university and the only operating university with a large library sufficient for study and research." Though many of the priests and professors are certainly liberal, and some are leftists, the embassy's cultural affairs section said that "the vast majority of students, professors and administrators are interested only in education, and stay aloof from politics."

EVERY six months the Reagan administration certified that the Salvadoran government was making a serious effort to respect human rights. The certifications were made in spite of continuing reports, by Amnesty International, by Americas Watch, and by a range of other organizations, from unions to doctors, that there was no improvement in the human rights situation, that the indiscriminate torture and murder of innocent Salvadorans continued at a shocking rate.

In defending the certifications, Elliott Abrams, head of the human rights bureau at State, argued that the issue of whether or not there was an improving human rights situation was inevitably a "subjective political judgment." While there may well be an element of subjectivity and politics involved in determining whether or not a government is complying with internationally recognized human rights standards, it seems that only the Reagan administration and its staunchest backers were able to find those standards being met in El Salvador. And it certainly was a political judgment, one that even some conservative Republicans had trouble reaching.

One of the principal arguments in support of the second certification (July 1982) was that the rate of indiscriminate killing by the government forces and paramilitary groups had declined. According to the church's legal aid office, 2,829 persons were killed by the government forces and paramilitary groups during the first six months of 1982, about half the 1981 rate. The Reagan administration said this was progress. But Representative Mickey Edwards, chairman of the American Conservative Union, declared after a visit to El Salvador that although the decline in assassinations "may look good on a computer printout . . . we don't see any progress that's been made at all." (Regarding the land reform, he added, "My impression is there has been no progress," an accurate conclusion that also ran counter to the President's certification.)

He was right. Fewer people were killed, not because there was a newfound respect for human rights but because there were fewer people to kill—"they were already killed or they got the hell out of the way," said a senior embassy officer. Another reason for the lower numbers at the time of the second, third, and fourth certifications was that there was less killing in urban areas and more in the countryside, in remote villages where Socorro Jurídico didn't have offices. And although the rate of killing had declined, it was still at the numbing level of about 100 a week in 1982 and 1983. A slaughter on the same scale in the United States would have eliminated 235,000 people in one year—or the equivalent of the population of St. Petersburg, Florida; Dayton, Ohio; or Fresno, California. The administration could use the declining numbers to support its subjective political judgment that there was an improving human rights situation. But there had been no significant changes in the structures, the institutions, the systems in El Salvador; they were pretty much the same as they had been before the coup in 1979. And the people being killed were not only "leftists" but union leaders, teachers, Christian Democratic party organizers, peasant leaders, and others who were part of the center the Reagan administration was trying to develop.

A few weeks before the second certification the embassy in El Salvador cabled Washington a grim account of how the National Police had tortured a volunteer for the Green Cross, a humanitarian organization in El Salvador. There wasn't anything particularly unusual about the torture; the embassy knew it happened all the time. What was different was that the victim was well known to many embassy personnel, having offered them the cover of the Green Cross to go into rural areas where there were guerrilla sympathizers. The embassy also sent the cable because "we wanted Washington to know what we were dealing with," said a diplomat involved in drafting the cable, which was highly classified so that only a few people would have access to it.

When Enders read the cable, he was furious—not with the National Police or the Salvadoran military but with the embassy for having recorded the incident in writing. Enders's fear was realized; the cable was leaked to Don Oberdorfer at *The Washington Post.*

The torture had been inflicted on the young man in a secret part of the National Police headquarters, in a soundproof room off limits to the International Red Cross and other groups that checked on the treatment of prisoners. In one torture session the victim was strapped to a rotating wheel, similar to the medieval rack. He was severely beaten and forced to inhale lime. During another torture, mockingly called the Carter, the victim was strung up by ropes tied to his hands and feet while severe pressure was applied to his testicles with a wire.

Abrams responded to the torture with the statement that it had to viewed "in the context of a steady improvement in human rights performance, especially on the part of the National Police." He said that the commander of the National Police, Colonel López Nuila, had "a strong commitment to human rights." The colonel was a member of the government's human rights commission.

The creation of this commission was heralded by the Reagan administration in its third certification (January 1983). But the seven-member commission, which had been formed under pressure from Washington, was little more than a public relations effort. "The Commission is really just a farce," the Salvadoran deputy minister for international organizations and human rights told U.S. embassy officers. The embassy relayed this view, along with other insights into the reality of the government's human rights commission, in a Confidential cable, one that was not provided under an FOIA request. Three months after being formed, the embassy reported, the commission still had virtually no resources; it lacked vehicles and even had to borrow typewriters. More seriously, "it has no specific authority over the military, even though National Police Director Col. López Nuila is a member," the embassy reported. Yet, it noted, "the investigation of disappearances almost inevitably includes the possibility of armed forces involvement, and in some cases leads to specific units or headquarters."

While Abrams and Enders were strong in their attacks on other human rights groups for being liberal or leftist, they failed to tell Congress what the embassy reported about the government's own commission. "Some members' objectivity is questionable," the embassy advised Washington. The commission's executive director was "a self-avowed rightist." Specific reference was made in the cable to the commission's report when the guerrillas seized the town of Berlín in early 1983, and the air force bombed the city and civilian population to dislodge them. "The Commission was quick to go to Berlín and denounce guerrilla atrocities, but their report did not even mention the alleged bombardment," the commission's executive director complained to the embassy. And when the commission staff gave information about human rights abuses to commission member Monsignor Fredy Delgado, a conservative bishop, Delgado "changes the facts and says what he wants," the executive director further complained.

To appreciate just how brutal and ruthless the government security forces were in 1983—when the Reagan administration twice more avowed human rights were improving—one must realize that the National Police under López Nuila was widely considered to be less ruthless than the National Guard and Treasury Police. Then consider the following, which is not an isolated incident. Shortly after midnight on April 4, 1983, national policemen, dressed in civilian clothes and some wearing masks, forced their way into the house of a seventy-four-year-old man and his wife. "Where is Paula?" they demanded. The older woman pointed to her granddaughter's room. Paula was taken from her bed and handcuffed. Then they seized the couple's thirty-one-year-old son and left. A few moments later the national policemen returned to take away Paula and to steal a television set, tape recorder, fan, and 60 colones (about $40). Two days later the bodies were found dumped at the entrance to the San Martín Cemetery. Paula, twenty years old, had been raped, had all her finger joints broken, and been shot in the head with a .38 caliber pistol. Ernesto, an employee at the Ministry of Agriculture, had also been shot in the back of the head. As part of his torture the National Police had beat him severely on the back and ground lighted cigarettes into his testicles. Both the victims were members of the Christian communities, and on Sunday Archbishop Rivera y Damas denounced the action. Reflecting its contempt for anyone who dared criticize the government forces, the National Police charged Rivera y Damas with "disseminating lies that contributed to hatred and confusion."

Horrendous stories about rape, torture, murder, and mayhem could fill pages, if not volumes. The simple fact is that the Salvadoran armed forces were no more respectful of human rights in 1983 than they had been before, and the administration knew it. In January 1983, at the time of Reagan's third certification, the CIA prepared a Secret analysis that more accurately reflected the manner in which the military operated. On the first page, under "Key Judgments," the agency concluded that "although some progress has been made in curbing abuses by the armed forces, El Salvador continues to have serious problems in this respect." In the body of its report the CIA provided details: "The tenuous and often nonexistent control of senior officers over elements of paramilitary security forces and civilian irregulars is a continuing cause for concern. . . . In isolated areas, especially, where lawlessness is a way of life, semiliterate personnel led by a corporal or sergeant all too often assume the roles of prosecutor, judge or executioner."

But it wasn't just in the rural areas, and it wasn't only semiliterate personnel who were culpable. The torture and brutality were ordered by senior commanders right in the capital. Political prisoners in government jails were sadistically tortured. In January 1983 a U.S. medical commission, under the auspices of the American Public Health Association, visited El Salvador. The members examined a woman with broken ribs and nose who told them the guards had stuffed pages from a telephone book in her mouth while they beat her on the back, stomach, and genitals, applied electric shock, and repeatedly raped her. One man had been burned with acid; the fingernails were yanked out of another; a third had been so savagely beaten that he had to be surgically castrated.

"Perhaps as many as 90 percent of detainees are being tortured during interrogation," the International Red Cross in Geneva informed the U.S. ambassador there in November 1983, according to a Confidential cable, which was not released under the Freedom of Information Act. In July 1983 the Reagan administration had for the fourth time certified an improving human rights situation in El Salvador. But the Red Cross, according to the cable, "has seen a continuing deterioration in the treatment of detainees since April."

While the issue of progress and an improving human rights situation might be a subjective political judgment, according to Abrams, there was one issue for which there were objective standards by which to measure the Salvadoran military's conduct. That related to the discipline of officers responsible for the brutality. Again, administration officials provided Congress with numbers that were misleading and with evasive answers.

"Since October 1979, the Salvadoran authorities have done much more than repeatedly emphasize to officers and men the need to protect human rights," Enders proclaimed to the House Subcommittee on Inter-American Affairs at the time of the first certification. "They have transferred, cashiered or punished 1,000 officers and men for various

abuses of military authority." Enders's assertion was not challenged
by any member of Congress. Had they done so, they might have discovered that his statement, made in 1982, was based on a report prepared
by the State Department covering 1980 and, moreover, that the 1980
report mentioned only enlisted men, not officers, as having been cashiered for various abuses. Furthermore, an embassy cable sent in July
1982, some six months after Enders had testified that officers had been
punished, reported that only 12 officers had been disciplined during
the period from January 1, 1982, to mid-July 1982. "To the best of our
knowledge," Ambassador Hinton wrote in the cable, "these are the
first instances where the Ministry of Defense has reported officers
have been arrested or investigated [emphasis added]." In spite of what
the embassy had reported to the State Department, Abrams asserted
before Congress, after the cable had been received, that *"several hundred* officers have been dismissed from the Armed Forces or have been
jailed [emphasis added]." On its face, the statement is somewhat preposterous. Excluding the 400-odd officer cadets who had just returned
from training in the United States, there were no more than 500 officers in the Salvadoran armed forces at the time.*

In July 1982 the administration once again certified that the Salvadoran government was achieving substantial control over all elements of its own armed forces, so as to bring to an end the indiscriminate torture and murder of its citizens by these forces. For the
preceding six months the administration claimed 109 members of the
armed forces had been disciplined. The information was supplied by
the embassy. But the embassy, in its cable, had noted that its information had come from Salvadoran military officials and cautioned that
it be used "with proper caveats." When Enders and Abrams testified
before House and Senate committees, they expressed no caveats.
Abrams even insisted that the majority of the offenses related to
human rights abuses. But the embassy cable indicates that fewer than
half were for murder, assault, and rape.

The whole issue of whether the Salvadoran military is gaining any

*In February 1982 the CIA reported that hundreds of military personnel had
been transferred, retired, or disciplined. Asked by the staff of the House Intelligence Oversight Subcommittee for the basis of this assertion, a CIA official
doubted whether any reporting could be found, the subcommittee noted in its
report. The CIA acknowledged that it had relied on what it had been told by the
Salvadoran minister of defense and moreover, that the offenses, according to
the report, "ranged from such infractions as drunkenness, cowardice, AWOL,
and disobedience, to desertion, thievery or murder; only a fraction of these were
the types of brutality considered politically motivated."

significant control over the violence by punishing soldiers and officers who torture and kill civilians has been obfuscated by imprecisely used statistics and ill-defined terms such as "detained," "disciplined," "punished."

Representative Don Bonker, Democrat of Washington, once tried to cut through to the guts of the issue when he asked pointed questions of Abrams during a congressional hearing.

"Is there one example where there has been a concerted effort by the Government to restrain the military and paramilitary forces from engaging in human rights violations? Has there been anybody imprisoned or been restrained from that kind of activity?" Bonker asked.

Abrams: "There are a number of directives from the President and from the Minister of Defense, General García. More importantly, because I agree with the notion you can issue directives as often as you want, military and security officers are being punished. That is important. That gets the message across to them."

Bonker, who had been briefed by his staff about the absence of any meaningful discipline within the military, pushed. "It is my understanding not one person has been tried or convicted of terrorist activity or human rights violations."

"Several hundred officers have been dismissed from the Armed Forces or have been jailed," Abrams responded. (There was no evidence to support the statement. Indeed, two weeks earlier the embassy had cabled the State Department that some officers had been arrested or investigated. The cable said nothing about "dismissed" or "jailed," and it wasn't several hundred but twelve.)

Bonker tried once more. "I mean convicted."

Abrams, still struggling to put the best face on the situation, first noted that the judicial system wasn't functioning. Then he said, "What is a better way of dealing with it in the Armed Forces than to put somebody in a military jail for a while as punishment? That is happening and dismissals from the security forces are happening."

That exchange was in July 1982. In October Bonker tried again, this time with a letter to Abrams asking for more detailed information about the 109 soldiers who the State Department said had been disciplined. Four months later Abrams replied that "the Embassy is now attempting to obtain additional information on each of the cases. . . . As soon as this additional information is received I will be back in touch with you." He never got back in touch. Understandably. In July 1983, a full year after Abrams had testified, Americas Watch reported that there had not been a single case of criminal punishment of a member of the Salvadoran armed forces for a human rights violation.

Congressional and human rights observers going to El Salvador pushed for more precise and meaningful information. What they learned from Salvadoran military officials contradicted what administration officials were saying. Democratic Congressmen Thomas Harkin (Iowa), James L. Oberstar (Minnesota), and William J. Coyne (Pennsylvania), along with their aides, once confronted Defense Minister García, as well as the commanders of the Treasury Police, National Police, and National Guard, demanding to know if anyone had ever been disciplined for a human rights violation. The congressmen were in El Salvador on a trip organized by John McAward, the staff director of the Unitarian Universalist Service Committee, the Boston-based nonsectarian, nonprofit organization founded in 1939. McAward, who led numerous trips to Central America, operated on the theory that for Americans, especially congressmen, to understand what was happening in Central America, they should be exposed to a wider range of views than were offered by the interviews carefully arranged by the U.S. embassy. To put it mildly, McAward was not popular with embassy officials in El Salvador. Recalling the delegation's meeting with García and the other commanders, McAward said, "The moment we entered the room, they all pulled out their tape recorders and slapped them on the table. Seven machines! So we pulled ours out, too—only two."

The congressmen demanded to know why soldiers and members of the security forces weren't punished for human rights violations. General Vides Casanova, commander of the National Guard, showed them a list of 926 persons he said had been punished. Examining the list closely, the delegation determined that 870 of the offenses were for drinking on duty, leaving a guard post, and the like, and the offenders received punishments of thirty days' confinement. No officers were on the list, and Vides Casanova admitted to the delegation that no member of the Guard had been punished for abuses of authority while on an official operation.

In interviews granted on the condition that they not be identified, because they are career Foreign Service officers and what they said contradicted what the Reagan administration was saying publicly, five diplomats whose time in El Salvador spanned early 1980 through mid-1983 all said that not a single officer and few, if any, enlisted men had ever even been tried, let alone convicted and punished, for anything that could be considered a human rights violation.

"Those who are disciplined are hopeless drunks, some are thieves, some are sodomists, some are discharged for failure to accept authority, and some are probably discharged for wanton murder, not politi-

cally motivated; but they just say 'shit' and write them off the books,"
said one diplomat, stressing that he was talking about enlisted men,
not officers. "If soldiers are being discharged for committing murder,
that's not much of a discipline," he added.

Another diplomat said he knew of soldiers who had been punished
"for rape and robbery and so forth, but not for doing something that
his bosses perceived as having needed done in the first place, which
is killing people."

"What about the bodies at El Playón, Puerto Diablo, tossed under
bridges, in the ravines?" I asked.

"They were perceived by someone as someone who needed killing.
Why? I don't know."

"And nobody was ever punished for that?" I continued.

"Oh, no, of course not. Never will be."

With another Foreign Service officer, who had been in El Salvador
from 1981 to 1983, I asked, "Have they ever tried anybody for a human
rights violation?"

He thought for several minutes, then said, "I can't remember one."
Then he added, "Well, again, you know, again, it's a question of mentality. For us, it's a human rights violation; for them, it's getting rid of
the enemy."

"Have they ever discharged anyone for a human rights violation?"
I asked.

"Yeah!" he exclaimed. "Well, they *arrested* a captain." His voice
rose with excitement. "First time. But it's a start! The son of a bitch
was guilty!"

That was in the spring of 1983. He was referring to Captain Carlos
Alfonso Figueroa Morales, commander of the elite Jaguar Battalion,
who was charged by the *government*'s human rights commission with
responsibility for the murder of at least eighteen peasant members of
the Las Hojas cooperative in February 1983. The victims, ranging in
age from seventy-six to a young child, were found lying along the
Cuyuapa River, their hands tied behind their backs. They had been
shot in the head by soldiers who arrived at the cooperative, where the
victims lived in simple mud-and-thatch huts. (The government's investigation was such a rarity, probably the first, that the story was on
page one of *The New York Times*.) "It pains us that the United States
is providing aid that does not get to us but instead comes to destroy us,"
Refugio Sánchez, a member of the cooperative, told Lydia Chavez of
The Times. "If they truly respect human rights why do they pay to kill
us?" Adrian Esquina, president of the National Association of Indigenous Salvadorans, said he thought the peasants had been killed be-

cause a landowner, whose request to build a road across the cooperative had been denied, had gone to his friends in the army and told
them that the peasants were subversives.

For some weeks before, ten U.S. military advisers had been training
soldiers at the army base in Sonsonate. After the American embassy
concluded that the captain and troops under his command had been
responsible for killing the peasants, the advisers were withdrawn. But
the diplomat's optimism that the Salvadoran government was actually
going to do something was misplaced. Yes, there had been an arrest
—of the father of an eighteen-year-old who was killed by the soldiers.
He was jailed on charges of trying to kill a civil defense guard, who
he thought had killed his son. Even the ever-cautious Magaña recognized that the charges were probably trumped-up when he told
Chavez, "I don't know if they were false charges."

But the *coup de grâce?* Captain Figueroa was placed in charge of
intelligence at the army base in Sonsonate. As for his supposed arrest,
Chavez noted wryly: "It now appears the writing of the press release
was as far as the arrest went." Captain Figueroa's commanding officer
at Sonsonate said that he had conducted an investigation of the
charges and found that his troops had not been guilty of any miscon-
duct. He accused the human rights commission and the National Association of Indigenous Salvadorans of a Communist plot to disgrace
the army.*

As certification has routinely followed certification, it seems to have
become apparent to Salvadoran officials that only cosmetic measures
are required on their part," *New York Times* reporter Charles Mohr
observed from El Salvador in August 1983, after the fourth human
rights certification. Then Mohr, who had spent four years covering the
war in Vietnam, added, "Much the same situation applied in Vietnam,
although the South Vietnamese authorities and security forces never
showed the same callousness that prevails here."

The Reagan administration has to share some of the moral responsibility for the callousness. Each time the administration issued another
certification, it was a message to the ruthless Salvadoran military
officers that they really didn't have to change their ways. Each time

*The Reagan administration still does not want all the facts of the Las Hojas
massacre known to the American public. In response to an FOIA request submitted in June 1983, the State Department, in February 1984, released six
cables relating to Las Hojas. There were substantial deletions in all of them,
including an entire page from one.

the administration insisted that officers were being punished when in fact, they weren't, it reinforced the military's belief that it did not have to punish officers. Each time the administration covered up atrocities and torture, it encouraged more. Each time the administration blamed the "extreme right" and the death squads, it was exonerating the military and the government. "Quiet diplomacy" didn't work.

Ambassador Hinton was the consummate practitioner of "quiet diplomacy." According to one of his senior aides, "He was certainly not blinded to the human rights abuses, but he was determined not to alienate the people in the government, to work behind the scenes, to try to make improvements that way, but not to speak out publicly." It was October 1983 before Hinton did finally speak out, in an address to the American Chamber of Commerce in San Salvador. "The Mafia must be stopped," Hinton told the stunned audience, which was not accustomed to this ambassador speaking so harshly about them. He was talking not about a criminal Mafia but about elements within the Salvadoran armed forces that carry out or tolerate the indiscriminate killing and torture. "The gorillas of this Mafia, every bit as much as the guerrillas in Morazán and Chalatenango, are destroying El Salvador."

Hinton was widely praised for his speech, in newspaper editorials and by members of Congress, who seemed to have forgotten that for a year and a half he had implicitly tolerated the "Mafia" and the "indiscriminate killing" by remaining silent.

But in Washington the Reagan administration again came to the defense of the Salvadoran military. One senior official, hiding behind anonymity, used *The New York Times* to rebuke Hinton for having spoken so bluntly, so honestly. The story appeared on page 1. Hinton, who had faithfully served his President, was angry, telling Christopher Dickey of *The Washington Post* some months later, "I think whoever went to The New York Times did the President of the United States a disservice." But it had been one of Reagan's closest advisers, Judge William Clark, at the time the director of the NSC, who spoke with *The Times.* Whether or not he had done a disservice to the President, he had clearly sent a message to the Salvadorans: They could continue with their murderous ways.

President Reagan himself sounded one of the most ringing defenses of the Salvadoran government when he took the extraordinary measure of addressing a joint session of Congress in April 1983.

Reagan praised the Salvadoran government for "making every effort to guarantee democracy, free labor unions, freedom of religion, and a free press. . . ." By contrast, he excoriated the Sandinista government in Nicaragua for censoring the press, interfering with the Catholic Church, acting against labor unions and free enterprise and for "mob action against Nicaragua's independent human rights commission" that drove the commission's director into exile. "It is the ultimate in hypocrisy," he added, "for the unelected Nicaraguan government to charge that we seek their overthrow when they are doing everything they can to bring down the elected government of El Salvador."

The President's speech was largely a success. Representative Clarence Long, Democratic chairman of the important Appropriations Subcommittee on Foreign Operations, praised it, calling the solutions proposed by Reagan "sound and just." And House Majority Leader Jim Wright said he was "absolutely, firmly and enthusiastically" behind Reagan's policy in El Salvador. Wright also criticized Senator Dodd, who had been chosen by other Democratic leaders to respond to the President's speech. Dodd attacked the Reagan policy as a "formula for failure" and called for a negotiated settlement.

Patt Derian, the head of State's human rights bureau under Carter, observed after Reagan's speech: "I thought it was the ultimate hypocrisy to list Nicaraguan human rights violations and portray El Salvador as a working democracy with a few little scratches."

One doesn't have to defend the antidemocratic practices and methods of the Sandinistas to recognize that there was more freedom—and less brutality—in Nicaragua than in El Salvador. "I don't understand how they call that government Communist, and say that this government is Christian and democratic," Monsignor Urisote once remarked about the two countries. In Nicaragua, "they don't shoot priests and workers, do they?"

In Nicaragua the Sandinistas censored the opposition newspaper *La Prensa.* In El Salvador opposition reporters and editors had been murdered, their newspaper facilities bombed into silence. There was no need for censorship in El Salvador because only the archconservative papers were functioning by 1983. In Nicaragua the government harassed the church. In El Salvador priests and nuns were murdered. In Nicaragua the human rights commission leader was driven into exile. In El Salvador human rights commission leaders weren't merely forced to leave the country; they were tortured and executed. Mutilated, decapitated bodies didn't show up daily on the dusty roads in Nicaragua.

Reagan had gone to Congress because his policy in Central America was not going well. He followed by naming Richard Stone, a conservative Democrat who had once been a registered lobbyist for the right-

wing Guatemalan government, as his special envoy to the region.*
And like the owner of a ball club that is losing too many games, Reagan also changed managers. Enders and Hinton were ousted, the former replaced by Langhorne A. Motley, with Thomas R. Pickering
becoming ambassador to El Salvador. In keeping with the pattern that
had marked Reagan's Latin American appointments when he came
into office, neither had any depth of experience in Latin American
affairs. Motley, a real estate magnate from Alaska—and a major financial supporter of Republican candidates—had never served in the diplomatic corps until Reagan awarded him the ambassadorship to Brazil in 1981. Pickering, a Foreign Service officer, had never served in
Latin America.

With a new team in place, the President appointed a special commission headed by Henry Kissinger, a person who knew little about
Latin America, to try to fashion a Central America policy. Kissinger's
appointment came days after the publication of *The Price of Power:
Kissinger in the Nixon White House,* by Seymour Hersh, a book that
some thought forever ended Kissinger's role in the making of U.S.
foreign policy. Hersh concluded that Kissinger, along with Nixon,
"remained blind to the human costs of their actions—a further price
of power. The dead and maimed in Vietnam and Cambodia—as in
Chile, Bangladesh, Biafra, and the Middle East—seemed not to count
as the President and his national security adviser battled the Soviet
Union, their misconceptions, their political enemies, and each other."

Reagan was now calling on Kissinger, who had played a role in
toppling a democratically elected leftist government in Chile a decade
earlier, to come up with a policy for dealing with a region where there
was already one leftist government in power, Nicaragua, and leftist
revolutionaries seeking power in Guatemala and El Salvador. Kissinger detested leftist political views and had contempt for Latin America. As recounted in Hersh's book, in 1969 Kissinger had bluntly told
the foreign minister of Chile, Gabriel Valdés, "Nothing important can
come from the South. . . . The axis of history starts in Moscow, goes to
Bonn, crosses over to Washington, and then goes to Tokyo. What happens in the South is of no importance."

Valdés responded during the luncheon in the Chilean embassy, "Mr.
Kissinger, you know nothing of the South."

"No," Kissinger replied, "and I don't care."

There was little, if anything, surprising in the Kissinger commis-

*Stone resigned in late February 1984. He was replaced by Harry W. Schlauder-
man.

sion's report about Central America.* It was for the most part a vindication of Reagan's policy. The commission recognized the indigenous causes of the revolutions, but then it asserted, "The Soviet-Cuban thrust to make Central America part of their geostrategic challenge is what has turned the struggle in Central America into a security and political problem for the United States and for the hemisphere."

Responding to the commission's report, Senator Daniel Patrick Moynihan, a New York Democrat who was not an outspoken critic of Reagan's policy in Central America—for example, he supported the covert funding of the military forces trying to topple the Sandinistas —said that the commission had adopted a doctrinal position. He noted that it had provided no evidence to support its position that the Soviet Union and Cuba presented a serious threat to U.S. security interests in the region.

In its report the Kissinger commission declared, "Beyond the issue of U.S. security interests in the Central America-Caribbean region, our credibility world-wide is engaged. The triumph of hostile forces in what the Soviets call the 'strategic rear' of the United States would be read as a sign of U.S. impotence."

The New York Times observed in an editorial: "The same fears about impotence and credibility were the stuff of a thousand speeches justifying American involvement for a generation in the lost war in Indochina." A litany of other countries in which the United States had asserted that its credibility and security were at stake was provided by Hodding Carter III in his column in *The Wall Street Journal.* "At one time, Somalia was supposed to be a test of our virility in the Horn of Africa and at a later time, Ethiopia," wrote Carter, who had been State Department spokesman during the Carter administration. "Both, when Soviet clients, were portrayed as daggers aimed at the vital oil arteries of the West. The oil continued to flow and continues to flow past their doors, as it has from Iran, and Iraq." Angola, Indonesia, Egypt, the Sudan, Ghana, and Chile were among other countries por-

---

*The manner in which the commission prepared its report was called "a lot of nonsense" by John Barlow Martin, a former ambassador to the Dominican Republic. Martin noted that in 1961, when President Kennedy was searching for a policy there, the President asked him to prepare a report. Martin spent nineteen days in the Dominican Republic, "screaming all the while at Under Secretary of State George W. Ball for limiting my stay to so short a time." In contrast, Martin noted, Kissinger spent barely a week in Central America. "And he is attempting to find out what's going on in six countries, not one! . . . How can he possibly find out what's going on in six countries in six days?"

trayed "as Marxist-Leninist threats to our national survival and sense of manhood," Carter continued.

As for El Salvador, the Kissinger commission, like the Reagan administration, opposed "power sharing" and said that "a true political solution in El Salvador can be reached only through free elections in which all significant groups have a right to participate." The commission overlooked the fact that the elections just two years earlier had not achieved peace and ignored the fate that would befall any leftist politician who entered the country to campaign. It also urged more military aid for El Salvador.

The Salvadoran church said that the Kissinger commission had "not listened" to its leaders. "We have been very clear in our opposition to more military aid," said a church spokesman. He added, "Mr. Kissinger has erred completely by ignoring the Christian forces, which are a force in the country. He has excluded the possibility of dialogue which Monsignor Rivera y Damas has proposed." And a senior leader of the Christian Democrats, Julio Rey Prendes, said that the Kissinger report "places too much emphasis on the military aspect," adding, "We don't need a triumph which flattens the enemy but rather one that integrates him."

The commission recommended that future military aid should be conditional on an improving human rights situation in El Salvador, including "termination of the activities of the so-called death squads, as well as vigorous action against those guilty of crimes and the prosecution to the extent possible of past offenders." These were essentially the same conditions of the certification law. Kissinger had opposed the conditionality provision; it was included at the insistence of the Democratic members of the commission.* But the potential impact of the conditions on the Salvadoran military was undercut by Chairman

---

*In addition to Kissinger, the other members were: Nicholas F. Brady, former Republican senator from New Jersey; Henry G. Cisneros, Democratic mayor of San Antonio; William P. Clements, former Democratic governor of Texas; Carlos F. Diaz-Alejandro, professor of economics at Yale; Wilson S. Johnson, president of the National Federation of Independent Business; Lane Kirkland, president of the AFL-CIO; Richard Scammon, the political scientist; John Silber, president of Boston University; Potter Stewart, retired associate justice of the Supreme Court; Robert Strauss, former chairman of the Democratic party; and Dr. William B. Walsh, founder and president of Project Hope, an international medical care and education organization. The commission's formal name was the National Bipartisan Commission on Central America; there were six Democrats and six Republicans. That it was widely referred to as the Kissinger commission was a reflection of Mr. Kissinger's personality and of the fact that he was chairman.

Kissinger and two other members of the commission, Nicholas F. Brady and John Silber. Dissenting from the majority opinion, the three argued that the conditions should not be imposed if doing so would result in a victory by the guerrillas.

The commission report declared that the conditions linking military aid to an improving human rights situation "should be seriously enforced." There was no reason to believe they would be, and on the basis of past performance, every reason to believe they would not.

17

ONE MORE TIME

THERE was at least one consistent element in the U.S. policy in El Salvador: the collective hand wringing about the level of violence. "Let me make clear," Assistant Secretary of State Enders said during the first certification hearings, "the control of violence is at the center of our relationship with the Salvadoran government." Six months later Reagan dispatched Undersecretary of Defense Fred C. Iklé to warn the Salvadoran military that U.S. military assistance would be terminated unless the human rights situation improved. At about the same time the Salvadoran high command got the warning from General Vernon Walters, the tough-talking conservative who was Reagan's ambassador at large. The purpose of Walters's meeting with the Salvadoran commanders, according to a diplomat who was in El Salvador at the time, "was to tell the goddamn military that if they didn't cut out these human rights violations, they were going to goddamn well pay some terrible price, and that the American military, although they're good friends, they couldn't possibly, they couldn't assess the ultimate damage that's going to be done to the Salvadoran military if they didn't cut that shit out." Six months after that even Secretary of State Shultz assured Congress that if the Salvadoran armed forces "don't clean up their act, the support is going to dry up, and they've been told that and they know that and that will happen."

They might have been told, but they knew it wouldn't happen. And it didn't. The Reagan administration lacked either the power or the will to convince the Salvadoran military to reform. The administration's actions spoke louder than its stern lectures. The financial spigot was never turned off; indeed, it was opened wider.

Within a few months of his arrival in El Salvador Ambassador Pickering, who was appearing to be more in the mold of Robert White than of Deane Hinton, went to the press with the evidence, which had long been known to the United States, that the death squads were run by senior military officers. The names of the majors, lieutenant colonels, and colonels were publicly released. Many of them were the same officers who had been transferred out of command positions or to foreign embassies under pressure from the Carter administration in December 1980. They had returned after Reagan had become President and the pressure to clean up the military had eased.

It wasn't just the military that had tightened its grip on the tiny country during the Reagan administration, but the most conservative elements, officers with "fascist" ideology, as even ranking U.S. officials described their political beliefs. Colonel Nicolás Carranza, the oligarchy's chief representative within the armed forces, was named head of the notorious Treasury Police. "He's not a thug; he's the Gestapo," said a U.S. diplomat. Ambassador Pickering, in an off-the-record comment to a reporter, described Carranza as a "fascist."* Lieutenant Colonel Mario Denis Morán, who had been present at the Sheraton Hotel when Hammer and Pearlman were murdered and whose bodyguard was one of the triggermen, was returned from diplomatic "exile"—where he had been sent after the murders—and given command of the garrison at Zacatecoluca, where the churchwomen's case was being investigated. Colonel Jorge Adalberto Cruz, one of D'Aubuisson's staunchest comrades, had command of troops in Morazán, a province where the guerrillas were particularly strong. Lieutenant Colonel Roberto Mauricio Stabén, who had been arrested along with D'Aubuisson for plotting a coup in 1980, was the executive officer of the cavalry unit. As such, noted Christopher Dickey, he was "responsible for patrolling—if not contributing to—the famous death squad dumping ground at El Playón a few miles from its headquarters."

The Reagan administration had tolerated the death squads for three years. And when, in late 1983, it began to denounce them publicly for what they were—part of the military—it stopped far short of taking action to match the rhetoric. During a visit to El Salvador in December 1983 Vice President Bush gave the Salvadorans a list of more than twenty-five military officers and civilians involved in the death squad activities. U.S. aid would be cut off if actions weren't taken against the individuals, Bush warned. The Salvadorans ignored the warning, responding with the military's time-honored

---

*Yet the CIA was paying Carranza more than $90,000 a year, a practice that had begun in the late 1970's, according to a story by Philip Taubman in *The New York Times* on March 22, 1984.

method of protecting its own. None of the officers named was criminally punished for his death squad activities. None was even discharged. The most severe "sanctions"—and then only for a very few —were transfer to attaché posts abroad or reassignment to key command posts. That there were no actions against other officers involved with death squads is understandable when one realizes the point with which Christopher Dickey concluded his article about the Salvadoran death squads: "And if the web of complicity tying the armed forces to death squad violence ever did unravel, you have to ask yourself, who would be left to fight the war?" Dickey's observation is a reminder that it is not entirely accurate to talk about "right-wing" death squads; though the officers commanding them and the businessmen funding them do have rightist political views, they should be described as "military" death squads.

Top administration officials, even the President himself, gave tacit approval to the ineffective actions by the military high command against the fascist commanders, the death squad leaders. They blamed the death squad activities on the guerrillas. "We learned some of the notorious elements in the death squads are in fact enjoying the protection of the communist guerrillas," declared Iklé, the number three man in the Pentagon, who was in El Salvador for twenty-four hours in late November 1983—when the links between the military and the death squads were finally being publicly acknowledged. "It is not the first time in history that fascists become the tools and accomplices of Leninist oppressors." Elliott Abrams was with Iklé, and he gave the more vicious elements within the Salvadoran military another green light. Three months earlier Abrams had insisted, "I really don't know who the death squads are." Now he asserted that the members of the death squads "are fairly well known." He blamed their continued existence on the guerrillas. "There's no action taken by the far left because they like to see Salvadoran society divided."

Abrams's statement caused the *Boston Globe* to editorialize: "Abrams is supposedly the voice of human rights in the Reagan Administration but he has consistently betrayed that trust. Rather than being an advocate of human rights policy in El Salvador, he has become apologist and smokescreen for a panoply of Administration Central America policies, many of which contradict human rights."

President Reagan went even farther toward exonerating the military death squads a few weeks later. Answering questions from schoolchildren on C-Span, a cable television network, Reagan said that some of the murders attributed to the rightists might actually be carried out by guerrillas who know "the right wing will be blamed for it."

Reagan had sent another clear message to the Salvadoran military a few days earlier, when he vetoed a congressional bill that would have extended the certification law, which had expired. (As for the Kissinger commission's recommendation that military aid be linked to an improving human rights situation, the White House said that Reagan "would be inclined" to ignore it.)

"Certification was in a way a charade," noted Laurence R. Birns, director of the liberal Council on Hemispheric Affairs. But, he added, "it was a charade that saved lives in that just before and after each certification the death tolls went down."

Congress also has to share some of the blame for the tragedy in El Salvador. The administration made a mockery of the certification law, but Congress was unable or unwilling to make it tougher. Congress didn't give the administration all the aid it wanted for El Salvador, but it did give enough so that the Salvadoran military felt no real pressure to reform itself.

If there were a phrase to describe the U.S. policy in El Salvador—and much of the congressional and public attitude toward it—it might well be "one more time." There was always the threat to cut off aid "if" . . . if the killers of the churchwomen weren't brought to justice, if the killers of Hammer and Pearlman weren't prosecuted, if Salvadoran military officers weren't disciplined, if there wasn't a significant reduction in violence. "Congress says one more massacre and no more aid. That was ten massacres ago," a Foreign Service officer appalled by the level of violence in El Salvador told me one day when I asked why he didn't think our threats to cut off aid had any impact.

Or as Senator Leahy, his voice rising in indignation, shot back after Secretary of State Shultz had assured the senators that the Salvadorans knew if they didn't improve their human rights performance, they would lose aid: "It is an open and shut case. El Salvador is thumbing its nose at us. It is saying, 'Give us a billion dollars and go to hell.' "

REVOLUTIONS are unsettling, but not inevitably Communist," *The New York Times* noted in an editorial. "If Communist, they are not inevitably pro-Soviet. If pro-Soviet, they are not irreversible. Only the Red Army keeps Eastern Europe Communist; Chinese and Yugoslav Communists have become America's friends. The idea that the whole world is tilting from right to left and threatening to bury the Americans in a Marxist avalanche is a dangerous delusion—just one more doctrine."

It is a doctrine that should—indeed, must—be discarded if the

United States is to have a sound foreign policy in El Salvador, as well as in other countries where revolutions are inevitable.

Among the leaders of the Salvadoran revolution are Marxists and hard-line Leninists, who would try to establish a dictatorship that represses human rights and crushes the human spirit. But within the opposition there are also many democrats. The challenge for U.S. policy is to work with and bolster the latter. The United States has worked hard to bring the Salvadoran right, including D'Aubuisson, into the political process. Surely the United States can reach out with the same effort to the left. A leftist government does not necessarily have to be anti-American and pro-Soviet. It probably would not be.

". . . I don't think the Soviets are very popular in Latin America," Jeane Kirkpatrick observed soon after being named ambassador to the United Nations. She's right.

But the United States won't have many friends in El Salvador or elsewhere either if it continues to prop up governments that brutally repress their own people. The debate should not be on whether the United States can achieve a military victory in El Salvador but rather on why we are seeking one. Why are we there? Can we accomplish what we profess to want, and above all, is our conduct morally justifiable in terms of the values the United States was founded to represent?

NOTES

The following notes are designed to supplement the attributions that appear in the text. I have not, however, identified the location of every statement and fact; to do so would result in a note section almost as long as the body of the book. As noted in the introduction, I relied heavily on the dispatches in *The New York Times* and *The Washington Post*, and except in a few instances, I have not footnoted them here. When there is not a full bibliographical reference in the notes, it will be found in the Bibliography.

---

1 THE STORY NOT TOLD

Ms. Foote and Mr. Bushnell testified before the Subcommittee on Foreign Operations of the House Committee on Appropriations on March 25, 1980. Their statements are as they appear in the transcript that was provided under the Freedom of Information Act (FOIA). The killings described in the paragraph beginning "On February 28, in the village of Villa Victoria . . ." are from a "Submission by Amnesty International to the Inter-America Commission on Human Rights of the Organization of American States," dated March 21, 1980. The attacks on the church noted in that paragraph were compiled by the Salvadoran archdiocese's legal aid office. Secretary of State Muskie's remarks were recorded by William Ford, who took notes of the meeting. They were inserted into the record during hearings before the Senate Foreign Relations Committee on March 18 and April 9, 1981. The statistics about the sizes of the various countries are from the *World Almanac*. The 1977 observation about U.S. interests in El Salvador by the American ambassador was made during hearings before the Subcommittee on International Organizations of the House Committee on International Relations on July 21, 1977, p. 11 ("Religious Persecution in El Salvador"; hereafter referred to as "Religious Persecution hearings —1977"). The head of the Latin American bureau at the State Department made his remark to the same subcommittee on March 9, 1977, p. 4 ("The Recent Presidential Elections in El Salvador: Implications for U.S. Foreign Policy." Hereafter referred to as "Election hearings—1977"). President Reagan's remark about the threat to "eventually, North America" was made at a news conference on March 7, 1981. The U.S. aid figures come from the Agency for International Development, published in *U.S. Overseas Loans and Grants and Assistance from International Organizations.* The remarks of Morales Ehrlich and Ambassador Lozano: "Election hearings—1977." Waghelstein's statement was during a briefing with reporters in San Salvador, a transcript of which was provided to the author. Abrams made his statement about Nicaragua to subcommittees on Human Rights and International Organizations and on Western Hemisphere Affairs of the House Committee on Foreign Affairs on August 3, 1983, p. 32.

2 ROOTS OF THE REVOLUTION

Major Harris's dispatch is quoted in Anderson, *Matanza,* pp. 83–84. Income distribution and other demographic figures in this chapter were compiled from a number of sources, including *Appendix, Nomination of Ambassador Robert E. White,* before Senate Foreign Relations Committee, February 5, 1980; "Evaluation of Sites and Services Projects, the Evidence from El Salvador," World Bank Staff Working Papers, Number 549 (1982); "El Salvador, Demographic Issues and Prospects," World Bank (1979); and the State Department's "Country Reports on Human Rights Practices." An important source for landownership statistics is Simon and Stephens, *El Salvador Land Reform 1980–1981, Impact Audit.* That only 6 percent earned more than $240 a month was reported by Christopher Dickey of *The Washington Post,* October 3, 1983. The number of doctors is from Dunkerley, *The Long War,* p. 68. Nutritional statistics, for El Salvador and other Latin American countries, are from the above-mentioned sources, plus "World's Children Data Sheet," prepared by the Population Reference Bureau, Inc., for the International Year of the Child 1979. The observations of the European ambassador are recorded in Ambassador Devine's book, *El Salvador: Embassy Under Attack.* The best single history of the taking of the Indian lands is found in Browning, *El Salvador.* The holdings of the Salvadoran oligarchy are detailed in Baloyra, *El Salvador in Transition,* pp. 22–32. Two valuable articles about the Salvadoran oligarchy were written by Paul Hoeffel; "The Eclipse of the Oligarchs," *The New York Times Magazine* (September 6, 1981), and "Autumn of the Oligarchs," in Schulz and Graham, *Revolution and Counter Revolution in Central America and the Carribbean.*

3 NO DEMOCRACY HERE

Hernández Martínez's prohibition on migration: Armstrong and Shenk, *El Salvador: The Face of Revolution,* p. 31; the march by blackshirts: Dunkerley, *The Long War,* p. 31; his statement about barefoot children: Didion, *Salvador,* p. 53. Duarte's interview with Buckley, "Letter from El Salvador," *The New Yorker* (June 22, 1981). Partial transcripts of the electoral fraud are in "Election hearings—1977." Unless otherwise noted, all congressional testimony referred to in this chapter are in those hearings and in "Religious Persecution hearings—1977." Vance's statement to Foreign Policy Association is quoted in Feinberg, *Central America: International Dimensions of the Crisis*, p. 81. A list of multinational development bank loans to El Salvador, and the U.S. position on them, is found in *Human Rights and U.S. Foreign Policy, Hearings Before the Subcommittee on International Organizations of the House Committee on Foreign Affairs*, 1979, p. 325. "Operation Rutilio" is described in Brockman, *The Word Remains*, p. 28; Lernoux, *Cry of the People*, pp. 61–62; Armstrong and Shenk, *The Face of Revolution*, pp. 93–94. Devine's role in securing the IDB loan is described in his book (p. 11). The bishops' statement about the *Ley de Orden*: "Human Rights in El Salvador—1978. Report of the Findings of an Investigatory Mission," Unitarian Universalist Service Committee, p. 37. Devine's statement about the *Ley de Orden* was reported by Riding, *The New York Times*, May 8, 1978. The Salvadoran soldier's description of the torture and murder of Richardson is contained in a cable released under the FOIA. Devine's views on human rights are in his book, p. 194. Additional statements in this chapter by Devine, and Lozano, were made in interviews with the author. Carter's use of the advisory board for diplomatic appointments is described in an article by Martin Tolchin in *The New York Times*, May 18, 1979, p. A15. The statistics about percentages of political appointments were reported in the "Briefing" column on the "Washington Talk" page of *The New York Times* on August 16, 1983. For a history of the creation of the human rights bureau at State, see Schoultz, *Human Rights and United States Policy Toward Latin America*, pp. 123–26. Todman's speech and the reaction were reported by Riding in *The New York Times*, May 8, 1978; and the Washington Office on Latin America, "Update," January–February 1978. The statement about the May downpours is quoted in Brockman, p. 156.

4 THE ARMY: THE LAW AND ABOVE THE LAW

Details of the murders of Hammer, Pearlman, and Viera are from AIFLD and cables. Hinton's statement about General Nutting's visit was made during a lengthy interview with James LeMoyne and Christopher Dickey at the ambassador's residence in San Salvador on April 28, 1983. A tape recording of the interview was provided to the author; hereafter referred to as "Hinton interview—April 1983"). D'Aubuisson's statement reported in *The New York Times*, October 21, 1982, p. A12. Córdoba incident related by former Ambassador Murat Williams. Gómez testified before the House Subcommittee on Inter-American Affairs, February 25, 1982. Christian's article, "El Salvador's Divided Military," appeared in *The Atlantic* (June 1983). Messing's view about corruption reported in the *Chicago Tribune*, March 29, 1983, p. 1. AID's evaluation of Salvadoran security forces: *Termination Phase-Out Study, Public Safety Project*, May 1974. OAS report: OEA/Ser.L/V/II.46; doc.23 rev.1; November 17, 1978. State's view of ORDEN: *Central America at the Crossroads, Hearings Before the Subcommittee on Inter-American Affairs of the House Foreign Affairs Committee*, September 11 and 12, 1979, p. 17. Kirkpatrick's statement was to a luncheon meeting of Members of Congress for Peace Through Law, February 26, 1981 (hereafter referred to as "MCPL—February 1981").

5 THE CHURCH: PERSECUTION AND REVOLUTION

Major sources for this chapter are: Lernoux, *Cry of the People,* especially chapter III: "Be a Patriot (in El Salvador) and Kill a Priest!"; two articles by Alan Riding: "The Sword and Cross," in *The New York Review of Books* (May 28, 1981); and "Latin Church in Siege," in *The New York Times Magazine* (May 6, 1979); and Brockman, *The Word Remains: A Life of Oscar Romero,* which, as the title implies, contains considerable detail about the archbishop's thinking and life. (Most of Romero's statements in this chapter and elsewhere in this book can be found in Brockman's account.) Romero's statement about having "evolved rather than changed" was made to Riding and reported in *The New York Times,* February 26, 1978. The Lawyers Committee for International Human Rights, in New York, has issued several reports about the murders of the four American churchwomen and the subsequent investigations. In addition, many of the statements by the National Guard soldiers who were charged with the murders are based on my examination of the court documents. Lewis's column appeared in *The New York Times,* March 29, 1981. White's statement about the involvement of higher-ups was to the Subcommittee on International Development of the House Committee on Banking, Finance, and Urban Affairs, July 23, 1981. Hinton's statement about higher-ups was made in "Hinton Interview—April 1983." Exchange between Studds and White is in *Presidential Certification on El Salvador,* Vol. I, *Hearings Before the Subcommittee on Inter-American Affairs of the House Committee on Foreign Affairs,* February and March, 1982. Hinton's rejection of the pope's plea for negotiations was reported by Juan Vasquez in the *Los Angeles Times,* March 8, 1983, p. 1.

6 THE OPPOSITION

Among the more comprehensive articles about the Salvadoran left that were used in writing this chapter: Riding, "Salvador Rebels: Five-Sided Alliance Searching for New, Moderate Image," *The New York Times,* March 16, 1982, p. 1 (including thumbnail sketches of various leaders); Dickey, "Unruly Salvadoran Left Appears to Coalesce," *The Washington Post,* July 8, 1983, p. 1; Leiken, "Anatomy of Resistance," *Worldview* (June 1983); Zaid, "Enemy Colleagues," *Dissent* (February 1982); Vallecillos, *"Fuerzas Sociales y Cambio Social en El Salvador,"* *Estudios Centroamericanos* (July–August 1979); and Christian, "The Other Side," *The New Republic* (October 24, 1983). White's testimony was to the Subcommittee on Inter-American Affairs, February 23, 1982, p. 228. Poor's article appeared on the Op-Ed page of *The New York Times* on March 27, 1981. Biographical information about the leftist leaders was compiled from a number of sources including profiles prepared by one of the U.S. intelligence agencies. Kirkpatrick's remarks about the Soviets was made to MCPL luncheon. Chavez's account of the Quebrada Seca killings appeared in *The New York Times,* June 4, 1983. The incident at the Costa Rican embassy is recounted by Devine in his book. The Gilman-Bray exchange is in "Election hearings—1977." The incident about the flag being carried across the stage is in Montgomery, *Revolution in El Salvador,* p. 128. Ana Guadalupe Martínez's account of her torture is in the 1978 OAS *Report on the Situation of Human Rights in El Salvador,* pp. 74–75. Krauss's four articles about his experiences in Chalatenango appeared in the *Atlanta Constitution,* February 7–10, 1982. Accounts of the massacre at the Sumpul River by Father Gallagher and the presbytery appear in Gettleman et al., *El Salvador: Central America in the New Cold War,* p. 148, and the *Congressional Record,* September 24, 1980, pp. S13375–79. *The Washington Post* front-page story about Nueva Trinidad appeared on February 4, 1982. Dillon's account about the guerrillas' executing eighteen appeared on the front page of *The Washington Post,* May 13, 1983; his account of the bodies discarded in the garbage dump appeared in the *Miami Herald,* May 11, 1983.

---

7 THE COUP: A LOST OPPORTUNITY

Many details of the coup and the weeks that followed were provided in interviews with René Guerra y Guerra, Román Mayorga Quiroz, Mario Andino, Héctor Dada, Guillermo Ungo, Rubén Zamora, and Frank Devine. While in El Salvador, I had discussed the events with Colonels Gutiérrez and Majano. The coup and subsequent events are examined by Devine in his book and Montgomery, *Revolution in El Salvador.* A detailed but yet unpublished account of the coup has been written by Dermot Keogh, professor of history at the University College, Cork, Ireland. Vaky testified to the House Subcommittee on Inter-American Affairs, September 11, 1979. That the CIA acted to block Guerra y Guerra from serving on the junta, see Montgomery, p. 196. The armed forces' Proclamation of October 15, 1979, is reprinted as Appendix II in *Report on Human Rights in El Salvador,* prepared by Americas Watch and the American Civil Liberties Union in January 1982. The State Department's accounts of the collapse of the first junta are in "Country Reports on Human Rights Practices for 1980," p. 427; ". . . for 1981," p. 424; ". . . for 1982," p. 492. The State Department's assessment of the strength of the guerrilla organizations is in *Hearings Before the House Subcommittee on Inter-American Affairs,* September 11 and 12, 1979.

---

8 A PLEA IGNORED

The statements by Bushnell to the Subcommittee on Foreign Operations of the House Committee on Appropriations on March 25, 1980, and the remarks of the members of the committee are as they appear in the transcript that was provided under the FOIA. The resignation letters and statements are excerpted in a report prepared by Cynthia Arnson and Delia Miller in June 1980 for the Institute for Policy Studies. The reports by Becklund and Pyes about D'Aubuisson's role in the murder of Archbishop Romero appeared in the *Los Angeles Times* and *Albuquerque Journal* on April 15, 1983. The details about Romero's last days and mass are in Brockman's book.

9 SEARCH FOR AN ELUSIVE CENTER

Feinberg's description of the U.S. role in El Salvador is in his book, *Central America: International Dimensions of the Crisis*, p. 74. Dickey's account of Romero's funeral appeared in *The Washington Post*, March 31, 1980; Treaster's in *The New York Times* on the same day. The bishops' statement was reported in a cable from the embassy. White's statement that Reagan was "right to concern himself with denying communism a new foothold . . ." is from his article, "Central America: The Problem That Won't Go Away," *The New York Times Magazine* (July 18, 1982). His statement that "we'd have a revolution here even if . . ." was made to reporters during a briefing in May 1980, and frequently repeated. Valuable reports on the Salvadoran land reform: "El Salvador Land Reform 1980–1981," by Simon and Stephens of Oxfam America; "Conference on Land Tenure in Central America," by the Washington Office on Latin America, March 1981; and two by Checchi and Company (under contract with AID), in December 1981 and January 1983. Nicaragua's land reform is examined in Marchetti and Deere "The Worker-Peasant Alliance in the First Year of the Nicaraguan Agrarian Reform," and Collins, *What Difference Could a Revolution Make?* The Nicaraguan and Salvadoran land reforms are compared by Carmen Diana Deere, a professor at the University of Massachusetts, Amherst, in "Comparative Analysis of Agrarian Reform in El Salvador and Nicaragua." On AIFLD's activities, in addition to Agee's book, *Inside the Company: CIA Diary*, there are two reports prepared by the Ecumenical Program for Interamerican Communication and Action (EPICA): Forche and Wheaton, "History and Motivations of U.S. Involvement in the Control of the Peasant Movement in El Salvador," and Sussman, "AIFLD: U.S. Trojan Horse in Latin America and the Caribbean." Prosterman's argument about Douglas MacArthur and land reform is contained in a letter he sent to *Barron's* on January 28, 1981 in response to an editorial in that newspaper. The El Peñón incident was related to me and Dickey, who reported it in *The Washington Post*, December 18, 1980; San Francisco Guajoyo was reported by the *Miami Herald*, June 5, 1980 (and in the classified "Memorandum to File"). Kirkpatrick's statement was made during the MCPL luncheon. Gómez testified to the House Subcommittee on Inter-American Affairs on February 25, 1982.

10 TRANSITION

Many of the details of the capture and killing of the FDR leaders are from embassy cables. The disfigurement of Chacón and Alvarez is described in Armstrong and Shenk, *El Salvador: The Face of Revolution*. Oakes's column appeared in *The New York Times*, April 3, 1981. The round-table discussion with *The New York Times* appeared on December 7, 1980. The Productive Alliance meeting with Kirkpatrick and others was reported in *The New York Times*, November 29, 1980. Kirkpatrick's statement about living and dying by the sword was made during the round-table discussion. Carter's diary entry about Duarte's becoming president is in his presidential memoirs, *Keeping Faith*, p. 585. The *Washington Post* story about the "boat landing" appeared January 15, 1981; *Newsweek*'s, January 26, 1981.

11 FROM A REVOLUTION TO THE COLD WAR

The news conference at which Reagan stopped short of saying that a coup would result in a cut-off in aid and "I inherited it" was reported in *The New York Times,* March 7, 1981, p. 1. Percy's statement was reported in *The Washington Post,* February 20, 1981, p. A20. Enders's statement was to the Subcommittee on Foreign Operations of the House Appropriations Committee, February 1, 1982, and to the House Subcommittee on Inter-American Affairs the next day, p. 35. The *Miami Herald* editorial appeared February 3, 1982. The view of the New York Foreign Policy Association was reported in the *Miami Herald,* March 7, 1982. Farer's article appeared in *The New York Review of Books* (March 19, 1981) and was reprinted in Gettleman et al., *El Salvador: Central America in the New Cold War.* Kirkpatrick's remarks about General Hernández Martínez were made in her article, "The Hobbes Problem: Order, Authority, and Legitimacy in Central America," published in *American Enterprise Institute 1980 Public Policy Week Papers,* p. 133. Her statement about congressmen who would like to see Marxists in power was reported in a Reuters dispatch in *The New York Times,* May 5, 1983. Hinton's statement "We've never been looking for a military victory" was reported in *The Washington Post,* January 30, 1982, p. 1. The views of Duarte and the Salvadoran military commanders about military aid were reported in *The New York Times,* February 21 and 25, 1981.

12 PURGE

The *Washington Post* article appeared on November 28, 1982. A general article about Reagan's ambassadors in Central America is by Dickey, "The Proconsuls," *Rolling Stone* (August 18, 1983). Enders's activities in Cambodia are examined in considerable detail by Shawcross in his book *Sideshow.* "The Can-Do Bombardier" was the title of a column by Sydney H. Schanberg in *The New York Times,* February 6, 1982. Enders was also the subject of an article, "The Tallest Gun in Foggy Bottom," by Phil Keisling, which appeared in *The Washington Monthly* November 1982. The *Boston Globe* and *New York Times* editorials appeared November 15, 1983. Lodge's views about the firing of Peter Bell appeared in his article on the Op-Ed page of *The New York Times,* December 17, 1983. For a longer examination of Bell's ouster and the naming of Doherty to the search committee, see Auferhide, "Reagan's Poor Excuse," *In These Times* (February 8–14, 1984), p. 11. The Abrams-Yatron exchange was on August 3, 1983, as were Abrams's statements about refugees being returned to El Salvador. The Abrams-Tsongas exchange was before the Senate Foreign Relations Committee on August 3, 1982, p. 42, as was Abrams's statement that the army had "several hundred prisoners . . . ," p. 17. His statement about "several hundred officers" having been dismissed or jailed was made during *Hearings and Markup before the House Committee on Foreign Affairs, July 29, 1982,* p. 93. For the Mexicans' view of Gavin's appointment, see, Juan M. Vasquez, "U.S. Envoy Gavin Presents Credentials in Mexico," *Los Angeles Times,* June 6, 1981; also, Vasquez, "Gavin Defends His Efforts as Envoy to

Mexico," *Los Angeles Times,* September 16, 1982. Kirkpatrick's remarks about being "rather overbearing" were made to the MCPL luncheon.

13 BLAMING OUTSIDERS

The text of the 1965 white paper was published in *The New York Times,* February 28, 1965. Secretary of State Kellogg's charges about Communists in Mexico are recounted in Ronald Steel, *Walter Lippmann and the American Century* (Boston: Little, Brown 1980), p. 237. Petras's article appeared in *The Nation* (March 28, 1981); Dinges's article appeared in the *Los Angeles Times,* March 17, 1981; McGehee's in *The Nation* (April 11, 1981); Kwitny's in *The Wall Street Journal,* June 8, 1981; Kaiser's in *The Washington Post,* June 9, 1981. Pyes's article about D'Aubuisson's role in supplying some of the white paper documents appeared in the *Albuquerque Journal,* December 22, 1983. Riding's article about weapons moving through Honduras appeared in *The New York Times,* February 5, 1982. The *Time* magazine cover story was March 22, 1982. A *Staff Report of the Subcommittee on Oversight and Evaluation of the House Permanent Select Committee on Intelligence* was printed on September 22, 1982; the matter of the ships and $17 million is on pp. 8–9. Pastor's observation about the command and control center is from his article in *The Atlantic.* The CIA's operation in El Salvador was revealed in an article by Philip Taubman, "U.S. Said to Have Large Spy Network in Latin America," *The New York Times,* March 20, 1983, p. 16. The *New York Times* editorial appeared February 19, 1981; the *Miami Herald*'s November 9, 1981.

14 WAGING WAR, REJECTING PEACE

A valuable comparison of the advisers in El Salvador and Vietnam is an unpublished thesis, "U.S. Military Advisers in Vietnam and Central America," by Andrew Owens Moore, submitted to Princeton University, May 12, 1983. Previous uses of 506 (a) authority are listed in the *Congressional Record,* March 2, 1982, p. E665. The statistics about multinational bank loans were provided by the Center for International Policy in Washington, D.C., which is the best single source of information about how the United States voted on the loans to South Africa and Nicaragua, as well as to other countries. For a study of the War Powers Act, see: *The War Powers Resolution, A Special Study of the Committee on Foreign Affairs of the House of Representatives,* April 15, 1982; and "War Powers Resolution: Presidential Compliance," prepared by the Congressional Research Service of the Library of Congress, Issue Brief Number IB81050, November 22, 1983. The GAO's report *Applicability of Certain U.S. Laws That Pertain to U.S. Military Involvement in El Salvador,* GAO/ID-82-53, July 27, 1982. Senator Glenn's charge about "tortured logic" was made during Senate Foreign Relations Committee hearings, March 18, 1981, p. 69. The *U.S. News & World Report* article appeared on October 11, 1982, p. 85. Safire's columns appeared in *The New York Times* on February 26, 1981, and June 18, 1982. The

Studds-Enders and Yatron-Enders exchanges were during hearings before the House Committee on Foreign Affairs, September 24, 1981, pp. 35, 16.

15 ELECTIONS SI, DEMOCRACY NO

Solarz's comment was reported in The *New York Times,* July 17, 1981, p. 1. The *Wall Street Journal* article about Casey and the CIA appeared on July 16, 1982, followed by an article in *The New York Times,* July 30. The number of voters as 1,551,687 is from a computer print-out from the Central Elections Council dated April 14, 1982. Media coverage of the election was examined by Jack Spence, "Media Coverage of El Salvador's Election," *Socialist Review* (April 1983). For a view of the media coverage in El Salvador in general, see the July/August 1983 issue of the *NACLA Report on the Americas;* Cynthia Brown and Fernando Moreno, "Force-Feeding the Press in El Salvador," *The Nation,* (April 1981); "Friendly Fire in San Salvador," *Columbia Journalism Review* (September/October 1982), p. 9; Michael Massing, "About-face on El Salvador," *Columbia Journalism Review,* (November/December 1983), p. 42. (My response to the article appears in *Columbia Journalism Review* [January/February 1984], p. 60). For a catalogue of media exclamations about the elections, see *Hearings and Markup Before the House Committee on Foreign Affairs and Its Subcommittee on Inter-American Affairs,* July and August 1982, pp. 504–07. I. F. Stone's reaction to the media's failure to protest more loudly the killing of the Dutch journalists appeared in "Deathly Silence," *The Nation* (May 1, 1982), p. 515. The American observer delegation's report was printed by the Senate Foreign Relations Committee, November 1982. Schuster's story appeared in *The Wall Street Journal,* March 17, 1982, p. 1. White's observation about "numbered ballots" was made in his article in *The New York Times Magazine* (July 18, 1982). Articles about the charges of an inflated vote total appeared in *The New York Times,* June 3, 1982 (Op-Ed page, "Salvador Vote Inflated, Study Is Said to Find," by Thomas Sheehan), June 4, 5, and 14, 1982; and in *The Washington Post,* June 19, 1982. For an attack on my reporting of the election fraud charges, see "Bonner's World," *National Review* (July 9, 1982). The two reports by the Catholic university about the inflated vote total are: *"Las Elecciones y la Unidad Nacional: Diez Tesis Criticas,"* Estudios Centroamericanos (April 1982), p. 233; and *"Las Elecciones de 1982. Realidades detras de las Apariencias,"* Estudios Centroamericanos (May/June 1982), p. 573. Carbaugh's contention that it took three minutes to vote is in *Hearing Before the Senate Committee on Foreign Relations,* August 3, 1982, p. 267. Pyes's comprehensive examination of the political right in El Salvador appeared in the *Albuquerque Journal,* December 18–22, 1983; Becklund's in the *Los Angeles Times,* December 18 and 19, 1983. D'Aubuisson's remark about the Germans' being "very intelligent" for having killed the Jews was quoted in a column by Mary McGrory, *The Washington Post,* April 27, 1982. That the U.S. intelligence agencies altered their biographical profiles of D'Aubuisson is reported in the *Staff Report of Subcommittee on Oversight and Evaluation of the House Permanent Select Committee on Intelligence,* p. 14. Wright's comments were reported in *The New York Times,* April 10, 1982. My front-page story about the land reform appeared on May 24, 1982. Hinton's charge that I was an "advocate journalist" appeared in

The New York Times, June 12, 1982. The *Wall Street Journal* editorial appeared February 10, 1982. Colonel Waghelstein's expletive to Dinges was reported in the *Columbia Journalism Review* (September/October 1982), p. 9. The La Florida incident is detailed in letters and statements by the Episcopal Church Center, in New York.

16 QUIET DIPLOMACY

Fiallos testified before the Foreign Operations Subcommittee of the House Appropriations Committee on April 29, 1981; reported in *The Nation,* May 16, 1981. The *Frontline* program, "Crossfire El Salvador," originally aired on PBS on June 27, 1983. Abrams's statement to the Western Hemisphere committee is on p. 46; Studds's on p. 41. The material about the Argentine advisers working with the Salvadoran military is from the Pyes-Becklund articles noted in the previous chapter. Hoge's article about the massacre at the Río Lempa appeared in *The New York Times,* June 8, 1981. The material about the killings at Cerros de San Pedro was provided by the Washington Office on Latin America. North's article appeared in *Newsweek* (April 25, 1983). Bourgois's article appeared in *The Washington Post,* February 14, 1982; he testified before House Subcommittee on Inter-American Affairs on February 23, 1982. Enders's testimony about the Mozote massacre was to the House Subcommittee on Inter-American Affairs on February 2, 1982, and to the Senate Foreign Relations Committee on February 8. Schanberg's column appeared in *The New York Times,* February 6, 1982, p. 19. Crossette's "News Analysis" appeared in *The New York Times,* February 4, 1982, p. 1. The *Wall Street Journal* editorial appeared on February 10, 1982. Three published volumes of House hearings directly relate to certification: *Hearings Before the Subcommittee on Inter-American Affairs,* February 2, 23, 25 and March 2, 1982; *Hearings and Markup Before the Committee on Foreign Affairs and Its Subcommittee on Inter-American Affairs,* June 2, 22; July 29; August 3, 10, and 17, 1982; *Hearings Before the Subcommittees on Human Rights and International Organizations and on Western Hemisphere Affairs,* February 4, 28 and March 7, 17, 1983. Senate Foreign Relations Committee hearings on certification: February 8 and March 11, 1982; August 3, 1982; February 2, 1983. At the time of the first certification, Americas Watch and the American Civil Liberties Union published a book, *Report on Human Rights in El Salvador.* The organizations followed with three supplements: July 20, 1982; January 20, 1983; and July 19, 1983. Enders's statement about the archbishop's legal aid office and about the "bias" of the Catholic university was made during *Hearings Before the Subcommittee on Inter-American Affairs,* February 2, 1982, p. 25; that the Documentation Center was a "leftwing organization" to the Senate Foreign Relations Committee, August 3, 1982, p. 76. Oberdorfer's story about the Green Cross cable and torture appeared in *The Washington Post,* July 26, 1982. Chavez's articles about the Las Hojas massacre appeared in *The New York Times,* February 28 and July 9, 1983. Moynihan's response to the Kissinger commission was reported in *The New York Times,* January 12, 1984. Former Ambassador Martin's observations appeared on the Op-Ed page of *The New York Times,* October 21, 1983. The *New York Times* editorial response to the Kissinger report appeared January 15, 1984. Hodding Carter's column appeared in *The Wall Street Journal,* January 19, 1984. The responses of the Salvadoran church and the Christian Democrats were reported in *The New York Times,* January 12, 1984.

17   ONE MORE TIME

Dickey's article about the Salvadoran death squads was in *The New Republic* (December 26, 1983). The *Boston Globe* editorial about Abrams appeared on November 15, 1983. The *New York Times* editorial about revolutions being "unsettling, but not inevitably Communist," appeared on July 24, 1983. Kirkpatrick's observation that the Soviets don't have much popular support was made during the MCPL luncheon.

BIBLIOGRAPHY

BOOKS

Agee, Philip. *Inside the Company: CIA Diary.* New York: Bantam Books, 1975.

Americas Watch Committee and the American Civil Liberties Union. *Report on Human Rights in El Salvador.* New York: Vintage Books, 1982.

Amnesty International. *Amnesty International Report 1982.* London: Amnesty International Publications, 1982.

———. *Amnesty International Report 1983.* London: Amnesty International Publications, 1983.

Anderson, Thomas P. *Matanza: El Salvador's Communist Revolt of 1932.* Lincoln: University of Nebraska Press, 1971.

———. *Politics in Central America.* New York: Praeger, 1982.

→ Armstrong, Robert, and Shenk, Janet. *El Salvador: The Face of Revolution.* Boston: South End Press, 1982.

Arnson, Cynthia. *El Salvador: A Revolution Confronts the United States.* Washington, D.C.: Institute for Policy Studies, 1982.

Baloyra, Enrique A. *El Salvador in Transition.* Chapel Hill: University of North Carolina Press, 1982.

Brockman, James R. *The Word Remains: A Life of Oscar Romero.* Maryknoll, N.Y.: Orbis Books, 1982.

Browning, David. *El Salvador: Landscape and Society.* Oxford: Clarendon Press, 1971.

→ Brzezinski, Zbigniew. *Power and Principle. Memoirs of the National Security Adviser, 1977–1981.* New York: Farrar Straus Giroux, 1983.

Buckley, Tom. *Violent Neighbors: El Salvador, Central America, and the United States.* New York: Times Books, 1984.

Carpio, Salvador Cayetano. *Secuestro y Capucha.* 6th ed. San Salvador: Editorial Universitaria Centroamericana, 1982.

Carter, Jimmy. *Keeping Faith: Memoirs of a President.* New York: Bantam Books, 1982.

Collins, Joseph, with Frances Moore Lappe and Nick Allen. *What Difference Could a Revolution Make? Food and Farming in the New Nicaragua.* San Francisco: Institute for Food and Development Policy, 1982.

Colindres, Eduardo. *Fundamentos Economicos De La Burguesia Salvadoreña.* San Salvador: Universidad Centroamericana José Simeón Cañas, 1977.

Devine, Frank J. *El Salvador: Embassy Under Attack.* New York: Vantage Press, 1981.

Didion, Joan. *Salvador.* New York: Simon & Schuster, 1983.

Dunkerley, James. *The Long War: Dictatorship and Revolution in El Salvador.* London: Junction Books, 1982.

El Salvador, A Country Study. Washington, D.C.: American University, 1979.

Erdozain, Placido. *Archbishop Romero: Martyr of Salvador,* trans. by John McFadden and Ruth Warner. Maryknoll, N.Y.: Orbis Books, 1981

Fagen, Richard R., and Pellicer, Olga, eds. *The Future of Central America: Policy Choices for the U.S. and Mexico.* Stanford: Stanford University Press, 1983.

Feinberg, Richard E. *The Intemperate Zone: The Third World Challenge to U.S. Foreign Policy.* New York: W. W. Norton & Company, 1983.

————, ed. *Central America: International Dimensions of the Crisis.* New York: Holmes & Meier Publishers, 1982.

Foreign Policy on Latin America 1970–1980. Boulder, Colo.: Westview Press, 1983.

Gettleman, Marvin E.; Lacefield, Patrick; Menashe, Louis; Mermelstein, David; and Radosh, Ronald, eds. *El Salvador: Central America in the New Cold War.* New York: Grove Press, 1981.

Hersh, Seymour M. *The Price of Power: Kissinger in the Nixon White House.* New York: Summit Books, 1983.

Keogh, Dermot. *Romero: El Salvador's Martyr.* Dublin, Ireland: Dominican Publications, 1981.

Kwitny, Jonathan. *Endless Enemies: The Making of an Unfriendly World.* New York: Congdon & Weed, 1984.

LaFeber, Walter. *Inevitable Revolutions: The United States in Central America.* New York: W. W. Norton & Company, 1983.

Leiken, Robert S. *Soviet Strategy in Latin America.* The Washington Papers/93, vol X. New York: Praeger, 1982.

————, ed. *Central America. Anatomy of Conflict.* New York: Pergamon Press, 1984.

Lernoux, Penny. *Cry of the People.* New York: Doubleday & Company, 1980.

McGehee, Ralph W. *Deadly Deceits: My 25 Years in the CIA.* New York: Sheridan Square Publications, 1983.

Millett, Richard. *Guardians of the Dynasty.* Maryknoll, N.Y.: Orbis Books, 1977.

Montgomery, Tommie Sue. *Revolution in El Salvador: Origins and Evolution.* Boulder, Colo.: Westview Press, 1982.

Newfarmer, Richard, ed. *From Gunboats to Diplomacy: New U.S. Policies for Latin America.* Baltimore: Johns Hopkins University Press, 1984.

The Report of the President's National Bipartisan Commission on Central America. New York: Macmillan Publishing Co., 1984.

Robbins, Carla Anne. *The Cuban Threat.* New York: McGraw-Hill Book Company, 1983.

Schoultz, Lars. *Human Rights and United States Policy Toward Latin America.* Princeton: Princeton University Press, 1981.

Schulz, Donald E., and Graham, Douglas H., eds. *Revolution and Counter Revolution in Central America and the Caribbean.* Boulder, Colo.: Westview Press, 1984.

Shawcross, William. *Sideshow: Kissinger, Nixon and the Destruction of Cambodia.* New York: Washington Square Press, 1979.

Vance, Cyrus. *Hard Choices: Critical Years in America's Foreign Policy.* New York: Simon & Schuster, 1983.

CONGRESSIONAL MATERIALS IN CHRONOLOGICAL ORDER

U.S. Congress. House. Committee on International Relations. *Human Rights in Nicaragua, Guatemala, and El Salvador: Implications for U.S. Policy. Hearings Before the Subcommittee on International Organizations,* 94th Congress, 2d session, June 8 and 9, 1976.

U.S. Congress. House. Committee on International Relations. *The Recent Presidential Elections in El Salvador: Implications for U.S. Foreign Policy. Hearings Before the Subcommittees on International Organizations and on Inter-American Affairs,* 95th Congress, 1st session, March 9 and 17, 1977.

U.S. Congress. House. Committee on International Relations. *Religious Persecution in El Salvador. Hearings Before the Subcommittee on International Organizations,* 95th Congress, 1st session, July 21 and 29, 1977.

U.S. Congress. House. Committee on Foreign Affairs. *Human Rights and U.S. Foreign Policy. Hearings Before the Subcommittee on International Organizations,* 96th Congress, 1st session, May 2, 10; June 21; July 12; and August 2, 1979.

U.S. Congress. House. Committee on Foreign Affairs. *Central America at the Crossroads. Hearings Before the Subcommittee on Inter-American Affairs,* 96th Congress, 1st session, September 11 and 12, 1979.

U.S. Congress. Senate. Committee on Foreign Relations. *Appendix. Nomination of Ambassador Robert E. White,* February 5, 1980.

U.S. Congress. House. Committee on Foreign Affairs. *Assessment of Conditions in Central America. Hearings Before the Subcommittee on Inter-American Affairs,* 96th Congress, 2d session, April 29 and May 20, 1980.

U.S. Congress. House. Committee on Foreign Affairs. *U.S. Policy Toward El Salvador. Hearings Before the Subcommittee on Inter-American Affairs,* 97th Congress, 1st session, March 5 and 11, 1981.

U.S. Congress. Senate. Committee on Foreign Relations. *The Situation in El Salvador,* 97th Congress, 1st session, March 18 and April 9, 1981.

U.S. Congress. House. Committee on Foreign Affairs. *Central America, 1981. Report,* 97th Congress, 1st session, March 1981.

U.S. Congress. House. Committee on Foreign Affairs. *U.S. Policy Options in El Salvador. Hearings Before the Committee on Foreign Affairs and Its Subcommittee on Inter-American Affairs,* 97th Congress, 1st session, September 24; November 5 and 19, 1981.

U.S. Congress. Senate. Committee on Foreign Relations. *Central America. Hearings Before the Subcommittee on Western Hemisphere Affairs,* 97th Congress, 1st session, December 14 and 15, 1981, and 2d session, February 1, 1982.

U.S. Congress. House. Committee on Foreign Affairs. *Salvadoran Refugees in Honduras. Hearing Before the Subcommittee on Inter-American Affairs,* 97th Congress, 1st session, December 17, 1981.

U.S. Congress. House. Committee on Foreign Affairs. *Presidential Certification on El Salvador,* Volume I. *Hearings Before the Subcommittee on Inter-American Affairs,* 97th Congress, 2d session, February 2, 23, 25 and March 2, 1982.

U.S. Congress. Senate. Committee on Foreign Relations. *Certification Concerning Military Aid to El Salvador. Hearings Before the Committee on Foreign Relations,* 97th Congress, 2d session, February 8 and March 11, 1982.

U.S. Congress. Senate. Committee on Foreign Relations. *El Salvador: The United States in the Midst of a Maelstrom. A Report to the Committee on Foreign Relations and the Committee on Appropriations,* 97th Congress, 2d session, March 1982.

U.S. Congress. House. Committee on Foreign Affairs. *The War Powers Resolution. A Special Study of the Committee on Foreign Affairs,* 97th Congress, 2d session, April 1982.

U.S. Congress. House. Committee on Foreign Affairs. *Presidential Certification on El Salvador,* Volume II. *Hearings and Markup Before the Committee on Foreign Affairs and Its Subcommittee on Inter-American Affairs,* 97th Congress, 2d session, June 2, 22; July 29; August 3, 10 and 17, 1982.

U.S. Congress. Senate. Committee on Foreign Relations. *Nomination of George P. Shultz. Hearings Before the Committee on Foreign Relations,* 97th Congress, 2d session, July 13 and 14, 1982.

U.S. Congress. Senate. Committee on Foreign Relations. *Presidential Certifications on Conditions in El Salvador. Hearings Before the Committee on Foreign Relations,* 97th Congress, 2d session, August 3, 1982.

U.S. Congress. House. Committee on Foreign Affairs. *Honduras and U.S. Policy: An Emerging Dilemma. Hearings Before the Subcommittee on Inter-American Affairs,* 97th Congress, 2d session, September 21, 1982.

U.S. Congress. House. Permanent Select Committee on Intelligence. *U.S. Intelligence Performance on Central America: Achievements and Selected Instances of Concern. Staff Report of the Subcommittee on Oversight and Evaluation,* 97th Congress, 2d session, September 22, 1982.

U.S. Congress. Senate. Committee on Foreign Relations. *Report of the U.S. Official Observer Mission to the El Salvador Constituent Assembly Elections of*

March 28, 1982. A Report to the Committee on Foreign Relations, 97th Congress, 2d session, November 1982.

U.S. Congress. Senate. Committee on Foreign Relations. *Presidential Certification on Progress in El Salvador. Hearing Before the Committee on Foreign Relations,* 98th Congress, 1st session, February 2, 1983.

U.S. Congress. House. Committee on Foreign Affairs. *U.S. Policy in El Salvador. Hearings Before the Subcommittees on Human Rights and International Organizations and on Western Hemisphere Affairs,* 98th Congress, 1st session, February 4 and 28; March 7 and 17, 1983.

U.S. Congress. House. Committee on Foreign Affairs. *Human Rights in El Salvador. Hearings Before the Subcommittees on Human Rights and International Organizations and on Western Hemisphere Affairs,* 98th Congress, 1st session, July 26, 1983.

U.S. Congress. House. Committee on Foreign Affairs. *U.S. Policy in Central America. Hearing before the Subcommittees on Human Rights and International Organizations and on Western Hemisphere Affairs,* 98th Congress, 1st session, August 3, 1983.

ARTICLES, PAMPHLETS, REPORTS

Allman, T. D. "Rising to Rebellion." *Harper's* (March 1981), p. 31.

————. "An American Tragedy." *Penthouse* (January 1984), p. 75.

The Americas at a Crossroads. Report of the Inter-American Dialogue. Woodrow Wilson International Center for Scholars, Washington, D.C., April 1983.

Applicability of Certain U.S. Laws That Pertain to U.S. Military Involvement in El Salvador. Report to Senator Edward Zorinsky by the Comptroller General of the United States. GAO/ID-82-53, July 27, 1982.

Arnson, Cynthia. *Background Information on El Salvador and U.S. Military Assistance to Central America.* Institute for Policy Studies, Washington, D.C., first published March 1980, with "Update" numbers 1–8.

Berryman, Phillip. *What's Wrong in Central America. And What to Do About It.* American Friends Service Committee, Philadelphia, 1983.

Bonner, Raymond. "The Agony of El Salvador." *The New York Times Magazine* (February 22, 1981), p. 26.

Buckley, Tom. "Letter from El Salvador." *The New Yorker* (June 22, 1981), p. 41.

"Central America." *The Nation.* Special issue (January 28, 1984).

"Central America: The Tortured Land." *San Francisco Examiner.* Special reprint of fifteen-part series that ran from July 25 to August 8, 1982.

Chace, James. "The Endless War." *The New York Review of Books* (December 8, 1983), p. 46.

Changing Course: Blueprint for Peace in Central America and the Caribbean; Policy Alternatives for the Caribbean and Central America. Institute for Policy Studies, Washington, D.C., January 1984.

Chavez, Lydia. "The Odds in El Salvador." *The New York Times Magazine* (July 24, 1983), p. 14.

———. "El Salvador: The Voices of Anguish in a Bitterly Divided Land." *The New York Times Magazine* (December 11, 1983), p. 53.

Checchi and Company. *Agrarian Reform in El Salvador.* Two reports presented to the Agency for International Development, Washington, D.C., December 1981; January 1983.

Christian, Shirley. "El Salvador's Divided Military." *The Atlantic* (June 1983), p. 50.

———. "The Other Side." *The New Republic* (October 24, 1983), p. 13.

Deere, Carmen Diana. "Comparative Analysis of Agrarian Reform in El Salvador and Nicaragua 1979–1981." *Development and Change* (Winter 1982), pp. 1–41.

DeYoung, Karen. "White Hand of Terror." *Mother Jones* (June 1981), p. 26.

Dickey, Christopher. "Death as a Way of Life." *Playboy* (October 1981), p. 109.

———. "The Proconsuls." *Rolling Stone* (August 18, 1983), p. 22.

———. "Behind El Salvador's Death Squads." *The New Republic* (December 26, 1983), p. 16.

Eisendrath, John, and Morrell, Jim. *Arming El Salvador.* Center for International Policy, Washington, D.C., August 1982.

El Salvador—Background to the Crisis. Central America Information Office (CAMINO), Boston, 1982.

"El Salvador. The Roots of Intervention." *The Nation.* Special reprint of articles that ran in 1981.

"El Salvador—Why Revolution?" *NACLA Report on the Americas* (March–April 1980).

"El Salvador—A Revolution Brews." *NACLA Report on the Americas* (July–August 1980).

El Salvador: Labor, Terror and Peace. A Special Fact-Finding Report by the National Labor Committee In Support of Democracy and Human Rights in El Salvador. New York, August 1983.

Fontaine, Roger; DiGiovanni, Cleto, Jr.; and Kruger, Alexander. "Castro's Specter." *Washington Quarterly,* (Autumn 1980).

Forche, Carolyn, and Wheaton, Philip. *History and Motivations of U.S. Involvement in the Control of the Peasant Movement in El Salvador: The Role of AIFLD in the Agrarian Reform Process 1970–1980.* Ecumenical Program for Interamerican Communication and Action (EPICA), Washington, D.C., undated.

Gleijeses, Piero. "The Case for Power Sharing in El Salvador." *Foreign Affairs,* vol. 61 (Summer 1983), pp. 1048–1063.

Gómez, Leonel, and Cameron, Bruce. "American Myths." *Foreign Policy,* vol. 43 (Summer 1981), pp. 71–78.

Hallin, Daniel C. *The American News Media from Vietnam to El Salvador: A Study of Ideological Change and Its Limits.* Presented at the 25th anniversary meeting of the International Association for Mass Communication Research, Paris, September 6–10, 1982.

Health and Human Rights in El Salvador. A Report of the Second Public Health Commission to El Salvador. Committee for Health Rights in El Salvador, New York, July 1983.

"Hemispheric Crisis: Issues and Options." *Foreign Policy,* vol. 52 (Fall 1983), pp. 42–117. Five articles, by Nestor D. Sanchez, Guillermo M. Ungo, Abraham F. Lowenthal, Ronald T. Libbey, and Tom J. Farer.

Hochschild, Adam. "Inside the Slaughterhouse." *Mother Jones* (June 1983), p. 19.

Hoeffel, Paul Heath. "The Eclipse of the Oligarchs." *The New York Times Magazine* (September 6, 1981), p. 20.

Keisling, Phil. "The Tallest Gun in Foggy Bottom." *The Washington Monthly* (November 1982), p. 51.

Keogh, Dermot. "The Coup d'Etat That Cost 657 Colones." Department of Modern History, University College, Cork, Ireland. Unpublished.

Kirkpatrick, Jeane. "Dictatorships and Double Standards." *Commentary* (November 1979), p. 34.

Leiken, Robert S. "Reconstructing Central America Policy." *Washington Quarterly* (Winter 1982), pp. 47–60.

———. "Anatomy of Resistance." *Worldview* (June 1983), p. 5.

LeoGrande, William M. "Drawing the Line in El Salvador." *International Security,* vol. 6 (Summer 1981), pp. 27–52.

———, and Robbins, Carla Anne. "Oligarchs and Officers: The Crisis in El Salvador." *Foreign Affairs,* vol. 58 (Summer 1980), pp. 1084–1103.

Marchetti, Peter, and Deere, Carmen Diana. "The Worker-Peasant Alliance in the First Year of the Nicaraguan Agrarian Reform." *Latin American Perspectives* (Spring 1981), pp. 40–73.

McColm, R. Bruce. *El Salvador: Peaceful Revolution or Armed Struggle?* Perspectives on Freedom, Number 1. Freedom House, Washington, D.C., 1982.

"The Media Go to War." *NACLA Report on the Americas* (July/August 1983).

Menges, Constantine C. "Central America and the United States." *SAIS Review* (Summer 1981), pp. 13–34.

Meislin, Richard J. "El Salvador: The State of Siege Continues." *The New York Times Magazine* (February 20, 1983), p. 34.

The Miami Report. Recommendations on United States Policy Toward Latin America and the Caribbean. The Miami Report, Coral Gables, Florida, undated; released January 1984.

Neier, Aryeh. "Tropic of Fire." *Mother Jones* (January 1982).

Pastor, Robert A. "Three Perspectives on El Salvador." *SAIS Review* (Summer 1981), pp. 35–48.

———. "Winning Through Negotiation." *The New Republic* (March 17, 1982), p. 13.

———. "The Target and the Source: El Salvador and Nicaragua." *Washington Quarterly* (Summer 1982), pp. 116–127.

———. "Our Real Interests in Central America." *The Atlantic* (July 1982), pp. 27–39.

Prosterman, Roy L. "Real Facts and True Alternatives." *Food Monitor* (November/December 1981), p. 13.

———. "The Unmaking of a Land Reform." *The New Republic,* (August 9, 1982), p. 21.

———; Riedinger, Jeffrey M.; and Temple, Mary N. "Land Reform in El Salvador: The Democratic Alternative." *World Affairs,* vol. 144 (Summer 1981), pp. 36–54.

———. "Land Reform and the El Salvador Crisis." *International Security,* vol. 6 (Summer 1981), pp. 53–74.

Pyes, Craig. "Salvadoran Rightists: The Deadly Patriots." Reprinted from a series that ran in the *Albuquerque Journal,* December 18–22, 1983.

Question of the Violation of Human Rights and Fundamental Freedoms in Any Part of the World, with Particular Reference to Colonial and Other Dependent Countries and Territories. Final Report on the Situation of Human Rights in El Salvador Submitted by Professor José Antonio Pastor Ridruejo in Discharge of the Mandate Conferred by Commission Resolution 32 (XXXVII). United Nations Economic and Social Council. E/CN.4/1502. January 18, 1982.

Report of a Medical Fact-Finding Mission to El Salvador, 11–15 January 1983. American Association for the Advancement of Science et al., January 1983.

Report on the Situation of Human Rights in El Salvador. Organization of American States, Inter-American Commission on Human Rights. OEA/Ser.L/ V/II.46., doc.23, rev. 1. November 17, 1978.

Riding, Alan. "Latin Church in Siege." *The New York Times Magazine* (May 6, 1979), p. 32.

———. "The Sword and Cross." *The New York Review of Books* (May 28, 1981), p. 3.

———. "The Central America Quagmire." *Foreign Affairs. American and the World 1982,* vol. 61 (1983) pp. 641–659.

———. "Revolution and the Intellectual in Latin America." *The New York Times Magazine* (March 13, 1983), p. 28.

Simon, Laurence R., and Stephens, James C., Jr., with Martin Diskin. *El Salvador Land Reform 1980–1981. Impact Audit.* Oxfam America, Boston, 1982.

Situation of Human Rights and Fundamental Freedoms in El Salvador. Note by the Secretary-General. Report of the Economic and Social Council, United Nations General Assembly. A/37/611. November 22, 1982.

Situation of Human Rights in El Salvador. Note by the Secretary-General. Report of the Economic and Social Council, United Nations General Assembly. A/38/503. November 22, 1983.

Smith, Wayne S. "Myopic Diplomacy." *Foreign Policy,* vol. 48 (Fall 1982), pp. 157–74.

Stein, Jeff. "Mystery Man of American Diplomacy [Vernon Walters]." *The Boston Globe Magazine* (August 29, 1982), p. 12.

"Struggle in Central America." *Foreign Policy,* vol. 43 (Summer 1981), pp. 70–103. Five articles, by Leonel Gómez and Bruce Cameron, W. Scott Thompson, J. Bryan Heir, Olga Pellicer, and Marlise Simons.

Sussman, Michael J. *AIFLD: U.S. Trojan Horse in Latin America and the Caribbean.* Ecumenical Program for Interamerican Communication and Action (EPICA), Washington, D.C., undated.

Termination Phase-Out Study, Public Safety Project. El Salvador. Agency for International Development, Washington, D.C., May 1974.

Human Rights in El Salvador—1978. Report of Findings of an Investigatory Mission. Unitarian Universalist Service Committee, Boston, 1978.

Central America 1980. Unitarian Universalist Service Committee, Boston, 1978.

Central America 1981. Unitarian Universalist Service Committee, Boston, 1981.

Central America 1982. Unitarian Universalist Service Committee, Boston, 1982.

El Salvador 1983. Unitarian Universalist Service Committee, Boston, 1983.

Waghelstein, John David. "A Theory of Revolutionary Warfare and Its Application to the Bolivian Adventure of Che Guevara." A Thesis Presented to the Faculty of the Graduate School of Cornell University for the Degree of Master of Arts. July 1973. Unpublished.

Conference on Land Tenure in Central America. Washington Office on Latin America, Washington, D.C., March 23, 1981.

U.S. Policy and Political Developments in El Salvador 1979–1983. A collection of articles reprinted from *Update: Latin America,* Washington Office on Latin America, Washington, D.C., 1983.

Wheaton, Philip. *Agrarian Reform in El Salvador: A Program of Rural Pacification.* Ecumenical Program for Interamerican Communication and Action (EPICA), Washington, D.C., undated.

White, Robert E. "Central America: The Problem That Won't Go Away." *The New York Times Magazine* (July 18, 1982), p. 21.

Zaid, Gabriel. "Enemy Colleagues: A Reading of the Salvadoran Tragedy." *Dissent* (Winter, 1982), pp. 13–40.

INDEX

Aaron, David, 183
Abrams, Elliott, 15, 163, 247,
    249–251, 305, 326, 327, 349, 351,
    354, 355, 367
ACLU (American Civil Liberties
    Union), 250, 309, 346
AD (Democratic Action), 304, 306n–
    307n
AECA (Arms Export Control Act),
    274, 275, 276
AFL-CIO, 45, 190, 192
Agee, Philip, 190–191, 258
agrarian reform, see land reform
    program
agriculture, Salvadoran, 19
    export crops and, 20–22, 25, 27,
    187, 188–189
    history of, 20–22
Aguilares:
    La Cabaña sugar mill strike in, 68
    Operation Rutilio in, 37–38
Aguirre Salinas, Osmín, 29–30, 95
AID (Agency for International
    Development), 55, 120, 190, 196,
    200, 201, 247, 315, 346
    AIFLD funded by, 191, 192
    election of 1982 and, 292, 293–294
AIFLD (American Institute for Free
    Labor Development), 45, 190,
    193–194, 197, 200, 201, 248–249
    AID's funding of, 191, 192
    as CIA cover, 190–191
    election of 1982 and, 292, 293,
    307
    murders of officials, 44–47, 50, 51,
    64, 76, 191, 212, 217, 249, 260,
    309, 344n, 368
    U.S. policy backed by, 192–194
AIM (Accuracy in Media), 316n

Air Force, Salvadoran, 279, 312–313
    civilians bombed by, 352
Alas, José Inocencio, 66n
Allende Gossens, Salvador, 89n, 155
Alliance for Progress, 25–27, 30, 192
Álvarez, Roberto, 346
Álvarez Córdova, Enrique, 100–101,
    102, 131, 160, 184, 190, 236
    assassination of, 213–214, 223,
    298
Álvarez family, 25
Álvarez Martínez, Gustavo, 282, 283
American Association for the
    International Commission of
    Jurists, 38
American Civil Liberties Union
    (ACLU), 250, 309, 346
American Friends Service
    Committee, 206
American Institute for Free Labor
    Development, see AIFLD
American Public Health Association,
    206, 353
American Security Council, 186
Americas Watch Committee, 259,
    325–326, 346, 347, 349, 355
Amnesty International, 172, 177, 206,
    259, 349
Ana María (Melida Anaya Montes),
    97–98, 134
Anderson, Thomas P., 23, 29, 61
ANDES (teachers' union), 86, 92,
    97–98
Andino, Mario Antonio, 163, 164
    in post-October 1979 coup junta,
    158–159, 161, 162, 167
ANEP (National Association of
    Private Enterprise), 34, 35, 37,
    161, 163, 169

393